Population Division
Department of Economic and Social Affairs

Population Bulletin of the United Nations

Living Arrangements of Older Persons:

Critical Issues and Policy Responses

Special Issue Nos. 42/43 2001

 United Nations   New York, 2001

NOTE

The designations employed and the presentation of the material in this publication do not imply the expression of any opinion whatsoever on the part of the Secretariat of the United Nations concerning the legal status of any country, territory, city or area or of its authorities, or concerning the delimitation of its frontiers or boundaries.

The term "country" as used in the text of this publication also refers, as appropriate, to territories or areas.

The designations "more developed", "less developed" and "least developed" countries, areas or regions are intended for statistical convenience and do not necessarily express a judgement about the stage reached by a particular country or area in the development process.

The views expressed in signed papers are those of the individual authors and do not imply the expression of any opinion on the part of the United Nations Secretariat.

Papers have been edited and consolidated in accordance with United Nations practice and requirements.

ST/ESA/SER.N/42-43

UNITED NATIONS PUBLICATION

Sales No. E.01.XIII.16

ISBN 92-1-151358-8

UN 2
ST/ESA/SER.N/42-43

PREFACE

An inevitable consequence of the demographic transition and the shift to lower fertility and mortality has been the evolution in the age structure of the world population. Many societies, especially in the more developed regions, have already attained older population age structures than have ever been seen in the past. Many developing countries in the midst of the demographic transition are experiencing rapid shifts in the relative numbers of children, population of working age and older persons.

Population ageing is expected to have a major impact on many aspects of life in the twenty-first century. According to United Nations population estimates and projections prepared by the Population Division of the Department of Economic and Social Affairs, persons aged 60 years or older comprised 10 per cent of the world's 6 billion inhabitants in 2000. This number is projected to increase to about 2 billion or 22 per cent of the world population by 2050, at which time it will be as large as the population of children. This historic crossover of an increasing share of older persons and a declining share of children will mark the first time that the number of children and older persons are the same.

Concerned by population ageing and a looming pension crisis, many Governments are promoting more self-reliance in income security for older persons and greater family responsibility for providing care. Consequently, patterns of caregiving and co-residence are emerging as pre-eminent issues related to the well-being of older persons.

In response to these concerns, the United Nations Population Division, with financial support from the United States National Institute on Aging, organized the Technical Meeting on Population Ageing and Living Arrangements of Older Persons: Critical Issues and Policy Responses, at United Nations Headquarters in New York from 8 to 10 February 2000. The purpose of the meeting was to bring together experts from different world regions to address the most pressing issues concerning population ageing and living arrangements of older persons and their historical and cultural contexts, the social process through which the living arrangements of older persons influence the demand for formal and informal support systems, and how Governments respond to these perceived needs. The meeting also aimed to improve the knowledge base, identify priorities for future research and raise the long-term visibility of ageing-related issues.

This volume contains the collected set of papers presented at the Technical Meeting. The papers examined demographic and policy dimensions of population ageing and living arrangements of older persons, living arrangements and the well-being of older persons in the past, living arrangements and family support, adapting to rapid societal transformation, poverty, health and living arrangements of older persons, future research directions and methodological issues. The sessions of the Meeting were organized along these major themes. Each session was supported by background papers, which reviewed the theme of that session.

The proceedings of the Meeting are here gathered as a special issue of the *Population Bulletin of the United Nations*. They include the papers presented to the Meeting after revision based on the discussion at the Meeting. The report on the Meeting, summarizing the discussion surrounding each agenda item and the conclusions reached, is contained in part one. The background papers are presented in part two.

CONTENTS

Explanatory notes

Symbols of United Nations documents are composed of capital letters combined with figures.

The following symbols have been used in the tables throughout this report:

Two dots (..) indicate that data are not available or are not separately reported.

An em dash (—) indicates that the amount is nil or negligible.

A hyphen (-) indicates that the item is not applicable.

A minus sign (-) before a figure indicates a decrease.

A point (.) is used to indicate decimals.

A slash (/) indicates a crop year or financial year, for example, 1994/95.

Use of a hyphen (-) between dates representing years, for example, 1994-1995, signifies the full period involved, including the beginning and end years.

Details and percentages in tables do not necessarily add to totals because of rounding.

Reference to "dollars" ($) indicates United States dollars, unless otherwise stated.

The term "billion" signifies a thousand million.

The group of least developed countries currently comprises 48 countries: Afghanistan, Angola, Bangladesh, Benin, Bhutan, Burkina Faso, Burundi, Cambodia, Cape Verde, Central African Republic, Chad, Comoros, Democratic Republic of the Congo, Djibouti, Equatorial Guinea, Eritrea, Ethiopia, Gambia, Guinea, Guinea-Bissau, Haiti, Kiribati, Lao People's Democratic Republic, Lesotho, Liberia, Madagascar, Malawi, Maldives, Mali, Mauritania, Mozambique, Myanmar, Nepal, Niger, Rwanda, Samoa, Sao Tome and Principe, Sierra Leone, Solomon Islands, Somalia, Sudan, Togo, Tuvalu, Uganda, United Republic of Tanzania, Vanuatu, Yemen and Zambia.

Part One

REPORT ON THE TECHNICAL MEETING ON POPULATION AGEING AND LIVING ARRANGEMENTS OF OLDER PERSONS: CRITICAL ISSUES AND POLICY RESPONSES

REPORT ON THE TECHNICAL MEETING ON POPULATION AGEING AND LIVING ARRANGEMENTS OF OLDER PERSONS: CRITICAL ISSUES AND POLICY RESPONSES

The Population Division of the Department of Economic and Social Affairs of the United Nations Secretariat, with financial support from the United States National Institute on Aging, organized a meeting of experts from 8 to 10 February 2000, to discuss the most pressing issues related to population ageing, living arrangements of older persons and possible government responses. Population ageing is expected to have a major impact on life in the twenty-first century. Concerned by the looming pension crisis, many Governments are promoting more self-reliance in income security for older persons and greater family responsibility for providing care. Consequently, patterns of caregiving and co-residence are emerging as pre-eminent issues related to the well-being of older persons.

The Meeting was opened by Joseph Chamie, Director of the Population Division. He emphasized that the two most important objectives of the Meeting were, namely, to address key issues related to the ageing process and how Governments were responding to them, and to improve our knowledge of patterns, determinants and consequences of living arrangements among older persons. Mr. Chamie observed that persons aged 60 years or older comprised 10 per cent of the world's 6 billion inhabitants. These older persons will increase to about 2 billion or 22 per cent of the population by 2050, a percentage already attained in the five "oldest" countries: Germany, Greece, Italy, Japan and Sweden.

The present report includes brief summaries of the papers presented in each of the meeting's sessions, along with comments by the discussant, a consolidated summary of the main points arising in the general discussions, and conclusions. The agenda, list of participants and list of documents are included in the annexes.

I. FORUM SESSION

For the opening session, members of United Nations missions, representatives of non-governmental organizations and members of the press were invited to attend. The forum was designed to create a background against which to cast the main theme of the meeting, namely, the living arrangements of older persons. Each of four experts was asked to consider what were the critical issues and policy responses to population ageing.

Barbara Crossette, moderator of the forum, acknowledged the important function played by the Population Division of the United Nations as a channel to disseminate information and as a useful source of interpretation of a number of statistics. She thanked the staff of the Population Division for also performing that role with regard to ageing and older persons' living arrangements.

Peter Peterson began by stating that ageing is not far away into the future, but is occurring now. It is also not just a local phenomenon but one that will take place in many societies around the world. Ageing will have a global impact, which he described as the "Floridization of the world". He called attention to the burden that ageing places on working age people, particularly in countries with pay-as-you-go pension systems. Furthermore, the growth of the older population implies an increased demand for health services, as the per capita consumption of health services is several times higher among older persons than for the rest of the population. The impact of falling birth rates and increased longevity, two phenomena that are occurring in developing countries as well, is likely to impose severe constraints. The fiscal and economic impact of ageing will have to be absorbed in a number of ways, affecting both the younger adult population and older persons. For example, we will face decisions about spending and tax increases, increased borrowing, longer duration of working life, importing labour, pronatalist measures, and cost reductions in pension and health plans, as well as their privatization.

The second forum member, Nana Araba Apt, deplored the absence of comprehensive planning to meet the challenges of an ageing world. In particular, she observed, we know little about the role of families, particularly where the family is under stress owing to severe economic crisis. In developing countries, with their extended family culture, households comprising four or even five generations could become common. It is not clear that we understand what the effects of those changes are on family relations. By the same token, we know little about how those processes affect the community. Ms. Apt called for more and better information on the social processes accompanying ageing and on the factors affecting the well-being of older persons.

The third forum member, Antonio Golini, pointed out that ageing resulted from two of humanity's greatest victories: increased longevity, or a victory over death and disease, and reduced birth rates, or a victory over unwanted childbearing. Yet, despite common sources, ageing processes are very diverse in different settings, particularly with respect to timing. Ageing has complex effects, involving many agents, activities and institutions. It is a silent process that evolves over the long term, producing consequences that are difficult to anticipate. It is also a new process in human societies, one for which there is no previous historical experience. Because ageing is global, it is necessary to create institutional mechanisms to deal with it. Mr. Golini proposed that countries establish supra-ministerial organizations to coordinate activities and planning that are relevant for ageing and that involve a number of traditional ministries that, as a rule, lack coordination. It is also important to take advantage of existing non-governmental organizations and redirect some

4

of their attention to ageing. Finally, there should be national research agencies focusing on ageing, such as those in the United States of America and Japan.

In preparing for an ageing society, he said that perhaps the most important need was for ideological change, in order to curb excessive individualism. There is a need for providing effective support to families, and this must include attention to the needs of the younger as well as of the oldest age groups. Secondly, more research is needed on morbidity, such as dementia and arthritis, to improve the quality of life of those surviving to older ages. Improvements such as these translate into actual slowdowns of the ageing process, and could conceivably reduce the burden on family budgets as well as on other persons. But ageing also creates problems for the young-adult generation, and attention should be directed to them as well. As social relations become more vertical than horizontal (most young adults will have fewer siblings than grandparents), there will be an increased family burden. Finally, as ageing occurs at different times in different places, it will create unique imbalances between countries. For example, as European countries move through a phase of high dependency ratios and labour shortages, developing countries will move through a phase of low dependency ratios and a surplus of young workers. How can these tensions be reduced? Increasing migration from labour surplus to labour deficient countries may be accompanied by political and ethnic tensions.

The fourth panellist, Elizabeth Mullen, reminded the audience that the image of ageing as a "problem" is misleading since it is usually based on a number of myths and stereotypes, rather than on empirical knowledge. The first myth is that older persons are homogeneous, which they are not. A second myth is that older persons are uniformly frail, dependent and vulnerable. As recent evidence in the United States indicates, older persons are less likely to be disabled or infirm than in the past. The older persons of today are not the older persons of yesterday, and will be different from the older persons of tomorrow. Differences are not just confined to health status but also include the kinds of activities older persons are able to perform, and the types of support they receive from families. Today, "intimacy at a distance" seems to be the preferred living arrangement with close family members — living apart but maintaining contact with close kin. A third myth is that older persons are only on the receiving end of exchanges. This is also inaccurate: research on intergenerational transfers shows that the flows are often from older persons to the young and not vice versa. An important programmatic issue that should have priority, whether it is related to co-residence or to other aspects of ageing, is the need to keep in place dynamic policies, flexible enough to adapt to the changing reality posed by older persons. The older population was very diverse, and aspects such as health, the financial situation and family and other social resources tended to differ according to age and between men and women. Sound data were required to monitor people's needs and the effects of policies, and it was important that data regarding the older population be tabulated by both age and gender.

Ms. Crossette began the discussion by asking Ms. Apt whether we in the West have excessively romanticized our view of extended families in Africa by attributing to the extended family a large and central role in the care of older persons when in fact it has less importance. Ms. Apt responded that the main problem faced by African societies was not the dissolution of the extended family — a phenomenon that was indeed occurring — and the growing trend towards family nuclearization, but the persistence and aggravation of poverty levels across the board, regardless of prevailing family types.

The discussion also raised the point that, although there were indeed too many negative stereotypes of older persons, paradoxically there were also a number of equally misleading and unfounded positive stereotypes that should be debunked. That is, just as it was untrue that the older population was uniformly dependent, it was also wrong to paint an overly bright picture that would lead to neglect of genuine needs for support.

Mr. Peterson pointed out that there were a number of feasible ways to induce adjustments to meet the special demands of an ageing world. For example, older people could work for longer periods of time. There was a prevailing myth that older people did not want, did not need or were not able to work. That was disproved by a number of concrete counter-examples, and should be taken into account in the design of programmes aimed at solving problems of labour shortages mentioned during the forum.

Mr. Golini emphasized the problem that would be created by the demand for labour in countries where ageing was most advanced, while a labour surplus existed in countries at an earlier stage of the demographic transition. He wondered what the political consequences and ideological fallout of such a confrontation of needs would be. On closing the forum, Mr. Chamie referred to the labour supply problem raised during the forum and informed the meeting that the question was being examined by the Population Division.

II. DEMOGRAPHIC AND POLICY DIMENSIONS OF POPULATION AGEING AND LIVING ARRANGEMENTS OF OLDER PERSONS

A statement contributed by the United States National Institute on Aging noted that a key issue that the world must grapple with was how countries with relatively few resources would cope with individual and population ageing. Comparative or cross-national research was an essential tool for understanding population ageing at a global level, and multilateral organizations and the international research community had a key role to play in advancing such research and in improving access to reliable statistical data on older populations. Since families provide most of the care when older people become disabled, living arrangements represent a key component in the link between individual and societal ageing.

The Chairman of the session, George C. Myers, introduced the main theme by reminding participants that almost 10 years ago a similar meeting, also organized by the Population Division, took place in Kitakyushu, Japan.

That meeting also looked at the residential arrangements of older persons. The differences in the approaches used then and those used now are, however, vast. Today, we have all but abandoned the aggregate approach, and focus more on individuals and individual behaviour. We also pay more attention to longitudinal rather than cross-sectional data, and attempt to identify better the social, political and cultural contexts within which ageing is occurring (contraction of the welfare state, reforms to pension systems, political mobilization of older persons and so on). These changes in approaches and perspectives have produced some tangible gains in knowledge, but have also raised additional questions. Some of these were posed in the two papers presented during the session.

Barry Mirkin of the Population Division presented the first background paper, on the demography of population ageing. The paper described global trends in population ageing. By 2050, it is expected that there will be nearly 2 billion people over the age of 60 years, or 22 per cent of the world population. This will mark the first time in history that the older population is larger than the child population. The growth of the older population often receives attention in connection with the developed countries. However, the older population is increasing at a substantially faster rate in the less developed regions than in the more developed regions. Because of the gender differential in mortality, there are currently 1.2 women for each man aged 60 years or older. Population ageing is caused not only by the decline in fertility, but also by the sharp reductions in mortality at adult and older ages. The impact of demographic ageing is clearly visible in the old-age demographic dependency ratio (the number aged 65 years or older per 100 persons of labour force age, 15-64 years), which is increasing both in more and less developed regions during the period from 1970 to 2050. Between 2000 and 2050, the old-age dependency ratio is expected to double in more developed regions and almost triple in less developed regions. Finally, the older population is unequally distributed between rural and urban areas. Whereas the majority of older persons in developed countries are urban dwellers, a significant proportion of older persons in developing countries — sometimes as high as 70 per cent — reside in rural areas.

Alberto Palloni presented the second background paper, which reviewed the state of knowledge about living arrangements and their implications for policy. He discussed the background conditions for ageing processes in developing countries, which are relevant for understanding the living arrangements of older persons. Ageing is occurring more rapidly in Latin America and Asia than in developed countries, and it is taking place within social and political contexts that are fragile and precarious. Some of the institutions providing social transfers to older persons either do not exist, are incipient or are being dismantled. Some examples are pension reforms in Latin America and the virtual absence of pension schemes in Asia. He argued that, contrary to many projections, the health status of older persons in Latin America, and possibly Asia as well, is likely to be worse than in developed countries. This implies higher levels of demands and needs, and heightens the importance of understanding living arrangements as it is through them that some of these demands are met.

The trend among older persons in Northern America and Europe has been towards increasing levels of living alone. Countries in Latin America and Asia continue to maintain very high levels of co-residence of older parents with children and, with the exception of Japan and the Republic of Korea, most societies have not yet shown clear indications of drastic changes in traditional patterns of co-residence. It is unclear when changes will occur, but there is a widespread belief that it will not take long before patterns found in the United States and Europe are adopted elsewhere as well.

A review of the literature revealed that remarkably little is known about the relationship between living arrangements and older persons' well-being. Most studies focus on the effects of poverty, income or wealth levels on the probabilities of older persons and children or other kin co-residing, while providing no information about other complementary, but perhaps more important, issues, namely, the degree to which co-residence with children or other kin enhances or depresses the well-being of older persons. In fact, the limited evidence available suggests that older persons living alone, particularly older widows, experience higher levels of poverty than those who co-reside. However, this finding is not universal and does not enable us to draw clear inferences about the direction of causality.

Despite new data, models and methods of inference, the determinants of living arrangements of older persons and the forces precipitating the sweeping changes in traditional co-residential arrangements in developed countries — and potentially in developing countries in the near future — are not well understood. It is believed that changes in income of both parents and children are very influential. It is also possible that some changes are due to changes in the prevailing characteristics of children available to co-reside (life cycle stages and income) and also to changes in preferences, which, in an era dominated by individualism, have turned towards living apart. Furthermore, we normally fail to consider simultaneously family and social transfers and co-residence, or to focus simultaneously on co-residence and on other older persons' social networks. In either case, the ability to understand underlying relations is severely impaired.

Comments by the discussant. Nikolai Botev noted that ageing is associated with distortions in the relative sizes of the cohorts. Indicators of kin availability are important and deserve to be monitored more widely, since they are strongly associated with living arrangements. The speed with which kin availability is decreasing has accelerated for countries with late demographic transitions. These countries will experience more sudden and rapid ageing processes than other countries. Other phenomena, such as war, massive migration and epidemics, can also distort kin availability.

Mr. Botev also underlined the point that, although co-residence is conventionally seen as a transfer of support and services from the young to the older generation, this is not always the case. As research has shown, co-residence can also be accompanied by a significant supply of services by older persons that benefit the younger population. The net flow within a household may go in either direction. Thus, it is important to examine co-residence in detail before making pronouncements about who receives net benefits. He also noted that a narrow focus on older persons' co-residence may be self-defeating as two important facts may be overlooked. On the one hand, the living arrangements of older persons are only one among many other social contexts within which older persons may develop social relations and connections. Not only does proximity without co-residence matter, but also living alone may be accompanied by social contacts outside the household, which may be instrumental in satisfying the basic needs of older persons. Thus, the linkages between co-residence, social networks and other family transfers should be studied together.

Mr. Botev also observed that demographers have not adequately explained population ageing and its implications to policy makers. Ageing occurs over a time horizon that is much longer than policy makers are accustomed to dealing with. Yet, despite its current speed in many parts of the world, the process of ageing will not continue indefinitely, and the proportion of older people in the population will eventually level off.

III. LIVING ARRANGEMENTS AND THE WELL-BEING OF OLDER PERSONS IN THE PAST

The Chairman of the session, Peter Lloyd-Sherlock, opened the session by emphasizing the importance of placing changes in the living arrangements of older persons in a historical perspective so as to shed light on future trends.

Steven Ruggles summarized his paper, which focused on the determinants of living arrangements of older persons in the United States from 1880 to 1990. Despite claims to the contrary, nearly all older persons in the United States prior to the period of full industrialization lived with children, provided that they had a living child. This does not conflict with the observation that only a small percentage of households contained multiple generations, since early death, late marriage and high fertility meant that few multigenerational households were possible. The prevailing household arrangement for older persons was of the extended type. This was the outcome of a stem-family system, whereby older children left the parental household upon marrying, while the youngest child remained at home with the parents. This pattern began to decline early in the twentieth century and further declined after 1940, a period during which there was a sharp increase in the prevalence of living alone among all older persons. The forces behind these momentous changes were most likely associated with the erosion of self-employment tied to the family farm. As new economic opportunities became plentiful and the main focus of production shifted from the farm to industry, wage labour overwhelmed the importance of family farm work. This weakened the links between the economic prospects of the young-adult generation and co-residence in the parental home. In the traditional arrangement, the co-resident adult child was subordinate to the parents but could expect eventually to take over the family farm or small business; the rise of wage and salary employment offered an alternative that was relatively attractive in financial terms and did not depend on the older generation. The decline of the family farm also meant that parents, themselves no longer farmers, had less need of children's labour. The rising income of older persons was not a factor in explaining the shifts that took place before 1950.

Different factors, however, were behind the shifts that took place after 1950. First, the rising income of older persons played a role by making possible greater independence, but this by itself could account for at most 30 per cent of the decline in co-residence since 1950. The rising income and education of the younger generation also had important effects. Indeed, the changing characteristics of the younger generation may be more important than the changes in the older generation for understanding the recent declines in co-residence.

Some analysts have suggested that the creation of the Social Security system fuelled the increase in living alone, by raising income and fostering financial independence; this view assumes that there was a pre-existing desire on the part of many older people to live on their own, and Social Security then provided the financial support for maintaining an independent household. Ruggles' analysis of the data did not support this contention. On the contrary, the creation of the Social Security system may better be understood as a response to changes in the family that had already taken place as a consequence of the decline of farming and the rise of urban wage labour.

Comments by the discussant. Jacques Légaré noted that the paper had broken new ground in several respects. He agreed that it was important to analyse both parents and children, given that living arrangements are likely determined by the characteristics of both these groups. Citing data from Canada, he noted that current co-residential arrangements are related to fertility — those living in multigenerational arrangements are more likely to have higher fertility — and that women who live alone are more likely to have higher socio-economic status, while the reverse is true for men. He also agreed that it was important to determine whether declining co-residence was due to rising parental income or the rising income of the younger generation and to compare actual to potential numbers of two- and three-generation households in order to show that co-residence was almost universal early on. He further concurred with the idea that the widening disparity in education between parents and children contributed to the erosion of co-residence, but questioned whether co-residence would increase once the education gap began to narrow. He suggested that more attention be paid to urban-rural differentials and gender issues.

Mr. Ruggles agreed that the paper gave little attention to gender; the topic was important and perhaps deserved attention in a separate paper. He believed that urban-rural differentials were not important in explaining declining co-residence, once farming employment was taken into account. He also noted that, while the positive relationship between number of children and co-residence has been observed in a variety of settings, in the United States this pattern emerged only after co-residence ceased to be near-universal and became a matter of choice.

Responding to a question concerning possible policy lessons that might be gleaned from the United States experience, Mr. Ruggles indicated that an incorrect understanding of the causes of historical trends could lead to unsound policy choices. As an example, he referred to a view that had gained prominence recently, that the rise of the Social Security system had provided an important impetus to the erosion of the multigenerational household; if this were so, a policy that weakened the Social Security system might be expected to produce a reversion to familial arrangements of the past. In fact, the causality was mainly in the opposite direction; that is, broad social and economic changes caused the decline in multigenerational living, and the Social Security system grew up in response to needs arising from those changes.

IV. LIVING ARRANGEMENTS AND FAMILY SUPPORT

The Chairperson, Elizabeth Mullen, observed that the theme of the session's two papers revolved around a key issue, namely, the relationship between the material and ideological basis of support for older persons. It is important to remember that there are a number of ideological constructs (such as prescriptions from religious teachings, Asian filial piety, and media emphasis on the need for support of older persons) that emphasize the support flowing from children to parents and that in some cases these ideologies remain, while the material basis for support has eroded. Under what conditions does this occur and how long can one expect an ideology that stresses support of older persons to persist while the material conditions that sustain it disappear?

Jay Sokolovsky summarized his paper on the living arrangements of older persons and family support in less developed countries. Developing countries will confront dramatic structural, economic and social changes over the coming decades as a result of population ageing. Powerful "discourses of neglect" regarding older persons are heard in many of these countries, including some, such as India, where living arrangements of older persons have been quite stable and seem to conform to traditional patterns of household formation despite demographic, social and economic changes. In some cases, these discourses act as narratives of caution, which can have deep cultural roots. The focus is on how families in developing countries are trying to adapt traditional patterns of living arrangements to powerful changes, and on how culture may be sufficiently flexible to respond to "modernization", in such a way that traditional systems survive within more modern contexts, when the necessary resources exist. In examining these issues, he reviewed some of the basic data on living arrangements and support for older persons in developing countries. Data from the author's longitudinal research in a village in central Mexico demonstrated the need to go below the surface of observed living arrangements in order to understand the changing circumstances in which developing countries find themselves.

Jenny de Jong Gierveld, in her paper on the living arrangements of older persons and family support in more developed countries, explored the major characteristics of older persons' living arrangements and family support in

11

developed countries. Marital status is an important determinant of living arrangements. Country differences in the distribution of older persons by marital status reflect differences in the timing of the "second demographic transition" affecting these countries. The latter term has been used to call attention to important shifts in patterns of norms and values, as well as in demographic behaviour, that have been observed in Europe during the past several decades. Among the most important demographic aspects are rising probabilities of never marrying and increasing frequency of divorce and of unmarried cohabitation. These changes have been viewed as linked to increased individualism and supported by underlying economic and social changes. In addition, some of the differences in older persons' living arrangements are associated with differentials in mortality at older ages. In general, living together as a couple is the most common living arrangement of older married persons in each of the four countries studied. While most older men live with a spouse, a large proportion of older women are widows, who have a higher propensity to live alone. There are marked contrasts among countries, with Finland and the United Kingdom of Great Britain and Northern Ireland exhibiting the highest proportions living alone and Italy and Hungary the lowest. Older divorced women show a marked tendency to live alone in all countries, although in Finland, at least, they do so to a lesser extent than widows. However, older divorced women experience higher rates of living in unmarried cohabitation or with lifelong acquaintances than do widows.

The second demographic transition is already leaving its mark and this is evident in the data, which clearly demonstrate the preferences of older people and young alike for living alone, though perhaps near to kin and with possibilities for other kinds of social and material support. However, there are — and always will be — situations that trigger co-residence. One of these is the health status of the older population. Identifying the transition to different living arrangements is important but requires longitudinal data.

An important finding in all countries, but particularly in Eastern Europe, is that co-residence is a social arrangement that favours both older persons and the young-adult generation. This is especially true in situations of severe housing shortages and poor housing quality. To the extent that the quantity and quality of housing improves, social security benefits increase and coverage expands to cover a larger portion of the older population, continued increases in the proportions living alone can be expected. It was noted, however, that there is clear evidence that some older persons, particularly widows and divorced older persons, are opting for flexible living arrangements, such as unmarried cohabitation and living "apart but together", that guarantee company and support without the need for remarriage. These types of arrangements provide important social and emotional benefits. Once again this points to the importance of studying social support networks rather than co-residence alone.

Comments by the discussant. Mohammed O. Rahman noted the possibility of an imminent second demographic transition in Hungary and Italy, which would imply an increase in the prevalence of living alone. He questioned whether this should be a matter of concern. Although the spread of such changes throughout Southern Europe is likely, it is also possible that this would not occur. The relationship between ageing of the population and decline in co-residence with children is not clear-cut: for instance, in Italy, the country with the highest proportion of older persons in the world, co-residence is much more common than in countries where the ageing process is not as advanced.

Mr. Rahman highlighted the phenomenon of living "apart but together" among widows and widowers. This type of arrangement merits attention, for it implies the emergence of household-based relationships that might escape notice if only conventional co-residential patterns are examined. This calls for new methods of data collection on emerging trends in living arrangements in Western Europe that are replacing co-residence with children or kin or living alone.

Mr. Rahman noted that the Sokolovsky paper raised an interesting issue regarding the validity of narratives of neglect, when co-residence and respect for older persons prevail. What do these narratives reflect? Anticipatory behaviour? Do they announce the demise of the traditional system? The evidence presented by the author suggests relative stability of co-residence arrangements in a highly changed community. This should alert us to the need for caution in using terms such as "ageing crisis", as there may not be a crisis, particularly when communities are able to adjust without dismantling traditional living arrangements.

V. ADAPTING TO RAPID SOCIETAL TRANSFORMATION

The Chairperson, Linda Martin, noted that the theme of the session involved immediate concerns, which have very relevant policy implications. The papers dealt with trends affecting older persons in a range of societies undergoing rapid change in socio-economic conditions. Perhaps it is here that the contrast between the ageing issues facing developed and developing countries is most stark.

In presenting his paper, Paulo Murad Saad discussed the possible impact of pension reforms on the living arrangements of older persons in Latin America. As these reforms have only recently been implemented, it is difficult to provide a quantitative assessment of their impact since most effects will be felt only in the long run. The degree to which pension reforms impact on the household structure of older persons will depend on the extent to which they affect the financial independence of older persons. It is expected that improvements in the value and/or coverage of pensions will lead to increases in the prevalence of independent living arrangements. Preliminary evaluations of the Chilean reform — the oldest in the region — do not point to any increases in older persons' financial autonomy. Most workers — especially those in the informal sector and those with lower incomes — do not contribute regularly to the system and will not receive benefits when they are older. On the other hand, the value of benefits paid by the Government, which still manages the old system, to the majority of current pensioners and retirees has dropped dramatically because of the huge outflow of income experienced by the public sector immediately following privatization. A basic lesson from the Chilean reform is that a private system tends to work well for high-income workers, but poorly for low-income workers. Thus, merely substituting a private system for one that was public is not likely to resolve problems associated with pension schemes in Latin America. Rather, pension reform should be part of a broader set of socio-economic reforms, capable of providing the necessary conditions for workers to fully participate in the system. Since pensions comprise an important component of older persons' income, even small changes in the value of benefits can potentially have a large impact on the living arrangements of older persons. At present, though, we do not know how living arrangements will respond to pension reforms.

The second paper in the session, presented by Vladislav V. Bezrukov, describes changes in the living arrangements of older persons in Ukraine during the country's political, social and economic crises. As a result of these crises, the situation of the older population has worsened. Within the past decade, population ageing in Ukraine has increased, mainly owing to the continuing decrease in fertility rates. The number of persons aged 60 years or older continued to grow, and they made up 19.5 per cent of the total population in 1998. Increases in the cost of living, inflation and low pensions have led to a larger gap between the economic provision of pensioners and the changing living standards of the working population. The lack of employment opportunities for older workers has aggravated the situation. The absolute number of workers aged 60 and over declined from 1.0 million people in 1989 to 0.6 million in 1995. Housing conditions were poor: fewer than half the older population lived in dwellings with connections to piped water and only about 40 per cent had access to hygienic sewage disposal. This gloomy social and economic context is worsened by two additional factors. First, the role of the family as providers of care for older persons has weakened during the past decade. This holds true particularly in rural areas, where older persons are most likely to live alone. Secondly, there is clear evidence of deteriorating health conditions among older persons, which is reflected in the sharp reduction of life expectancy at age 60. Unfortunately, the present economic situation does not allow the delivery of appropriate health and social welfare services to the older persons who need them. In the final section, the paper explores alternative public interventions to improve the economic, social and health status of the older population.

Zeng Yi presented a paper on extremely rapid ageing and living arrangements in China. Both the official Chinese and the United Nations most recent projections confirm a rapid increase in the proportion of older persons, the large absolute numbers of older persons, an extraordinarily rapid increase of the oldest old after 2020, and sharper increases of the older population in rural than in urban areas. More than 70 per cent of Chinese older persons live with children. Among those who live with offspring, about three fourths live in family households comprising three or more generations. The proportion of older persons living alone is relatively small, and very few old people live in institutions. In general, older women are disadvantaged, for they are economically more dependent than men yet are also much more likely to be widowed and thus to live alone. Considerable differences exist between rural and urban areas. The pattern of living arrangements of older persons changed little, if at all, between 1982 and 1990. Drawing upon empirical findings discussed in the paper, the authors review selected policy recommendations for strengthening the family support system, establishing an old-age insurance programme in rural areas, and designing programmes to increase the level of benefits for disadvantaged older persons (particularly widows), and to smooth the transition to a "two-child plus spacing" policy to replace the current one-child policy.

The paper presented by Nana Araba Apt focused on rapid urbanization and living arrangements of older persons in Africa. A number of drastic changes have occurred in the recent past, some of which would have been unthinkable until recently. First, systems of authority and dominance favouring elders have weakened as they play less important roles within the extended family. This is mainly the result of the erosion of rural production and of the household as the unit of production. Massive migration flows towards urban areas undermine the traditional system in which older persons commanded respect and authority. As older persons become more dependent within an altered social and economic context, and widespread poverty. persists, families find it more difficult to support their older members. Thus, care of older and dependent parents, a task that in Africa only children can perform, will burden young adults well into the twenty-first century.

The troublesome fact is that, in Africa, ageing and the situation of older persons is not really felt or acknowledged as a problem by political leaders or other interested parties. Africa is still demographically very young, and issues related to the care of older persons have less priority amid a number of more urgent problems. African countries not only lack resources that can be diverted to increase older persons' well-being but national Governments themselves are unlikely to act efficiently either to generate new resources or to allocate efficiently those that exist. Thus, at least in the near future, the well-being of older persons will be entirely dependent on the ability of children to provide for parents. A key issue is how to mobilize support in an environment where co-residence is threatened by large migration flows, where diseases and epidemics (including HIV/AIDS) are eroding the demography of households and families, and where there is massive unemployment of the young. Older people may have to continue working well past what in the West are considered ages of retirement. Given that, in the foreseeable future, Africa is unlikely to be able to build a comprehensive welfare system, limited measures are worth considering, such as tax breaks for those taking care of older relatives, and construction of community centres that can be used as meeting places or clubs for older people. The paper concludes with a number of policy recommendations for Ghana, including promotion of rural development, strengthening older persons' income-earning opportunities, promoting village-based small industry and business development, encouraging and facilitating older persons' participation in the labour force and securing additional education and vocational training.

Comments by the discussant. John E. Dowd, the discussant for the session, noted that all four papers made clear the need to utilize all the demographic information available, including information on health and disability, on risk factors and on chronic illnesses, before one could make an assessment of the situation of older persons according to co-residence status. Although in most cases those data do not exist, sometimes minimal data sets are available for making appropriate inferences. In the absence of well-integrated and coherent data sets, we need to work on a piecemeal basis, trying to assemble various segments of information from different sources.

Mr. Dowd found commonalities in the policy recommendations proposed by the authors of all four papers, but also questioned whether some of the measures were feasible. For example, all four authors agreed on the need to ensure better pensions for workers in all sectors of the economy as a way to ensure less dependency on children or relatives. He questioned whether this was realistic for many poor countries, where social security systems either do not exist or have very limited coverage. A second common thread in the papers was the recommendation that older persons be given a chance to participate more fully in the labour market under a variety of schemes to secure economic support as well as social integration.

VI. POVERTY, HEALTH AND LIVING ARRANGEMENTS OF OLDER PERSONS

Jenny de Jong Gierveld opened the session by noting that the papers to be discussed focused on the relation between well-being and residential arrangements but from a somewhat different perspective. The question now was whether there is any evidence that different co-residential arrangements lead to different health or poverty status among older persons.

Emily Grundy described evidence of the relations between living arrangements and characteristics of older persons, focusing on studies in the United Kingdom. Although there are theoretical reasons to suggest that living alone might have adverse effects on the health of at least some older people, the empirical evidence shows that those living alone are generally in the best health. However, in interpreting this fact it is essential to take into account the importance of selective moves to institutions and to relatives' households. In particular, among the very old, living alone may only be an attractive or possible option for those in reasonably good health or with good support systems. Given that surviving spouses, attentive daughters and personality cannot be randomly allocated, it is unlikely that the "true" effects of living arrangements on the health of older adults can ever be quantified. Moreover, these are certain to vary between populations and individuals. The psychological effects of living alone, for example, may be damaging for older people who regard this situation as undesirable or stigmatizing but beneficial for those who regard it as an indication of independence and autonomy. Empirical studies have shown that having a close relationship with someone seen only two or three times a week was just as protective as having a confidant in the same household. It was those who had no close relationship at all who were at more serious risk of clinical depression. One might hypothesize that possibilities of economies of scale associated with co-residence may lead to adverse consequences for older persons who live alone and are poor, but may have no measurable effects among those who are well off. Another important point is that the health statuses of members of households where older persons reside are correlated. And, obviously, the health characteristics of those who share a household are important for the health of older individuals. Thus, it is important to consider the household's characteristics rather than just those of individuals when deciding on allocation of services.

Mohammed O. Rahman discussed the results of his research in Bangladesh. There is very little information about the impact of living arrangements on patterns of morbidity for older adults in developing countries. The paper employs newly collected comprehensive data to examine the impact of living arrangements — particularly the presence of various family members — on self-reported general health and limitations in activities of daily living for adults aged 59 years and over in rural Bangladesh. The results suggest that the gender difference in the impact of spouses on self-reported general health is consistent with the notion of spouses being more important for older women than for their male peers in a social setting where women have limited access to resources. These cross-sectional results need to be viewed with some caution because having a co-resident spouse appears not to affect limitations in activities of daily living for either older men or women, while earlier longitudinal mortality studies in the same population found that the impact of spouses was greatest for older men and was mixed for older women in terms of mortality. These discrepant findings reflect either differences owing to variations in study design or outcomes that vary according to the specific dimensions of health status examined. The results help underscore the complex dynamics of the relationship between living arrangements and the health status of older persons in developing countries.

Peter Lloyd-Sherlock summarized the results of his ethnographic work on poverty, old age and living arrangements in slums in Argentina and Brazil. Although the numbers of older persons were found to be lower in slum neighbourhoods than in other urban districts, there is fragmentary evidence that this gap is being reduced. Older people in the study districts were more likely to be living in large household units than were older persons in general, but co-residence did not necessarily mean support from other household members. In many cases older persons were significant net contributors to household welfare. In some cases support from relatives living outside the home was more important than support from inside. Many older people are homeowners. This often represented a significant contribution to family welfare, but was rarely recognized by those concerned. The results of the microstudies are highly context-specific and may not apply to poor older people living in other urban communities. However, they draw attention to the complexity of older people's living arrangements and to the dangers of making assumptions about socio-economic relations from raw demographic data.

Finally, Mapule F. Ramashala described conditions of older persons in South Africa, using the 1996 South African population census. The projected growth in the number of persons aged 75 and over is of particular concern, because this group has the greatest number of needs that must be met: economic security; access to essential health and human services; adequate housing and personal safety. Of particular importance in South Africa is the problem of housing, which, combined with large rural to urban migration outflows of the young, leads to drastic alterations in patterns of living arrangements of older people. We know little about the existence and feasibility of alternative living arrangements, especially for older persons who are frail, the slightly impaired, and those who need sheltered housing but not nursing care.

Inadequate housing conditions are particularly problematic for older people who are disabled. In South Africa, one policy response to the severe reduction in public expenditures supporting nursing homes has been the concept of "ageing in place", whereby older people remain in their homes, with their kin or children. Providing support services to permit people to remain in their homes is considered the best option by many in the field of gerontology and appears to be a feasible solution for South Africa. To the extent that such policy is complemented by public assistance to meet the basic needs of older persons and the members of their households, programmes for "ageing in place" may take advantage of kin and young adults who can remain with older people, thus providing an array of services while in turn receiving shelter and sharing household goods in compensation for their services. These mixed strategies that combine familial support and state-based support to sustain familial care are likely to be, on the whole, less costly and probably more effective than strategies exclusively based on one or the other.

Comments by the discussant. The discussant, Martha Pelaez, noted that the four papers were tied together by a common attempt to understand either the extent to which certain characteristics of older persons (health, disability and poverty) affect co-residence or the degree to which living arrangements and marital status influenced older persons' characteristics such as health status and disability. Furthermore, the existence of two-way relations — for example, health affecting living arrangements and vice versa — has been repeatedly mentioned, warning us to be cautious in making causal inferences. With the exception of the paper by Ms. Ramashala, which is based on census data, all the papers highlight the importance of social networks beyond those created through co-residence. The papers also stress the influence of housing availability and housing characteristics. Throughout the meeting participants emphasized the need to examine the complete set — or as complete a set as possible — of older persons' social relations rather than confining attention to those in the household. Less attention was paid to issues of housing location and housing quality. Location and quality of housing may directly affect the health and well-being of older persons, and it might also determine the locus of control and therefore the likelihood that older persons can live with the younger generations. Clearly, special communities developed to house older persons by definition exclude multigenerational living arrangements.

An important issue highlighted by the papers is the need to study the dynamics of living arrangements. The papers give examples in which a cross-sectional picture could not possibly inform us about the changes that occur as a result of health conditions, including physical and mental health. The dynamics of transitions may differ by social class and by location of residence, as shown by Mr. Lloyd-Sherlock.

Linked to this is the theme of institutionalization and the creation of specialized hospitals and health-care facilities. The living arrangements of older persons will follow a different dynamic when Governments — as they are beginning to do in many countries — and private businesses — as they emerge in some places — begin to develop alternative arrangements that are not stigmatized. These linkages are important with regard to mental health. It is known, for example, that mental health impairments are especially likely to lead to institutionalization. Similarly, living alone may be a precursor to institutionalization, once serious physical or mental health problems develop.

VII. FUTURE RESEARCH DIRECTIONS

Douglas A. Wolf, the Chairman of the session, observed that over the past decade there has been a substantial amount of research on living arrangements but important questions remained unanswered.

Victoria Velkoff summarized her paper discussing priorities for future research. She noted several observations emerging from a cross-national comparison of living arrangements: women in developed countries are much more likely than men to live alone as they age, mainly because women are more likely to be widowed; there has been an increase in the proportion of the older population living alone in developed countries; in developing countries, both older men and women usually live with adult children; and the use of institutional care for the frail elderly varies widely among countries but is relatively low everywhere. She focused on three main areas where research was needed: (a) changing family structure; (b) familial resource transfers; and (c) older people's preferences in terms of living arrangements and care. First, research on changing family structure should take into account alternative and changing family forms — including "blended families" that result from divorce and remarriage — and their possible consequences for living arrangements later in life. Changes in kin availability also needed attention. Grandparent-and-child families are increasingly common in some countries, particularly where HIV/AIDS has orphaned many children. With regard to the second point, little is known at present about the complex decision-making process behind transfers of physical, emotional and economic support among family members. Co-residence often offers benefits to both the adult parents and the adult children, but flows of support from kin outside the household are also important. Even though in most societies support is likely to flow in both directions — from parents to children as well as the reverse — the balance is likely to differ from place to place. For instance, by comparison to those in developed countries, older people in developing countries appear less likely to provide financial help to children — probably they lack the means to do so — although older parents clearly make substantial contributions in other ways ranging from socialization to housekeeping and child care. With respect to the third point, there is a need for more research on the preferences and attitudes of older people regarding living arrangements. Assumptions are often made about older people's preferences for living arrangements that are based on past or traditional norms. Recent research in the Philippines found that many older people, although co-residing with children, would prefer to live alone or with a spouse. This is similar to results reported from Brazil and Ecuador. More frequently than not older persons live with children either because of their needs, the needs of their children or a combination of both.

Several participants provided information about ongoing activities related to population ageing. Richard Leete presented a note on the United Nations Population Fund's research focus in the area of population and ageing, including examples of projects supported by the Fund. It was noted that while the bulk of the Fund's programmable resources are earmarked for reproductive health services in developing countries, including family planning and sexual health, about 30 per cent of the Fund's resources are devoted to programmes and projects in the area of population and development strategies. This includes the linkages between population and development, of which population ageing is one of the areas of focus.

Alexandre Sidorenko described the activities of the Programme of Ageing of the Department of Economic and Social Affairs of the United Nations Secretariat during the period from 1999 to 2002. The three major activities were (a) revising and updating the International Plan of Action on Ageing; (b) developing a long-term strategy on ageing; and (c) convening of the World Assembly on Ageing in 2002. He stressed the important role of the World Assembly, not only as a follow-up to the goals and recommendations agreed to in the International Plan of Action on Ageing elaborated in 1982 at the first World Assembly on Ageing, but also as a forum for launching the research agenda on ageing for the twenty-first century. He also spoke of the European regional conference on ageing, which is also expected to be convened in 2002.

Nikolai Botev described the work programme of the Population Activities Unit of the Economic Commission for Europe (ECE). There were four areas of work: (a) international migration and migrants; (b) population ageing and older persons; (c) fertility, family and reproductive health; and (d) follow-up to population conferences. A major project deals with the status of older persons in ECE countries, especially economic conditions, living arrangements and gender. The main objectives are to assemble a set of cross-nationally comparable microdata samples based on the 1990 round of national population and housing censuses conducted in the member States of ECE and to use these samples to study the economic and social conditions of older persons.

Comments by the discussant. The discussant for the session, Antonio Golini, observed that the marked contrast in living arrangements for older men and women pointed to the need to study living arrangements by marital status, as others had also noted. Similarly, we need to understand why levels of institutionalization differ as much as they do among the developed countries.

Is it because institutional living is still stigmatized in many societies and demand is low, or is it because there are not enough incentives for private capital to satisfy the existing demand? And, if this is so, how can the supply shortage be addressed? As more options for co-residence become available, patterns of co-residential arrangements will affect aggregate characteristics and have important ecological and spatial consequences. Finally, living arrangements are indeed a form of transfer and, as such, should be studied together with the occurrence of other transfers.

A second dimension of interest is healthy ageing. What are the factors that affect it and what are the most useful interventions? An important point has to do with the intensity and speed of ageing. To the extent that intensity and speed are high, the lead time for society and Governments to act will be shorter, with corresponding consequences for the health of older persons. A complicating issue is that speed and intensity will vary across countries and within regions in the same country. Focusing on the factors affecting healthy ageing is also complicated since the determinants of interest are not just proximate but also distant. For example, it is one thing to know that current co-residential arrangements may affect depression a few years from now, and another to know that health conditions during older ages are determined by social and health conditions early in life. Whereas in one case we could act, in the other the policy options may be more limited. Mr. Golini suggested additional studies and research on determinants of physical health and disability as well as mental health. In particular, we need to know with some certainty whether the future will be characterized by expansion or compression of morbidity.

A third dimension of ageing has to do with availability of kin. Mr. Golini suggested that the ratio of persons aged 75 or over to the population aged 50 to 64 was a useful approximate indicator of the number of oldest old, those most likely to need support, in relation to the number of children available to provide that support. The value of this indicator is projected to rise rapidly in all countries, and in some countries, including Italy, by 2050 there will be more than one person aged 75 for each person aged 50 to 64.

Fourth and finally, he observed that the ideological superstructure that rationalizes relations between older persons and younger generations had drifted too far in the direction of individualism. To the extent that individualistic values become dominant, the care of older persons will become disconnected from familial concerns.

VIII. SYNOPSIS OF THE DISCUSSIONS

Research issues and policy concerns

The living arrangements of older persons are of interest for both policy and scientific reasons. First, living arrangements may influence the material and psychological well-being and health status of the older generation. Co-residence with older parents may also affect the well-being of the other family members, typically adult children and grandchildren. A second major reason for policy concern is the potential trade-off between public (e.g., social

21

security) and private, family-based support for older persons. Traditionally, most, though certainly not all, family support has been delivered within a co-resident family unit, and a decline in such arrangements is likely to coincide with a rising demand for public provision of some of the services formerly provided by family members. More generally, individuals' "micro" decisions about co-residence have, in the aggregate, "macro" effects in such areas as demand for social services and energy, water and other resource consumption; that is, a trend towards the establishment of more numerous but smaller households can be expected to increase consumption and associated privately and publicly borne costs. Finally, there is a broader scientific interest in understanding major shifts in family and household composition over time and place, and in trying to understand how family relationships are affected by economic and other social changes in the course of development. There is a particular interest in understanding the current situation and in forecasting trends in developing countries, where mechanisms and resources for non-familial support for the older population are few.

Data on living arrangements need to be supplemented by other information in order to understand the implications of changing residential patterns for older (and younger) persons' welfare. First, we need to know about preferences of older persons and of their kin. Secondly, for a comprehensive picture of support provided within the family, it is important to investigate the role of kin living elsewhere, since relatives, and even non-relatives, living nearby may be an important source of emotional support and assistance, and even distant kin may provide significant financial assistance. Thirdly, for sound policy decisions, we need a better understanding of the nature of intra-family transfers and their relationship to the system of pensions and social welfare. Fourthly, there is also a demographic context that is relevant. The younger old are more likely to be in good health, can still be economically active and may provide substantial assistance — both financial and personal (e.g., child care) — to their children and grandchildren. In such cases, support may flow mainly from the older generation to the younger. With advancing age and with the onset of chronic disease or disability, the older generation becomes more likely to depend on others for both financial support and personal care. It is also important to note that the family caregivers for a population aged 80 or over are typically individuals aged 55 to 60 or older. That is, those providing care and, especially, emotional support for the oldest old are themselves part of the older population.

Participants agreed that, based on present knowledge, it is difficult to argue convincingly what is best for older persons in terms of residential arrangements and, therefore, to choose cogently between alternative policy options. At present, even on apparently self-evident matters such as the relation between co-residence and feelings of loneliness and isolation, we have no decisive data. It is difficult to determine the effects of living arrangements on health, since ill health almost certainly affects living arrangements; only those who remain in moderately good health are likely to be able to live independently. There is really no sure way to tell what the causal relation between well-being and living arrangements is since we cannot perform randomized experiments. Longitudinal data can help answer some of the questions, but some difficult issues of interpretation of cause and effect cannot be settled even if the sequence of events is clearly known. More particularly, current and future behaviour depend to an unknown degree on people's expectations about the future and cannot be fully understood by studying events that have taken place up to the time of observation.

It is important to recognize that the relationship between co-residence and levels of well-being depends on the social context and macroeconomic conditions, not just on individual characteristics and preferences. Thus, co-residential arrangements are constrained by housing markets and quality of housing stocks, so that the choice of co-residence is not always freely made. In this connection, it was reported that, in Ukraine, older persons who were assigned to places that they considered undesirable experienced higher mortality, morbidity and disability. Similarly, the ability of older persons to be satisfied and live without stress is likely to be a function of characteristics such as gender and education.

Because of their low rates of participation in the formal labour market, women are most vulnerable economically and their well-being may be more dependent on co-residence than is that of men. Also, since roles within families differ according to characteristics such as gender, age and marital status, co-residence will have different effects according to the status of the older persons regarding those characteristics.

The characteristics of the adult children are also important in determining living arrangements. It was reported that, in Brazil, older persons' own expectations are that their daughters, not sons, will take care of them in old age. A similar division of labour between sons and daughters has been observed in some countries of Asia, although in others a daughter-in-law traditionally provides most day-to-day assistance. Trends affecting the younger generation, such as increases in divorce, cohabitation and women's labour force participation, could limit the willingness or the capacity of children to provide support to parents through co-residence. The strength of bonds established earlier in life may also have an important effect. For example, the prevalence of living alone among divorced men in several European countries was higher than among divorced women. This could be due to the stronger childhood bonds formed between mothers and children than between divorced fathers and children.

Several participants remarked that the option of institutionalization is often ignored in discussions of living arrangements of older persons and seemed not to be regarded as a realistic or satisfactory option. Is this because there is a stigma attached to it? Or is it really a matter of lack of demand? Is it possible that the supply of acceptable institutional options is limited and insufficient but that the latent demand is substantial? Meeting participants confirmed that institutionalization was indeed stigmatized in many developing countries, including China. Yet, the issue is of relevance to older persons everywhere, not just in developed countries. It was noted that, especially for the younger old, institutionalization was often linked to health problems, while for the oldest old it was more often related to social situations, including a lack of potential family caregivers. Because the needs of older persons who are infirm and debilitated may outstrip the resources of members in a joint family, long-term care and institutionalization will become the only alternative for some people, and this too is a matter for design of adequate policies. Institutions provide a different array of care than co-resident families can or are willing to provide. If the development of robust pension systems is desirable, so is the development of policies to support affordable and good-quality institutional living arrangements.

In some areas of the world, there are creative alternatives to both home-based care and institutionalization. Thus, for example, in a few countries older persons are beginning to reside in communities specially designed for them. Older persons should have a say in determining the location and functioning of these communities; for instance, a location near downtown areas may be preferred because it provides easier access to cultural activities and a range of shops and services. These communities help resolve some of the social integration problems referred to earlier. However, whether they become widespread or not will depend on social, economic and, ultimately, cultural conditions.

This also raises the question of costs: Governments will become interested in the issue only to the extent we are able to show the costs associated with each set of options. In many settings families are currently providing care that would be costly to replace. For instance, a study in Ukraine made approximate estimates of the cost of providing paid caregivers for older persons to meet all the needs of the elderly for outside care, which is currently partly covered by family members and the formal sector. In this case, to care for the needs of older persons, using only outside providers, it was estimated that the Government would need an amount close to the total health budget of Ukraine.

Whereas in developed countries, pensions and social security expenditures are an important source of income for the older population, in most developing countries, the majority of older persons do not have coverage of any type, as their labour experience revolves around the informal economy. In these cases, providing broad coverage would require the establishment of social security systems that cover the informal economy. Another approach is South Africa's programme of assistance that subsidizes the family or close kin for care provided to older persons.

At present, living with children and other kin may be the only option available to the majority of older persons in developing countries, and those who lack this option may face destitution. Even in those countries, though, co-residence is not a panacea. To the extent that older persons contribute to the household, joint living arrangements may be tolerated and considered advantageous to all members of the household. But as older persons' contribution begins to decrease and as they become more a source of demand for services, there is reason for concern that co-residence arrangements may begin to weaken. When co-residence becomes increasingly difficult or is simply not an option, some older people will necessarily have to enter institutions.

Data and research needs

Meeting participants also discussed data needs and methodological approaches for answering many of the unresolved questions noted above. Assessment of data needs and design of data-collection instruments must take into account policy concerns and should be informed by theories of social functioning and social and economic change. In this regard, some participants regretted that the meeting had devoted relatively little time to theoretical issues.

In many developing countries, even basic descriptive information from a cross-sectional survey or case study is difficult to come by, especially given the inevitable competition for scarce research funds. One way to deal with this is demonstrated by John E. Dowd and colleagues at the World Health Organization, who are working on the design of data-collection systems (minimal data sets) sufficient to monitor and gauge the situation by tracking key indicators, without necessarily generating information to unravel complicated causal processes. To go further, to reveal the dynamic characteristics of household arrangements over time usually requires longitudinal studies and a focus on transitions over the life course of individuals, with attention to both older persons and their close kin.

There is value to be gained by combining survey-based data with information collected through focus groups and ethnographic research. Ethnographic approaches were employed in obtaining the results reported at the meeting by Peter Lloyd-Sherlock and Jay Sokolovsky. One important strength of ethnographic approaches is their ability to obtain information in depth about the process and reasons that underlie changes in living arrangements. For example, did the parent(s) move in with, or away from, adult children, or vice versa, and was the move impelled more by the needs of the older or of the younger generation? Was a move motivated by health problems, by financial considerations, or by needs for companionship, or for help in managing the household? Have living arrangements in fact changed, or did the parents and children remain together continuously after the children married?

It was noted that even in structured single-round surveys it was possible to pose questions that would ascertain basic information about the situation surrounding changes in living arrangements (and other major life events) and the reasons for those transitions. Such information could be of great value for interpretation and would be relevant to policy concerns, yet this type of data has rarely been gathered in surveys so far.

There is a tendency for surveys to focus on the older population only, or on the younger population only, and to ask such different questions of each group that it is not possible to compare the older and younger generations' desires and needs or their contributions to one another's well-being. Researchers and groups providing support for research on intergenerational family relations and intergenerational support should ensure that a core of questions is posed to both older and younger adults. Results also need to be tabulated in a way that facilitates comparison between the groups.

A number of research initiatives were discussed, including longitudinal studies conducted in developed countries.

Census microsamples have increasingly been used to study living arrangements, their social and economic correlates, and trends over time. There is still much potential for further work of this sort. Steven Ruggles described a new project at the University of Minnesota to preserve and make more widely available census microsample data from the 1960s and later for a range of countries. The Economic Commission for Europe has also been engaged in work in this area, involving census microsample data for a range of countries in Europe and Northern America. However, not all countries have made such data available for research use. Participants voiced a plea to the scientific community to encourage those who are in charge of gathering and managing data from national or regional censuses to make them available for sampling and analysis. Census microsamples can, and should, be structured in a way that preserves confidentiality.

Demographers have contributed to an understanding of the demographic constraints on the formation of extended households through the use of simulations. There have been two major approaches: microsimulation, which involves using a computer to answer specific questions about the individual life course, through sampling and model-based assumptions; and macrosimulation, which applies a set of deterministic assumptions in order to project aspects of the life course for a group of people. Zeng Yi presented illustrative results from a new macrosimulation model, ProFamy, to project transitions in household types, and also mentioned other macrosimulation models. Douglas Wolf gave an overview of microsimulation approaches.

The meeting discussed relative strengths and weaknesses of the macro- and microsimulation approaches. Within each general approach, a number of core models and computer programs have been developed. In general, microsimulation offers more flexibility, including the potential to investigate questions that were intractable by other methods. However, some participants criticized most of the analytic efforts in this area for failing to make the assumptions of the model clear and/or convincing to the reader. The sheer complexity of many such simulations makes them difficult to present in a way that is understandable and convincing to an audience of researchers or policy makers. A fundamental problem is that empirical information about some of the key relationships included in microsimulation models — such as correlated risks among family members — is generally not available, and in this case assumptions of unknown validity have had to be made; this has inevitably led to questions about the validity of the outcome of the simulations. Other participants stressed that the approach was indeed useful in certain situations. For instance, it could show the implications of making alternative assumptions, including assumptions about unmeasured heterogeneity in the population with respect to key risk factors such as frailty. It had also been useful in giving insights about kinship networks under different regimes of mortality and fertility. There was a further suggestion that different types of simulation might be employed in a complementary way to address specific aspects of issues such as kin availability.

26

IX. General Conclusions of the Meeting

Papers presented at the meeting and accompanying discussions facilitated the identification of a number of research and policy-relevant themes regarding the living arrangements of older persons. Many of these are due to insights produced by recent research and findings uncovered in the past 10 years. Although the living arrangements of older persons have always been an important dimension of the study of ageing, it is only in the past few years that researchers in the area have reached what may be termed a strategic point in the accumulation of knowledge, one that enables us to make certain statements with confidence and that sheds light on key areas for future research.

Pervasiveness of trends

Despite great intercountry variability in pace and timing, all developed countries have experienced increases in the prevalence of living alone among older persons. These trends are expected to continue. The contour of trends may not be exactly the same from place to place but they are quite close, and in the short run at least it is more likely that we will see a convergence towards even higher levels of living alone than any drastic reversals of recent trends.

With a few exceptions (such as the Republic of Korea), the same cannot be said of developing countries. There, the prevalence of older persons' co-residence with children and kin continues to be high — usually over 80 per cent — and these levels have changed very little in the past few decades. Yet, however small they may have been, changes during the decade 1980-1990 towards higher levels of living alone may point to the beginning of a major shift in the developing world as well. For a number of reasons discussed below, most researchers working in this area believe that many developing countries have reached a turning point beyond which the traditional living arrangements of older persons are being eroded.

Forces behind changes

Demographic determinants can be expected in the future to contribute to increases in the prevalence of living alone among older persons in the more developed countries, though they are not a major reason for the trends observed to date. Sharp fertility reductions will produce lower levels of demographic availability of children and other kin. In order for joint living arrangements between children and older persons to be possible, only one surviving child per couple is needed. But having only one child is probably not sufficient to provide the full array of choices for older persons as would a larger number of children; indeed, in a number of countries, parents with more children have been found to have a higher probability of co-residence. Thus, even though among the more developed countries Italy has one of the highest levels of joint living arrangements among those aged 60 or older, the current levels may not be sustainable with a demographic regime such as that in

27

northern Italy, where about 25 per cent of women above age 30 are childless and fully 50 per cent have only one child.

Mr. Ruggles argued persuasively that the turning point marking the beginning of the end of traditional living arrangements in the United States occurred as a result of transformations in the economy, and the same forces are believed to have operated in Europe. These changes simultaneously weakened the household economy and tightened the relation between human capital and social and economic returns and achievement. Social constructions such as the emergence of the welfare state reinforced changes that had begun to occur earlier but were not themselves the trigger that precipitated change. Finally, these changes have been reinforced by shifts in the ideological superstructure — reflected in stated preferences and values — with stronger emphasis on individual development, less reliance on family and kin networks, and an increase in the value placed on independent living.

Such trends are not the only factors influencing the dissolution of traditional living arrangements. Economic prosperity makes it more feasible for older people to live alone, while external constraints such as availability of housing and labour market rigidities for the younger generations can modify the extent to which living arrangements move in tandem with the set of economic, social and ideological conditions identified earlier.

Apart from a few Asian societies favoured by rapid industrialization, most other countries in the developing world face conditions that may retard the transition to higher levels of living alone. First, intergenerational solidarity and a sense of obligation towards older persons continue to be strong everywhere, or at least so it appears from survey information on preferences. Secondly, incipient, poorly developed, or non-existent systems of social transfers continue to place older persons at a disadvantage, even in cases where they may prefer to live independently, rather than with their children or other kin. Thirdly, apart from areas where migratory outflows are massive, conditions for the younger generations are not always conducive to situations where the pooling of resources and the economies of scale reaped from joint living arrangements can easily be forgone. Finally, only in a few of these societies have demographic and economic transformation led to rigidities in the life cycle of younger individuals — owing to career demands, dual-earning couples and marital disruption — to constrain the field of choice for living arrangements of older persons.

At the same time, if the above explanation of trends in the more developed countries is correct, this has major implications for developing countries as well. Their economies will, necessarily, in the course of development, undergo similar structural changes away from family farms and family enterprise. Nana Araba Apt reported that such changes were already tending to undermine the traditional authority of older persons in Africa. These changes are occurring more rapidly in developing countries than they have in the West, and the generational gap in education and earnings — two other factors thought to be important — is even wider in many developing countries than it has ever been in the West.

28

Co-residence and well-being

There are a number of reasons to be concerned about patterns of older persons' living arrangements. First, older persons' living arrangements have spillover effects. That is, individual decisions about joint or separate living affect social and contextual characteristics. Thus, they have an impact on aggregate demand for housing and housing services as well as on the size and type of demand for social services and caregiving for older persons. Secondly, it is widely believed that living arrangements are one factor, among many others, that influence older persons' well-being.

In the meeting a number of interventions identified the first reason as one of some importance but also made it clear that it was a neglected area of research. The second reason for examining older persons' living arrangements attracted much more attention. Yet, even though more research has focused on it, the kinds of inferences we can normally make are remarkably weak and tentative. The simple question "Are older persons who live alone better or worse off than those who live with children or relatives?" cannot be answered in a straightforward way. First, there are issues pertaining to identification of causal relations that are simply insurmountable with the data normally available. Thus, unless one has longitudinal observations, it is difficult, if not impossible, to decide whether conditions defining older persons' well-being lead to a particular type of residential arrangement or vice versa. Some may go so far as to say that without the ability to perform a randomized experiment, we will never be able to make unequivocal statements about this question.

Secondly, if living arrangements influence older persons' health conditions, socio-economic standing, emotional well-being or other dimensions of individual welfare, the effects could be highly contingent — that is, dependent on the presence or absence of other conditions. Thus, it is known, but rarely investigated, that the existence of social connections to individuals other than those in the immediate family has an important effect on emotional conditions such as loneliness. Familial transfers such as cash, periodic caregiving and so on could satisfy many of the needs that would normally be taken care of in situations of joint living.

In summary, in addition to the many problems presented to us by actually measuring the levels of older persons' well-being (how many dimensions? which ones?), there are serious difficulties associated with causal inferences. Some of these can be resolved by widening the scope of our inquiries, including an assessment of social relations other than those with family members, and measuring family transfers other than those that are part of co-residence.

Alternative living arrangements

The living arrangements of older persons need not involve a choice between living alone and living with family members only. For example, living alone but with a companion appears to be increasingly common among widows and widowers in Europe. We do not know whether this type of living arrangement will become widespread, nor do we understand the conditions (availability of housing; pension systems) that make it feasible.

The emergence of communities designed for older persons within or close to central cities is another form of living arrangement that emerges as a feasible alternative in the more developed and in some developing countries. But we do not yet completely understand either their financial implications or the type of older persons who are attracted to them. The idea that joint living arrangements of older persons and children could be reinforced by granting government subsidies to families, as is occurring in South Africa, is an innovative approach that may support continued co-residence as a solution in societies where there are no other feasible alternatives.

Finally, even in countries where the institutionalization of older persons is still highly stigmatized, it will not be possible to avoid altogether the development of institutionalization as an alternative. The current low levels of use of such an arrangement to provide care to older persons who are disabled and infirm could reflect social avoidance as much as a lack of adequate supply. It is likely that as soon as adequate financial incentives are introduced in the market, private initiative will develop and exploit this niche, first catering to pre-existing demand among the more affluent and then creating through diffusion and imitation a much larger demand. Older persons living in poverty and, more generally, all those who cannot afford good-quality institutional services will require different facilities and, in all likelihood, these will have to be financed through public transfers.

ANNEXES

ANNEX I

Agenda

1. Opening of the Meeting
   Forum on Critical Issues and Policy Responses to Population Ageing
2. Demographic and policy dimensions of population ageing and living arrangements of older persons
3. Living arrangements and well-being of older persons in the past
4. Living arrangements and family support
5. Adapting to rapid societal transformations
6. Poverty, health and living arrangements of older persons
7. Future research directions
8. Conclusions and closing of the formal sessions

ANNEX II

List of participants

Nana Araba Apt, Centre for Social Policy Studies, University of Ghana, Legon, Ghana

Vladislav V. Bezrukov, Institute of Gerontology, Academy of Medical Sciences, Kiev, Ukraine

Nikolai Botev, Population Activities Unit, Economic Commission for Europe, Geneva, Switzerland

Barbara Crossette,* New York Times, New York, New York, United States of America

Jenny de Jong Gierveld, Netherlands Interdisciplinary Demographic Institute, The Hague, Netherlands

Susan De Vos, Center for Demography and Ecology, University of Wisconsin, Madison, Wisconsin, United States of America

John E. Dowd, Ageing and Health Programme, World Health Organization, Geneva, Switzerland

Antonio Golini, Departimento de Scienze Demografice, University of Rome, Rome, Italy

Emily Grundy, Centre for Population Studies, London School of Hygiene and Tropical Medicine, London, United Kingdom of Great Britain and Northern Ireland

Joachim Holzenberger, German Foreign Office, Berlin, Germany

Jacques Légaré, Analytical Studies Branch, Statistics Canada, and Département de démographie, Université de Montréal, Montréal, Canada

Peter Lloyd-Sherlock, University of East Anglia, Norwich, United Kingdom of Great Britain and Northern Ireland

Linda Martin, The Population Council, New York, New York, United States of America

Elizabeth Mullen, International Activities, American Association of Retired Persons, Washington, D.C., United States of America

George C. Myers, Center for Demographic Studies, Duke University, Durham, North Carolina, United States of America

Alberto Palloni, Center for Demography and Ecology, University of Wisconsin, Madison, Wisconsin, United States of America

Martha Pelaez, Division of Health Promotion and Protection, Pan American Health Organization, Washington, D.C., United States of America

Peter Peterson,* The Blackstone Group, New York, New York, United States of America

Mohammed O. Rahman, Department of Population and International Health, Harvard School of Public Health, Boston, Massachusetts, United States of America

Mapule F. Ramashala, University of Durban-Westville and Medical Research Council, Durban, South Africa

Steven Ruggles, Department of History, University of Minnesota, Minneapolis, Minnesota, United States of America

Jay Sokolovsky, University of South Florida, Bayboro Campus, Florida, United States of America

Victoria Velkoff, International Programs Center, United States Bureau of the Census, Washington, D.C., United States of America

Douglas A. Wolf, Center for Policy Research, Syracuse University, Syracuse, New York, United States of America

Zeng Yi, Center for Demographic Studies, Duke University, Durham, North Carolina, United States of America

United Nations Population Division
Joseph Chamie, Director
Larry Heligman, Assistant Director
Mary Beth Weinberger, Chief, Population and Development Section
Barry Mirkin, Population Affairs Officer
Paulo Murad Saad, Population Affairs Officer
Karoline Schmid, Population Affairs Officer

United Nations Division for Social Policy and Development
Brigid Donelan
Alexandre Sidorenko

United Nations Population Fund
Rene Desiderio, Technical and Policy Division
Richard Leete, Technical and Policy Division

---

* Participated in the Forum only.

ANNEX III

List of documents

Symbol	Agenda item	Title/author
UN/POP/AGE/2000/1	2	The demography of population ageing Barry Mirkin and Mary Beth Weinberger Population Division
UN/POP/AGE/2000/2	2	Programmatic and policy aspects of population ageing and living arrangements Alberto Palloni
UN/POP/AGE/2000/3	3	Living arrangements and well-being of older persons in the past Steven Ruggles
UN/POP/AGE/2000/4	4	Living arrangements of older persons and family support in less developed countries Jay Sokolovsky
UN/POP/AGE/2000/5	4	Living arrangements of older persons and family support in more developed countries Jenny de Jong Gierveld, Helga de Valk and Marieke Blommesteijn
UN/POP/AGE/2000/6	5	Impact of pension reform on living arrangements of older persons in Latin America Paulo M. Saad, Population Division
UN/POP/AGE/2000/7	5	Political, social and economic crises and living arrangements of older persons: the case of Ukraine Vladislav V. Bezrukov and Natalia A. Foight
UN/POP/AGE/2000/8	5	Extremely rapid ageing and the living arrangements of older persons: the case of China Zeng Yi and Linda George

33

Symbol	Agenda item	Title/author
UN/POP/AGE/2000/9	5	Rapid urbanization and living arrangements of older persons in Africa Nana Araba Apt
UN/POP/AGE/2000/10	6	Living arrangements and the health of older persons in more developed countries Emily Grundy
UN/POP/AGE/2000/11	6	Living arrangements and the health of older persons in less developed countries: evidence from rural Bangladesh Mohammed O. Rahman
UN/POP/AGE/2000/12	6	Living arrangements of older persons and poverty Peter Lloyd-Sherlock
UN/POP/AGE/2000/13	6	Living arrangements, poverty and the health of older persons in Africa Mapule F. Ramashala
UN/POP/AGE/2000/14	7	Future research directions Victoria Velkoff
UN/POP/AGE/2000/15	-	Note on statistical analysis and microsimulation for studying living arrangements and intergenerational transfers Douglas A. Wolf

Information papers

UN/POP/AGE/2000/INF.1		Provisional organization of work
UN/POP/AGE/2000/INF.2		Provisional list of participants
UN/POP/AGE/2000/INF.3		Provisional list of documents

Part Two

BACKGROUND PAPERS

THE DEMOGRAPHY OF POPULATION AGEING

*Barry Mirkin and Mary Beth Weinberger**

An inevitable consequence of the demographic transition and the shift to lower fertility and mortality has been the evolution in the age structure of the world population. Many societies, especially in the more developed regions, have already attained older population age structures than have ever been seen in the past. Many developing countries in the midst of the demographic transition are experiencing rapid shifts in the relative numbers of children, working-age population and older persons.

DEMOGRAPHIC ASPECTS

The number of persons aged 60 years or older in the world is estimated to be 605 million in 2000. This number is projected to grow to nearly 2 billion by 2050, at which time it will be as large as the population of children (0-14 years). This historic crossover of an increasing share of older persons and a declining share of children will mark the first time that the number of children and older persons are the same.

Persons aged 60 or older currently comprise 10 per cent of the world population (see table 1). The percentage is much higher in the more developed regions (20 per cent) than in the less developed regions (8 per cent), which are at an earlier stage of the demographic transition. It is especially low in the least developed countries (5 per cent). Among individual countries, the most aged are Greece and Italy, where 24 per cent of the population is aged 60 or older in 2000. Many European countries, as well as Japan, have percentages nearly as high. By 2050, the older ages will make up a projected 22 per cent of the world population — 33 per cent in the more developed regions, 21 per cent in the less developed regions and 12 per cent in the least developed countries.

In terms of major regions, the majority of the world's older persons (53 per cent) reside in Asia, while Europe has the next largest share, 24 per cent (see table 2 and figure I). Asia's share of the older population will increase to 63 per cent by 2050, while the share of Europe will show the greatest relative decrease of any region, shrinking from 24 per cent to 11 per cent.

---

* Population Division, United Nations Secretariat.

TABLE 1. ESTIMATED AND PROJECTED PERCENTAGE OF THE POPULATION
IN SELECTED AGE GROUPS, BY REGION

Region	1970	2000	2025	2050
Children: under age 15				
World total	37	30	23	20
More developed regions	26	18	16	15
Less developed regions	42	33	25	20
Least developed countries	44	42	35	24
Africa	45	42	35	24
Asia	40	30	22	19
Europe	25	17	15	14
Latin America and the Caribbean	42	32	24	20
Northern America	29	21	18	17
Oceania	32	25	21	19
Youth: ages 15-24				
World total	18	18	15	13
More developed regions	17	14	11	11
Less developed regions	18	19	16	14
Least developed countries	18	20	20	17
Africa	18	20	20	17
Asia	18	18	15	13
Europe	16	14	10	10
Latin America and the Caribbean	19	20	16	13
Northern America	17	13	12	12
Oceania	18	15	14	13
Older persons: ages 60 or over				
World total	8	10	15	22
More developed regions	15	20	28	33
Less developed regions	6	8	13	21
Least developed countries	5	5	6	12
Africa	5	5	6	12
Asia	6	9	15	24
Europe	15	20	28	35
Latin America and the Caribbean	6	8	14	22
Northern America	14	16	26	28
Oceania	11	13	20	24

Region	1970	2000	2025	2050
	Oldest old: ages 80 or over			
World total	1	1	2	4
More developed regions	2	3	5	9
Less developed regions	0.4	1	1	3
Least developed countries	0.3	0.3	1	1
Africa	0.3	0.4	1	1
Asia	0.4	1	2	4
Europe	2	3	5	9
Latin America and the Caribbean	1	1	2	4
Northern America	2	3	4	8
Oceania	1	2	3	6

Source: The Sex and Age Distribution of the World Populations: the 1998 Revision, volume II: Sex and Age (United Nations publication, Sales No. E.99.XIII.8), medium variant projections.

TABLE 2. ESTIMATED AND PROJECTED REGIONAL DISTRIBUTION OF THE POPULATION AGED UNDER 15 YEARS AND THE POPULATION AGED 60 YEARS OR OVER — 1970, 2000 AND 2050 (PERCENTAGE)

Region	Under age 15			Aged 60 or over		
	1970	2000	2050	1970	2000	2050
World total	100	100	100	100	100	100
More developed regions	19	12	10	47	38	19
Less developed regions	81	88	90	53	62	81
Least developed countries	10	15	20	5	5	9
Africa	12	19	24	6	6	11
Asia	63	61	57	45	53	63
Eastern Asia	27	20	15	23	27	26
China	24	18	14	18	21	22
South-eastern Asia	9	9	9	5	6	9
South Central Asia	24	29	28	15	17	25
India	16	19	17	11	13	16
Western Asia	3	4	5	2	2	3
Europe	12	7	5	33	24	11
Latin America and the Caribbean	9	9	9	6	7	9
Northern America	5	4	4	10	8	6
Oceania	0.4	0.4	0.5	1	1	1

Source: The Sex and Age Distribution of the World Populations: the 1998 Revision, volume II: Sex and Age (United Nations publication, Sales No. E.99.XIII.8), medium variant projections.

Figure I. Geographic distribution of the population aged under 15 and 60 or over, 2000 and 2050

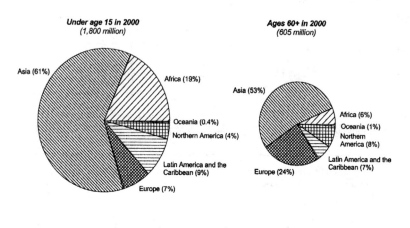

Under age 15 in 2000
(1,800 million)

Asia (61%)
Africa (19%)
Oceania (0.4%)
Northern America (4%)
Latin America and the Caribbean (9%)
Europe (7%)

Ages 60+ in 2000
(605 million)

Asia (53%)
Africa (6%)
Oceania (1%)
Northern America (8%)
Latin America and the Caribbean (7%)
Europe (24%)

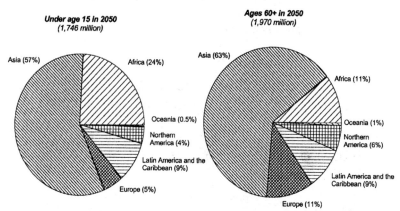

Under age 15 in 2050
(1,746 million)

Asia (57%)
Africa (24%)
Oceania (0.5%)
Northern America (4%)
Latin America and the Caribbean (9%)
Europe (5%)

Ages 60+ in 2050
(1,970 million)

Asia (63%)
Africa (11%)
Oceania (1%)
Northern America (6%)
Latin America and the Caribbean (9%)
Europe (11%)

Source: *The Sex and Age Distribution of the World Populations: the 1998 Revision, volume II: Sex and Age* (United Nations publication, Sales No. E.99.XIII.8), medium variant projections.

40

The oldest old, persons aged 80 years or older, currently number 70 million, the majority of whom live in more developed regions. Thirty-three million are estimated to be living in less developed regions. They make up about 1 per cent of the world's population and 3 per cent of the population of the more developed regions. This oldest age group is the fastest growing segment of the older population. By 2050, the number of the oldest old is projected to be five times as large as at present. By that date, the oldest old will be 4 per cent of the total world population, and in the more developed regions, one person out of 11 is projected to be aged 80 or older. In the less developed regions, 3 per cent of the population will be 80 years or older.

It is necessary to look beyond 2050 to see the full consequences for population ageing of ongoing trends towards lower fertility and mortality rates. A range of alternative scenarios presented in the United Nations long-range population projections (United Nations, 1999a) show that future populations will reach a significantly older age structure than the populations of the present, or even of the populations of 2050. Figure II shows projected trends in the proportion of the world's population aged 60 or older through the year 2150, from the medium fertility scenario, which assumes that fertility in all major areas will stabilize at replacement level around 2050, and that mortality rates will continue to improve. By 2150, persons aged 60 or older are projected to number 3.0 billion, nearly one person out of every three alive at that time. Over 1.2 billion people, or one in every 10 persons, will be aged 80 or older. Only 18 per cent of the population will be children aged under 15 years, as compared to 30 per cent at present.

Speed of ageing

The growth of the older population often receives attention in connection with the developed countries. However, the tempo of ageing is more rapid in the less developed regions than in the more developed regions (see figure III). Because rapid changes in age structure may be more difficult for societies to adjust to than change that is spread over a longer time horizon, the speed of population ageing has important implications for government policies, such as pension schemes, health care and economic growth. Figure IV shows, for selected countries, the dates when the population reached, or is expected to reach, the point when 7, 14 and 21 per cent of the population was aged 65 or older. (Currently, 6.9 per cent of the world's population is aged 65 or older.) Typically, the transition from 7 to 14 per cent took longer for countries that reached the 7 per cent level at an earlier date. For example, France and Sweden, which reached the 7 per cent point before 1900, took 114 years and 82 years, respectively, to reach 14 per cent. That same transition required only 24 years in Japan, from 1970 to 1994. Several developing countries shown in figure IV will also make a rapid transition from 7 to 14 per cent aged 65 or older. Brazil, Indonesia, the Republic of Korea and Tunisia are projected to make this transition in a time-span of under 25 years, and the two most populous countries, China and India, may require only 25 and 28 years, respectively.

Figure II. Percentage of world population by age group, medium scenario, 1950-2150

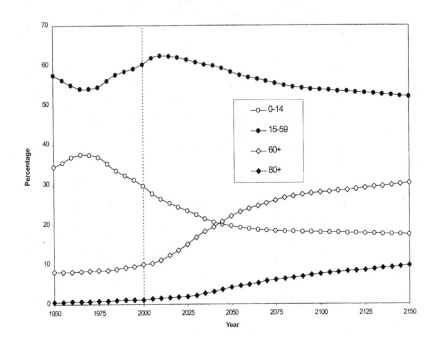

Source: Population Division of the Department of Economic and Social Affairs of the United Nations Secretariat, Long-range world population projections, based on the 1998 revision (ESA/P/WP.153), 1999.

Figure III. Growth in population size and age-specific annual growth rates, for the child, youth and older populations, 1970-2050

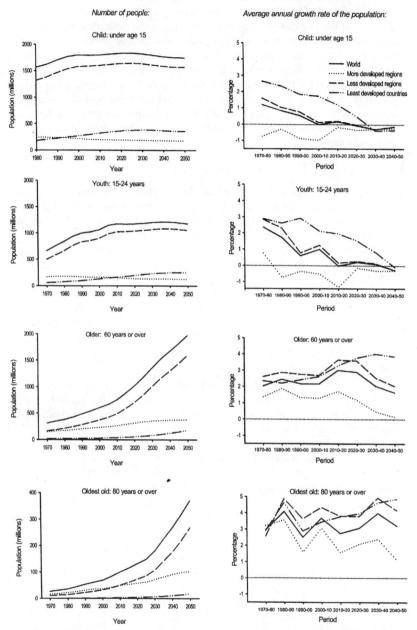

Source: The Sex and Age Distribution of the World Populations: the 1998 Revision, volume II: Sex and Age (United Nations publication, Sales No. E.99.XIII.8), medium variant projections.

In many cases, it will take substantially less time for the transition from 14 to 21 per cent aged 65 years or older than it took to move from 7 to 14 per cent (see figure IV). Although no country has yet reached the point where 21 per cent of the population is aged 65 or older, some countries, including Italy and Japan, are expected to reach that point before 2015; in Japan, the transition from 14 to 21 per cent will have taken only 16 years, and in Italy, 23 years. At a later date, Canada and the United States of America are also expected to make a rapid transition from 14 to 21 per cent aged 65 or older as the large "baby boom" cohorts enter the higher ages. Thus, in the near future, some societies will be faced not only with older populations than have ever existed at the national level, but also with populations that are ageing at an extremely rapid pace.

Ageing and gender

Population ageing is, in basic demographic respects, not "gender-neutral". The evolution to an older age structure changes the balance in numbers of men and women in the whole population. Men's higher mortality over the life course means that women typically outnumber men at older ages, and the difference is quite large among the oldest old (see table 3). At ages 60 or older, there were an estimated 81 men for every 100 women globally in 2000, and at ages 80 or older there were only 53 men for every 100 women. The sex ratios of older age groups are lower in the more developed regions than in the less developed regions, since there are larger differences in life expectancy between the sexes in the more developed regions. In addition, the sex ratio in the oldest age groups in the more developed regions retains the effect of the heavy loss of males in some countries during the Second World War.

Given the age patterns of the sex ratio, the rapid growth of the elderly population and the increase in the proportion in older age groups imply a decrease in the sex ratio for the total population and a greater increase in the number of older women than of older men. Projected increases between 2000 and 2050 in the number of persons aged 60 or older are 636 million for men and 729 million for women in the world as a whole. Projected increases during the same period in the number of persons aged 80 or older are 116 million for men and 185 million for women.

Figure IV. Time when the percentage of the population aged 65 or over reached or will reach 7, 14 and 21 per cent: selected countries

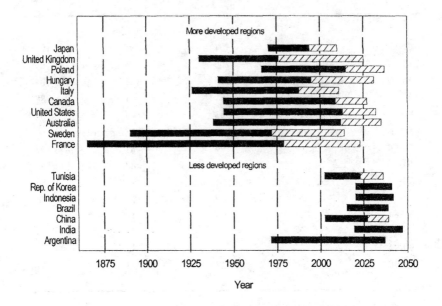

Percentage 65 or over:

■■ Period from 7% to 14%
▨▨ Period from 14% to 21%

Note: For countries where the percentage aged over 65 years will reach 21 per cent after 2050, only the period between attainment of the 7 and 14 per cent points is shown.

Sources: The Sex and Age Distribution of the World Populations: the 1998 Revision, volume II: Sex and Age (United Nations publication, Sales No. E.99.XIII.8); United States Bureau of the Census, *An Aging World II,* International Population Reports, P95/92-3 (Washington, D.C., Government Printing Office, 1992).

TABLE 3. SEX RATIOS BY AGE IN THE MORE AND LESS DEVELOPED
REGIONS, 2000
(Men per 100 women)

Age	World	More developed regions	Less developed regions
	For broad age groups		
Total	101	95	103
<15	106	105	106
15-59	103	101	104
60+	81	71	88
80+	53	44	64
	For 5-year groups, ages 60 or over		
60-64	94	87	97
65-69	89	82	93
70-74	81	72	86
75-79	69	59	78
80-84	60	51	69
85-89	48	41	59
90-94	36	32	46
95-99	27	23	37
100+	25	19	38

Source: *The Sex and Age Distribution of the World Populations: the 1998 Revision,
volume II: Sex and Age* (United Nations publication, Sales No. E.99.XIII.8).

Concomitant with dramatic improvements in average lifespan has been the widening differential over time between male and female longevity. By 1995-2000, the female advantage in life expectancy at birth has grown to almost eight years in more developed regions and three years in less developed regions. The advantage, however, diminishes during the life course and by age 60, the male-female differential has narrowed to four years in more developed regions and to only two years in less developed regions. At current mortality rates (for 1995-2000), almost 40 per cent of girls and about one quarter of boys born can expect to survive to the "oldest old" ages, 80 years or older. While the increased likelihood of surviving to older ages is obviously due to mortality declines at younger ages, recent decades have also seen significant mortality improvements among the older population, including the oldest old, and these trends so far have been more beneficial to women than to men (Kannisto, 1994).

At older ages, women are less likely to be married and more likely to be widowed than are men, not only because they survive on average to higher ages, but also because most women marry men several years older than themselves. While more than three quarters (79 per cent) of older men are married, on a global basis, less than one half (43 per cent) of older women are married (United Nations, 1999b). The longer-term effect of gender differences in marriage age on later widowhood is only one of many ways in which demographic, as well as economic and social circumstances in early life have diverging ramifications for men and women in old age.

Demographic causes of population ageing

The process of population ageing is determined primarily by trends in fertility rates and secondarily by mortality rates. Any population with a long history of high fertility has a "young" age structure, similar in its general features to the present age structure for the group of least developed countries (see figure V). The average age of the population starts to rise when fertility rates decline. For the period 1995-2000, 61 countries in the world, representing 44 per cent of the world's population, are at or below replacement fertility. By 2015, the world's population is projected to reach 7.2 billion, of which about two thirds will be living in countries at or below replacement fertility (United Nations, 1999c). The impact of mortality decline is more variable, depending on whether the decline in mortality operates mainly at younger or at older ages. In fact, the first stages of mortality decline have usually particularly benefited infants and children, and have often served to make the population younger. However, changes in mortality may assume a greater importance for population ageing later in the demographic transition. In countries where mortality rates at young ages are already low, further declines have tended to affect mainly the adult and older ages, and have contributed to population ageing. For example, Caselli and Vallin (1990) have demonstrated the growing impact of mortality change in population projections of France and Italy. They concluded that even if Italian fertility remained at a very low level of 1.4 children per woman through the year 2040, more than half the increase in the proportion of the population aged 60 or older would be due to mortality change, and less than half to the earlier fertility trends.

Trends in dependency ratios

Demographic dependency ratios are used as approximate indicators of the relative sizes of the non-working-age and working-age populations. The youth-dependency ratio (the number of children per 100 persons of labour force age, ages 15-64 years) and the elderly-dependency ratio (the number aged 65 years or older per 100 persons of labour force age) indicate the dependency burden on workers and how the type of dependency shifts from children to older persons during the demographic transition. The potential economic implications of falling or rising burdens of demographic dependency have been an area of active research.

47

Figure V. Population pyramids: age and sex distribution, 2000 and 2050

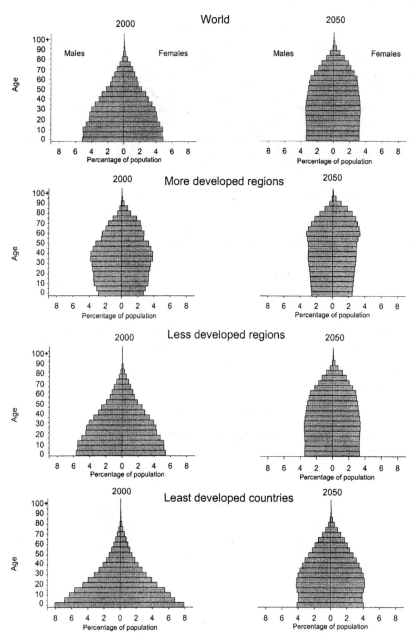

Source: The Sex and Age Distribution of the World Populations: the 1998 Revision, volume II: Sex and Age (United Nations publication, Sales No. E.99.XIII.8), medium variant projections.

Since 1970, the youth-dependency ratio has been declining in all regions, while the over-65 dependency ratio is rising (see table 4). Trends for the total ratio in different countries and regions depend upon the relative size and speed of these countervailing trends in the older and younger components. In general, the total dependency burden declined between 1970 and 2000. In the more developed regions, the total dependency ratio decreased over that period from 56 to 48 dependent-aged persons per 100 aged 15 to 64. The ratio will increase between the present and 2025 and is projected to rise further, to 70, by 2050. In the less developed regions, the overall dependency ratio in 1970 was 84, much higher than in the more developed regions, but it decreased rapidly to 60 by 2000, is projected to decline further to 50 by 2025 and then to increase slightly between 2025 and 2050. The impact of demographic ageing is clearly visible in the old-age dependency ratio, which is increasing in both more and less developed regions during the period from 1970 to 2050. Between 2000 and 2050, the old-age dependency ratio will double in more developed regions and almost triple in less developed regions.

The amount and pace of change in demographic dependency ratios varies greatly between countries. Large swings in dependency ratios are typically initiated or accentuated by rapid fertility declines, but those effects take many years to play out. Four examples are shown in figure VI to illustrate a range of situations and trends:

Argentina has experienced a gradual fertility decline, with relatively minor fluctuations over a long period. It is projected to experience only minor changes in the total dependency ratio, which will remain near 60 over the entire period from 1970 to 2050.

In Italy, the total fertility rate plummeted after the mid-1970s to reach the unprecedentedly low level of 1.2 by the early 1990s. The total dependency ratio initially declined, but increases in the over-65 dependency ratio will dominate the trend into the future, and will produce an especially rapid rise in demographic dependency after 2020.

The Republic of Korea experienced a rapid fertility decline after 1970, and the total dependency ratio fell to an unusually low level of 39 by 2000. The overall ratio will not begin to rise appreciably until after 2015, but it will then increase rapidly.

Kenya shows an extremely high child-dependency ratio, with a total dependency ratio of 115 in 1980. Kenya had one of the highest levels of fertility in the world, estimated at 8.1 children per woman during the period from 1960 to 1980, before beginning a rapid fertility decline, which is projected to continue. By 2000, Kenya's under-15 and over-65 ratios were similar to those seen in the Republic of Korea 30 years earlier.

TABLE 4. TRENDS IN AGE-DEPENDENCY RATIOS, BY REGION — 1970 TO 2050 (PERCENTAGE)

Region	1970	2000	2025	2050
	Dependency ratio: total			
World total	75	58	51	56
More developed regions	56	48	58	70
Less developed regions	84	60	50	54
Least developed countries	90	82	63	47
Africa	92	84	63	47
Asia	80	56	48	57
Europe	56	48	56	72
Latin America and the Caribbean	87	59	50	58
Northern America	62	51	59	64
Oceania	65	54	56	60
	Under age 15			
World total	66	47	36	31
More developed regions	41	27	25	26
Less developed regions	77	52	37	31
Least developed countries	84	77	56	35
Africa	86	78	56	35
Asia	73	47	33	30
Europe	39	26	23	25
Latin America and the Caribbean	79	50	35	32
Northern America	46	32	29	28
Oceania	53	39	33	30
	Ages 65 or over			
World total	10	11	16	26
More developed regions	15	21	33	44
Less developed regions	7	8	13	23
Least developed countries	6	6	6	12
Africa	6	6	6	12
Asia	7	9	15	27
Europe	16	22	33	47
Latin America and the Caribbean	8	9	14	27
Northern America	16	19	30	36
Oceania	12	15	23	30

Note: The ratios show the ratio of the numbers of persons aged under 15 years and over 65 years to the number aged 15 to 64 years, expressed as a percentage.

Source: The Sex and Age Distribution of the World Populations: the 1998 Revision, volume II: Sex and Age (United Nations publication, Sales No. E.99.XIII.8), medium variant projections.

Figure VI. Estimated and projected trends in age-dependency ratios in selected countries

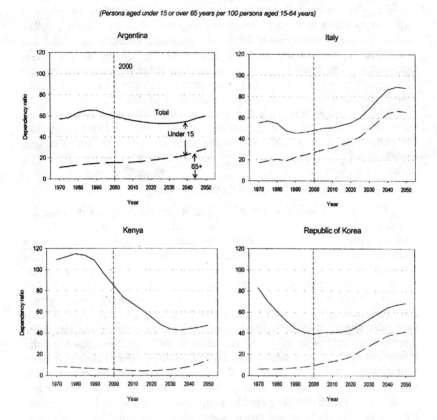

(Persons aged under 15 or over 65 years per 100 persons aged 15-64 years)

*Source: The Sex and Age Distribution of the World Populations: the 1998 Revision,
Volume II: Sex and Age* (United Nations publication, Sales No. E.99.XIII.8), medium variant
projections.

Urbanization

Consistent with the global trend of urbanization, the older population is becoming more concentrated in urban areas. By 2000, the majority of the world's older persons (51 per cent) will live in urban areas; by 2025, this is expected to climb to 62 per cent of older persons (United Nations, 1993). These figures, however, mask the large divergence between more and less developed regions. In the more developed regions, 74 per cent of older persons are urban dwellers, while in the less developed regions, which remain predominantly rural, slightly more than one third (37 per cent) of the elderly reside in urban areas. Despite the increasing urbanization of the older population, rural areas remain disproportionately older than urban areas in many countries as a result of migration of young persons to urban areas and the return migration of older persons to rural areas (Martin and Kinsella, 1994).

CONCLUSIONS

There can be little doubt that changes in age distribution have complex social and economic implications at the societal and individual levels. An excess supply of workers could for instance turn into an acute shortage of new entrants within a few years. Likewise, the departure of older workers from the labour force is a source of serious pressure on national economies through its impact on pension schemes. An important issue is the question of how best to allocate limited resources among public sectors. Accordingly, planning may have to reflect greater sensitivity to expected demographic changes. This is especially important in the light of an increasingly competitive and integrated international economic environment, as well as a re-examination of the limitations of the welfare state. Conventional wisdom is that if change is slow, countries can more easily adapt. As the experience of developed countries has shown, despite an ageing process that has occurred over many years, adjustment to the challenges posed by population ageing has not been smooth. Given that large shifts in age structure are being compressed into a relatively short period in developing countries, these countries will have less time than the developed countries to adapt to the problems posed by the changing age structure.

On the individual level, the goal is to enable older persons to maintain their dignity, self-esteem and physical and mental well-being in order to facilitate their continued participation in society and recognize their valuable contribution to their families and communities. The challenge for countries and communities is to provide conditions that promote quality of life and enhance the ability of older persons to work and live independently as long as possible.

REFERENCES

Caselli, Graziella and Jacques Vallin (1990). Mortality and population ageing. *European Journal of Population* (Amsterdam, Netherlands), vol. 6, No. 1, pp. 1-25.

Kannisto, Vaino (1994). *Development of Oldest-Old Mortality, 1950-1990: Evidence from 28 Developed Countries.* Odense, Denmark: Odense University Press.

Martin, Linda and Kevin Kinsella (1994). Research on the demography of aging in developing countries. In *Demography of Aging*, Linda Martin and Samuel Preston, eds. Washington, D.C.: National Academy Press.

United Nations (1993). Urban and rural areas by sex and age: the 1992 revision. ESA/P/WP/120.

_____ (1999a). Long-range world population projections, based on the 1998 revision. ESA/P/WP/153.

_____ (1999b). *Population Ageing, 1999.* Sales No. E.99.XIII.11.

_____ (1999c). *World Population Prospects: the 1998 Revision, vol. II, Sex and Age.* Sales No. E.99.XIII.8.

United States Bureau of the Census (1992). *An Aging World II.* Washington, D.C.: Government Printing Office. International population reports, P95/92-3.

LIVING ARRANGEMENTS OF OLDER PERSONS

*Alberto Palloni**

INTRODUCTION

During the past decade, there has been a surge of interest in the living arrangements of older persons. The theme has been part of the demography and sociology of the family, but only as an outcome subordinate to the broader issue of household and family organization. It has received new impetus owing to three interrelated factors: first, the rapidity and demographic inevitability of ageing in the developed world and its even more accelerated pace in countries that have experienced recent demographic transitions; secondly, the increasing availability of data and deployment of procedures to extract information from older sources and to analyse new ones; and thirdly, an upsurge of research in the economics of intergenerational transfers, an area that for a long time has been inextricably linked to the explanation of fertility changes but that now, paradoxically, experiences a revival in order to understand the consequences, rather than the causes, of fertility change.

The present paper takes stock of recent developments in the literature, summarizes key findings, provides a synthesis of theories and models, and reviews issues pertaining to statistical inference. It also suggests a road map for further research and identifies what appear to be the most salient problematic issues and likely solutions.

The term "living arrangements" or "co-residential arrangements" is used interchangeably to refer to the household structure of the elderly. When living with at least one child (or other kin), the term "co-residence" is used. Unless otherwise noted, when the elderly live with a spouse but no other kin or are unmarried and living with no other kin, the term "living alone" is used. The paper is divided into six sections. Section II reviews briefly some well-known and other lesser-known characteristics of the ageing process in both developed and developing countries. Using the case of Latin America as an example, the section highlights conditions of the ageing process that will constrain the social and demographic space where changes in future living arrangements of the elderly can take place. Section III examines the nature of recent trends in living arrangements and the current situation in both developed and developing countries, and reviews evidence regarding the relation between

---

* Center for Demography and Ecology, University of Wisconsin, United States of America.

co-residence and well-being. Section IV locates elderly living arrangements in a theoretical niche carved out by the literature on households, families and intergenerational transfers, and identifies the most important findings for both developing and developed countries. Section V offers an examination of the theoretical issues to be addressed, promising model formulations, and a synthesis of the kinds of data required to shed light on important issues with policy relevance. The concluding section poses three strategic themes to be considered for future research.

PREAMBLE: THE INSTITUTIONAL AND DEMOGRAPHIC CONTEXT OF RAPID AGEING

With the notable exception of the African continent, the populations in most countries of the world are ageing rapidly. Commonly used indicators of ageing are the fraction of the population attaining age 60 or 65 and indices, such as the dependency ratio, comparing the size of the elderly to the younger population. Table 1 shows the values of the proportion of the population over age 60 and availability ratios[1] estimated in 1990 and projected in 2020-2025 for selected major regions of the world. An interesting feature of the table is the increased homogeneity projected to prevail in 2020-2025 as opposed to the heterogeneity in 1990. Countries with post-1970 demographic transitions and countries where the demographic transition was well established in the 1930s are much closer to one another in terms of both indices. Convergence of indicators of ageing is not just the result of the smoothing effects embedded in the persistence of a demographic regime, but also an outcome of more rapid ageing in countries with late demographic transitions. Figure I provides an illustration of the relative speed in the ageing process of selected countries in Latin America and compares values of the mean ages of various populations (see, also, Palloni, De Vos and Pelaez, 1999).

The factors explaining population ageing are well known and will not be repeated here. Instead, the focus is on two characteristics of the ageing process in developing countries. These deserve attention because they can affect patterns of co-residence, and because they have a bearing on future levels of well-being of the elderly. The data compiled are for Latin America but, in principle, these conditions may be shared by other regions of the world.

Incongruence between the speed of the ageing process and the institutional context

There are a number of reasons why labelling ageing as a "problem" may well describe the conditions found in developing countries, rather than being an excessively charged characterization. The point is a simple one: the forces responsible for ageing in most developing countries, sharp fertility decline after 1970 and mortality decline after 1950, lead to relatively fast and concentrated changes in the age structure. The changes take place before the social and economic conditions that facilitate and secure transfers of wealth towards the elderly have a chance to emerge, develop or consolidate. Instead, the institutional context is characterized by insufficiently developed capital

55

markets, high risk and uncertainty that inhibits adequate private savings, insecure property rights, high inflationary pressures, as well as a lack of social security schemes, the absence of private pension plans and insufficient health insurance.

TABLE 1. PROPORTION OF THE POPULATION OVER AGE 60 (P) AND AVAILABILITY RATIOS (AR), 1990-2025[a]

Region	1990		2020-2025	
	P	AR	P	AR
Sub-Saharan Africa	0.047	12.8	0.048	11.8
Eastern Africa	0.044	12.3	0.048	13.6
Central Africa	0.049	10.9	0.046	12.7
Northern Africa	0.059	10.4	0.093	7.9
Southern Africa	0.055	11.5	0.066	10.6
Western Africa	0.047	11.6	0.051	12.1
Eastern Asia	0.103	7.2	0.178	4.6
South Central Asia	0.067	9.4	0.101	7.3
South-eastern Asia	0.067	9.9	0.112	6.8
Western Asia	0.068	9.3	0.097	7.2
Eastern Europe	0.171	4.6	0.236	3.6
Northern Europe	0.202	4.0	0.204	3.2
Southern Europe	0.206	4.1	0.278	3.1
Western Europe	0.202	4.1	0.278	3.1
Caribbean	0.093	7.4	0.141	5.4
Central America	0.062	10.1	0.106	6.9
South America	0.077	8.7	0.126	6.0
Northern America	0.163	4.8	0.235	3.5
Oceania	0.132	5.6	0.184	4.2

Source: United Nations, World Population Prospects, 1998 Revision.

[a] AR is the ratio of population aged 15-59 to the population aged 60+. A more precise indicator of availability requires establishing average length of generations, $t(x)$, between the elderly aged x and their children aged $x-t(x)$. One can then form the age-specific availability ratio for age x, $AR(x)$, as the ratio of population aged x to the population aged $x-t(x)$. The adjusted availability ratio is the weighted average of $AR(x)$.

Figure I. Mean age of population

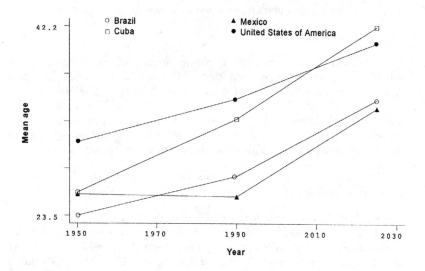

In these countries, there is a sharp incongruence between the advance of the ageing process and the social and institutional context within which it takes place. The consequences of this dislocation are two: first, the demands associated with rapid ageing are less likely to be met in these areas than elsewhere and, secondly, levels of well-being of the elderly will be endangered in the best of cases and will decline in the worst.

Social security

In the vast majority of countries in Asia and Latin America, social security systems are non-existent or poorly developed, and coverage extends to a privileged sector of the workforce only. Even though social security systems were established in some Latin American countries much earlier than in the United States of America, they are currently in disarray and are experiencing reforms that will drastically alter the programmes' coverage and contract their safety net components (Barrientos, 1997; Palloni, De Vos and Pelaez, 1999).

Human capital

Populations attaining age 60 or 65 now and in the near future belong to cohorts whose wage-earning history is fragile. These are cohorts whose levels of education are far lower than they are among the elderly in developed countries. With a few exceptions, in Latin American countries, not less than 30 per cent of those attaining age 60 are illiterate. Massive literacy campaigns did not begin in earnest until the late 1950s so their effects cannot be felt until after 2025. Even then, the composition of the elderly by levels of education will be lopsided towards incomplete primary and secondary levels, far from assuring access to sources of income derived from accumulated assets, savings and the private pension plans that are just now coming into existence.

Gender differentials

Male and female mortality disparities in developing countries are at roughly comparable levels with those in developed countries. In Latin America, just over two thirds of those surviving to age 60 are women and about half of them are widows. Women's levels of education lag far behind those of males, and their patterns of labour-force participation have historically stayed at very low levels. Their wage-earning history is precarious and leaves them totally dependent on others in their families for income.

Health status of the elderly: where does the growth of the elderly population come from?

At least in Latin America, the rapid growth of the older population that will take place between now and 2025 or so has two main sources: the transient increase in fertility that took place between 1955 and 1965 and, most important, the massive mortality decline that began in 1950. Thus, the cohorts that attain their sixtieth birthday between 2000 and 2025 are the beneficiaries of unusually large improvements in survival, particularly during early childhood. For example, individuals born in 1960 experienced lower levels of early childhood mortality than those born in 1955. This will increase the size of the cohort attaining age 60 in 2020 relative to cohorts that reach age 60 five years earlier.

Empirical estimates of the contribution of mortality decline to the growth of the elderly

To assess the importance of mortality decline as a contributor to the growth of the elderly population, we select three countries that roughly represent the diversity of regimes of mortality decline in the region. For each of them, we estimate the profile of mortality decline over the period from 1900 to 1990, and calculate a projected life-table to assess future changes during the period from 1990 to 2020. We then proceed to estimate the absolute magnitude of the contribution of mortality changes to the rate of increase of the population in several quinquennial age groups at various points in time and for the years 2000 and 2020. Figure II shows the estimated magnitude of these changes for age groups 50-54, 55-59 and so on for the year 2020. The vertical axis represents the total cumulated change of mortality rates experienced by cohorts reaching ages in the horizontal axis during the year 2020. Thus, for example, compared to those who will be in the age group 60-64, Chileans who attain ages 65-69 in 2020 will experience reductions in mortality rates after birth of the order of 0.0125. For Chileans aged 70-74 in 2020, the figure is about 0.028. Since the bulk of mortality decline, particularly during early childhood, occurred in the post-Second World War years, the peak is attained among the cohorts born during those years (who will be aged between 70 and 80 in 2020). Older cohorts also experience mortality changes but, since they are not the beneficiaries of the typically larger gains accruing to early childhood, the magnitude of the changes is smaller.

Graphs for other countries in the region look similar to that in figure II. The only difference is that in cases where mortality decline occurs later than in Chile or Mexico, the curves are displaced towards the left, and their peaks are associated with younger cohorts. Furthermore, in countries where mortality changes are less gradual and more concentrated in time (as in Bolivia, Peru, Ecuador or Paraguay), the curves are narrower and more spiked.

The estimates plotted in figure II enable us to informally gauge the magnitude of the contribution of past mortality changes to current and future ageing. In Chile, for example, about 43 per cent (0.015/0.035) of the total rate of increase of the population 60 or over by 2020 is due to mortality changes. In Mexico, the corresponding values are slightly lower. Thus, a substantial fraction of future ageing is attributable to mortality changes experienced during the period from 1930 to 1990. The remainder (about 57 per cent in the case of Chile) is associated with either changes in the size of the birth cohorts, or, to a lesser extent, with changes in mortality at ages above 60.

Figure II. Cumulated mortality change by age, 2020

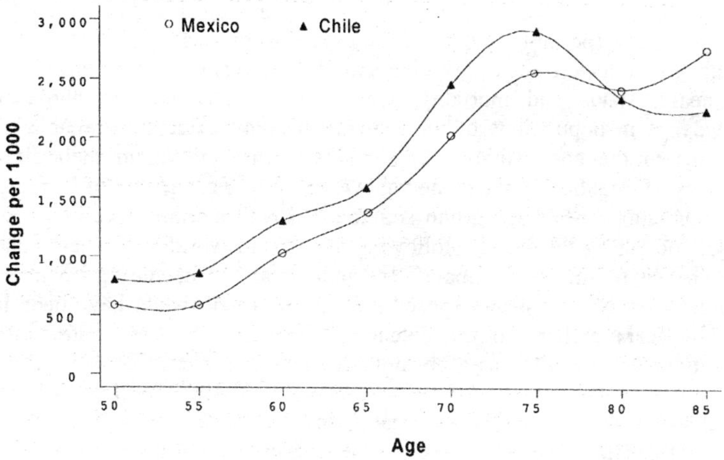

As shown elsewhere (Palloni and Lu, 1995), about 70 per cent of the mortality decline that occurred between 1940 and 1980 was due to changes in mortality associated with infectious diseases in the first 10 years of life. This statistic suggests that the relatively compressed schedule of ageing in the region can, in part at least, be traced to the medical and public health revolution that triggered the mortality decline nearly half a century ago. This legacy may have important implications for the health and disability status of the elderly population after 2000.

Even if there are significant improvements in mortality at older ages, it is worth asking how healthy the extra years of life will be, and what will be the magnitude of health-care costs associated with them. The following paragraphs contain a brief discussion of what the future trends in health status among the elderly are likely to be.

Prospective changes in mortality and health status

Even if it is true that additional gains in survivorship are possible, it is not at all clear that the added years of life will be healthy ones. The health status of the elderly will depend on two conditions. The first is access to satisfactory health or medical care. Health status will be worse for populations with limited access to health or medical care and better elsewhere. The second condition is the composition of the population at any age according to risk profiles. This is a complex result of three factors: early childhood exposure (perinatal and first five years' growth and development), lifetime behavioural risk profiles (smoking, drinking, diet and exercise), and past purchase of health inputs (possibly dependent on occupation, education and assets). Although we have some knowledge about the effects of each of these factors on health status and mortality, we know virtually nothing about their prevalence in populations of the region. The only evidence available to us pertains to the composition of the cohorts who will attain their sixtieth birthday after 2000. As mentioned above, about half of the rate of increase of the population in this age group is associated with mortality decline in early childhood during the decades following the Second World War. These cohorts will be increasingly dominated by individuals who, during their early childhood, may have been exposed to conditions that would have been fatal several years earlier. To the extent that exposure to and contraction of conditions early in life has a physiological effect that endures and plays out many years later (Fogel, 1986; Fogel and Costa, 1997; Barker, 1997), we should expect that the health status of the corresponding cohort will deteriorate. These effects are likely to be stronger among populations that are more vulnerable or that have less opportunity to purchase adequate health inputs. As documented elsewhere (Palloni, De Vos and Pelaez, 1999), an important fraction of the elderly in the region will live in rural areas and will belong to the lowest social classes, that is, they will be exposed to conditions characterized by little, if any, access to satisfactory health-care facilities and to mediocre informal care. Reforms in the public sector, the wholesale revamping of pension systems, and past trends in labour-force participation will only worsen the situation by hampering the ability to purchase acceptable health services.

Elsewhere (Palloni, De Vos and Pelaez, 1999), the examples of respiratory tuberculosis, osteoporosis and dementia are cited as three conditions tightly linked to health status in the past that are likely to affect the health status of the elderly in the near future to a larger extent than they do now or than they ever did in developed countries.

The foregoing considerations suggest the conjecture that future increases in life expectancy above age 60 in countries of the region are unlikely to be accompanied by corresponding decreases in the prevalence of ill health. A more likely scenario is one where an increasing fraction of years of life gained are spent in disability or ill health.

Empirical assessment of recent conditions

Is there any empirical evidence directly or indirectly supporting the conjecture stated above?

The only two sources of information about health conditions among the elderly in the region are a multi-country study coordinated by the Pan American Health Organization in the early 1980s and two recent surveys carried out in São Paulo, Brazil and Mexico City. For a number of reasons, self-reports on health status are the only comparable item that provides useful variability across countries in the region. Table 2 shows the percentage of sample population aged 60 and above reporting their health in various categories in a continuum from "poor" to "very good". Although age distinctions would have been desirable, sample sizes do not permit us to compute reliable age-specific estimates. The table also includes comparable percentages calculated from the Health and Retirement Survey (HRS) and Asset and Health Dynamics among the Oldest Old (AHEAD), two of the most important data sources on the elderly in the United States of America. Figures in the table are shown by gender and, in the case of the United States, by ethnic group. Table 2 includes data for four additional countries (Colombia, El Salvador, Jamaica and Venezuela), where the categories for self-reporting employed originally did not allow us to make a distinction between "poor" and "average" or between "good" and "very good". In addition, results from two recent studies carried out in São Paulo, Brazil and Mexico City are included. In order to compare all countries, we merged "poor" and "fair" on the one hand, and "good" and "very good" on the other.

.

TABLE 2. PROPORTIONAL DISTRIBUTION OF POPULATION 60+
ACCORDING TO SELF-REPORTED HEALTH STATUS: SELECTED
COUNTRIES IN LATIN AMERICA AND THE CARIBBEAN,
AND THE UNITED STATES, 1980-1995

Country	A. Unabbreviated categories			
	Poor	Fair	Good	Very good
Males				
Argentina	3.4	33.6	53.4	9.7
Brazil	22.2	-	62.2	15.6
Chile	20.2	37.9	36.3	5.6
Costa Rica	17.7	38.5	33.1	10.6
Mexico	19.6	47.0	27.8	5.6
Trinidad and Tobago	26.6	32.6	32.6	7.9
USA black population (HRS)	12.6	22.5	30.6	39.3
USA black population (AHEAD)	20.4	30.0	28.0	21.6
USA white population (HRS)	7.7	12.3	28.8	51.2
USA white population (AHEAD)	12.5	21.0	32.0	34.6
Females				
Argentina	10.0	42.7	40.8	6.6
Brazil	34.9	-	50.6	14.5
Chile	27.6	42.9	34.7	4.9
Costa Rica	20.7	42.8	27.8	8.7
Mexico	22.6	48.5	24.8	4.1
Trinidad and Tobago	37.6	37.1	19.8	5.3
USA black population (HRS)	12.0	22.7	33.1	32.2
USA black population (AHEAD)	19.7	29.7	27.6	22.9
USA white population (HRS)	6.7	14.3	25.8	54.6
USA white population (AHEAD)	11.5	22.5	30.4	35.8

TABLE 2 (continued)

Country	B. Abbreviated categories	
	Poor/fair	Good/very good
Males		
Argentina	37.4	63.0
Brazil	61.4	38.6
Chile	58.1	41.9
Colombia	55.3	44.7
Costa Rica	56.2	43.7
El Salvador	78.8	22.2
Jamaica	66.6	33.4
Mexico	79.7	20.3
Trinidad and Tobago	59.2	40.8
Venezuela	82.7	17.3
USA black population (HRS)	35.1	64.9
USA black population (AHEAD)	50.4	49.6
USA white population (HRS)	20.0	80.0
USA white population (AHEAD)	33.5	66.6
Females		
Argentina	52.7	47.4
Brazil	72.8	27.2
Chile	70.5	29.6
Colombia	66.7	33.3
Costa Rica	63.5	36.5
El Salvador	77.6	18.4
Jamaica	86.0	14.0
Mexico	71.1	28.9
Trinidad and Tobago	74.7	25.3
Venezuela	77.3	22.7
USA black population (HRS)	34.7	65.3
USA black population (AHEAD)	49.4	50.5
USA white population (HRS)	21.6	80.4
USA white population (AHEAD)	34.0	66.0

Sources: Pan American Health Organization, 1989a, 1989b, 1989c, 1990, 1993, except Brazil and Mexico (see Palloni, De Vos and Pelaez, 1999). For Brazil, see Ramos and others (1998); for Mexico, see Gutierrez (1998); for USA, see Smith and Kingston (1995).

HRS = Health and Retirement Survey.
AHEAD = Asset and Health Dynamics among the Oldest Old.

While self-reported health status is not an ideal indicator of health conditions, it can be shown to be surprisingly accurate and a good predictor of subsequent ill health and mortality (Idler and Kasl, 1991; Idler and Benyamini, 1997; Mare and Palloni, 1988). Three features stand out in the table.

First, in all countries of the region, except Argentina, the fraction reporting that they are not in good health status ("poor" or "fair") is two to three times higher than comparable figures for the white population in the AHEAD study. It should be remembered that the sample studied in AHEAD corresponds to an older age bracket (70+), whereas those of HRS correspond to a younger age bracket (51-61). Thus, in the AHEAD study, the population reporting to be in poor/fair health is 33.5 per cent among white males and 34.0 per cent among white females. In the best case in the region (Argentina), the corresponding numbers are 37.4 per cent among males and 52.7 per cent among females. In all other countries, the percentages are much higher, from about 55.3 per cent among males in Colombia to about 86.0 per cent among females in Jamaica. As would be expected, the comparison is more favourable if one takes as reference the United States black population. But even then, only Argentina seems to fare better. Secondly, the heterogeneity within the region is substantial and appears to be only weakly correlated with mortality levels. Thus, the lowest percentage reported to be in average or worse health occurs in Argentina (37.0 and 52.7 per cent), while the highest occurs in Jamaica (79.7 and 86.0 per cent) and Venezuela (82.7 and 77.3 per cent). Thirdly, there are large gender disparities and, with the exception of Venezuela, all of them favour males. The differences can be as large as 15.2 percentage points in Argentina and as small as 1 or 2 percentage points in El Salvador. It should be noted that in the United States and other developed countries the male-female differences are insignificant or exhibit the opposite pattern. If these gender differentials in self-reports do indeed reflect unobserved differentials in underlying health conditions, the patterns displayed are of importance since, as suggested earlier, elderly women not only represent close to two thirds of the elderly population but are also at higher risk of experiencing worse economic conditions.

TRENDS IN OLDER PERSONS' LIVING ARRANGEMENTS AND WELL-BEING

The living arrangements of the elderly are just one element among many others included in a package of transfers towards the elderly originating within the boundaries of the kin group or family. These are referred to as familial or family transfers. In turn, these transfers are just one part of the totality of transfers towards the elderly that also include societal resources such as pensions, disability income, health payments and transfers in the form of subsidies for institutionalization, home care and housing. These are referred to as social transfers. Thus, co-residence of the elderly with their children (or other kin) is just one among many transfer flows involving the elderly. Social transfers and family (kin group) transfers are the most important sources of support for the majority of the elderly. Other sources include assets, wages and private pension plans.

The observed prevalence of co-residence with children may be related to the magnitude of other flows, but the exact direction of causality is not always clear. The demand for co-residence with children or other kin is probably heightened in societies with a precarious institutionalization of social transfers, with traditionally low levels of human capital investments, and where the health and disability of the elderly require large expenditures on care and health services.

Trends in co-residence of the elderly

The availability ratio is the ratio of the population aged 60 and over to the population between ages 15 and 59. The latter population is the pool of available individuals with whom the elderly could co-reside. Two dimensions of co-residence of the elderly are of interest: the overall levels of living alone, and the age patterns of living alone. Each of these is discussed below.

Overall levels of living alone among the elderly

Census information for the United States of America in 1990 shows that about 75 per cent of white males and females older than 65 lived alone or with a spouse. Roughly two thirds, or 65 per cent, of unmarried white women and men live alone (Kramarow, 1995; Ruggles, 1994; Schoeni, 1998). For African Americans, the figures are 51 and 48 per cent, respectively. In Western and Northern Europe, as in the United States, the prevalence of the elderly population, regardless of marital status, living in a single-person household is between 15 and 40 per cent (Keilman, 1988; Kinsella, 1990). Moreover, the prevalence of living alone in these countries is anticipated to be much higher in the short run since recent trends point to a rapid increase in this type of living arrangement (Pampel, 1992), with all the consequences that this transformation may entail (Reher, 1998).

This is in contrast to the situation in most countries of Asia and Latin America where the proportion of all elderly living alone rarely exceeds 10 per cent. Countries in the Caribbean occupy an intermediate position, with the prevalence of living alone ranging from 10 to 20 per cent (Kinsella, 1990). The aforementioned figures for these countries are calculated using as reference the entire elderly population and, therefore, conceal higher levels of living alone among those who do not have a spouse. Since the fraction of all elderly over 60 or 65 who are unmarried ranges between one third and one half, the fraction of all unmarried elderly who live alone cannot be much higher than 0.20 in the countries of Asia and Latin America, and less than 0.40 in the Caribbean.[2]

Current levels of living alone among the elderly in the United States of America and in Western and Northern Europe are the result of changes that may have begun in earnest before 1900 but whose full effects are felt only after 1950. By contrast, and with only few exceptions, the observed changes in Asia, Latin America and the Caribbean are of only recent origin and of considerably lower magnitude. The two most noticeable exceptions are Japan and Taiwan Province of China. In Japan, a society with traditionally high levels of elderly co-residence, the proportion living alone has increased steadily since 1960, at an estimated rate of about 1 per cent per year, and has reached values close to 0.30 in 1990. It is projected to increase even more (Hirosima, 1997). Similarly, in Taiwan Province of China and the Republic of Korea, two Asian populations with traditionally high levels of co-residence, the trend towards higher levels of living alone is unequivocal (Hermalin, Ofstedal and Lee, 1992; Hermalin, Ofstedal and Chang, 1992; De Vos and Lee, 1988). Other countries in Asia and Latin America reveal less change in patterns of co-residence. Table 3a shows the fraction among all unmarried elderly living alone in the United States. Table 3b summarizes comparable information available for European countries, whereas table 3c gives comparable figures for a sample of countries from the developing and developed world, with available data for two or three points in time. While the largest changes have undoubtedly occurred in the United States of America and Europe, the situation in some Asian populations (Japan and Taiwan Province) has already destabilized. In Latin America and the Caribbean, observed changes are quite muted, and there are no indications of a massive break with the past (see, also, De Vos, 1990; Palloni and De Vos, 1992). Table 4 contains more detailed information at one or two points in time for selected countries in Latin America and the Caribbean. Altogether, the figures in tables 3c and 4 show that changes in the same direction, albeit of smaller magnitude, as those experienced by forerunners are occurring in the developing world as well.

Not only are changes in developing countries of small magnitude but they also start from lower baseline values. Yet, researchers and policy makers alike suspect that much larger changes are in the making, and that patterns similar to those experienced by the United States of America and Europe will soon engulf Asia and Latin America alike, while Africa, in all likelihood, will continue to lag behind.[3]

Age patterns of living alone among the elderly

Age patterns of living alone among the elderly are a somewhat less studied aspect of the phenomenon. With a few exceptions (see Liefbroer and de Jong Gierveld, 1995), the prevalence of the elderly co-residing with children (or kin) decreases from about age 50 to about age 75 or 80 and then increases again (Kinsella, 1990). This age pattern is clearly exhibited among all the elderly in the United States microcensus data from 1880 on (Ruggles, 1994), and among elderly widows in the 1960-1990 Current Population Survey (CPS) time-series (Macunovich and others, 1995). Over time, the increase in living alone has been proportionately higher among the oldest old (over 85) than among the young old (Ruggles, 1994; Tuma and Sandefur, 1988). This age pattern of living alone is less pronounced but still detectable in Canada (Légaré, 1998) and in data for Japan (Hirosima, 1997) and a number of European countries (Kinsella, 1990).

TABLE 3a. PROPORTION OF UNMARRIED ELDERLY (65+) LIVING ALONE IN
THE UNITED STATES, 1910-1990

| Year | Unmarried elderly living alone | |
	White	Non-white
1910	0.12	0.16
1940	0.21	0.15
1960	0.39	0.30
1980	0.66	0.47
1990	0.70	0.49

Sources: Ruggles (1994). Estimates for 1990 calculated from Kramarow (1995).

TABLE 3b. PROPORTION OF UNMARRIED ELDERLY (60+)
LIVING ALONE IN EUROPE, 1975-1990[a]

| Country or area | Year | |
	1975	1990
France	0.74	0.86
Belgium	0.72	0.85
Netherlands	0.72	0.87
West Germany	0.60	0.77
Italy	0.46	0.66
Luxembourg	0.55	0.73
Denmark	0.84	0.92
Ireland	0.37	0.56
Great Britain	0.75	0.87
Northern Ireland	0.49	0.68
Finland		0.70
Czech Republic (1991)		0.66
Estonia (1989)		0.51
Romania (1992)		0.51
Bulgaria (1992)		0.50

Sources: Figures for Western Europe calculated from Pampel (1992). Figures for Eastern
Europe from Devos and Sandefur (1999).

[a] No comparable time trends are available for Eastern Europe. Estimates for Eastern
Europe refer to elderly population 60+.

TABLE 3c. PROPORTION OF ELDERLY POPULATION LIVING ALONE
IN OTHER COUNTRIES OR AREAS

Brazil: unmarried elderly 55+		Mexico: all elderly 65+	
1960	0.11	1976	0.07
1980	0.20	1994	0.07
Chile: unmarried elderly 60+		Argentina: unmarried elderly 60+	
1970	0.06	1970	0.10
1982	0.08	1982	0.11
Japan: unmarried elderly 65+		Thailand: all elderly 65+	
1970	0.15	1986	0.06
1980	0.27	1994	0.08
1990	0.35		
Taiwan Province of China: all elderly 65+ (living alone or with spouse)			
1976	0.09		
1989	0.23		

Sources: For Argentina, Pan American Health Organization (1989a); for Brazil, Agree (1993); for Chile, De Vos (1990); for Japan, Hirosima (1997); for Mexico, Solis (1999); for Taiwan Province, Hermalin, Ofstedal and Chang (1992); and for Thailand, Knodel, Amornsirisomboon and Khiewyoo (1997).

TABLE 4. PROPORTION OF ALL ELDERLY AND OF UNMARRIED[a]
ELDERLY (60+) LIVING ALONE, BY SEX, SELECTED
LATIN AMERICAN COUNTRIES

	Year	All			Unmarried		
		Total	Men	Women	Total	Men	Women
Argentina	1970	10	10	11	21	31	17
	1980	11	9	12	22	29	20
Bolivia	1976	12	10	13	23	28	21
Brazil	1970	7	5	9	17	24	14
	1980	8	7	10	21	31	17
Chile	1970	6	7	6	12	18	9
	1982	8	7	8	15	22	13
Colombia	1973	6	6	6	10	15	8
	1985	6	6	6	12	19	9
Costa Rica	1973	6	5	6	12	18	9
	1984	8	8	8	17	25	13
Dominican Republic	1970	7	8	6	12	21	8
	1981	7	9	6	15	26	9
Ecuador	1974	8	8	7	15	23	12
	1982	9	9	8	19	27	14
Guatemala	1981	5	5	6	12	20	9
Mexico	1970	8	6	10	17	23	15
Nicaragua	1971	8	9	7	14	27	10
Panama	1970	12	15	9	21	35	13
	1980	12	15	9	24	38	15
Paraguay	1972	7	7	8	14	23	11
	1982	7	5	8	14	20	12
Venezuela	1981	8	9	7	14	23	9

Source: Microsamples of decennial censuses.
[a] Unmarried refers to individuals not in a union.

69

Furthermore, in most cross-sectional studies, the estimated effects of parental age on the probability of co-residence are either increasing or display the non-linear form present in the United States data. Let us assume for a moment that these patterns remain constant. Since the difference between the minimum and maximum values of the fraction co-residing by age can be fairly large (of the order of 10 to 15 per cent in the United States), modest changes in the age distribution of the elderly could have non-trivial effects on the overall fraction living alone, even in the absence of changes in the age-specific probabilities of living alone. The direction and magnitude of these effects will depend on the relative size of consecutive cohorts of elderly. In turn, the overall magnitude of the difference between them will be a function of the past history of fertility and mortality. In the developing world, the size of the first few cohorts attaining age 60 by 2020 will create a bulge that will surely inflate the overall proportion living alone. This effect will increase for a number of years before it reverses or is attenuated as the same cohorts attain ages 75 or 80, the age interval where the age-specific rates of living alone begin to decrease again.

It is unlikely that observed age patterns will remain constant for too long. For one thing, they may reflect cohort effects: the oldest old of today belong to cohorts with less education and more modest wage-earning history. This makes them less likely to have a wide variety of choices available other than co-residence with children. Also, the oldest old have a higher prevalence of disability and chronic illnesses and are more likely to be offered care by kin or children (see below). If the age of onset of the most prevalent forms of disability increases (or decreases), age patterns of co-residence could experience a downward (or upward) shift at younger ages. Finally, there is a relation between length of generation and co-residence (see below). If the age difference between parents and the youngest of their children changes — as a result of delaying or anticipatory fertility tactics — the age patterns of co-residence will also be affected.[4]

Co-residence and levels of well-being

A concentrated research focus on the living arrangements of the elderly is a relatively new theme. It is driven by concerns raised around the world in general, and in developed countries in particular, about consequences of rapid ageing. To the extent that co-residence with adult children or other family members is seen as a fundamental strategy to bolster the overall levels of well-being of the elderly, trends pointing to a dissolution of traditional living arrangements, where most elderly live with children or relatives, are seen as worrisome and threatening.

This preoccupation is exacerbated in recently industrialized countries and in developing countries alike, where these trends are of more recent origin. They take place, however, within more fragile institutional contexts, where social transfers towards the elderly are non-existent or not well established, and whose prospects appear increasingly compromised by institutional reforms and tight fiscal discipline. It is well known that levels of poverty everywhere have historically been higher among elderly people, and this is probably even more pronounced in developing countries now than it was in the past in more developed countries (Ramashala, 1997; Townsend and Wedderburn, 1965; Townsend, 1979). Given the current conditions of overall poverty in most developing countries, there is little evidence to suspect that this state of affairs could change any time soon (Gwatkin, 2000).

The combination of fiscal restraint and insufficiently developed mechanisms of social transfers could constrain even more the range of options during an epoch of swelling demand caused by the sheer increase in the size of the elderly population, even if their patterns of illnesses and disability were to remain unchanged. Thus, the argument goes, poverty among the elderly is likely to increase.

It is widely thought that the erosion of a traditional norm whereby the elderly commonly reside with children or relatives will reduce the well-being of the older population. This outcome is likely if the onset of a newer regime with lower co-residence is not accompanied by improvements in the elderly's command over private income, does not trigger changes in other elements of familial transfers, or does not induce an improvement of existent social transfers. Indeed, central Governments in many countries have undertaken explicit campaigns to reassert family obligations towards the elderly (Martin and Kinsella, 1994; Knodel, Amornsirisomboon and Khiewyoo, 1997; Reher, 1998).

In the developed world, industrialization and modernization may have eroded familial bonds but they have simultaneously fostered a system of social transfers that effectively operates as a compensatory mechanism to reinforce transfers towards the elderly. The onset and evolution of this system of institutionalized transfers may itself have reduced even further the need for and discouraged the continuation of family transfers, including co-residence. In addition, through investments in human capital, older individuals are able to command higher levels of income while, as insurance or as a complement, they are open to and actively pursue the option of continuing to participate in the labour force. Competing with other needs and demands, the efficiency and sufficiency of compensatory social transfers, however, has been questioned in the United States (Preston, 1984), and are even less likely to be seen as a feasible solution in the less developed world.

In developing countries, older people's access to sources of income is usually far below what is necessary to secure self-sufficiency, while their continued participation in the labour force, for a long time a necessity rather than an option, may be endangered by rapid economic change and growing obsolescence of human capital. Furthermore, in both the developed and the developing world, the overall demand for care and attention for the elderly will be a function of the prevalence of illness and disability, and of the amount of time lived in good health at older ages. Recent research suggests that disability and ill health have not worsened over time in some developed countries (Crimmins, Hayward and Saito, 1994; Crimmins, Saito and Ingegneri, 1997; Manton, Corder and Stallard, 1993). But this may be a transient phase and, as suggested above, may not hold true at all in developing countries, where the available evidence suggests that the elderly could be far

71

worse off than their counterparts in developed countries. Thus, even if there were compensatory changes in social transfers and improvements in private sources of support were feasible, the well-being of the elderly might remain compromised. In this pessimistic scenario, co-residence with children and relatives is seen as a mechanism of last resort.

Are observed changes in co-residential arrangements of the elderly associated with other changes affecting this subpopulation? The study of patterns of elderly co-residence is not just a theoretical exercise to understand the historical evolution of families and households. It is also an area of concrete concern for policy makers. Implicitly or explicitly some constituencies hold the strong belief that a reduction of elderly co-residence with kin can and will translate into deterioration of the elderly's levels of well-being.[5] What evidence is there to support this conjecture?

In order to construct a robust test, it is necessary to have time trends on indicators of levels of well-being for the elderly by residential arrangements. At least some foundation is also needed to assess the precise direction of causality or, to use in the technical jargon, to determine whether well-being is endogenous. The author is not aware of any comparative studies of changes over time of the older population's levels of well-being according to living arrangements and, despite many efforts, the problem of endogeneity appears to remain intractable.[6] It is possible, however, to use a number of disparate data sources that do shed some light on the issue. Although these data sources provide information on a rather large number of indicators, it suffices to focus on the relations between a handful of them.

Let us say that a satisfactory indicator of well-being is some demarcator enabling us to distinguish the older population living in poverty. Suppose the fraction of the elderly living below poverty level is ρ and the fraction below poverty level and living alone and co-residing are ρ_a and ρ_c, respectively. Let the probability of living alone among those above and below poverty be π_r and π_p respectively. The following equalities are straightforward:

$$\rho_a = (1 + \rho/(1-\rho)(\pi_r/\pi_p))^{-1}$$

and

$$\rho_c = (1 + \rho/(1-\rho)((1-\pi_r)/(1-\pi_p)))^{-1}$$

Thus, differences in the values of ρ_a and ρ_c over time (or across countries) depend on the overall levels of poverty among the elderly as well as on the relative magnitude of the probabilities of living alone among those above and below the poverty level. A decrease in poverty among those who live alone could be the result of either a decrease in the overall poverty rate (independently of living arrangements), an increase in the probability of living alone among those who are not poor, or a combination of the two. As a result, even under conditions guaranteeing strict comparability of the poverty measure, changes over time or over units of observations, cannot be interpreted unequivocally. Admittedly, these elementary equalities assume the analytic problem away since we implicitly assumed that decision making about co-residence — π — is correctly estimated as a function of poverty rather than the other way around.

Very few studies provide information on the values of ρ_a and ρ_c at one point in time and, even more rarely, over several periods of time. In some cases, one can obtain estimates of ρ but little or no information on anything else. Most studies report estimates of the π values but say nothing about ρ, ρ_a or ρ_c. In these cases, the values of π are usually not directly observed but can be retrieved indirectly by converting estimates of the effects of measures of wealth on the probabilities of living alone, while controlling for a host of other quantities. A complicating problem is that measures of socio-economic conditions — which we take as proxies for well-being — vary a great deal. Often, the indicator is income, and, in some cases, researchers use property ownership or "soft" proxies such as education levels, occupation and occupational status. Rarely, if ever, are estimates of π obtained using a dichotomous indicator of poverty as we have argued here. In sum, inferences and comparison across studies are hindered by a number of factors, even if one could agree on the rather dubious proposition that levels of well-being are indeed well captured by using only measures of socio-economic standing.

The longest string of evidence the author knows of is the United States microcensus samples starting in 1880. These data appear to corroborate the existence of a direct relation between indicators of wealth for the elderly in different co-residential statuses. Indeed, the data show that in the past it was among the better-off that one found the highest probability of co-residence with children or kin, whereas living alone was more likely among the poor, the propertyless and the destitute. The relationship reverses, however, after 1950 or 1960, just at the time of onset of the sharp upturn in the prevalence of living alone. Thereafter, the association between the probability of living alone and measures of wealth or socio-economic status among the elderly becomes strong and positive. Upon careful examination of these data, Ruggles infers that, in 1850, for example, there was a strong positive relationship between real property of the elderly and co-residence, and the richest 10 per cent lived with their adult children 50 per cent more often than did the propertyless. For the post-Second World War period, information on income, home value and years of education verifies the finding that multigenerational families are most frequent among the poorest and least educated (Ruggles, 1994, 1996).

In another study on conditions in the United States, Pampel finds evidence supporting the idea that π_r is higher than π_p (Pampel, 1983). He uses the 1960 and 1970 Public Use Samples (PUS) as well as the March 1976 Current Population Survey and confirms the effect of income on the probability of living alone but finds little evidence to support the idea that this has increased, at least in the 15 years or so covered by his data.

The information from these two studies refers to trends in values of π, not of ρ.[7] However, we can combine it with other sources to arrive at cleaner conclusions. The estimated (official) poverty rate among the elderly in the United States (ρ) declined from about 27 per cent in 1959 to about 12 per cent in 1990 (Holtz-Eakin and Smeeding, 1994). A drop in overall poverty rates among the elderly raises the fraction who are above poverty level both among those living alone and among those co-residing. However, since we know that π_r increased, it must be the case that levels of poverty among the elderly living

73

alone dropped faster than levels of poverty among the elderly who co-reside. From this very elementary exercise one could conclude that, in the United States at least, living alone has not translated into deterioration of levels of well-being. Without a precise time-series of π, we cannot say, however, whether one group is now better off than the other, or whether the differential in well-being by co-residence status has increased or contracted.

Although there are no long-time trends of levels of well-being among the elderly by co-residential arrangements in other countries, some information can be obtained from an examination of recent conditions. The main findings are summarized below.

Europe, United States, Canada and Australia

In a study of microdata for nine countries from the Luxembourg Income Study, Smeeding and Saunders find that the fraction of elderly women below the poverty line (defined as 50 per cent of the median disposable income) is substantially higher among elderly women living alone than among all elderly women in all countries in the sample (Smeeding and Saunders, 1998). The ratio of elderly women who live alone and are below the poverty line to those co-residing who are below poverty ranges from 1.2 in Hungary to about 2.0 in Canada. In the United States, the ratio is about 1.6, a figure rather difficult to reconcile with our previous conclusion, though not necessarily inconsistent with it.[8] Overall, this information supports the idea that living alone among the elderly is accompanied by more widespread poverty, although it is not clear whether poverty is triggered by solitary living or vice versa.

In a cross-national study of European countries spanning the years from 1975 to 1989, Pampel (1992) shows that the fraction living alone among the unmarried has increased over time and approximately at the same rate in all countries in his sample. The two proxies for individual socio-economic conditions, education and occupation, have a trivial influence on the probabilities of living alone, suggesting that π_p and π_r are probably quite similar to each other.

The bulk of studies carried out with recent data for the United States (Soldo, Wolf and Agree, 1990; Bishop, 1986; Wolf, 1990; Wolf and Soldo, 1988; Kramarow, 1995; Kotlikoff and Morris, 1990; Michael, Fuchs and Scott, 1980; Ruggles, 1994, 1988) confirm the existence of a positive effect of income on the probability of living alone. Even though qualifications regarding the form of the relation, the appropriate set of control variables and the existence of contingencies are in order, the finding that the probability of living alone is higher among those who are better off is fairly generalized. Again, these estimates simply refer to the relative magnitude of π_r and π_p (or, better yet, to the ratio $\pi_r/(1-\pi_r)/\pi_p/(1-\pi_p)$) and are not directly or easily transformed into estimates of contrasts between levels of well-being among those living alone and those co-residing.

It is well known that in Asian countries filial piety and a strong sense of obligation towards parents and the elderly alike are still widespread and dominant. These cultural prescriptions translate into norms of support that reinforce intergenerational transfers towards the elderly and produce a robust tendency to live with parents. As documented earlier, the fraction of the elderly living alone is low, and those who do so constitute a population perceived to be much like they were in the United States at the beginning of the twentieth century, that is, largely composed of the infirm, poor and destitute. But the evidence available for the most recent period is remarkably elusive on this score. The summary of various studies that follows shows that the empirical evidence from several countries is not always consistent with this imagery. The first two studies summarized below provide estimates of quantities analogous to ρ_a, whereas all the others only enable us to retrieve values of π_r.

The Luxembourg study cited above includes information for Taiwan Province of China, where the ratio of women living alone and below poverty level to those co-residing and below poverty is in the neighbourhood of 2.8. This is by far the largest ratio, and its magnitude is all the more remarkable since levels of poverty among all elderly Taiwanese are higher than in countries such as Canada or Germany, two of the countries where high ratios of poverty among those living alone were identified.

In a recent study of nationally representative data in Thailand, Knodel and colleagues uncover a more mixed picture that, although not entirely inconsistent with the belief that the elderly living alone may be worse off, suggests that the relations are more complicated. Thus, Knodel and colleagues conclude that the image of the elderly being increasingly deserted to live on their own or being neglected if they do live with their family is reinforced by media conveying the same idea. Unfortunately, it appears to be based more on preconceptions and anecdotal evidence than on hard facts (Knodel, Amornsirisomboon and Khiewyoo, 1997). In fact, their data reveal that while there are some differences in indicators of well-being (income, perceived sufficiency of income, recent financial problems, and household possessions), these are hardly large enough to substantiate the idea that those living alone are a particularly fragile group. It is only in rural areas where the differences are sufficiently strong to merit special attention.

Table 5 summarizes the information regarding the effects of indicators of well-being (socio-economic status) in a number of Asian and Latin American countries. The best way to characterize these results is that they are somewhat inconclusive, even though positive relations are more common than negative ones. The studies define different focal populations (unmarried versus unmarried and married elderly), and they differ in terms of indicators of socio-economic standing and types of controls used. Overall, and perhaps unsurprisingly, the estimated effects are somewhat inconsistent. In some cases (Brazil, Malaysia, Mexico and the Republic of Korea), the effects of income or home ownership are equivalent to those already verified in the United

States and Europe. In other countries, the effects of indicators of well-being can be in the opposite direction, or statistically insignificant, as is the case of home ownership in Brazil.

TABLE 5. EFFECTS OF INDICATORS OF WELL-BEING ON THE PROBABILITY
OF LIVING ALONE, ASIA AND LATIN AMERICA

Study	Country or area (year)	Indicator of well-being[a]	Direction of effect[b]
Martin (1989)	Republic of Korea (1984)	Ownership	Positive
	Malaysia (1984)	Ownership	Positive
	Philippines (1984)	Ownership	Not significant
	Fiji (1984)	Ownership	Not significant
Casterline and others (1991)	Philippines (1984)	Education	Not significant
	Singapore (1986)	Education	Not significant
	Taiwan Province of China (1989)	Education	Positive
	Thailand (1986)	Education	Not significant
Chan and Da Vanzo (1996)	Malaysia (Malay) (1988/89)	Income	Positive
	Malaysia (Chinese) (1988/89)	Income	Positive
	Malaysia (Indian) (1988/89)	Income	Positive
	Malaysia (Malay) (1988/89)	Education	Not significant
	Malaysia (Chinese) (1988/89)	Education	Not significant
	Malaysia (Indian) (1988/89)	Education	Not significant
Da Vanzo and Chan (1994)	Malaysia (1988/89)	Income	Positive
Solis (1999)	Mexico (1994)	Income/ education	Not significant
Agree (1993)	Brazil (1960)	Income	Positive
	Brazil (1960)	Education	Negative
	Brazil (1980)	Income	Positive
	Brazil (1980)	Ownership	Negative

[a] Ownership refers to home ownership.
[b] Unless explicitly noted, all effects are statistically significant.

76

Finally, there are studies focusing on the effects of children's characteristics on the probabilities of co-residence with their parents. If one assumes that indicators of wealth across generations are strongly correlated and that the within-family (across offspring of the same parents) variance in wealth is trivial, then a high probability of not living with parents among children above the poverty line would suggest that parents above poverty are more likely to live alone. This is a fragile inference, particularly since often key parental characteristics are not controlled for. One of these studies (Martin and Tsuya, 1991) shows that in a sample of Japanese middle-aged individuals indicators of high socio-economic status correlate negatively with co-residence with parents. Similarly, in a study of middle-aged people in Turkey, Aykan and Wolf (1998) find that education of children is negatively related to co-residence with parents. By contrast, in a study of 10 counties scattered widely throughout eastern China, Parish and colleagues find that higher income among sons leads not to decreased co-residence in favour of financial aid but to more of both co-residence and aid (Parish, Shen and Chang, 1995).

What can one conclude from these disparate findings? The most robust inference is that the evidence supporting the claim that living alone among the elderly is associated with lower levels of well-being is not always consistent with the evidence. What we know for sure is that, with a few exceptions, there is some support for the contention that the probability of living alone is higher among those who are better off, and that in a few countries in Europe and in Taiwan Province, elderly women who live alone experience higher poverty levels than do those who co-reside, although this contrast is not confirmed by roughly comparable data in other countries (e.g., Thailand). Finally, while most of the studies attempt to estimate the effects of measures of economic standing on the probability of living alone, they do not shed light on the complementary, but quite distinct, issue of whether the elderly living alone are better off than those who co-reside or, more fundamentally, they cannot confirm the counterfactual that they would be better off if they did.

Given this rather negative conclusion, combined with the fact that throughout this exercise we intentionally overlooked endogeneity issues and systematically dodged considerations regarding the meaning and measurement of well-being, it seems fair to say that, to put it mildly, our state of knowledge in this key area for public policy is fairly primitive.

EXPLAINING TRENDS IN CO-RESIDENCE PATTERNS
OF THE ELDERLY

Why did the prevalence of older people's living alone (or with spouse only) rise so much in the United States and Europe, and why should one expect that a similar phenomenon will occur in Asia, Latin America and the Caribbean? This question remains important even though the previous assessment does not reveal a close connection between co-residence arrangements and the elderly's well-being, nor does it justify gloomy scenarios associated with the increased prevalence of living alone. It is suspected that research in the area has not been properly focused to make a connection that indeed exists. Thus, understanding the factors responsible for trends in living arrangements will help us to identify conditions that are, at least in theory, related to the elderly's well-being, and thus clarify not just the theoretically interesting issue of family and household transformations, but also some of its more concrete and practical implications.

To identify factors that explain past trends of intergenerational co-residence and the possible relation to the well-being of older persons, the paper first locates the theme within the broader and distinguished tradition of studies of families and households. There is then a discussion of a general framework to sort out conditions that could account for observed trends. Finally, the paper reviews some of the empirical evidence available to adjudicate between alternative explanations.

Living arrangements of the elderly, living arrangements of children and household types

The study of levels, patterns and changes of living arrangements among the elderly has been an important though not always central feature of sociology and demography of the family. The literature on transformations of the family and household living arrangements that accompany or follow industrialization and modernization is dense with references to a transition entailing drastic reductions of joint co-residence of members of different generations. The debate on whether such a transition has indeed taken place, rather than being an illusion created by demographic constraints, has generated a vast literature directly or indirectly documenting a number of changes of living arrangements of older persons (Wall, 1989a, 1989b; Smith, 1993; Laslett, 1972; Ruggles, 1987, 1988, 1994; Kobrin, 1976; Wachter, Hammel and Laslett, 1978; Levy, 1965; Berkner, 1972, 1975; Kertzer, 1989, 1991). There is a long tradition in sociology and social history that deals with this effect of industrialization and modernization on the nature of family bonds and on the related issue of household organization. The central problem is whether industrialization and modernization triggered a transition from a system largely dominated by extended households and families to one dominated by simple households and nuclear families. As an offshoot of this transition, the prevalence of the elderly's co-residence with children and other kin decreases, and living alone or with a spouse becomes the norm. Early formulations emphasize the existence of such a transition, while revisionists assert that the transition is merely apparent, an artifact created by an effectively low prevalence of extended families in pre-industrial societies to begin with. Such low prevalence could be the product of either a strong adherence to normative patterns inconsistent with more than minimal household extension, or to constraints imposed by the demographic regime characteristic of such societies, regardless of what the cultural norms or individual preferences were. A revision of this revisionist approach, however, makes it clear that, at least in some pre-industrial societies, a regime of extension did in fact exist, it can be identified if proper measures are used, and there is an observable transition to the elementary household and family forms (Ruggles, 1994).

By and large the empirical evidence brought to bear on this problem is in the form of distributions of households by type, that is, by categories of households defined according to classes of kin (or non-kin) relations that members in the household share. In particular, the level of co-residence of multiple generations is assessed using measures of the proportion of households that include parents and children (Wachter, Hammel and Laslett, 1978; Ruggles, 1987; King and Preston, 1990). In societies where the distribution of surviving offspring has a high mean, and where many adults do not survive to old age, the fraction of all households containing aged parents and their children cannot be too high, even if, for example, a stem family regime prevails (Ruggles, 1994; Kertzer, 1989, 1991). As shown in the previous section, redefining units of analysis and focusing instead on the living arrangements of the elderly (rather than directly on households) leads to clear evidence of a shift from prevalence of co-residence with children to living alone. This shift takes place even in the presence of a powerful demographic tug originating in sharp increases of survival among both parents and children.

This tension between different types of units of observations also exists if one insists that measurement should be centred on children rather than on parents. In this case, the focus is on the distribution of children (rather than of households) by co-residential arrangement with parents. From first principles one can derive a number of relations between the two (Preston, 1976; Freedman and others, 1991), but the key idea is that for some research objectives only one of them will do.

The argument for focusing on the elderly rather than on children is the same as the one given in favour of a focus on the elderly rather than on all households. That is, the assessment based on children — as was the one based on household types — is subject to confounding effects produced by demographic forces that affect strongly the distribution of surviving offspring. If one is interested in the elderly's well-being, it is advantageous to define direct measures that reflect the characteristics of the elderly, not those reflected in the characteristics of offspring.[9] As discussed below, this does not mean that the characteristics of children are unimportant and should be neglected, but rather that they should be regarded as affecting outcomes of interest among the elderly. Thus, co-residence among the elderly should have theoretical priority over the alternatives of studying household distributions or children's co-residence patterns.

Frameworks to explain trends in the elderly's living arrangements

Co-residential arrangements of the elderly are a strategic element of broader patterns of household organization and part of a much larger set of intergenerational transfers. It is sensible then to look for interpretative insights using ideas borrowed from the stock of theories and models designed for the study of these two phenomena.

A number of recently developed frameworks link intergenerational transfers to formulations based on evolutionary theories. These suggest that strong kin networks, familial bonds and the prevalence of household extension were dominant in pre-industrial societies where they operated as mechanisms to spread the high costs of childbearing and sustain a high fertility regime that offset high infant and childhood mortality. These arguments stress the role of the grandparental generation as an important source of support to younger relatives (Turke, 1989, 1991; Fricke, 1990; Lee, 1997; Kaplan, 1994, 1997; Stecklov, 1997; Kobrin, 1976). To the extent that children and grandparents (and other kin) were able to support the care and nurturing of siblings and grandchildren, they maximized reproductive potential under precarious conditions. Strong family bonds and household organization are designed to decrease the costs of these activities for everybody involved. Co-residence, and other forms of exchanges largely realized within the household, represent the context in which most support took place. Without invoking evolutionary principles, Caldwell's theory of intergenerational flows (Caldwell, 1976) also links strong multigenerational family ties and support to the maintenance of high fertility.

However, while Caldwell chooses to emphasize the importance of transfers from the younger to the older generation, recent evidence suggests that even in pre-industrial societies the direction of net transfers is probably from the old to the young and not vice versa (Turke, 1989; Fricke, 1990; Lee, 1997; Kaplan, 1994, 1997; Stecklov, 1997).

Industrialization and modernization subvert the system of transfer flows by concentrating production outside the household and privileging returns to human capital. The fall in mortality makes unnecessary the maintenance of very high levels of fertility and instead gives way to the need for investing heavily in children. Thus, the props for a system of intergenerational exchange — and the household organization that sustained it — are weakened and, with them, the entire system of family bonds and exchanges. The direction of intergenerational flows reverses and alternative forms of social support acquire importance as compensating mechanisms, simultaneously freeing the younger generation from obligations towards the elderly and securing for them minimal levels of well-being. The whole ideological superstructure is revamped as the nuclear family becomes a legitimate arrangement and ceases to be a deviant behavioural alternative subject to social sanctions. The new arrangements rest on an individualist ideology that replaces strong familistic sentiments and asserts individual welfare and self-development over the kin group or the clan.

This evolutionary interpretation has much to recommend it. But it fails on a number of counts. First, it is not altogether clear that the flow of intergenerational transfers in pre-industrial and high-fertility societies is upward at all. Utilizing a simple accounting procedure, Lee documents that in some high-fertility settings the direction of flows is, unexpectedly, towards the younger generations, with the consumption needs of children dominating over the consumption needs of the elderly (Lee, 1994a, 1994b, 1995; Lee and Paloni, 1992; Stecklov, 1997). Instead, in industrialized societies, the direction of transfers is upward, from the younger to the older generation (Lee and Palloni, 1992).[10] Secondly, as discussed above, the statement that everywhere in the pre-industrial world extended co-residential arrangements were pervasive has proved to be incorrect, at least in some key pre-industrial societies where the nuclear family was the norm, not the exception. Thirdly, and more importantly, the explanation based on an evolutionary argument is excessively loose as it does not identify precise mechanisms ensuring the persistence of networks, bonds and exchanges that result in a high density of transfers towards the elderly and, as part of these, co-residence with children and kin. As a consequence, it is difficult if not impossible to formulate defensible hypotheses, much less testable ones, accounting for diversity over time and space.

In a much less ambitious attempt but one that contains the specificity that the evolutionary approach lacks, Burch and Matthews (1987) identify a number of factors that could account for the persistence (or change) of household arrangements. Their suggestion is to define key principles, stipulate a few axioms and formulate explicitly a number of testable explanations for observed changes. The main disadvantage of the approach is that it lacks generality as it is intended to account only for household arrangements and overlooks the totality of intergenerational flows, of which co-residence is a part. However, this shortcoming may become less relevant to the extent that one can blend their framework with theories of intergenerational transfers.

The object to be explained is household status. Co-residence of the elderly with their children is just one among several possible household statuses. The main axiom in this perspective is that household type is a composite good that can be chosen by individuals. In doing so, they choose some combination of a set of goods, including privacy, companionship, domestic services, and consumption economies of scale. The household arrangement is thus not a goal in itself but an instrumental good, a means to an end. This departs somewhat from the traditional microeconomic formulations that emphasize household arrangements as an expression of demand for only one of these goods, namely, privacy and independence. A number of other formulations insist on the centrality of the idea of household as a composite good (Ermisch, 1981; Lam, 1983, 1984, 1988). The difference between the Burch-Matthews formulation and these revisionist microeconomic approaches is that the former contains a more thorough identification of the classes and types of goods produced by household sharing.

This axiom is fundamental as it implies a key principle for investigation. This is that, to the extent that household arrangements may produce a variety of goods, it must also be the case that factors explaining the persistence or change of household arrangements will be found among (a) those that change individual preferences for these goods, (b) those that alter their prices, and (c) those that determine individuals' ability to purchase them.

Three qualifications are in order. First, the effect of these factors is tightly related to the nature of each good appropriated or consumed in a household. Shelter, for example, is a public good "produced" by the household that is very sensitive to changes in private income. Not so domestic service or

81

recreation. Thus, fine-tuning the definition of goods to establish their relations and classifying them as public versus private, as complementary or substitutes, and as inferior, superior or mixed, is of some importance to formulate hypotheses explaining change and persistence in household arrangements. As we will see below, this is done in most research on co-residence of the elderly, but mostly in an ad hoc, unsystematic fashion.

Secondly, the ability of individuals to pay for these goods involves income from labour and from income-producing transfers, household labour, and a number of less tangible modes of payment such as affection, deference, or credits from past services. The intrinsic value attached to each of these payments may wax and wane and will alter conditions of individual decision-making about living arrangements.

Thirdly, the tug of traditional sentiments and the social sanctions reinforcing them may be strong. Thus, although changes in conditions that affect prices, preferences and income could lead to decision-making where nuclearization is the optimal strategy for individuals, the observed household arrangements may not reflect this at all. Instead, they may lag behind, sustained by social sanctions that continue to reinforce more traditional household arrangements. Consequently, time lags are relevant and they will routinely play a role in groups where social sanctions to prevent deviations from a traditional norm operate with some efficiency.

This very simple schema is sufficient to pose a number of alternative hypotheses to explain the observed trend towards the increased prevalence among the elderly in the United States and Europe of living alone, and to anticipate what may happen in the rest of the world. What follows is a review of the main factors that have been invoked to explain increasing trends of living alone. Two shortcomings need to be highlighted. First, not all of these factors occupy the same level of abstraction. Thus, for example, income is a characteristic that can be associated with the elderly or their children. The same applies to preferences or to other social transfers. Health status, on the other hand, is more likely to be relevant when it refers to the elderly rather than to their children. Secondly, only in a few cases is the evidence derived from time trends; the bulk comes from cross-sectional studies. These two classes of evidence are not strictly comparable, do not have the same empirical weight and may and finally do lead to different inferences.

The role of income

A number of analyses lead to the conclusion that the rising real income among older persons is no doubt one of the main reasons that the proportions living alone have reached such high levels, especially among single or previously married women (Burch and Matthews, 1987; see, also, Michael, Fuchs and Scott, 1980; Kobrin, 1976; Soldo and Lauriat, 1976; Wolf, 1984). As individual real income increases, some goods traditionally produced by households become more affordable. Goods produced outside households, such as recreation, become private goods and replace others that are produced by households. Increases in real income are thought to decrease the propensity of individuals to rely on the public good component contained in the basket of household-produced goods.

This explanation implicitly assumes that goods associated with separate living (privacy and independence) are indeed superior and that, when budgetary constraints are relaxed, individuals tend to consume them instead of those produced by shared living. The assumption is tantamount to stating that the preference for these goods preceded the changes that made their consumption feasible, in much the same way as explanations of fertility decline that invoke the importance of knowledge and availability of contraception implicitly assume that a desire for smaller families preceded their advent.

The empirical evidence for an income effect on co-residence among the elderly does exist but it is not altogether convincing. In a cross-national study based on individual data, Pampel (1992) shows that effects of variables proxying for income are in the expected direction, but they are of trivial magnitude, and that the increasing trend in proportions living alone remains largely unexplained by well-identified conditions. In a decomposition analysis of trends in living alone among elderly widows in the United States, Kramarow (1995) also finds that proxies for income account for a fraction of all changes during the twentieth century, although, as mentioned earlier, the key variable does not behave as expected. In an important paper advocating a microeconomic framework, with income as the key variable, Michael, Fuchs and Scott (1980) attribute increases in prevalence of living alone largely to the increased ability to purchase privacy and to support independent living afforded by higher incomes. Finally, in a study of CPS data for the United States from 1965 to 1990, Macunovich and colleagues find that the effect of retirement income on the probability of living alone among elderly widows is positive and very strong (Macunovich and others, 1995). However, their analysis does not provide estimates of the amount of change (increase) in the proportion living alone attributable to changes in income and to other factors. Estimation using limited time trends leads Kobrin (1976) and Soldo (1981) to argue that, although changes in income may have an important influence, it is to the decrease in the availability of children that one should attribute primary responsibility for observed increases in living alone (see, also, Soldo, Wolf and Agree, 1990).

Some of the limited success in explaining time trends using income as an explanatory factor may be attributable to poor measures of real income among the elderly, or to inappropriate controls for relevant variables. Furthermore, the effects of income appear to be highly non-linear (Wolf and Soldo, 1988), and only in a few studies do the models allow for non-linearities.

In developing countries, most studies are of the cross-sectional variety and have not shed any light whatsoever on the nature of changes. We do know, however, that cross-sectional data are not always consistent with the hypothesis that higher income promotes living alone (see above), at least in the simplified models used so far.

More serious than the lack of consistency between theoretical expectations and observable regularities is an interpretative problem. Increases in income among the elderly have taken place as a result of large institutional changes that eroded attachment to traditional norms, transformed individual preferences and reinforced social transfers. These broader social changes have also led to increases in income of children, and this may also have an influence on decisions about shared living.

Finally, the choice of wealth indicators matters, as is the case with property ownership, for example. All three situations (settings where ideologies change simultaneously with material conditions, with children's income and with the meaning of property ownership) lead to a danger of overinterpreting the effects of parental wealth on co-residential arrangements: it will be hard to establish whether the association between income and living alone is a spurious one, making parental income changes endogenous, not an exogenous causal factor.

There is some evidence that effects of income (or other indicators of wealth) do indeed reflect artifacts. For example, in the study by Kramarow cited above, changes in the effects of variables have more salience than do changes in the variables themselves. A similar finding is reported by Chan and DaVanzo (1996) who find that among unmarried individuals in Malaysia, ethnic differentials in living alone are largely attributable to differences in the effects of variables, not to differences in the values of the variables. Patterns of this sort are typically found in the presence of endogenous effects, although, of course, this is not the only possible interpretation.[11]

Thus, although there are strong reasons to suspect that income affects the elderly's co-residence, and that increasing income over time may partially explain the large changes in levels of co-residence in the post-Second World War era, the empirical evidence is mixed and the interpretation of findings is not straightforward.

The role of social and other alternative transfers

One of the factors responsible for the increase in real income among the elderly is the institutionalization of social transfers through pension funds and safety-net programmes. More generally, it is widely stated in the literature that a central motive for the maintenance of a net flow of family transfers and co-residence with the elderly is associated with needs emerging in social contexts with poorly developed capital markets, precarious private savings rates, high levels of risk and uncertainty, and devoid of institutionalized mechanisms for social transfers. In view of this, one would expect that accounting for social changes that alter such contexts and for the presence and strength of social transfers would provide some leverage to explain observed changes in levels of living alone. But this is not the case. In the study by Pampel (1992) in Europe, his study of United States data (Pampel, 1983), and in one by Keilman (1988) on European countries, the role of social transfers is of trivial importance and cannot account for the observed diversity in levels of co-residence across countries in Europe and over time in the United States.

Similarly, co-residence and other family transfers from children to parents continue to dominate even in societies such as Malaysia and Taiwan

Province of China, where, albeit in the absence of significant social transfers towards the elderly, the social and economic contexts are conducive to very high levels of private savings rates (Lillard and Willis, 1995, 1997; Lee, Mason and Miller, 2000).

In contrast to these negative findings, Chan and Cheung (1997) report that among Singaporean retirees the availability of social transfers significantly decreases the propensity to cite children as the main source of financial support. They conclude that as coverage of CPF (a form of social transfer) widens, reliance on children as the main source of financial support will probably decrease. Although the main outcome of their investigation is not co-residence, it is likely that the same conclusion applies to it as it does to other forms of transfers.

In Latin American countries, the aggregate relation between, for example, levels of coverage and proportion of elderly living alone is close, but it is so partly because countries with a well-developed social security system are also those where fertility is lower, where industrialization and modernization have advanced the most, and where changes in the traditional norms may be further ahead. In such conditions, aggregate data will tell us very little about the mechanisms actually involved (Palloni, De Vos and Pelaez, 1999). Deterioration in the real value of social transfers and drastic changes in the mechanisms to enforce them have already led to erosion of wages and pension among the elderly. Future trends are anticipated to only get much worse (Margulis, 1993; Barrientos, 1997). If these changes are indeed accompanied by a decrease in the fraction of elderly living alone, one would have a better case to argue for income effects. This is so because it is unlikely that changes in preferences could operate fast enough to be responsible for the potential decrease in co-residence.[12]

Social transfers are not the only source of alternative support for the elderly. Another source is within-family transfers, consisting of actual flows of cash or services provided by the younger generations. The institutional changes that facilitate increases in the elderly's income are also responsible for increasing real income among their children, and for changes in their consumption priorities. If income of adult children rises, it is more likely that co-residence with parents could be substituted for other private transfers. Admittedly, this requires the relaxation of a regime where stigma or disapproval is attached to children living away from their parents.

In order to test this hypothesis, we must examine jointly patterns of co-residence and the entire array of family transfers towards parents. As a rule, however, this is not done in the studies surveyed.[13] Instead, researchers focus either on the probabilities of co-residence among the elderly, without considering other transfers from their children, or on the flow of transfers from children to the elderly, without considering co-residence. And if they do, co-residence is a control variable, not an outcome variable. For example, in an interesting paper on intergenerational transfers in the United States, Hogan, Eggebeen and Clogg (1993) identify three latent patterns of transfers towards the elderly among younger adults. But since co-residence is not considered as an explicit transfer, the patterns identified in their latent class model are subject to measurement error. It would have been desirable to identify latent classes using co-residence as well as other family transfers. The point is that both should be modelled simultaneously as they are complementary to and may substitute for each other. Whether this occurs or not, and to what extent, may vary across social and economic settings.

Although not explicitly designed to deal with co-residence, the accounting framework elaborated by Lee (1994a, 1994b) could, in principle, take account of both co-residence and other transfers. For example, in the estimation exercise performed by Stecklov (1997) for Côte d'Ivoire, family transfers could be decomposed into those associated with shared living and those originating in other sources. Weights could be assigned to co-residence as a function of the nature of consumption of household goods. This could lead to identification of the relative magnitude of all family transfers. If this exercise is carried out with different social groups, it is possible to describe the variability in co-residential arrangements simultaneously with the variability in other transfer flows (social and family-related).

The role of preferences

The role of preferences is a thorn in the side of research on co-residence arrangements, for their effects can rarely be identified when they are not measured directly (Myers, 1996). The idea that changes in tastes for privacy and independence are causing rapid changes in the living arrangements of the elderly is a plausible one. But there are few studies that measure preferences directly. For the most part, preferences are assumed away, as happens in most research that focuses on changes in the role of income.

Lesthaeghe has argued in favour of the hypothesis that a number of demographic changes, including low fertility, are attributable to the rise of individualism. This emerges as an ideological consequence of the advent of a post-modern society, the spread of affluence and the availability of enhanced social transfers and government-sponsored safety nets (Lesthaeghe and Meekers, 1986; Inglehart, 1981; Lesthaeghe, 1983).

An individualistic superstructure, however, may not suffice without subverting the household as a unit of production of goods, a consideration that is especially important in rural areas of the developing world. Growth of individualism is facilitated by reorganization of production and by technological developments that make possible an ample supply of goods, such as recreation and companionship, traditionally produced by households. Other goods, such as personal care for children and the elderly, housekeeping and meal preparation, also become available outside the household, and the opportunity costs for the production of these goods by individuals within a household become steeper. If, as some empirical research shows (Lesthaeghe and Meekers, 1986), this connection between individualistic ideology and technological and material development is a plausible one, we face, here again, an endogeneity problem, as both income and preferences for living alone are similarly responsive to other factors, without necessarily influencing one another.

Despite these massive changes, traditional ideas appear to change very slowly. Investigations on attitudes of young adults towards the elderly and of elderly people towards their children reveal an important regularity, namely, a strong sense of reciprocity and altruism on the part of both young adults and the elderly alike. In a study not directly focused on co-residence but on motives for intergenerational exchanges, Logan and Spitze (1995) find that, in the United States at least, there is a high degree of consensus across ages on responses that favour older persons' interests. They conclude that, in contrast to a public image of selfishness and self-interest, age differences in the attitude studied highlight intergenerational solidarity: older people's attitudes seem to give greater weight to the needs of younger generations, and vice versa. Relations across age groups apparently have an altruistic character — not only in the family, where economists have come to expect it, but also in the interpersonal realm of governmental programmes. These findings are not necessarily inconsistent with higher probabilities of living alone among the elderly, provided that the "losses" incurred by establishing separate living arrangements are indeed compensated by other transfers, either social or familial. But they give less credence to arguments pointing to a shift in ideology as the main causal factor responsible for trends in living arrangements.

In an analysis of attitudes expressed in focus group interviews in four Asian societies (Philippines, Singapore, Taiwan Province and Thailand), Ingersoll-Dayton and Saengtienchai (1997) report that, while expressions and manifestations of bonds of solidarity with the elderly are changing, respect remains a central value. While strict obedience is on the decline, focus group participants acknowledge that deference and respect are embedded in many other behaviours. Their findings suggest that, far from being neglected, traditional feelings for the elderly are very much in place.

Similar work with focus groups by Knodel and colleagues in Thailand points to a widespread norm of support for the elderly and the elderly's preferences of co-residence with children. They conclude that fertility decline, and the entire ethos that accompanies the change, may have limited effects on co-residence, largely owing to the relative flexibility among Thais with respect to the gender of co-resident adult children and particularly with respect to the gender of the child who eventually remains with the elderly parents once all others have left the parental household (Knodel, Chayovan and Siriboon, 1992, p. 96). Opinions by participants in their focus groups reflect that young adults and the elderly alike seem to hold co-residence and other forms of support in high esteem, and they are not about to abandon them even if smaller families are accepted as the norm.

In apparent stark contrast, a study of the elderly in the city of São Paulo, Brazil carried out by Ramos finds that multigenerational arrangements are not necessarily appreciated by the elderly. In fact, he confirms the existence of a positive gradient between the probability of living alone and levels of poverty but also discovers that the perceptions of those living in three-generational households, in particular, were often negative. They expressed less satisfaction with life and with family relations, and referred to fewer confidants and people to visit than the average for the sample. This was despite the fact that they were receiving more personal and nursing care (Ramos, 1994). On the other hand, those in living arrangements with children (but not jointly with grandchildren) appear to be more satisfied. It is unclear from this whether lack of satisfaction is a result of overall living conditions in three-generational families or the outcome of an inconsistency between actual living arrangements and the elderly's (or children's) preferences. In a comparison of conditions among Dutch and Tuscan elderly, de Jong Gierveld and colleagues find that those living alone were more likely to feel isolated and lonely (de Jong Gierveld, Van Tilburg and Lecchini, 1997). Isolation and loneliness are two important indicators of emotional dissatisfaction and depression among the elderly. However, living with children was less protective against loneliness than was the presence of a spouse, and having a wide social network and other sources of emotional support helped protect against loneliness, independent of living arrangements. This suggests that shared living with children may not always lead to a higher likelihood of emotional satisfaction.

This is all very sketchy and fails to address the main point, namely, whether preferences for living alone — rather than respect for the elderly — have indeed changed. However, these findings cannot be ignored since, if anything, they suggest that there is no compelling and convincing proof of the admittedly more general hypothesis that individualism and self-centredness could be eroding norms of co-residence. If it has changed, preferences for co-residence with the elderly is unlikely to be the product of an overhaul of the ideological foundation of family solidarity. Even if verified on a massive scale, ideological changes are not sufficient proof, as it would be difficult to reject the alternative hypothesis that new values regarding co-residence are more a rationalization of new behavioural patterns than their cause.

The multiplying effect of diffusion

An idea that has attracted remarkably little attention is that norms of living arrangements among the elderly may be diffused and adopted even when the whole set of material conditions that led to their emergence elsewhere are not yet realized in a particular place and time.

The sudden and large fertility decline that took place in the developing countries after 1970 cannot be explained without recourse to a diffusion explanation. The key is not the diffusion of the availability of contraception but of the social acceptance of a low-fertility norm. Similarly, it could well happen that under a minimum set of conditions regarding social transfers, for example, the norm of living alone becomes accepted and practised among groups that have not yet completely developed all conditions that lead to a higher prevalence of living alone in other places. The lure of what is "Western" is generalized and powerful, and is not just manifested in completed fertility but in family size as well. It may turn out to be even stronger under the onslaught of rapid ageing itself (Wolf, 1994a). It is not implausible, then, to think that one of the components of Westernization, the nuclearization of families, becomes embedded even in local traditional cultures, much as the low-fertility norm is absorbed wholeheartedly by those whose material living conditions lag behind the behavioural innovation.

Admittedly, testing this hypothesis is difficult as it requires long time-series or, alternatively, microdata for different social groups at two or more points in time, a simultaneous assessment of material conditions, and knowledge of co-residential preferences.

Demographic availability of kin

A constraint on the observed prevalence of co-residence with children is the availability of surviving children. In theory, only one surviving child suffices for co-residence to occur. Thus, the fertility decline experienced in Western societies, Asian countries and the majority of the developing world should not, in principle at least, precipitate higher levels of living alone since it takes place simultaneously with an equally sharp increase in child survival. Admittedly, the distribution of children surviving per mother has shifted towards lower values and contains much less dispersion than in the past. But declines in fertility could exert immediate pressure on co-residence only if they are accompanied by widespread childlessness. This is a scenario that could become a fact in industrialized societies but it is not yet so, and it is far from the reality in developing countries. With a few exceptions, the observed desired family size in many countries and across all cohorts of women does not suggest a future of sharp increases in voluntary childlessness.

The literature on co-residence, however, systematically shows that the number of surviving children does matter for the probability of the elderly to co-reside. In particular, it suggests that elderly persons with a larger number of surviving children are more likely to co-reside. In a thorough review, Wolf (1994a) shows that in most studies carried out before 1993 in the United States and European countries, the probability of living alone is negatively related to the availability of children. Similarly, in an interesting study of United States historical patterns, the authors venture a prediction of future increases in living alone based solely on oscillations in the number of surviving children (Macunovich and others, 1995). But these large effects are also seen in Asia (Casterline and others, 1991; Knodel, Amornsirisomboon and Khiewyoo, 1997) and in Latin America (Solis, 1999; Agree, 1993). How can this regularity be interpreted?

One explanation is that families with higher numbers of children surviving are selected for characteristics that motivate stronger adherence to the traditional norm of co-residing with parents. In this scenario, the explanatory variables (availability) are endogenous and their effects cannot be interpreted as liberally as is frequently done in the literature (Myers, 1992). A second explanation requires us to invoke auxiliary elements that are, strictly speaking, not part of demographic availability per se. A higher number of children surviving implies a larger and more diverse pool of resources so that either the costs (for children) associated with co-residence can be spread over a larger number of individuals or, alternatively, parents are more likely to find a desirable set of choices (Wolf, 1994a). If only one child is available, the brunt of the costs has to be absorbed by one person, and the range of options narrows down to only two. When the number of surviving offspring is higher, there is far more room for adjustment, including the possibility of rotating co-residence. And if there is variance in the characteristics of children, it is more likely that a desirable choice can be at least approximated. This argument assumes a number of conditions regarding bargaining among children, which, for the moment, is intentionally overlooked.

A third explanation suggested by Knodel is that a larger number of children surviving is likely to be associated with higher variance in the ages of children. In particular, families with higher numbers of surviving children are more likely to contain relatively young ones when their parents are older than, say, 60 or 65. To the extent that younger children are less likely to be encumbered by parental responsibilities, they are more likely to co-reside. It follows from this that it is not the availability of children per se that matters, but the characteristics of those available. Although Knodel suggests that the key feature is the age of the youngest, this is but a proxy for the relevant target conditions, namely, those associated with the stage of the life course experienced by all relevant children. Knodel's conjecture finds support in other Asian countries as well (DaVanzo and Chan, 1994; Casterline and others, 1991).

This finding has a few implications. The most important one is that as the length of generations rises — childbearing becomes increasingly concentrated at older ages — the proportion living alone will systematically vary by age of parents: it should be lower at younger ages (young old) and will increase thereafter (oldest old). Thus, the overall proportion living alone will depend strongly on the age distribution of the elderly. In developing countries at least, the cohorts who reach age 60 or 65 by 2020 are relatively large cohorts, a result of transient increases in fertility in the 1950s and 1960s and of steadily declining mortality. But these are the same cohorts adopting norms of concentrated childbearing. Therefore, one would expect that, if everything else is constant, the proportion living alone will decrease for a period of time after 2020 but then increase steadily as these larger cohorts age and their children reach stages in their life cycle that make co-residence with parents increasingly difficult.

If extensively verified, the effects of the age of the youngest child need to be interpreted by examining the life course characteristics of available children, an idea that has been posed and pursued by Wolf in several papers (Wolf, 1994a).

In addition to their age distribution, a characteristic of surviving children systematically omitted from analyses is their composition by migrant status. A demographic measure of availability only reflects a potential for co-residence but conceals the unavailability of those who are migrants. The migration of children from rural to urban areas or from one country to another may reflect household strategies whereby co-residence is replaced by income transfers in the form of remittances. If this is so, controlling for children's migration status will attenuate the effects of pure availability. This is because migrant children are more likely to come from households with a higher number of children among which migration and other income-generating strategies are pursued simultaneously.[14]

The idea that it is not sheer availability that matters has a flip side that has not gone unnoticed. This is that spatial proximity and the ability to establish frequent and easy contact with children and kin may ultimately matter more than shared living in the same dwelling (Wolf, 1994a; Choe, 1987; Florentina, 1991; Cai, 1991; Kendig, 1987; Knipsheer and others, 1995). It may also solve some of the potential problems of co-residence that may lead to the elderly's dissatisfaction (Ramos, 1994). Spatial proximity to children and the elderly's density of social networks involving children (and other kin) and friends or acquaintances could be considered as substitute transfers, just as are help with income or with provision of services.

Finally, it is worth considering another characteristic of children, namely, their composition by marital status. Although in some research a measure of availability of children is the number of unmarried surviving children, the bulk of investigations uses number of children, frequently controlling for their marital status. At least in the United States, the effects are unequivocal: availability of unmarried children matters more than sheer availability (Wolf and Soldo, 1988). Recent work has begun to explore this theme in depth but from the point of view of parents, namely, assessing the effects of parental marital history on the patterns of exchanges flowing from children to parents (Pezzin and Schone, 1999). In most countries in Asia and Latin America, marital status matters less as co-residence seems to take place equally among parents and unmarried and married children.[15]

The issue has importance if trends towards a new form of family organization involving high levels of divorce and consensual unions materialize throughout the developing world. This is because the budgetary, spatial and social constraints imposed by these new types of family arrangements of children are bound to affect their (and their parents') preferences for co-residence, and constrain (or enhance?) shared living even more than the reduction in sheer availability of surviving children.

Health status of the elderly

In virtually all cross-sectional studies of the probability of living alone (or co-residing with children or kin) there is mention of the role of the health status of the elderly. The conjecture is simple: since the needs of elderly persons who are disabled or ill are greater, co-residence should be more likely (keeping everything else constant). The empirical record is not at all clear on this score; although the effects are usually in the expected direction (for example, Haaga, Peterson and DaVanzo, 1993), their magnitude pales relative to the magnitude of other determinants. In a few studies, the findings are inconsistent with those expected and no relation at all is found (Martin, 1989). In yet others, the effects are as expected for some elderly (married) but not for others (unmarried) (DaVanzo and Chan, 1994).

If health status and disability status do have an independent impact, their role in the overall reduction of the probability to co-reside should be investigated. In view of the conjecture posed earlier about the possible increase in disability and chronic illnesses among the elderly in Latin America, one would expect that the trend towards solitary living promoted by other factors would be counterbalanced by the expected deterioration of health status.

Finally, most studies that use health measures rely heavily on self-reports. These are subject to some measurement error but, more importantly, may reflect a state achieved as a result of co-residence. That is, some elderly among those who co-reside may have been ill and temporarily disabled in the recent past, but recovered after the onset of a co-residence spell.

Residential arrangements as a coping mechanism

As is plain from the theoretical framework reviewed earlier, patterns of co-residence of the elderly have traditionally been studied with excessively static lenses, as if they were part of inflexible social arrangements or exchanges and lacking in plasticity. As a consequence, we know little about the social use of co-residence as a transient adjusting mechanism to cope with crises, however short-lived, triggered by income or property loss, death of a spouse, or health deterioration, or as a defensive resource to offset deleterious consequences of shifts in social conditions that suddenly alter demographic profiles, institutional settings or property regimes. In all these cases, living arrangements may be temporarily adjusted and tinkered with until conditions in existence before the adjustment are restored, a point in which they may return to their initial state.

An important example of this type of phenomenon is taking place in countries in Africa, as a consequence of the HIV/AIDS epidemic. About 10 years ago, simple simulation models suggested that a major adjustment in patterns of co-residence would need to occur to accommodate not just for the steep increases in adult mortality, but also for the completely changed adult health profile that would ensue (Lee and Palloni, 1992). This has proved to be true, but the author knows of only one effort to assess what the adjustments are for the elderly in the case of Thailand (Wachter, Knodel and VanLandingham, 1999) and none in Africa.

A second example of short-term changes in co-residence patterns of the elderly in response to social shifts may be occurring in a number of countries in Latin America. The most demographically advanced among them (Argentina, Chile and Uruguay) are also the ones where the ageing process is proceeding most rapidly and where currency and inflationary crises and draconian restructuring programmes have undermined the earnings of the elderly population. They are also those in which reforms of traditional pension systems and publicly funded health insurance programmes have been thoroughly dismantled. Although there is abundant anecdotal evidence indicating that there are significant increases in co-residence of the elderly, I know of no study assessing the impact that these changes have had on the elderly's living arrangements. This may undermine our ability to predict what will inevitably occur in other countries, such as Brazil and Mexico, that could rapidly join the ranks of countries such as Argentina, Chile and Uruguay.

The present section reviews several classes of models for the study of the living arrangements of the elderly. Some of them have been conventionally used in the literature and will continue to be used for a time to come. Others are less developed and their use is much less widespread, but they offer a great deal of promise and their properties and implications should be studied further. The section also contains a discussion of the role of simulation and data needs to shed light on issues that remain poorly understood.

The review is necessarily selected and driven by two rather narrow concerns. First, as mentioned above, one of the central motivations for studying the living arrangements of the elderly is a practical one, namely, the belief that they have a bearing on the elderly's levels of well-being. We are normally content with assessments about what the prevalent living arrangements are, an examination of the nature of time trends, and the identification of key factors that determine them. Most of the time, however, we neglect to consider related issues regarding residential preferences of parents and children alike, or whether they suffice for satisfying basic necessities. It seems fair to ask whether our models enable us to pass judgements about the extent to which the welfare of the elderly is affected by living arrangements.

Secondly, as reiterated several times in this paper, the living arrangements of the elderly are just one among many other alternative resources, and may not even be the most important one. Furthermore, the availability of other resources may condition the role played by living arrangements, when they play a role at all. Yet, as noted earlier, living arrangements are studied as an outcome in itself, neglecting the entire bundle of resources that the elderly "consume", including savings, bequests, assets and rents, wages and family and social transfers. Thus, an important question to ask is whether the models we use enable us to understand complementarities, substitutability and contingencies of living arrangements and other resources, particularly those associated with other family and social transfers.

Types of models

Five classes of models are distinguished: reduced forms for co-residence (simple and complex), structural forms for co-residence (conditional and unconditional) and structural forms for intergenerational transfers.

Reduced forms for co-residence: simple representations

The conventional way of studying the living arrangements of the elderly is to use observable information at one point in time or from pooled time-series data, and then to model the observed probabilities of living alone versus a number of alternative options. If the alternatives are just two, a logit (or probit) model is used. If there are more than two, a multinomial logit is the preferred choice.

The specification of the models usually proceeds by including co-variates in the model that are considered to be good indicators of properties identified in a number of alternative theories about co-residence (old-age security hypothesis, parental repayments, risk and insurance, altruism, exchange motive and so on). In addition, appropriate controls are included. Often, empirical specifications include characteristics of the elderly but only on rare occasions do they also include selected characteristics of a sample of their surviving children.

The estimation of these models results in a set of regression coefficients, usually in the form of estimates of effects on the log odds of living alone (versus one or a number of alternative co-residential arrangements). The validity of a theory is then judged by examining the statistical significance of the regression coefficients of the set of indicators associated with it.

The shortcomings of this kind of modelling are many. The paper focuses on three of them that are closely related to the two main concerns stated at the outset of the present section.

(a)   *Lack of a decision-making model*

Perhaps the most important drawback of these models is that they never explicitly pose a representation of what the decision-making process for co-residence is. Even if one neglects the existence of other transfers and ignores their influence on co-residence, the estimated coefficients are largely uninterpretable since we do not know what they refer to, other than to an empirically found association. It is certainly not enough to say, for example, that the effects of the variable income or property ownership are statistically significant and properly assigned as we have no theoretical model within which they are assigned some meaning. One consequence of this lack of theoretical specificity is that endogeneity problems plague these studies and, frequently, the researcher pays only passing attention to them. The second drawback is that to the extent that the decision-making process leading to observable co-residential patterns is opaque, comparability of estimated effects over time or over units of analyses is impossible, for one does not know how differences in estimates should be interpreted. They may simply reflect changes in the importance of the degree to which a variable is endogenous to the process, or be the result of shifts in the social contexts where decisions about co-residence are made. Finally, individual preferences are never explicitly introduced, and frequently the whole issue of preferences is hardly mentioned at all. The result is that these models cannot even begin to address whether the elderly's residential arrangements increase, decrease or are neutral with respect to their well-being.

(b)   *Absence of representation of entire sets of options*

An equally troublesome feature of these models is that, more often than not, there is no consideration of alternative co-residence options offered by the array of children and kin available to the elderly. This is not just a difficulty that can be solved by controlling for the demographic availability of children (using the number of children surviving) or kin (using frequencies of available close kin). The problem is that what matters for co-residential arrangements has more to do with the joint characteristics of children vis-à-vis their parents than with the sheer number of surviving children. Their marital status, their labour-force status, their education and their income are all of considerable importance and should be taken into account in suitable ways.

(c)   Lack of consideration of other family and social transfers

A final shortcoming is that the role of other family and social transfers is overlooked. In the rare examples when this is not the case, they are represented as co-variates that enter the specification of the model in the same way as any other co-variate. Instead, the actual utilization of other transfers could be a function of co-residence (rather than the other way around) as children and the elderly may substitute one for the other. More generally, the availability and feasibility of alternative transfers may be an integral part of the decision-making process that leads to living alone or to co-residence. They should then be considered as joint outcomes about which individuals make decisions. The lack of a solution to this problem leads to difficulties analogous to those described earlier regarding the availability of children. This is not surprising since they are tightly related to each other. For example, accounting for children's educational effects on the probability of the elderly's co-residence has relevance for assessing the validity of the hypothesis according to which increased co-residence with the more highly educated among the children reflects the existence of repayment of parental investments in children's education.

Reduced forms for co-residence: complex representations

To resolve the problem summarized in (b) above, Wolf and Soldo (1988) formulate a more nuanced model that incorporates all co-residential arrangements that are possible with surviving children. This formulation consists of a multinomial model simultaneously considering all options available to the elderly and making them functions of both the elderly's and, potentially, all of their children's characteristics. It can be applied in cases where there is substantial simultaneous co-residence with children, or when the prevailing rule is one of co-residence with a single child. Estimates of such models can be interpreted more freely than can the conventional reduced logit (or probit) approach as they are potentially informative about the influence of all possible parent-children pairings and about their relevant characteristics. So far, however, the actual estimation of these models has been carried out in the absence of a theoretical formulation that makes explicit the underlying decision-making process, and that considers the non-additive influence of alternative forms of transfers.[16]

An important advantage of the model proposed by Wolf is that, with appropriate information, one could include explicit consideration of other family transfers (as associated characteristics of children), as well as other social transfers. In this sense, the model also opens the door to solve problem (c). However, since it still does not solve (a), it is unlikely that one could interpret meaningfully the effects of variables measuring the existence of other family (via child) transfers.

Structural forms for co-residence: conditional model

Kotlikoff and Morris (1990) were the first to derive an estimable model of co-residence from a stylized yet informative and potentially rich decision-making framework for co-residence between parents and one available child (or kin). The detailed description of the framework is beyond the scope of this paper but its core aspects can be briefly summarized. One starts from first principles, namely, two utility functions, one for a child, $U(c)$, and one for the parent, $U(p)$. Each of them depends on levels of consumption, C, housing services, H, and a pair of coefficients capturing preferences for shared living arrangements, A and B, for the child and parent, respectively. In addition, there is a utility function that applies when they choose to live together. This is a weighted average of $U(c)$ and $U(p)$, where the weight is a parameter θ chosen jointly by the pair. This parameter reflects the bargaining process between parent and child. However, knowledge of the particular value of θ chosen by the pair if they decide to live together is not necessary to infer their preferences for shared living arrangements. All that is needed is that there be a set of possible values of θ such that, in each case, parent and child are better off living together than living apart. This property is key since it means that the analyst can separate the preferences of the elderly parent and adult children from the unknown dynamics of the bargaining process that makes shared living possible.

A final step in the construction of the model is the formulation of a pair of equations for A and B, the unmeasured preferences for the child and the parent. These are made functions of measured characteristics and associated effects, and of individual heterogeneity:

$$A=\alpha_c X_c+\varepsilon_c$$

$$B=\alpha_p X_p+\varepsilon_p$$

where A and B are the child and parent preferences for shared living, X_c and X_p are vectors of child and parental characteristics, α_c and α_p are effects, and ε_c and ε_p are child and parent unmeasured factors.

Co-residence is an event that will occur if, and only if, a simple condition, K, is met. Condition K can be expressed as a function of A and B and, therefore, determined by the vectors of measured characteristics, associated vectors of estimable effects and, lastly, by unmeasured individual heterogeneity. The precise form of the function on which shared living depends is contingent on the precise parameterization of the εs. The important point is that, under a normal approximation, the final formulation is a model quite different from a conventional reduced-form probit or logit.

There are a number of advantages to this approach. The first is that the final functional form for the probability of co-residence that the analyst needs to estimate empirically is entirely determined by the decision-making model.

This is in contrast to the reduced form models researchers usually use, where the functional form is defined a priori as probit or logit or tobit. The second advantage is that the way in which co-variates affect the decision about co-residence is not arbitrarily specified but depends on the nature of the decision-making model. To the extent that the assumptions and properties of this model are altered, so will the form in which individual characteristics or social settings affect the probabilities of finding co-residence for a particular parent-child pair.

The Kotlikoff-Morris model is elementary since it only allows for effects of a limited set of characteristics, and their utility functions are, perhaps intentionally, excessively simplistic. However, neither of these shortcomings is fatal as the model can be expanded to accommodate, for example, more complex utility functions and to include the effects of numerous parental and child characteristics omitted in their first application. It is because of this that their model solves problem (a). It does not, however, solve problem (b) and, consequently, cannot solve problem (c).

Structural forms for co-residence: unconditional model

The most important disadvantage of the Kotlikoff-Morris model is that it is limited to one pair, the parent and one available child. In this sense, the model is conditional on the choice of one pairing. For most interesting cases, this will not do since within each family there might be a number of possible pairs that could lead to shared living between parents and children.

The solution to this shortcoming consists of extending the Kotlikoff-Morris model to multiple pairs and then adopting the two-sided logit (TSL) model proposed by Logan (1996) and Logan, Hoff and Newton (1999) to determine the empirically observable co-residence pairs. The resulting model is unconditional (on the pair chosen for co-residence). An outline of the solution follows. First, we extend the Kotlikoff-Morris model to consider every possible pair that can be formed between parents and each surviving (available) child. This means that there will be as many U(c) functions as there are children and as many total (family) utility functions as there are possible pairs.[17] As a consequence, there will be as many parameters θ as there are possible pairs for shared co-residence. Each of these captures the bilateral bargaining between a child and the parent, as well as the dynamic of any between-sibling bargaining process.

The second step consists of the implementation of the two-sided logit approach proposed by Logan and others (1999) to determine the equilibrium (stable) solution to the matching problem and to estimate the effects of vectors of parental and children's characteristics. The TSL approach was designed to increase the tractability of problems involving a match between two sides. Each side is assumed to have preferences that are functions of the characteristics of each member of the pair. The empty set option (no pair formed) is equivalent in our case to choosing the option of living apart.

Estimation of the TSL model is numerically very difficult when the set of pairs that can be formed is large. However, in the case of co-residence, we have a rather small number of possible pairs per family, unless the number of surviving children is extremely large. Therefore, the numerical estimation problems should be considerably reduced.

Structural forms for intergenerational transfers

The main disadvantage of the extension of Kotlikoff-Morris type models is that they are not designed to deal with the totality of intergenerational transfers, of which co-residence is a part. An admittedly ad hoc solution that preserves the main properties of the model is to include family or social transfers as part of the vector of parent-child characteristics. However, this is unappealing and unlikely to get us too far in assessing theories regarding joint motives for co-residence and other transfers between parents and children.

The only feasible solution is to build models for overlapping generations such as those proposed by Lillard and Willis (1995), and the richer ones suggested and estimated by Rosenzweig and Wolpin (1993). They are, in principle at least, well designed for addressing the problem of decision-making about co-residence as part of the bundle of intergenerational exchanges, but are difficult to specify, are data demanding, and complicated to estimate, all of which limits their more generalized application.

Further developments

While the modelling issues discussed above and their implications for data collection could mean significant advances in the field, more modest undertakings can also improve our understanding of the living arrangements of the elderly. The present section concludes at a lower level of abstraction, with a brief discussion of desirable analyses of easily obtainable aggregate data. Also identified are some improvements in our existing analytic schemes and their application to extant longitudinal data.

Aggregate data analysis

A number of interesting issues discussed earlier could be studied with data already available to us, particularly those in the form of microsamples from national censuses. For example, it is not difficult to create comparable (across time and social settings) measures of poverty from census data, and to cross-tabulate the elderly population by poverty status and a number of relevant characteristics. This will enable us to establish levels of poverty by living arrangements and, when two or more censuses are available, to assess time trends. Modelling of these data for causal inferences is difficult but a subordinate goal, that of understanding the status quo as well as anticipating where future trends are heading, could be attained.

Similarly, cross-classification of the elderly by living arrangements and number of surviving children is a useful exercise to understand patterns of living arrangements by demographic availability and according to life-cycle stages of children. The goal is not to produce precise causal inference but rather a detailed demographic accounting to establish whether theoretically interesting relations conjectured by researchers are at least weakly supported.

Finally, cross-national studies of microsamples linked to contextual data pertaining to institutional contexts can be useful for identifying the variability of older persons' living arrangements according to conditions that normally constrain observed patterns of social and family transfers.

Analytic improvements

A plea for collecting and using individual longitudinal data is customary at the end of many papers on living arrangements. There are many reasons for this plea, including the enhanced ability to identify the existence and quantify past transfers and living arrangements. There is a different reason to focus on longitudinal data (even if only in the form of limited panels), namely, the enhanced ability to assess the influence, however transient, of changes in individual or social conditions on co-residential arrangements.

A simple example is the one regarding the relation between elderly health status and living arrangements. With access to longitudinal data, we can estimate reduced form multistate hazard models that, with all their limitations, will shed light on the issue of plasticity of living arrangements. It could well be, for example, that although the norm of shared living loses its appeal, another norm remains in effect, namely, one that calls for co-residence if and when the health status of a parent deteriorates. Under what conditions associated with individual characteristics (parents' and children's) and their social context (existence of health insurance schemes and so on) this occurs, and under which ones it is less likely to materialize is of relevance for understanding how levels of well-being of the elderly may fluctuate. These studies can also support the projection of future living arrangements as a function of the health status of the elderly.

The plea for using microsimulation models is also well known but less frequent. For the most part, microsimulation is a tool sparsely used to quantify the effects of demographic conditions on availability (De Vos and Palloni, 1989; Wachter, Knodel and VanLandingham, 1999; Wachter, Blackwell and Hammel, 1999; Wolf, 1999). The outcomes of microsimulation, however, are silent on issues regarding preferences and propensities and without them their application is of limited reach.

However, as suggested and implemented by Wolf in several papers (1994b, 1999), microsimulation models can be combined with empirical estimates of the probabilities of co-residence, given the characteristics of the parent-child pair. If models regarding co-residence were designed to deal with other transfers, there is no reason why microsimulation could not incorporate modules designed to represent jointly the effects of demographic availability, the effects of individual characteristics and the interplay of co-residence and other transfers. This is a powerful tool that can make tractable thorny issues regarding feedbacks and may, if properly used, provide the needed link between micromodels of intergenerational transfers (including co-residence) and aggregate demographic accounting of the sort promoted by Lee and colleagues.

CONCLUSIONS

Throughout this paper the author stresses the important point that our concern with the living arrangements of the elderly should be subordinate to the larger concern for welfare among them. This requires that we pose the problem differently from the way in which it has been treated historically. To do so we need to address three interrelated problems. The solution to each of these problems presents its own demands in terms of theories, model formulations and data-collection protocols.

The first problem is to link living arrangements more tightly to levels of well-being of the elderly. This requires that we emphasize as much the precise measurement of the elderly's (and children's) preferences and desires as we do observed living arrangements. Simultaneously, our data-collection efforts should also include objective assessments of levels of well-being by compiling lists of goods consumed and needs that may depend on health status, residential location and other individual or contextual characteristics. Making inferences about the elderly's living arrangements that have indeterminate implications for their levels of well-being is a somewhat empty exercise.

The second problem is to understand how living arrangements change as a function of the increase in the aged population itself, the improving (or deteriorating) health status of the elderly and the processes that alter the opportunities and constraints of their children (or other kin). In concluding a review of the literature on living arrangements, Wolf (1994a) conjectured that perhaps the largest concern of all has to do with feedback effects: as ageing of societies proceeds, the growth of the elderly population itself could create conditions for changes in the norms of co-residence and of relations between generations. If they occur, these feedback effects will require time before they can percolate and influence observable living arrangements and other social and familial transfers. Although some of them may be interpretable by way of diffusion-like models, where trends in one social context directly affect trends in others, their full understanding will require fine-tuning of our frameworks, as well as collecting much more detailed information on actual preferences and characteristics of the social, political and economic settings than we do now.

By the same token, larger demographic changes that include but are not restricted to rapid ageing will influence the characteristics of the life cycle of adult children. Higher prevalence of divorce and consensual unions, shifts in the timing of marriage and of first birth cannot occur without having an impact on patterns of relations between generations. What influences, for example, will the massive prevalence of divorce and disrupted families of adult children have on opportunities and desire to co-reside with parents?

Finally, a major part of the prospective changes in modern demographic regimes could be substantial increases in longevity. The conditions under which this will occur will necessarily differ among countries. In some, increased longevity may go hand in hand with better health and longer duration lived as healthy at older ages. In others, this may not be the case at all. The consequence could be an increasing demand for care among a much larger stock of elderly people living much longer. What changes will this bring in patterns of living arrangements and what effects will they have on the levels of well-being of the elderly?

The third and final problem has to do with locating living arrangements of the elderly within a larger context constituted by other family and social transfers. Changes in education and technology will affect productivity and human capital and thus alter the basis of within-family transfers. The diffusion of Western-like institutions will provide opportunities for materializing social transfers in societies that did not have them, and globalization of the economy will offer numerous opportunities for changing the nature of capital markets, altering the levels of risks and uncertainties in local economies, and modifying private and governmental savings patterns. Decisions about the living arrangements of the elderly will be affected by these changes, which will surely alter the likelihood, magnitude and direction of family and social transfers made possible by the new or reshaped institutional contexts. Without considering co-residence and other transfers simultaneously, as complements or substitutes for each other, our knowledge about levels and patterns of the elderly's living arrangements will continue to lag behind their historical transformations.

NOTES

[1] The availability ratio is the ratio of the population 60 and over to the population between ages 15 and 59. The latter population is the pool of available individuals with whom the elderly could co-reside.

[2] It is suspected that the prevalence of living alone among the elderly in Africa, though varying widely across countries, is at lower levels than in Asia and Latin America. This could be changing rapidly, particularly in countries with high levels of HIV prevalence.

[3] Co-residence regimes in sub-Saharan Africa are undergoing sustained stress and may quickly become destabilized as a consequence of the massive effects of the HIV/AIDS epidemic.

[4] For a view imputing changes in age patterns of living alone to past oscillations in fertility, see Macunovich and others, 1995.

[5] The eighth five-year plan in Thailand makes this explicitly a governmental concern (NESDB, 1995, cited in Knodel, Amornsirisomboon and Khiewyoo, 1997). See, also, Reher (1998) for a statement regarding the consequences, and state of affairs they reflect, of co-residence in Europe.

[6] This is one area where improvements through purely descriptive endeavours are feasible and useful. In fact, we now have available a large number of microcensus data for several areas in the world from which one could compute indicators of levels of well-being for the elderly by household type. These estimates could be compared across countries and over time to assess changes in the joint distribution of the elderly by co-residence and levels of well-being. Admittedly, the most difficult task here is to construct comparable indicators of well-being from census data.

[7] In a more recent analysis of the United States microcensus samples, Kramarow finds that the effects of home ownership, the most important among a handful of indicators of individual wealth, on the probability of living alone among elderly widows are trivial before 1940 but turn very strong and negative between 1960 and 1990 (Kramarow, 1995, p. 343). This is a somewhat surprising result because, as the author notes, we expect that home ownership reflects wealth which is associated with living alone in the second half of the twentieth century (Kramarow, p. 344). Home ownership is a variable that behaves erratically in most analyses of living alone in developing countries, at times depressing the probability of living alone (Agree, 1993, for Brazil) and at times enhancing it (Solis, 1999, for Mexico). To the extent that older persons' home ownership encourages children to move in with parents, there will be a positive association between it and probabilities of living alone. Without being able to explicitly address the endogeneity problem associated with the use of this variable, one needs to also examine relations between co-residence and other indicators of wealth. Similarly, it is possible that the relationship between wealth and co-residence, at least as embedded in π values, is gender-specific and that Kramarow's results apply only to women, not to men.

[8] The finding is consistent with Kramarow's findings. As mentioned in note 7, one possibility is that there are sharp gender differentials in the relations between poverty and co-residence, a conjecture that Smeeding's data do not confirm. A second possibility is that the relationship between poverty levels and co-residence involves complicated non-linearities not captured by the coarse categorization of poverty level used here.

[9] There is another possibility, which is to measure expectancies rather than distributions. Thus, for example, Schoeni (1998) shows that the fraction of the elderly living alone and the expected duration of living alone behave in somewhat different ways. But, since the differences between the two are hardly consequential and the latter is harder to compute, I will choose to focus on the distributional measure.

[10] This statement refers to overall transfers. Family transfers in industrialized societies are still downward but are more than offset by large social transfers mostly realized through the public sector.

[11] An interpretative problem of a different nature from that posed by endogeneity has to do with model specification. Thus, Kotlikoff and Morris (1990) show that the interpretation of income effects at one point in time is highly sensitive to the nature of the underlying decision process about shared living. They show, for example, that effects of increase of parental income on the probability of co-residence are a function of both parents' and children's preferences for shared living.

[12] However, in the study by Lesthaeghe and Meekers (1986), the authors find that short-run oscillations in the inflation rate have a visible impact on value judgements associated with preferences.

[13] A noteworthy exception is the analysis of Malaysian data carried out by Haaga and colleagues where they verify that, at least among those in poor health, family transfers are larger in the absence of co-residence. Similarly, Rosenzweig and Wolpin (1993) explicitly develop a model where co-residence and other transfers are considered simultaneously. The estimates they derive from United

States data, however, do not provide a basis for assessing the relations between one and the other since they do not investigate the latter stages of the life cycle.

[14] In reference to the previous discussion on the relation between co-residence and well-being, it should be noted that areas of high migration may be among those where parents' and children's co-residential status is a misleading indicator of quality of living and well-being of the elderly.

[15] In their study in Malaysia, however, DaVanzo and Chan (1995) find that there are important differentials according to marital status and gender.

[16] In a generalization of this approach to continuous but truncated variables, Wolf and colleagues suggest using a simultaneous tobit equation model (Wolf, Freedman and Soldo, 1997).

[17] A more complicated alternative is to consider a unique but composite family utility function including all children and the parents.

REFERENCES

Agree, Emily Miriam (1993). Effects of demographic change on the living arrangements of the elderly in Brazil: 1960-1980. Durham, North Carolina: Duke University. Ph.D. dissertation.

Aykan, Hakan, and Douglas A. Wolf (1998). Traditionality, modernity, and household composition: parent-child co-residence in contemporary Turkey. Syracuse, New York: Syracuse University, Maxwell Center for Demography and Economics of Aging. Paper No. 17.

Barker, D. J. P. (1997). *Mothers, Babies and Health in Later Life*. London: Churchill-Livingston.

Barrientos, Armando (1997). The changing face of pensions in Latin America: design and prospects of individual capitalization pension plans. *Social Policy and Administration*, vol. 31, No. 4, pp. 336-353.

Berkner, Lutz K. (1972). The stem family and the developmental cycle of the peasant household: an eighteenth century Austrian example. *American History Review*, 77 (April), pp. 398-418.

_____ (1975). The use and misuse of census data in the historical analysis of family structure. *Journal of Interdisciplinary History*, 4 (spring), pp. 721-738.

Bishop, C. E. (1986). Living arrangements choices of elderly singles: effects of income and disability. *Health-care Financing Review*, vol. 7, No. 3, pp. 65-73.

Burch, Thomas K., and B. J. Matthews (1987). Household formation in developed societies. *Population and Development Review*, vol. 13, No. 3, pp. 495-511.

Cai, Wenmei (1991). Changing family structures in the process of aging population in rural and urban China. *Population Aging: Review of Emerging Issues*, 108, pp. 123-125.

Caldwell, John C. (1976). Toward a restatement of demographic transition theory. *Population and Development Review*, vol. 2, Nos. 3-4, pp. 321-366.

Casterline, John B., and others (1991). Differences in the living arrangements of the elderly in four Asian countries: the interplay of constraints and preferences. Ann Arbor: University of Michigan, Population Studies Center. Research report 91-10.

Chan, Angelique, and Paul Cheung (1997). The interrelationship between public and private support of the elderly: What can we learn from the Singaporean case? Ann Arbor: University of Michigan, Population Studies Center. Research report 97-41.

Chan, Angelique, and Julie DaVanzo (1996). Ethnic differences in parents' co-residence with adult children in peninsular Malaysia. *Journal of Cross-Cultural Gerontology*, vol. 11, No. 1, pp. 29-59.

Choe, Ehn Hyun (1987). Current and future prospects on problems of aging in the Republic of Korea. *Population Aging: Review of Emerging Issues*, 80, pp. 44-52.

Crimmins, Eileen, M. Hayward and Yasuhiko Saito (1994). Changing mortality and morbidity rates and the health status and life expectancy of the older population. *Demography*, vol. 31, No. 1, pp. 159-175.

Crimmins, Eileen, Yasuhiko Saito and Dominique Ingegneri (1997). Trends in disability-free life expectancy in the United States, 1970-1990. *Population and Development Review*, vol. 23, No. 3, pp. 555-573.

DaVanzo, Julie, and Angelique Chan (1994). Living arrangements of older Malaysians: who coresides with their adult children? *Demography*, vol. 31, No. 1, pp. 95-113.

de Jong Gierveld, J., L. Van Tilburg and L. Lecchini (1997). Socio-economic resources, household composition, and the social network as determinants of well-being among Dutch and Tuscan older adults. *Genus*, vol. LIII, No. 3-4, pp. 75-100.

De Vos, Susan (1990). Extended family living among older people in six Latin American countries. *Journal of Gerontology*, vol. 45, No. 3, pp. S87-94.

_____, and Y. Lee (1988). Change in extended family living among the elderly in South Korea, 1970-1980. Madison: University of Wisconsin, Center for Demography and Ecology. Working paper 88-43.

_____, and Alberto Palloni (1989). Formal models and methods for analyzing kinship and household organization. *Population Index*, vol. 55, No. 2.

_____, and Gary Sandefur (1999). Elderly living arrangements in Bulgaria, the Czech Republic, Estonia, Finland, and Romania. Madison: University of Wisconsin, Center for Demography and Ecology. Working paper 99-14.

Ermisch, J. F. (1981). An economic theory of household formation. *Scottish Journal of Political Economy*, 28, pp. 1-19.

Florentina, Subartinah (1991). Social welfare services for the elderly in Indonesia. *Population Aging: Review of Emerging Issues*. Asian Population Studies Series, No. 80. Bangkok: Economic Commission for Asia and the Pacific, pp. 44-52.

Fogel, R. W. (1986). Nutrition and the decline of mortality since 1700: some preliminary findings. In *Long-Term Factors in American Economic Growth*, S. L. Engerman and R. E. Gallman, eds. Chicago: University of Chicago Press.

_____, and Dora L. Costa (1997). A theory of technophysio evolution, with some implications for forecasting population, health-care costs, and pension costs. *Demography*, vol. 29, No.1, pp. 49-66.

Freedman, V. A., and others (1991). Intergenerational transfers: a question of perspective. *The Gerontologist*, vol. 31, No. 5, pp. 640-647.

Fricke, Thomas E. (1990). Darwinian transitions? a comment. *Population and Development Review*, vol. 16, No. 1, pp. 107-119.

Gutiérrez, Luis M. (1998). Relación entre el deterioro funcional, el grado de dependencia y las necesidades asistenciales de la población envejecida en Mexico. En *La Población de Mexico al Final del Siglo XX: Serie Investigación Demográfica en Mexico*, H. Hernandez and C. Menkes, eds. Mexico: Universidad Nacional Autónoma de Mexico.

Gwatkin, Davidson R. (2000). Health inequalities and the health of the poor: What do we know? What can we do? *Bulletin of the World Health Organization*, vol. 78, No. 1 (January), pp. 3-17.

Haaga, John, Christine Peterson and Julie DaVanzo (1993). Health status and family support of older Malaysians. Santa Monica, California: Rand Corporation, Labor and Population Program. Working paper No. 93-17.

Hermalin, Albert I. (1997). Drawing policy lessons for Asia from research on ageing. *Asia-Pacific Population Journal*, vol. 12, No. 4.

_____, Mary Beth Ofstedal and Mei-Lin Lee (1992). Characteristics of children and intergenerational transfers. Ann Arbor: University of Michigan, Population Studies Center. Research report 92-21.

Hermalin, Albert I., Mary Beth Ofstedal and Ming-Cheng Chang (1992). Types of supports for the aged and their providers in Taiwan. In *Aging and Generational Relations: Life-Course and Cross-Cultural Perspectives*, Tamara K. Hareven, ed. New York: Aldine DeGruyter.

Hirosima, K. (1997). Projection of living arrangements of the elderly in Japan: 1990-2010. *Genus*, vol. LIII, No. 1-2, pp. 79-111.

Hogan, Dennis P., David J. Eggebeen and Clifford C. Clogg (1993). The structure of intergenerational exchanges in American families. *American Journal of Sociology*, vol. 98, No. 6, pp. 1428-1458.

Holtz-Eakin and T. M. Smeeding (1994). Income, wealth, and intergenerational economic relations of the aged. In *Demography of Aging*, L. Martin and S. H. Preston, eds. Washington, D.C.: National Research Council.

Idler, Ellen L., and Yael Benyamini (1997). Self-rated health and mortality: a review of twenty-seven community studies. *Journal of Health and Social Behavior*, 38, pp. 21-37.

Idler, Ellen L., and S. Kasl (1991). Health perceptions and survival: do global evaluations of health status really predict mortality? *Journal of Gerontology*, vol. 46, No. 2, pp. S55-65.

Ingersoll-Dayton, Berit, and Chanpen Saengtienchai (1997). Respect for the elderly in Asia: stability and change. Ann Arbor: University of Michigan, Population Studies Center. Elderly in Asia research report, series 97-46.

Inglehart, R. (1981). Post-materialism in an environment of insecurity. *American Political Science Review*, 75, pp. 880-900.

Kaplan, Hillard (1994). Evolutionary and wealth flows theories of fertility: empirical tests and new models. *Population and Development Review*, vol. 20, No. 4, pp. 753-791.

_____ (1997). The evolution of the human life course. In *Between Zeus and the Salmon: The Biodemography of Longevity*, Kenneth W. Wachter and Caleb E. Finch, eds. Washington, D.C.: National Academy Press.

Keilman, N. (1988). Recent trends in family and household composition in Europe. *European Journal of Population*, 3, pp. 297-326.

Kendig, Hal L. (1987). Roles of the aged, families and communities in the context of an aging society. *Population Aging in Asia: Review of Emerging Issues*. Asian Population Studies Series, No. 80. Bangkok: Economic Commission for Asia and the Pacific, pp. 75-83.

Kertzer, David I. (1989). The joint family household revisited: demographic constraints and household complexity in the European past. *Journal of Family History*, 14, pp. 1-15.

_____ (1991). Household history and sociological theory. *Annual Review of Sociology*, 17, pp. 155-179.

King, Miriam L., and Samuel Preston (1990). Who lives with whom? Individual versus household measures. *Journal of Family History*, 15, pp. 117-132.

Kinsella, Kevin G. (1990). *Living Arrangements of the Elderly and Social Policy: A Cross-National Perspective*. Center for International Research, paper No. 52. Washington, D.C.: US Bureau of the Census.

Knipscheer, C. P. M., and others, eds. (1995). *Living Arrangements and Social Networks of Older Adults*. Amsterdam, Netherlands: Vrije University Press.

Knodel, John, Pattama Amornsirisomboon and Jiraporn Khiewyoo (1997). Living arrangements, family support and the welfare of the elderly: findings and implications of the 1994 survey of elderly in Thailand. Ann Arbor: University of Michigan, Population Studies Center, Research report 97-43.

Knodel, John, Napaporn Chayovan and Siriwan Siriboon (1992). The impact of fertility decline on familial support for the elderly: an illustration from Thailand. *Population and Development Review*, vol. 18, No. 1, pp. 79-103.

Kobrin, F. E. (1976). The fall in household size and the rise of the primary individual in the United States. *Demography*, vol. 13, pp. 127-138.

Kotlikoff, L. J., and J. Morris (1990). Why don't the elderly live with their children? A new look. In *Issues in the Economics of Aging*, D. A. Wise, ed. Chicago: University of Chicago Press.

Kramarow, Ellen (1995). The elderly who live alone in the United States: historical perspectives on household change. *Demography*, vol. 32, No. 3, pp. 335-352.

Lam, David (1983). The economics of household composition in developing countries. Berkeley: University of California. Ph. D. dissertation.

_____ (1984). *Household Public Goods and the Shadow Price of Privacy: A Framework for Modeling the Interaction of Household Composition and Economic Behavior*. Minneapolis, Minnesota: Population Association of America.

_____ (1988). Marriage markets and assortative mating with household public goods. Ann Arbor: University of Michigan, Population Studies Center. Research report 88-120.

Laslett, Peter (1972). Introduction. In *Household and Family in Past Time*, Peter Laslett and Richard Wall, eds. London: Cambridge University Press.

Lee, Ronald D. (1994a). Fertility, mortality and intergenerational transfers: comparisons across steady states. In *The Family, the Market and the State*, J. Ermisch and N. Ogawa, eds. Oxford: Oxford University Press.

_____ (1994b). The formal demography of population aging, transfers, and the economic life cycle. In *Demography of Aging*, Linda G. Martin and Samuel H. Preston, eds. Washington, D.C.: National Academy Press.

_____ (1995). A cross-cultural perspective on intergenerational transfers and the economic life cycle. *Intergenerational Economic Relations and Demographic Change*. IUSSP. Papers from a seminar. Honolulu, Hawaii, 12-15 September.

_____ (1997). Intergenerational relations and the elderly. In *Between Zeus and the Salmon: The Biodemography of Longevity*, Kenneth W. Wachter and Caleb E. Finch, eds. Washington, D.C.: National Academy Press.

_____, A. Mason and T. Miller (2000). From transfers to individual responsibility: implications for savings and capital accumulation in Taiwan and the U.S. Paper presented at the Population Association of America meeting, Los Angeles, California, March.

Lee, Ronald D., and Alberto Palloni (1992). Changes in the family status of elderly women in Korea. *Demography*, vol. 29, No. 1, pp. 69-92.

Légaré, Jacques (1998). *Living Arrangements of Older Persons in Canada: Effects on Their Socio-Economic Conditions*. New York: United Nations, and Ottawa: Statistics Canada.

Lesthaeghe, R. (1983). A century of demographic and cultural change in Western Europe: an exploration of underlying dimensions. *Population and Development Review*, vol. 9, pp. 411-435.

_____, and D. Meekers (1986). Value changes and the dimension of familism in the European Community. *European Journal of Population*, 2, pp. 225-268.

Levy, Marion J., Jr. (1965). Aspects of the analysis of family structure. In *Aspects of the Analysis of Family Structure*, Marion J. Levy, Jr. and others, eds. Princeton: Princeton University Press.

Liefbroer, Aart, and Jenny de Jong Gierveld (1995). Living arrangements, socio-economic resources, and health. In *Living Arrangements and Social Networks of Older Adults*, C. P. M. Knipscheer, and others, eds. Amsterdam, Netherlands: Vrije University Press.

Lillard, Lee, and Robert J. Willis (1995). Intergenerational transfers in Indonesia. *Intergenerational Economic Relations and Demographic Change*. Papers from a seminar. Honolulu, Hawaii, 12-15 September.

_____ (1997). Motives for intergenerational transfers: evidence from Malaysia. *Demography*, vol. 34, No. 1, pp. 115-134.

Logan, John Allen (1996). Opportunity and choice in socially structured labour markets. *American Journal of Sociology*, vol. 102, No. 1, pp. 114-160.

Logan, John R., Peter D. Hoff and Michael Newton (1999). Estimation for the marriage model. Madison: University of Wisconsin, Center for Demography and Ecology. Working paper 99-31.

Logan, John R., and Glenna D. Spitze (1995). Self-interest and altruism in intergenerational relations. *Demography*, vol. 32, No. 3, pp. 353-364.

Macunovich, Diane J., and others (1995). Echoes of the baby boom and bust: recent and prospective changes in living alone among elderly widows in the United States. *Demography*, vol. 32, No. 1, pp. 17-28.

Manton, Kenneth, L. S. Corder and E. Stallard (1993). Estimates of change in chronic disability and institutional incidence and prevalence rates in the U.S. elderly population from the 1982, 1984 and 1989 National Long Term Care Survey. *Journal of Gerontology*, vol. 48, pp. S153-166.

Mare, Robert D., and Alberto Palloni (1988). Couple models for socioeconomic effects on the mortality of older persons. Madison: University of Wisconsin, Center for Demography and Ecology. Working paper 88-07.

Margulis, Mario (1993). Envejecimiento y pobreza: la movilización de los jubilados. IV Conferencia Latinoamericana de Población: La Transición Demográfica en America Latina y el Caribe. Mexico, 23-26 marzo.

Martin, L. G. (1989). Living arrangements of the elderly in Fiji, Korea, Malaysia, and the Philippines. *Demography*, vol. 26, pp. 627-643.

_____, and N. O. Tsuya (1991). Interactions of middle-aged Japanese with their parents. *Population Studies*, vol. 45, pp. 299-311.

Martin, L. G. and Kevin Kinsella (1994). Research on the demography of aging in developing countries. In *Demography of Aging*, Linda G. Martin and Samuel H. Preston, eds. Washington, D.C.: National Academy Press.

Michael, R. T., V. R. Fuchs and S. R. Scott (1980). Changes in the propensity to live alone: 1950-1976. *Demography*, vol. 17, pp. 39-53.

Myers, G. C. (1992). Demographic aging and family support for older persons. In *Family Support for the Elderly*, H. L. Kendig, A. Hashimoto and L. C. Coppard, eds. Oxford: Oxford University Press.

_____ (1996). Aging and the social sciences: research directions and unresolved issues. In *Handbook of Aging and the Social Sciences*, R. H. Binstock and L. George, eds. New York: Academic Press.

Palloni, Alberto, and Susan De Vos (1992). Changes in families and households in Latin America since 1950. Paper presented at the Population Association of America meeting, Pittsburgh.

_____, and Martha Pelaez (1999). Aging in Latin America and the Caribbean. Madison: University of Wisconsin, Center for Demography and Ecology. Working paper 99-02.

Palloni, Alberto, and Hsien-Hen Lu (1995). Patterns of adult mortality in Latin America: 1950-1990. Paper presented at the Population Association of America meeting, San Francisco, April.

Pampel, Fred C. (1983). Changes in the propensity to live alone: evidence from consecutive cross-sectional surveys, 1960-1976. *Demography*, vol. 20, pp. 433-449.

_____ (1992). Trends in living alone among the elderly in Europe. In *Elderly Migration and Population Redistribution*, Andrei Rogers, and others, eds. London: Belhaven Press.

Pan American Health Organization (1989a). *A Profile of the Elderly in Argentina*. Technical Report No. 26.

_____ (1989b). *A Profile of the Elderly in Guyana*. Technical Report No. 24.

_____ (1989c). *A Profile of the Elderly in Trinidad and Tobago*. Technical Report No. 22.

_____ (1990). *A Profile of the Elderly in Costa Rica*. Technical Report No. 29.

_____ (1993). Analysis Comparativo del Envejecimiento en Brasil, Colombia, El Salvador, Jamaica, y Venezuela. Technical Report No. 38.

Parish, William L., Shen Chonglin and Chang Chi-hsiang (1995). Family support networks in the Chinese countryside. Chicago: University of Chicago, Population Research Center. Discussion paper 95-7.

Pezzin, Liliana E., and Barbara Steinberg Schone (1999). Parental marital disruption and intergenerational transfers: an analysis of lone elderly parents and their children. *Demography*, vol. 36, No. 36, pp. 287-298.

Preston, Samuel H. (1976). Mortality Patterns in National Populations. New York: Academic Press.

_____ (1984). Children and the elderly: divergent paths for America's dependants. *Demography*, vol. 21, pp. 435-457.

Ramashala, Mapule F. (1997). Poverty and ageing: implications for health. In *Eliminating Poverty in Old Age*, James Calleja, ed. Malta: International Institute on Aging.

Ramos, Luiz R. (1994). Family support for the elderly in Latin America: the role of the multigenerational household. In *Ageing and the Family*. United Nations International Conference on Ageing Population in the Context of Family, Kitakyushu, Japan, 15-19 October 1990. Sales No. 1994.XIII.4.

_____, and others (1998). Two-year follow-up study of elderly residents in São Paulo, Brazil (Epidoso project): methodology and preliminary results. *Journal of Public Health*, vol. 32, No. 5, pp. 397-407.

Reher, David Sven (1998). Family ties in Western Europe: persistent contrasts. *Population and Development Review*, vol. 24, No. 2, pp. 203-234.

Rosenzweig, Mark R., and Kenneth I. Wolpin (1993). Intergenerational support and the life-cycle incomes of young men and their parents: human capital investments, co-residence, and intergenerational financial transfers. *Journal of Labor Economics*, vol. 11, No. 1, pp. 84-112.

Ruggles, Steven (1987). *Prolonged Connections: The Rise of the Extended Family in Nineteenth Century England and America*. Madison: University of Wisconsin Press.

_____ (1988). The demography of unrelated individuals: 1900-1950. *Demography*, vol. 25, pp. 521-536.

_____ (1994). The transformation of American family structure. *American Historical Review*, vol. 99, pp. 103-128.

_____ (1996). Living arrangements of the elderly in America. In *Aging and Generational Relations Over the Life Course: A Historical and Cross-Cultural Perspective*, Tamara K. Hareven, ed. New York: Walter de Gruyter and Co.

Schoeni, Robert F. (1998). Reassessing the decline in parent-child old-age co-residence during the twentieth century. *Demography*, vol. 35, No. 3, pp. 307-313.

Smeeding, Timothy M., and Peter Saunders (1998). How do the elderly in Taiwan fare cross-nationally? Evidence from the Luxembourg Income Study (LIS) Project. Syracuse, New York: Syracuse University, Working paper No. 183.

Smith, Daniel Scott (1993). The curious history of theorizing about the history of the Western nuclear family. *Social Science History*, 17, pp. 325-353.

Smith, J., and D. Kingston (1995). Race, socioeconomic status and health in later life. Santa Monica, California: Rand Corporation, Labor and Population Program. Working paper No. 95-10.

Soldo, Beth J. (1981). The living arrangements of the elderly in the near future. In *Aging: Social Change*, S. B. Kiesler, J. N. Morgan and V. K. Oppenheimer, eds. New York: Academic Press.

_____, and P. Lauriat (1976). An analysis of living arrangements among the elderly through log-linear models. *Journal of Comparative Family Studies*, special issue (summer), pp. 351-367.

Soldo, Beth J., Douglas A. Wolf and Emily M. Agree (1990). Family, households, and care arrangements of the frail elderly: a structural analysis. *Journal of Gerontology: Social Sciences*, vol. 45, pp. S238-249.

Solis, Patricio (1999). Living arrangements of the elderly in Mexico. Paper presented at the Population Association of America meeting, New York.

Stecklov, Guy (1997). Intergenerational resource flows in Côte d'Ivoire: empirical analysis of aggregate flows. *Population and Development Review*, vol. 23, No. 3, pp. 525-553.

Townsend, P. (1979). Poverty in the United Kingdom. *A Survey of Household Resources and Standards of Living*. Harmondsworth, United Kingdom: Penguin.

_____, and D. Wedderburn (1965). *The Aged in the Welfare State*. Occasional Papers on Social Administration, No. 14. London: Bell.

Tuma, Nancy B., and Gary D. Sandefur (1988). Trends in the labor force activity of the elderly in the United States, 1940-1989. In *Issues in Contemporary Retirement*, Rita Ricardo-Campbell and Edward P. Lazear, eds. Stanford, California: Hoover Institution Press.

Turke, Paul, W. (1989). Evolution and the demand for children. *Population and Development Review*, vol. 15, No. 1, pp. 61-90.

_____ 1991. Theory and evidence on wealth flows and old-age security: a reply to Fricke. *Population and Development Review*, vol. 17, No. 4, pp. 687-702.

Wachter, Kenneth, Debra Blackwell and Eugene A. Hammel (1999). *Testing the Validity of Kinship Microsimulation: An Update*. Berkeley: University of California.

Wachter, Kenneth, E. Hammel and Peter Laslett (1978). *Statistical Studies of Historical Social Structure*. New York: Academic Press.

Wachter, Kenneth, John E. Knodel and Mark VanLandingham (1999). AIDS and the elderly of Thailand: projecting familial impacts. Bay Area Colloquium on Population. California, 4 November.

Wall, R. (1989a). Living arrangements of the elderly in contemporary Europe. In *Later Phases of the Family Life Cycle*, E. Grebenik, C. Hohn and R. Mackensen, eds. Oxford: Clarendon.

_____ (1989b). Leaving home and living alone: an historical perspective. *Population Studies*, vol. 43, pp. 369-390.

Wolf, Douglas A. (1984). Kin availability and the living arrangements of older women. *Social Science Research*, vol. 13, pp. 72-89.

_____ (1990). Household patterns of older women: some international comparisons. *Research on Aging*, vol. 12, pp. 463-486.

_____ (1994a). The elderly and their kin: patterns of availability and access. In *Demography of Aging*, Linda G. Martin and Samuel H. Preston, eds. Washington, D.C.: National Academy Press.

_____ (1994b). Co-residence with an aged parent: lifetime patterns and sensitivity to demographic change. In *Ageing and the Family*. United Nations International Conference on Ageing Population in the Context of Family, Kitakyushu, Japan, 15-19 October 1990. Sales No. 1994.XIII.4.

_____ (1999). *Microsimulation as a Tool for Population Projection*. Syracuse, New York: Syracuse University, Center for Policy Research.

Wolf, Douglas A., Vicki Freedman and Beth J. Soldo (1997). The division of family labor: care for elderly parents. *Journal of Gerontology*, series B, vol. 52B (special issue), pp. 102-109.

Wolf, Douglas A., and Beth J. Soldo (1988). Household composition choices of older unmarried women. *Demography*, vol. 25, pp. 387-403.

LIVING ARRANGEMENTS AND WELL-BEING OF OLDER PERSONS IN THE PAST

*Steven Ruggles**

INTRODUCTION

Analysis of long-run changes in the living arrangements and economic well-being of the aged is limited by the lack of consistent data sources across time and space. Some fragmentary evidence on the living arrangements of the aged in several European and North American countries before the mid-twentieth century is summarized in table 1. The numbers should be interpreted cautiously. The earliest estimates are especially suspect, since we generally lack information about the enumeration procedures or completeness of the surviving pre-nineteenth century listings of inhabitants. Even in the nineteenth century, there was significant variation in census concepts and definitions among countries and across time (Ruggles and Brower, forthcoming). Moreover, the processing of the existing historical data has not followed standardized procedures from study to study, and we have little information of the representativeness of the local studies. Therefore, it would be premature to make too much of the apparent trends and differences shown in table 1. Despite all these qualifications, however, we can be confident that prior to the twentieth century most elderly persons in Europe and North America resided with their children and that residing alone was exceedingly rare.

Today, the great majority of the aged populations of North America and Europe reside alone or with only their spouse. Moreover, recent studies suggest that the percentage of the aged who live alone has also begun to rise in many Asian and Latin American countries (Hermalin and Ofstedal, 1996; Uhlenberg, 1996; Martin, 1989; De Vos, 1995). Taken as a whole, the evidence suggests that the shift towards independent residence of the aged is a worldwide phenomenon.

---

* University of Minnesota, United States of America.

TABLE 1. PERCENTAGE OF PERSONS AGED 65 OR OLDER RESIDING WITH CHILDREN
OR RESIDING ALONE, SELECTED COUNTRIES, 1599-1921

Place/time		With children			Alone			N^a
		Males	Females	All	Males	Females	All	
Belgian industrial								
1830	Verviers	58.8	56.1	57.5	6.4	5.6	6.0	996
French Pyrenean								
1793	Bour de Bigorre	85.7	70.0	79.1	0.0	0.0	0.0	46
1846	Esparros	86.2	86.6	85.7	0.4	0.3	0.5	95
1876	Esparros	72.0	76.7	65.6	10.6	6.9	15.6	117
1906	Esparros	54.2	55.8	52.6	18.5	14.7	35.9	105
Irish rural								
1901	4 villages	72.3	69.1	76.4	3.7	3.3	4.2	325
1911	4 villages	77.1	76.9	77.3	3.5	3.1	3.6	542
England								
1599-1796	Rural communities	49.0	37.0	43.1	2.0	16.0	8.9	205
1692	Lichfield	54.0	34.0	41.1	3.0	15.0	10.7	104
1701	Stoke	54.0	46.0	50.0	5.0	8.0	6.5	78
1891	13 communities	48.0	47.0	47.4	5.0	11.0	8.3	3 808
1901	13 communities	51.0	50.0	50.4	4.0	11.0	7.9	4 008
1911	13 communities	52.0	52.0	52.0	6.0	10.0	8.2	4 962
1921	13 communities	52.0	52.0	52.0	6.0	11.0	8.8	5 886

Place/time			With children			Alone			N^a
			Males	Females	All	Males	Females	All	
Canada									
	1871	National	80.0	74.0	76.7	13.0	36.0		836
Hungary (age 60+)									
	1762-1816	4 villages	92.6	90.9	92.0	0.0	0.0	0.0	142

Sources: Alter, Cliggett and Urbiel (1996); Fauve-Chamoux (1996); Guinnane (1996); Wall (1995); Dillon (1997); Andorka (1995).

[a] Number of observations.

113

According to the consensus of scholarly opinion, the simplification of the living arrangements of the aged during the twentieth century has resulted primarily from an increase in the resources of the aged, which has enabled increasing numbers of elderly to afford independent living. The author's analysis suggests the opposite: he argues that the decline of the multigenerational family occurred mainly because of increasing opportunities for the young and declining parental control over their children.

Eventually, the author intends to test this interpretation for several different countries, but at present his analysis is limited to the United States. Only for the United States is there a continuous series of high-quality compatible data on the living arrangements and economic well-being of the aged over the very long run. In the conclusion, there is a description of a new data project that will eventually allow similar analysis for a variety of other countries.

Data

The present study is based on the Integrated Public Use Microdata Series (IPUMS).[1] IPUMS is a coherent national database describing the characteristics of 55 million Americans in 13 census years, spanning the period from 1850 through 1990. It combines census microdata files produced by the United States Census Bureau for the period since 1960 with new historical census files produced at the University of Minnesota and elsewhere. By putting the samples in the same format, imposing consistent variable coding, and carefully documenting changes in variables over time, IPUMS is designed to facilitate the use of the census samples as a time-series. IPUMS allows us to circumvent most of the incompatibilities and errors in published census tabulations and to extend the series on household and family composition backwards in time for 150 years.

The most important innovation of IPUMS, for the present purpose, is a set of consistently constructed family interrelationship variables for all years. These variables identify the location within the household of each individual's spouse, mother and father. The family interrelationship pointers provide the essential building blocks to construct virtually any standard measures of household composition. Because the family interrelationship variables were designed to be as compatible as possible across census years, the resulting measures of household and family composition are far more useful for the study of long-run change than are any of the tabulations generated by the Census Bureau.

Thousands of scholarly books and articles have been written on the family. Most of these works make implicit or explicit assumptions about long-term changes in family composition. However, there is remarkably little research that makes consistent comparisons of family composition over the very long run, because until recently most census statistics on family composition began in 1960.[2] During the 1970s and 1980s, historians carried out studies of family composition limited to particular nineteenth-century communities, but the analyses were not, in general, compatible with modern census statistics. Thus, our understanding of long-run trends in American family composition has been based on a little knowledge leavened with a lot of speculation. Now, for the first time, we have the tools to measure changes in American family composition in a consistent fashion over a very long span of time. This new information forces us to rethink many of our ideas about the sources of change in the family.

MULTIGENERATIONAL FAMILIES IN THE
NINETEENTH CENTURY

Overview

The living arrangements of the aged in the United States shifted dramatically during the past 150 years. The key changes are summarized in figure I. In the mid-nineteenth century, about 70 per cent of persons aged 65 or older lived with their children or children-in-law. In addition, about a tenth of the elderly lived with other relatives — mainly grandchildren, siblings, nephews and nieces. Another tenth lived with non-relatives; most of these were boarders, but some were household heads who kept boarders or servants. Only 11 per cent of the elderly in 1850 lived alone or with only their spouses, and only 0.7 per cent lived in institutions such as almshouses and homes for the aged.

After 1860, residence with children began to decline. Increasingly, the elderly began to live alone, with their spouses only, or in old-age homes. The trend was gradual until 1920, but then began to accelerate. The decline in residence with children was most rapid during the period from 1940 to 1980, when more than half the total change took place. By 1990, less than 15 per cent of the aged lived with their children, while 6.8 per cent lived in institutions and almost 70 per cent lived alone or with their spouses only.

The timing of change in the living arrangements of the elderly was not greatly influenced by sex or marital status. Among whites, widows, widowers and married couples all lived mainly with children in the nineteenth century, as shown in figure II. Widows were slightly more likely to reside with children than were widowers, but the difference was not great and the shift to residence alone or in institutions during the twentieth century was common to both. Elderly blacks, however, shown in figure III, were considerably less likely than were whites to reside with their children in the nineteenth century. This was particularly true for unmarried black men, fewer than 50 per cent of whom lived with their children.

Figure I. Distribution of living arrangements: elderly white individuals and couples in the United States, 1850-1990

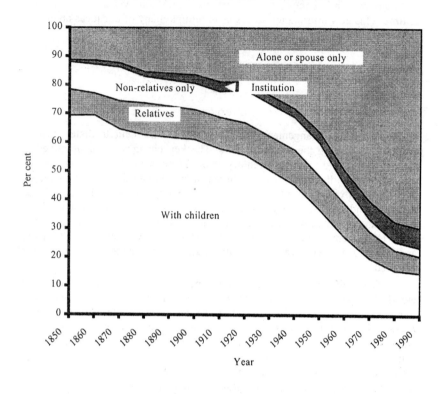

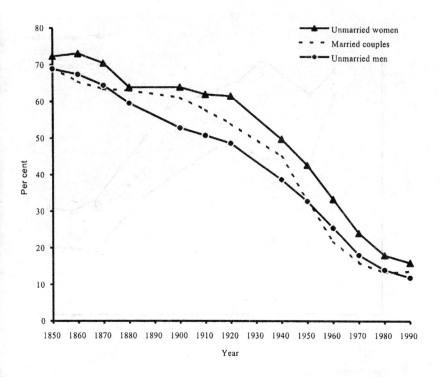

Figure II. Percentage of elderly whites residing with own children, by sex and marital status: United States, 1850-1990

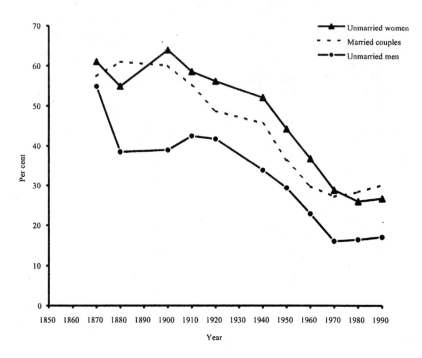

Figure III. Percentage of elderly blacks residing with own children, by sex and marital status: United States, 1850-1990

Among the 30 per cent of the elderly who lived without children in 1860, about a third had children living next door.[3] Thus, 80 per cent of the elderly resided either with children or in an adjacent dwelling. The high percentage of elderly persons who resided with or adjacent to children in the nineteenth century is especially striking when we consider that not all the elderly had the possibility of residing with their children. About 7 per cent of the elderly had never married, and with few exceptions this meant that they had no children with whom to reside. Another 8 per cent married, but the marriage produced no children. Some 5 per cent of the elderly had children, but all of them had died. Taking all this into account, then, somewhere on the order of a fifth of the elderly in 1860 had no living children. About 8 in 10 elderly persons resided with their children or immediately next door in 1860; thus, as near as we can measure, the practice was essentially universal.[4]

Despite the universality of elderly persons living with or next door to their children, the consensus of historians is that the elderly in the past always preferred to live alone, just as they do today. Tamara K. Hareven, the most prominent analyst of the history of generational relations, is representative of the mainstream of historical opinion:

Aging parents and children [in the nineteenth century] rarely co-resided in multigenerational households ... Despite this overall commitment to residence in nuclear households, common to members of various ethnic groups and native-born Americans alike, nuclear households expanded to include other kin in times of need, during periods of accelerated migration or housing shortage. The most notable extension of the household occurred when elderly parents and especially widowed mothers were unable to maintain themselves in their own residences. In such cases, aging parents had an adult child return to live with them, or they moved into a child's household (Hareven, 1994; p. 442).

The idea that the aged have always preferred to live alone and that multigenerational families were only resorted to in cases of dire necessity stems from Peter Laslett's findings some four decades ago that the overwhelming majority of pre-industrial English households were nuclear in structure (Laslett and Harrison 1963; Laslett 1972). But, as I have argued at length, the percentage of households containing extended kin has limited relevance for the analysis of the living arrangements of the aged (Ruggles, 1986, 1987, 1994, 1996a, 1996b). Long generations, short life expectancy and high fertility before the demographic transition meant that there was a small population of elderly people spread thinly among a much larger younger generation. Under these circumstances, the percentage of households with elderly kin was necessarily small.[5] Indeed, if every elderly person in the United States in 1850 who was living apart from kin — whether alone, in the almshouse or as a servant or boarder — moved in with kin, that would increase the total number of multigenerational families by only 20 per cent.

Hareven was among the first to discover that the elderly in the past usually resided with their grown children. Because she was already firmly convinced by Laslett's argument that there had always been a strong preference for nuclear family composition, she downplayed the significance of the finding. She maintained instead that three-generation families were rare before the industrial revolution and were only resorted to in cases of necessity, "primarily when elderly parents were too frail to maintain a separate residence" (Hareven, 1996; pp. 1-2). Virtually all historians who have written on this subject in recent years agree with Hareven. Nineteenth-century elderly persons only moved in with their children, they argue, when they were widowed, infirm or impoverished and had no other alternatives.[6]

The formation of multigenerational families in the nineteenth century

In the nineteenth century multigenerational families were usually formed when one child remained in the parental home after reaching adulthood to work on the family farm or business, with the anticipation of eventually inheriting it. Even though most households did not include multiple generations at any given moment, the great majority of families went through a multigenerational phase if the parents lived long enough. The multigenerational family was a normal stage of the pre-industrial family cycle.

Families were typically multigenerational only for a brief period, after the younger generation reached adulthood and before the older generation died.[7] This multigenerational phase nevertheless played an essential role in the functioning of the pre-industrial family economy. It ensured continuity of the labour supply on farms and for other traditional livelihoods and provided economic security in old age. The two generations were interdependent; the elders needed their children to continue to operate the farm, but as long as the elders held the property they were ultimately in control. With the replacement of the pre-industrial family economy by a wage-labour system, the incentives for multigenerational families disappeared.

Most other historians working in this area have a very different interpretation of the formation of multigenerational families in the nineteenth century. Kertzer (1995) has dubbed the dominant interpretation the "nuclear reincorporation theory". The theory states that all children ordinarily left home when they got married. Then, when the elderly parents became widowed, infirm or impoverished, they moved into their children's household. Thus, most historians maintain, the elderly in the multigenerational family were usually the dependent generation, and the younger generation took in their needy elders because of altruism. This theory allows family historians to reconcile their belief that a nuclear family system predominated in the nineteenth century, with the empirical finding that the elderly ordinarily resided with their children. It also provides a neat explanation for the decline of multigenerational families in the twentieth century: with rising incomes, more and more of the elderly could afford to maintain themselves, and did not have to move in with their children.

It matters who moved in with whom, because the formation of multigenerational families sheds light on the motivations of both generations, and has powerful implications for the disappearance of the multigenerational family in the twentieth century. It is difficult to study the formation of families in the nineteenth century, because our sources are limited. Qualitative sources — such as letters and diaries — provide many examples of both children remaining with their parents and of elderly parents moving in with their children, but they cannot tell us which pattern predominated. Nor can the available quantitative sources answer the question unambiguously. The census is a cross-section of the population at a given moment, so it cannot directly tell us how multigenerational families came about. But the quantitative evidence does provide some revealing clues.

If children established independent households upon reaching adulthood and their parents moved in with them later on, that implies that parents and children ordinarily resided separately for a period. Thus, one would expect to find that the proportion of persons residing with children would decline in late middle age as the children left home, and then increase again in old age as the parents moved in with their children. By contrast, if the co-resident child had never left home, one would expect no increase in co-residence of the elderly with increasing age. Figure IV shows the percentage of persons residing with their children by age for selected years from 1850 to 1980. In recent census years, there has been the expected rise in co-residence among the very old.

This pattern is most clearly evident in 1980, when persons aged 80 or over were almost twice as likely to reside with children as persons aged 65 to 69. The hypothesis that multigenerational families were formed when dependent elderly moved in with their children fits reasonably well with the evidence from the twentieth century. But in 1850 and 1880, there was no increase in co-residence with increasing age. This finding is consistent with the interpretation that the elderly did not typically move in with their children for support; instead, the children never moved out.

Figure IV. Percentage of persons residing with their own children, by age: United States, 1850-1990 (selected years)

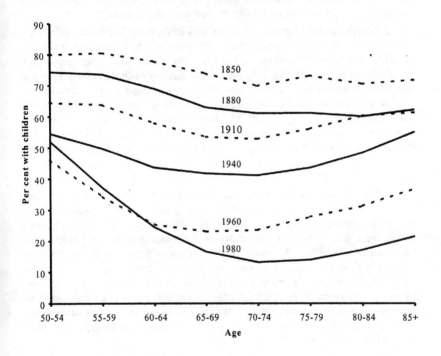

Headship patterns offer a second clue to the formation of multigenerational families. The federal census directed enumerators to list the head of household first on the census schedule, so enumerators had to identify which individual was the head. It seems implausible that dependent elderly who moved into the household of a child for assistance would assume the household headship. On the other hand, in families where the child remained in their parental household after marriage, we know that the child often assumed headship when the father retired or died. Thus, when the elderly are listed as head, we can reasonably assume that they did not move in with their children; if a child is listed as head, however, that does not necessarily mean that the household was formed independently by the child. The proportion of elderly listed as head can therefore reasonably be regarded as a lower-bound estimate of the proportion remaining in their own households.

In every census year between 1850 and 1900, over 75 per cent of elderly men residing with a child were listed as the household head. This suggests that in multigenerational households with elderly men, the older generation ordinarily retained authority. It is doubtful that many of these elderly men had moved in with their children because they could no longer support themselves; it is far more plausible that the younger generation remained in the parental household after reaching adulthood. About one third of unmarried elderly women in multigenerational households were listed as household heads, but this does not mean that the elderly mother necessarily moved in with her children after she was widowed. In many cases, property and authority shifted to the male heir upon the death of the father.

Even if most multigenerational families were formed when children remained in their parental home after reaching adulthood, there is evidence that some elderly did move in with their children. The clearest indication comes from information on marital status. Although both married elderly and widowed elderly ordinarily resided with children, widows did so slightly more frequently than did married couples. In 1880, the earliest year for which we have full information on marital status, about 68 per cent of elderly widows lived with children, compared with only 63 per cent of married couples. This suggests that a significant minority of elderly widows either moved in with a child when their husbands died, or a child who had previously left home moved back upon the death of the father.

The censuses demonstrate unequivocally that the great majority of nineteenth-century elderly who had a living child resided with a child. Did the parents move in with their children, or did the children remain in their parental household after reaching adulthood? The evidence on headship and on the age pattern of co-residence indicates that in most cases the children were remaining in their parental household. Still, some elderly clearly did move in with children in old age. The most plausible interpretation is that both patterns were fairly widespread: usually, adult children remained in their parental households, but occasionally, the elderly — especially widows — did move in with their children.

Parental widowhood and the marriage of children

Only a minority of married elderly persons in the nineteenth century resided with married children. More often, married elderly resided with unmarried children and unmarried elderly resided with married children. About 17 per cent of married couples in the mid-nineteenth century resided with married children; by contrast, 56 per cent of widowed elderly resided with married children.

Some analysts have interpreted this pattern as evidence supporting the nuclear reincorporation hypothesis. They reason that married elderly resided with their unmarried children, but the younger generation departed upon marriage and established independent households. Then, when the older generation became widowed or infirm, they moved in with their married children. But the evidence on headship and on the age pattern of co-residence suggests that nuclear reincorporation was not the dominant mechanism of multigenerational families.

There is an alternate interpretation of the association between parental widowhood and the marriage of children. The most important determinant of marriage for the younger generation in multigenerational families was not the marital status of the parents, but rather property ownership of the children. As illustrated in figure V, members of the younger generation in multigenerational households seldom married before they obtained property. Historians have long argued that in pre-industrial Western society, marriage was contingent on economic circumstances: young couples were usually forced to delay marriage until they were economically independent (Hajnal, 1965).

The younger generation in multigenerational families could obtain the family property by either inheritance or gift. It appears that only a minority of nineteenth-century male property holders transferred their property to their children while they were still alive, although it clearly did happen from time to time (see, for example, Gross, 1993). In 80 per cent of multigenerational households with a surviving father between 1850 and 1870, all the property was in the hands of the father, but in the other 20 per cent of cases, the younger generation held at least some of the property. When the father died, the property was usually split between the widow and the children. Widows were almost always entitled to a share of the family property, whether or not their husbands left wills, and this no doubt helped to protect their position in the family.[8] The largest share of land, however, ordinarily went to the co-resident child.

Figure V. Per cent of younger generation married, by value of real estate owned: persons residing with elderly parents, 1850-1990

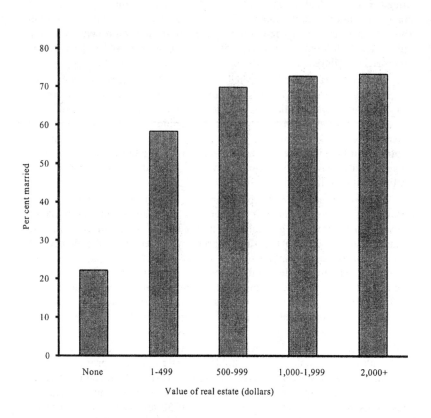

It is clear, then, why the death of a father was associated with marriage of the younger generation. In most cases, the children had to wait for the death of the father in order to inherit, and in most cases they could not marry without the inheritance. But widowed men were also more likely to reside with married children than were married men. Maternal death did not ordinarily lead to an inheritance when the father survived. Thus, we would not expect the adult children of widowed men to be in any better position to marry than were the adult children of married men. Why, then, did widowed men tend to live with married children, while married men lived with single children?

The answer is connected to the rigid sexual division of labour in nineteenth-century households. Some essential tasks — including food storage and preparation, housekeeping, and clothing manufacture and repair — were only performed by women. It was therefore essential to have an adult woman in every household, and the need for an adult woman was especially critical in farm households. Thus, if an elderly man living with an unmarried son was widowed, he had two options: he could either remarry himself, or he could provide the resources for his son to marry. In most cases, he did the former: in 1910, the earliest year for which we have information, about 63 per cent of ever-widowed men had remarried. When, for whatever reason, the patriarch did not remarry, however, he had little choice but to allow his son to marry.

If an elderly man living with an unmarried daughter became widowed, there was much less need to allow the daughter to marry. As long as the father was fit to carry out the male tasks, the family could survive with one adult man and one adult woman. The result of this pattern is evident in figure VI, which shows the percentage of children married, by sex and by sex of parent. In families with a widowed father and a daughter, only 38 per cent of the daughters were married in 1850-1860. By contrast, in families with a widowed father and a son, 64 per cent of the sons were married. This dramatic difference in the percentage married between sons and daughters supports the interpretation that the ability of the younger generation to marry was contingent on the resources provided by their parents.

Sickness, wealth and living arrangements of the aged

The evidence on the formation of multigenerational families does not resolve the issue of the reasons for multigenerational family composition: was it a mutually beneficial arrangement, as I maintain, or was it a system of old-age support resorted to only out of necessity, as most other historians believe? To assess whether the elderly lived with their children because they were dependent on them, we must explore evidence on sickness and wealth.

Most historians agree that nineteenth-century elderly lived with their children for one of two main reasons: either they were too sick or frail to adequately care for themselves in their own residence, or they were too poor to afford a place of their own. The nineteenth-century censuses provide sufficient information to test both of these hypotheses.

The 1880 census included a unique inquiry: "Is the person on the day of the Enumerator's visit sick or temporarily disabled, so as to be unable to attend to ordinary business or duties? If so, what is the sickness or disability?" This question cannot be expected to capture all cases of frailty, but the responses are full of entries like "old age and rheumatism", "enfeebled by years", "helpless from age and infirmity", and "dotage". Even if the question is not perfect, it is the most comprehensive question on health ever to appear in an American population census. If ill-health were a significant motivation for the elderly to reside with their children in the nineteenth century, we would expect to find that sick elderly would reside with children more frequently than did healthy elderly.

Figure VI. Per cent of sons and daughters married by sex and marital status of elderly parents: United States, 1850-1860

It turns out that sickness and disability were not associated with multigenerational family composition. Among elderly persons listed with a chronic illness in 1880, 56.0 per cent resided with a child; by contrast, 60.5 per cent of healthy elderly resided with a child.[9] The same pattern prevailed for women and men alike among both blacks and whites. If anything, then, sickness among the elderly actually discouraged residence in multigenerational families. This makes sense if the younger generation was usually dependent on the older generation, since chronically ill elderly probably had less to offer as incentive to stay around.

We also have good information on wealth. In 1850, the census included a question on the value of real estate owned by each individual; in 1860 and 1870 the census asked about both real estate and personal property.[10] The relationship between value of property and living arrangements is given in figures VII and VIII. By both measures, the wealthiest elderly were the ones most likely to reside in multigenerational families. This is exactly what we would expect if the younger generation ordinarily remained on the family farm with the hope of eventually inheriting it; if the parents had little property, the children had little incentive to remain behind. If nineteenth-century multigenerational families were mainly formed to assist destitute elderly parents, however, we would expect that the wealthy would be the group most likely to live alone.

Figure VII. Per cent of elderly residing with adult children by value of real estate held: United States, 1850

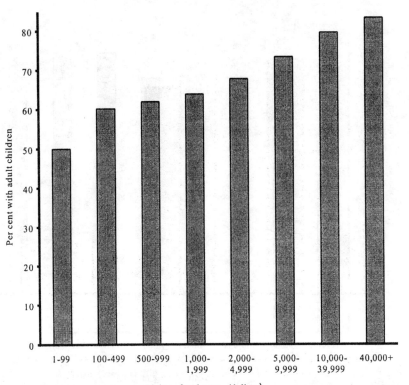

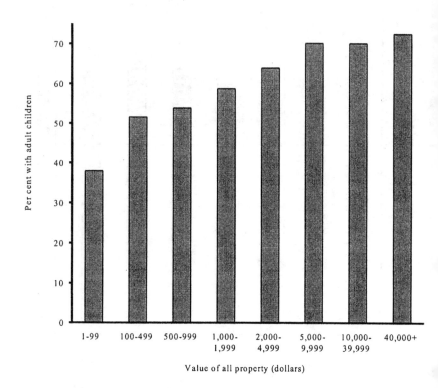

Figure VIII. Per cent of elderly residing with adult children by value of all property: United States, 1860-1870

Other indicators of socio-economic status confirm the finding that high economic status was associated with multigenerational family composition in the nineteenth century. In the nineteenth century, middle- and upper-income families almost always had live-in domestic help. Several historians have argued that dependent elderly kin — particularly mothers or mothers-in-law — in the nineteenth century took the place of servants, by providing child-care services and helping with housekeeping in exchange for their maintenance. Thus, one might expect to find that multigenerational households had fewer servants than other households. In fact, as shown in figure IX, residence with servants was strongly associated with residence in multigenerational families, and the effect is virtually as strong for women as for men. The reason is simple: it was the rich who most often resided in multigenerational families.

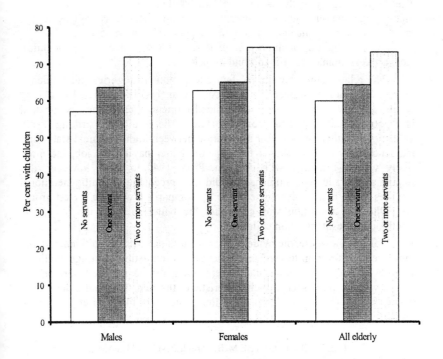

Figure IX. Per cent of elderly residing with children, by presence of servants: United States, 1880

The only indicator of socio-economic status consistently available for the entire period from 1850 to 1990 is occupation. Unfortunately, this measure is only available for a minority of the elderly. For nineteenth-century women, occupational information is seldom available and even when it is it often provides little insight into economic well-being. Moreover, with the rise of the wage-labour system, men began to retire when they reached old age. Thus, by 1920, occupational information is unavailable for 37 per cent of elderly men. Despite these limitations, the occupational data is invaluable because it provides our only means of tracing the long-run trend in the relationship between economic status and multigenerational family composition.

Our census database classifies the occupational information in all census years into 280 job titles defined by the Census Bureau for the census of 1950. To analyse the living arrangements of the elderly, four occupational groups are defined based on the median income of persons with each occupational title in 1950. Category one is the lowest, and it includes all titles with median incomes that fell in the bottom quarter of the 1950 income distribution, such as domestic servants, newsboys, waiters and waitresses, laundresses and farm labourers. Category two, which represents the second quarter of the income distribution, includes cashiers, stenographers and typists, apprentices of various sorts, telegraph messengers, shoe repairmen, barbers and teamsters. The third category includes most of the skilled artisans, such as bakers, blacksmiths, carpenters, mechanics, plumbers and tailors, as well as skilled factory workers, policemen and bookkeepers. The highest quarter of the income distribution includes engineers, lawyers, doctors, academics, stockbrokers, managers, officials and proprietors.

The relationship between the four occupational categories and residence with adult children is given in figure X. The analysis is restricted to elderly employed males. The author also excluded farmers, because their occupation is a poor indicator of their economic status. The results are striking. From 1880 to 1920, there was a clear association between high economic status and residence in multigenerational families: the better paying the job, the more likely was co-residence with children. From 1940 to 1970, however, this relationship gradually diminished, as did the percentage of multigenerational families in the highest economic group by comparison with the lowest group. By 1980, the transition was complete: the better the job, the lower the likelihood of residence with children.

Taken as a whole, the evidence on the class patterns of multigenerational family composition in the nineteenth century is irresistible. Multigenerational families in the nineteenth century were not a refuge for the poor; on the contrary, they were especially characteristic of the rich. The poor elderly, who had little to offer their children, were the group most likely to end up living alone.

THE DECLINE OF THE MULTIGENERATIONAL FAMILY

Dimensions of change

The United States in the mid-nineteenth century was already one of the leading industrial nations in the world. It was among the top producers of boots and shoes, cotton textiles, liquor, paper, agricultural implements, guns and ships. As early as 1840, more horsepower was generated by steam engines in the United States than in any other country, and more than half of the world's railroad mileage was in the United States. The improvements in transportation — not just the railroads, but also canals and turnpikes — opened up vast new tracts of land in the interior to commercial farming. Farmers began to sell most of what they produced, and they used the proceeds to buy all sorts of tools and consumer products they could not previously afford, such as magazines, almanacs, whale-oil lamps, wallpaper, clocks, scissors and woven cloth. By mid-century, the innovations in manufacturing, transportation and commerce touched the lives of virtually all Americans.

Figure X. Percentage of elderly employed men residing with adult children by occupational rank: United States, 1850-1990

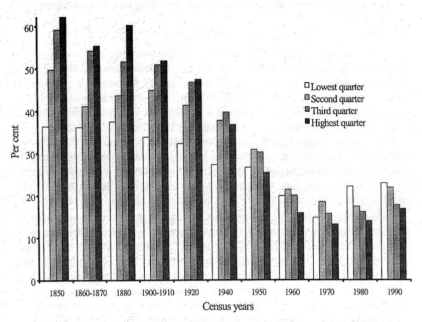

Notes: Elderly defined as 65+; adult defined as 18+; 1850-1860, restricted to white population only; low-density samples (1860, 1870 and 1900, 1910) combined to obtain sufficient cases in all occupational groups.

Even though the transformation of the economy was well under way, the United States in 1850 was still a fundamentally agricultural society. The great majority of Americans still lived in rural areas and most earned their living from agriculture. Wealth was reckoned in land and slaves. American families grew most of their own food and made most of their own clothes. Despite the early growth of the factory system, even manufacturing was still mostly carried out within the household: artisans and their families typically lived together adjacent to the shop where they produced such products as leather goods, flour or furniture. The system of household production also predominated in the service sector, especially in retail trade.

The gulf that separated Americans from the Victorians is apparent in figure XI, which shows the estimated percentage of the population residing in rural areas and the percentage of the labour force engaged in non-agricultural pursuits from 1790 to 1990. Employment in agriculture began to fall after 1810, when about 85 per cent of the labour force worked in farming. For the next 17 decades, agricultural employment dropped steadily by an average of 5 per cent per decade; by 1980, only 2 per cent of workers remained in farming.

Few Americans lived in towns in the mid-nineteenth century; as late as 1840, 9 out of 10 Americans resided in places with less than 2,500 population. Through most of the nineteenth century, the majority of those who did not work on farms still lived in rural areas, often providing services to farmers.

The rise of male wage labour and the decline of the multigenerational family

The multigenerational family system of mid-nineteenth century America provided benefits for both the older generation and the younger generation. Elderly farmers needed an adult child or child-in-law to do heavy work when they were no longer capable of doing it themselves. The younger generation eventually inherited the farm. As wage work replaced family labour, this system eroded. Wage labour undermined the family economy through two mechanisms. First, rising opportunities attracted young men off the farm or away from the family business. Then, when those lifelong wage earners aged, they had no need for their children to remain and operate the family business, and they had no incentives to offer for the next generation to stick around.

The chronological fit between the shift from male self-employment to wage work and the shift from multigenerational to solitary residence among the aged is fairly good. Figure XII shows the percentage of white and black men who were employed in wage or salaried jobs from 1850 to 1990, and figure XIII compares the percentage of elderly whites and blacks living without their children. Among whites, the most rapid rise in wage labour occurred before 1920, whereas the change in family composition was most rapid after 1920. Perhaps this is because there was a lag between the disappearance of the economic incentive for multigenerational families and the shift to separate residence.

Among blacks, the chronological fit between wage labour and separate residence of the elderly is less perfect. The percentage of black men who were wage workers actually declined from 1870 to 1920, and rose sharply thereafter. The percentage of elderly blacks living without children, however, rose continuously except for a slight downtick between 1880 and 1900. This points to a problem in using a crude index of self-employment. The rise in black self-employment in the late nineteenth century reflects the adoption of the sharecropping system in the South. Sharecropping replaced wage agricultural labour because it increased profits for planters, not because it offered anything to the workers. The system did not provide blacks with incentives to adopt multigenerational family composition; older sharecropping blacks ordinarily had few assets and were frequently saddled with debt. The economic circumstances of both older and younger blacks were dismal during the late nineteenth and early twentieth centuries, and they did not improve greatly until the northward migration of the mid-twentieth century. Because of the prevalence of sharecropping, we would not expect self-employment to be a good predictor of co-residence for blacks in this period.

Figure XI. Per cent of rural population and per cent of the labour force employed in agriculture, 1790-1990

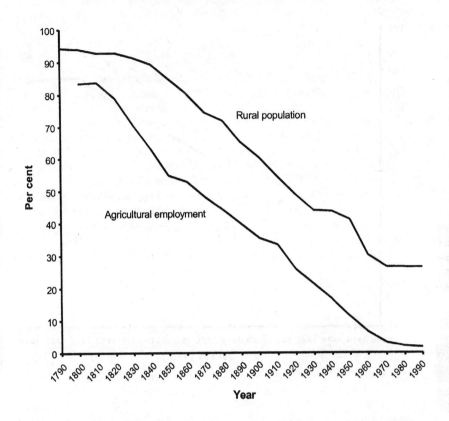

Sources: Agricultural employment, 1790-1840, Lebergott (1964); 1850-1950, IPUMS; rural population, United States Bureau of the Census (1975).

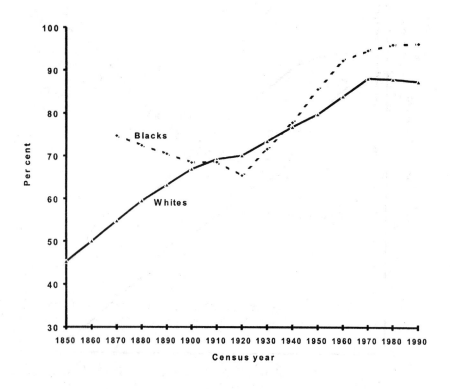

Figure XII. Percentage of men employed in wage and salary work,
by race: 1850-1990

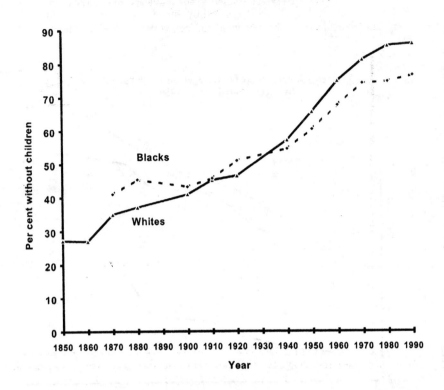

Figure XIII. Percentage of elderly residing without children, by race: United States, 1850-1990

The black pattern of rising self-employment in the late nineteenth and early twentieth centuries highlights an important point. Some self-employed jobs — including such titles as hucksters, peddlers and bootblacks, as well as sharecroppers — provided little incentive for the younger generation to remain at home and work in the family business. Only those family businesses that represented better opportunity than wage-labour employment were sufficient to keep the younger generation at home. Similarly, the availability of wage employment was not by itself sufficient to attract young men off the farm; there had to be jobs that paid decent wages. Wage labour had always existed. In the mid-nineteenth century, however, most wage labour involved backbreaking work for little pay; the biggest wage-labour occupations were agricultural labour and domestic service.

Increasingly, however, well-paid wage jobs were being created in factories, railroads and offices. Figure XIV gives the percentage of black and white men in "good" wage and salary jobs from 1850 through 1990. Good jobs are defined as those occupations with earnings of $2,200 or more in 1950. Adjusted for inflation, this is equivalent to the poverty line for a family of four in 1998, but in 1950 and before it was considered a decent middle-class wage.

The percentage of both white and black men with good jobs rose dramatically from the nineteenth century until 1970, with only a brief interruption during the depression. In all periods, the gap between blacks and whites has been enormous, but it has diminished slightly since the Second World War. Between 1980 and 1990, the percentage of men with good jobs began to fall.

Figure XIV. Percentage of men aged 18+ with "good" jobs, by race: United States, 1850-1990

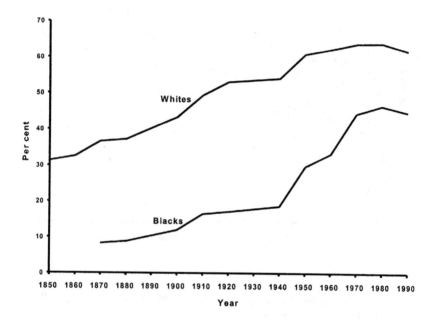

The rise of well-paid wage-labour jobs did not occur evenly across the country. In some parts of the country — like Rhode Island and Massachusetts — industrialization was well under way by 1850. Other areas — like Arkansas, Alabama and Mississippi—remained rural backwaters well into the twentieth century. The combination of great geographical variation and rapid chronological change in the economy allows us to test the hypothesis that the rapid decline of co-residence between the elderly and their children was connected to the rise of good wage-labour jobs for the younger generation.

In the mid-nineteenth century, wage labour had been concentrated in Rhode Island and Massachusetts, where the earliest textile mills had been established, together with California, which was dominated by mining. Then the wage-work system spread, first to other New England States and the Mountain States, then to New Jersey, Pennsylvania, Delaware and Maryland. In the early twentieth century, industries like meat packing, steel making and automobile manufacturing turned Illinois, Ohio and Michigan into wage-labour States. After the war, regional differences began to diminish, and self-employment became rare outside the agricultural States of the Great Plains.

For the period from 1850 through 1950, the geographic distribution of multigenerational families was closely correlated to the geographic distribution of self-employment. For example, multigenerational families in 1920 were concentrated in the southern tier and to a lesser extent in the upper Midwest, the same regions that retained the highest percentage of self-employment.

The combined geographic and chronological association of work and family composition can be seen in figure XV, which is a scatter plot of self-employment percentage and multigenerational families in four census years. The vertical axis shows the percentage of elderly whites residing with children, and the horizontal axis shows the estimated percentage of men self-employed.[11] Each symbol represents a State in a particular census year. For example, the rightmost symbol on the graph represents Illinois in 1850, where 67 per cent of men were self-employed and 75 per cent of the elderly resided with children. Different symbols are used for each census year. To maximize comparability over time, the graph is limited to the 17 States with a sufficient number of elderly in all census years.[12]

Figure XV. Scatter plot of residence with children and self-employment, 1850-1940

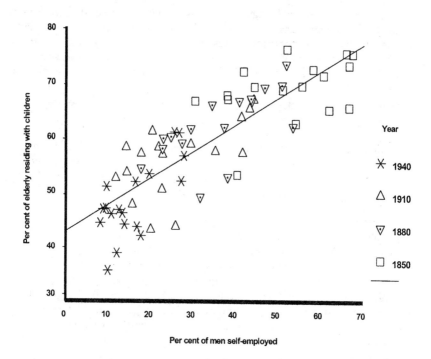

By analysing State differences in family composition, we can examine the relationship between change in self-employment and change in family composition. The results of this analysis, detailed in table 2, are striking. Three State-level regression models are shown. The first model shows simply the effect of the census year on the percentage of elderly whites residing with children between 1850 and 1940. The "reference category" is 1850, so the coefficients reflect the difference between co-residence of the elderly in 1850 and in the indicated year. For example, the coefficient for 1940 is -21.0, indicating that the average percentage of elderly persons with children was 21 percentage points lower in 1940 than it had been in 1850.[13]

The second model introduces two variables describing occupational composition. The first of these variables, "farmers", is simply the percentage of white males aged 16-64 listed as farmers in each State. The second variable, "self-employed", is the percentage of white males aged 16-64 in the occupations that were most frequently self-employed in 1910 and that yielded earnings of at least $2,200 in 1950.[14] The residual occupational category (not included because of multicollinearity) consists of the predominantly wage and salary occupations. Model 2 shows that if we hold these variables constant across time, the difference between 1850 and 1940 disappears entirely.

TABLE 2. STATE-LEVEL OLS REGRESSIONS OF OCCUPATIONAL STRUCTURE ON PER CENT OF ELDERLY RESIDING WITH CHILDREN: POOLED DATA, STATES WITH SUFFICIENT CASES IN ALL CENSUS YEARS, 1850-1940

	Model 1		Model 2		Model 3	
	B	Std. error	B	Std. error	B	Std. error
Census year						
1850	(reference category)		(reference category)		(reference category)	
1880	-7.10	2.38[a]	4.35	2.39	2.70	2.81
1910	-12.47	2.38[b]	2.57	2.65	1.05	3.43
1920	-14.25	2.38[b]	3.17	2.92	1.13	3.87
1940	-21.00	2.38[b]	1.67	3.51	-1.15	4.90
Occupational structure						
Per cent farmers			0.69	0.09[b]	0.61	0.14[a]
Per cent self-employed			1.49	0.28[b]	1.06	0.42[c]
State effects	No		No		Yes	
Constant	67.77	1.68[b]	14.50	8.27	26.63	13.07[c]
R square	0.52		0.74		0.85	
Adjusted R square	0.50		0.72		0.81	
N	85		85		85	

Notes: OLS = ordinary least squares; B = slope; N = number of observations; P = probability.

[a] p<0.01.

[b] <0.001.

[c] <0.05.

The third model is subtler: it controls for State differences in living arrangements. By controlling for State effects, we are accounting for any State differences in residential behaviour that persist over time.[15] As a result, instead of analysing the absolute effects of occupational structure on family composition, model 3 assesses the effects of changes in occupational structure on changes in family composition. Model 3 reveals that the timing of the decline of farming and other self-employment in each State is an excellent predictor of the timing of change in family composition. Indeed, the association between changing self-employment and changing family composition is so strong that it is implausible that the two are not causally related.

We lack sufficient cases to carry out a similar geographic analysis for blacks. Our historical census samples are quite large; to date, our data-entry operators at Minnesota have transcribed information about some 3 million individuals. Blacks, however, have historically comprised less than a tenth of the elderly population. Moreover, blacks were geographically concentrated in the South for most of the period under consideration, and they are still under-represented in the Plains, the Mountain States and northern New England. Thus, we cannot carry out a comparable analysis for blacks. Even if we could, however, it is doubtful whether we could distinguish the effects of changing black opportunities on the living arrangements of the elderly, since we cannot identify sharecroppers in the census database. Nevertheless, the overall trends in the living arrangements of elderly blacks are consistent with an economic interpretation. In the nineteenth century, elderly blacks were less likely to reside with their children than were elderly whites, and this is probably because they had less to offer them. In the twentieth century, as multigenerational family composition became associated with low socio-economic status, the percentage of elderly blacks residing with their children began to exceed that for whites.

Alternate interpretations for change, 1850-1940

We should bear in mind that the close relationship between change in family composition and change in self-employment is merely a statistical correlation, and does not absolutely prove that the decline in self-employment was responsible for the decline of multigenerational families. Historians and sociologists have suggested other explanations for the changing family composition that might also fit the observed geographical and chronological pattern of family change. Urbanization, rising geographic mobility, rising income and changing attitudes have all been proposed to account for the decline of the multigenerational family. None of these factors, however, show the same chronological and geographic fit with family composition as do farming and other forms of self-employment.

Urbanization occurred at the same time as the shift to independent residence of the elderly, but once we control for the effects of farming there is no independent relationship between rural residence and multigenerational family composition in any period (Ruggles, 1996b). Geographic mobility actually declined between 1850 and 1950, and so cannot be invoked to explain the decline of the multigenerational family in that period. As shown in figure XVI, the percentage of Americans who migrated across State lines declined steadily from 1850 to 1950, and then rose sharply.[16] Even today, however, inter-State migration is less frequent than it was in the mid-nineteenth century. Nor can rising income explain any shift to separate residence before the recent period. As demonstrated above, before 1950, high economic status of the elderly was associated with residence with children; thus, it is not plausible that rising incomes would have contributed to separate residence of the elderly in this period.

**Figure XVI. Per cent of persons migrating between States by age 50-59:
United States, 1850-1990**

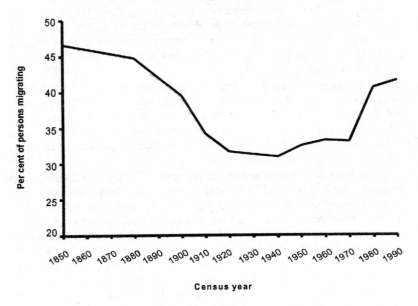

Census year

Note: Standardized to control for the changing size-distribution of State of birth.

Source: Patt Kelly Hall and Steven Ruggles, "Moving through time: lifetime internal migration patterns of Americans, 1850-1990", presented at the Social Science History Association, Fort Worth, Texas, 11-14 November 1999.

The effects of attitudinal change are more difficult to assess. Clearly, social norms were changing, and it was becoming increasingly expected that the elderly and their children would reside apart. The real question is whether changing attitudes towards co-residence of the generations were a driving factor in the shift of family composition, or whether the change in attitudes merely reflected changing behaviour. In the latter case, cultural inertia might operate as a brake on changes in the family, keeping some families together after there was any economic incentive to reside in multigenerational families. Since we lack systematic evidence about the precise geographic and chronological patterns of shifting attitudes in the first half of the twentieth century, we cannot tell for sure whether change in attitudes generally preceded or lagged behind changes in the family. The author suspects, however, that attitudes are more likely to have slowed the changes in the family than to have accelerated them.[17]

The effect of rising incomes, 1950-1990

By 1950, the great bulk of the workforce was engaged in wage and salary work, and farming had become a minor occupation. Nevertheless, the shift in the living arrangements of the elderly did not cease. On the contrary, the change in family composition accelerated: from 1950 to 1990, the percentage of elderly persons residing with their children dropped from 37 per cent to 15 per cent.

Sociologists generally attribute the rapid post-war shift in the living arrangements of the elderly to rising incomes. The Social Security programme and the growth of private pension plans meant that more and more of the elderly had good incomes, even though fewer and fewer had their own farms or businesses. Thus, analysts argue, the elderly increasingly had the economic means to maintain separate residences.

For the recent period, unlike the nineteenth century, this theory makes sense. As noted above, until relatively recently the elderly with the highest economic status were the group most likely to reside with their children. Thus, for the period from 1850 through 1940, it is highly doubtful that an increase in the economic security of the aged would have led to an increase in the percentage of elderly who lived alone. In the second half of the twentieth century, however, the pattern reversed: the elderly with the greatest economic resources were the ones most likely to live alone or with their spouse only. Thus, for the late twentieth century, it is plausible that the rising income of the elderly was responsible for at least some of the change in their family composition.

Since 1950, the census has included a direct inquiry on income, so it is fairly straightforward to estimate the effects of income on family composition. Figure XVII gives the percentage of elderly residing with adult children, by income group for each census year from 1950 through 1990. The income amounts are adjusted for inflation and expressed in 1990 dollars. In all years, the highest-income elderly were least likely to reside with children. The elderly with no income whatsoever were likely to reside with children in 1950 and 1960, but this effect has diminished in more recent years. The pattern was essentially identical for elderly widows, widowers and married couples.[18] There was, however, a significant difference between blacks and whites: among blacks, the relationship between income and family composition was considerably weaker than it was for whites.

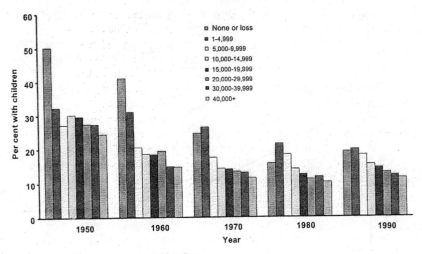

Figure XVII. Per cent of elderly persons residing with children by total income, 1950-1990

Note: Income expressed in 1990 dollars.

How much of the decline of the multigenerational family should be attributed to rising income? Let us assume for the moment that the sole reason why the elderly with higher incomes were more likely to reside alone was because they could better afford it.[19] Then it is a straightforward matter to calculate the percentage of the elderly that would have lived with children in each period assuming no change in the income distribution. In figure XVIII, the solid line shows the percentage of elderly who resided with their adult children from 1950 through 1990. The dashed line shows what the percentage would have been had there been no change in the distribution of income.[20] It turns out that the effects of rising income are fairly modest. Overall, less than 30 per cent of the change in elderly family composition can be attributed to this source.[21]

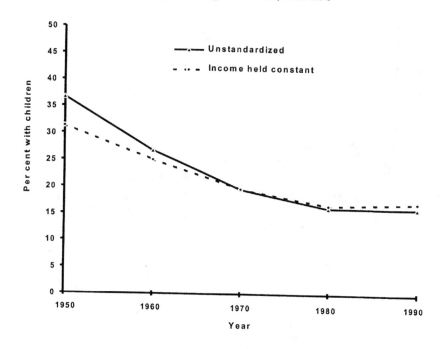

Figure XVIII. Percentage of elderly residing with own children, controlling for changes in income, 1950-1990

The effect of Social Security on family composition

Some analysts have attributed the shift in the living arrangements of the elderly to the introduction of the Social Security programme of old-age assistance. The Social Security programme began in 1936 during the depths of the Depression, and it has become the most substantial legacy of Roosevelt's New Deal. The programme was modest in the early years; because it was conceived as a pension plan, each person's benefit depended partly on his or her contributions. Benefits and coverage expanded dramatically from the early 1940s to the late 1970s, however, and Social Security eventually became the largest expenditure of the federal Government, amounting to 22 per cent of total spending by 1997. Figure XIX traces the expansion of average Social Security benefit levels, and figure XX shows the percentage of elderly receiving benefits from the programme. By 1990, the Social Security programme covered approximately 95 per cent of the elderly, and they received an average benefit of $559 per month (*Survey of Current Business*, 1998; p. 7). This has had a dramatic impact on the economic well-being of the elderly. Social Security now accounts for a third of the total income of the elderly, and if Social Security were abolished, the number of elderly in poverty would rise fivefold, to just over 50 per cent (Social Security Administration, 1996; pp. 133, 151).

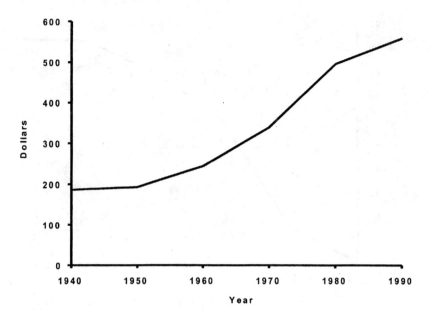

**Figure XIX. Average monthly benefit of Social Security recipients:
United States, 1940-1990 (1990 dollars)**

Source: McGarry and Shoeni (1998), table 3.

Figure XX. Percentage of elderly receiving Social Security benefits: United States, 1940-1990

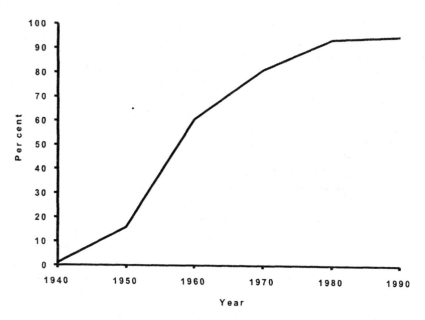

Source: McGarry and Shoeni (1998), table 3.

The Social Security programme is the most massive social policy enterprise ever undertaken in the United States. How much did it affect family composition? This question is complicated, because we lack a crucial piece of information: we do not know how much private savings and pensions would have grown if Social Security had not existed.[22] Certainly, some elderly would have saved more if they thought that they would have to live entirely from savings, and probably unions and employers would have developed larger pension programmes. But because we do not know how much lower savings and pensions would have been in the absence of Social Security, we cannot tell just how much the Social Security programme has raised the income of the elderly.

What we can do is make an upper-bound estimate of the impact of Social Security on the living arrangements of the elderly. Suppose we assume that Social Security had no impact whatsoever on savings or pensions. If that were the case, then we could calculate what the income distribution of the elderly would be in the absence of Social Security simply by subtracting their Social Security income from their total income. Figure XXI shows the effect of Social Security on the income of the elderly in 1990, based on this assumption. If we count Social Security income, only 4 per cent of the elderly in 1990 earned under $2,500; without Social Security, over 35 per cent would have fallen in the under-$2,500 category.[23] The percentage of elderly in every one of the higher income groups declines if we exclude Social Security income.

Given our assumption, we can now predict what percentage of elderly would have lived with their children in the absence of Social Security benefits.[24] We can only carry out the analysis for the period since 1970, because before that we lack census information on Social Security income. The solid line in figure XXII shows the percentage of elderly residing with their adult children from 1950 to 1990. The dashed line shows the predicted percentage residing with children if we exclude Social Security income from 1970 through 1990. The analysis suggests that Social Security has had a significant effect on living arrangements, but in the context of the long-run change in living arrangements, that effect is rather small. Overall, Social Security might explain no more than about 20 per cent of the total drop in residence with children since 1936. Even this effect is surely overstated, since it exaggerates the impact of Social Security on the income of the elderly.

The establishment and expansion of the Social Security programme is not, however, unrelated to the revolution in the living arrangements of the elderly; in fact, the two historical trends are closely related. The problem is that many analysts have the direction of causality reversed. As we have seen, the changes in family composition of the elderly began about 1860, long before the advent of Social Security. By 1936, some 40 per cent of the elderly already lived without kin. This created a new social problem of destitute elderly, and the Social Security programme was a solution.

The creators of the Social Security programme uniformly believed that the need for old-age assistance had greatly increased because of the rise of wage labour, the decline of farming and the resulting change in the family. Thomas H. Eliot, Counsel for the Committee on Economic Security, which drafted the Social Security bill, put it this way:

> In the old days, the old-age assistance problem was not so great so long as most people lived on farms, had big families, and at least some of the children stayed on the farm. It was customary when the old people got too old to do their share of the work they would stay on the farm and the sons or daughters would keep them there in the home. That pattern changed slowly but continuously from the early part of the century as more and more of the young, rural population left the farms. The three-generation household (aged parents, children, and grandchildren), perfectly common 50 years ago, had begun to become very rare indeed. By the time people got old, the children had already left and gone to the city. There was no one to take care of them. Hence, an increase in the problem of the needy aged (Eliot, n.d.).

Figure XXI. Percentage distribution of income among elderly, 1990: total income compared with non-Social Security income

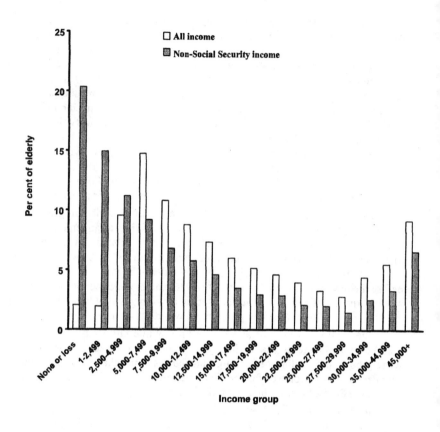

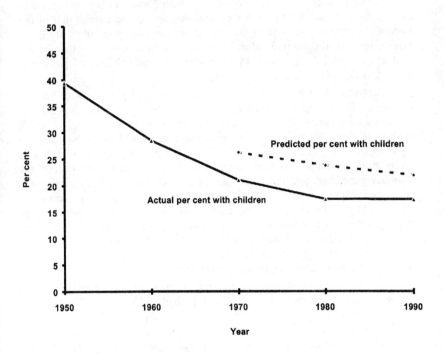

Figure XXII. Predicted percentage of elderly residing with children if Social Security income is excluded, 1950-1990

Another drafter of the original Social Security legislation, J. Douglas Brown, spoke of the problems created when older people had been left behind as young people moved to the cities (Brown, 1969). Nelson Cruikshank, another early advocate of Social Security, explained that before the 1930s most people thought all a family needed for a secure old age or to ride out a period of depression was a quarter section of good land and a couple of sons to help farm it, or even a couple of daughters through whom able-bodied sons-in-law might be acquired (Cruikshank, 1978). And Ewan Clague, who joined the Social Security Board in 1936, wrote that earlier in the century, old people simply lived on the farm until they died; consequently, the modern old-age problem had not developed (Clague, 1961).

Thus, Social Security did not cause the major changes in the family composition of the elderly; rather, it was a consequence of such changes. The creators of the Social Security system saw it as a response to changes in the family that had already taken place as a consequence of the decline of farming and the rise of urban wage labour.

Rising income can account for no more than 30 per cent of the decline in the residence of the elderly with their children during the second half of the twentieth century, and perhaps two thirds of this change resulted from the Social Security programme. What, then, was the source of the other 70 per cent of change? To understand what happened, we must shift our focus to the characteristics of the younger generation.

Between 1950 and 1970, the income of the elderly doubled, but the income of the younger generation rose even faster. In constant dollars, the income gap between the elderly and their children grew rapidly. In 1950, persons in their 30s and 40s made an average of $4,900 more than persons aged 65 or older, in 1990 dollars; by 1970, the gap had grown to $10,000. Even more dramatic was the growing disparity in education between the younger generation and the older one. In the early twentieth century, when secondary education was expanding gradually, the younger generation was only slightly better educated than their elders. In 1925, the elderly had an average of only 1.1 fewer years of schooling than did their children. With the rapid rise of secondary education after the turn of the century, however, that education gap expanded dramatically: by 1960, the elderly had an average of 3.0 fewer years of schooling than did their offspring.[25]

The author contends that the growing disparity in income and education between elderly parents and their children had profound implications for generational relations. The traditional authority of the patriarch had depended largely on control over economic resources. But the authority of the older generation — women as well as men — also depended on respect for their knowledge and experience. In the rapidly changing world of the mid-twentieth century, longevity no longer was the key to useful knowledge. The younger generation increasingly regarded their elders as relics of a bygone age.

The growing educational and economic gap between generations compounded the decline in the authority of the old. It also meant a dramatic expansion of economic opportunity for the young. The generation that reached adulthood after the war had unprecedented success early in life, especially in contrast to their Depression-era parents.

Social gerontologists have consistently argued that the decline in residence of the elderly with their children reflects the preferences of the elderly. This argument has its roots in the pioneering surveys carried out in 1957, 1962 and 1975 by Ethel Shanas, in which the elderly consistently maintained that they did not want to move in with their children (Shanas, 1962, 1968). The elderly say that they do not want to be a burden to their children. When the elderly do live with their children, they are now usually dependants of their children, a living arrangement that is considerably less attractive than the dominant position of the elderly in the nineteenth-century family.

There has been much less attention paid to the preferences of the younger generation, but they are clearly just as reluctant to live with their parents as their parents are to live with them. The rise of secondary and higher education eroded the remaining economic incentives for the younger generation to defer to their elders. In the mid-twentieth century, after most people had begun to work for wages and agriculture had become a minor sector of the economy, young people often found jobs through parents or other family connections. The growing gap in education between generations meant that the younger generation sought higher-status jobs, and their parents often could not help. The increased pace of social and economic change in the twentieth century, compounded by the growing differences in education level, led to a growing cultural gap between the generations. Thus, the residential preferences of the young may have shifted even more dramatically than did those of the old.

To assess the effects of changing income and education on the living arrangements of elderly whites between 1950 and 1990, I again turned to geographic analysis. The results reveal that throughout the period, the States with the highest income and education of the younger generation tended to be the States with the lowest percentage of elderly residing with children.

Just as in the analysis of self-employment described earlier, we can control for State differences in family composition in order to focus on the relationship between change in education and income and change in family composition. The analyses presented in table 3 are similar to those in table 2, but the period covered is 1950 through 1990 and the explanatory variables are measures of income and education instead of measures of occupational structure. Model 1 shows the overall change in the percentage of elderly residing with children, without controlling for any of these factors. The model shows a decline of 38 percentage points in residence of the elderly with children between 1950 and 1990. This figure is somewhat larger than the true change in the percentage living with the elderly, since it represents the average change across 48 States and the District of Columbia.

The second model in table 3 adds two income variables: the percentage of elderly (age 65+) with incomes of $13,000 or more, and the percentage of the younger generation (ages 30 through 49) with incomes of $13,000 or more. State effects are also controlled, so the model predicts the effects of changes in income on changes in the family composition of the elderly. The coefficients for both income measures are significant, but not in the expected direction: high income of the elderly was associated with co-residence, not with separate residence as we would expect. High income of the younger generation, as expected, was associated with separate residence. Model 2 explains little of the change over time, as the rising income of the elderly nearly cancels out the effects of rising income for the younger generation; only about 10 per cent of the change over the period 1950 through 1990 disappears when we control for the income of both generations.

TABLE 3. STATE-LEVEL OLS REGRESSIONS OF EDUCATION AND INCOME
ON PER CENT OF ELDERLY RESIDING WITH CHILDREN: POOLED DATA,
STATES WITH SUFFICIENT CASES IN ALL CENSUS YEARS, 1950-1990

	Model 1		Model 2		Model 3	
	B	Std. error	B	Std. error	B	Std. error
Census year						
1950	(reference category)		(reference category)		(reference category)	
1960	-25.96	1.05[a]	-19.94	3.07[a]	-15.34	2.78[b]
1970	-33.17	1.05[a]	-26.39	3.89[a]	-15.14	3.75[b]
1980	-37.67	1.05[a]	-32.52	4.19[a]	-11.53	4.66[c]
1990	-38.02	1.05[a]	-34.22	4.57[a]	-6.42	5.51
Income and education						
Elderly $13,000+			0.29	0.08[b]	0.06	0.08
Younger $13,000+			-0.24	0.09[b]	-0.14	0.08
Younger high school+					-0.54	0.07[b]
State effects	No		Yes		Yes	
Constant	51.15	0.75[a]	50.68	1.30	74.60	3.43[b]
R square	0.88		0.97		0.98	
Adjusted R square	0.88		0.96		0.97	
N	244		244		244	

Notes: OLS = ordinary least squares; B = slope; N = number of observations;
P = probability.

[a] $p<0.001$.

[b] $p<0.01$.

[c] $p<0.05$.

Model 3 adds an educational variable: the percentage of the younger generation (ages 30 through 49) with 12 or more years of schooling. The results are dramatic: changing educational levels of the younger generation are far better predictors of changing family composition of the older generation than are either of the income measures. Indeed, when we add education to the model, it swamps the effects of the income measures, and both lose their statistical significance. Moreover, this analysis suggests that the rising education of the younger generation can explain most of the rise of solitary residence among the aged. By contrast, the usual explanation for the change, the rise in income of the aged themselves, does not appear to have an independent effect on living arrangements.

This sort of geographic analysis has the potential to yield misleading results. The evidence clearly reveals that the States with the greatest increases in education for the younger generation were the ones with the greatest shift to independent residence for the elderly. This relationship is so strong that it could be sufficient to explain most of the decline in co-residence of the elderly since 1950. This does not, however, prove that the education of the younger generation was actually responsible for the change in the living arrangements of their parents. Instead, it could be that some unmeasured characteristic of the States with high education actually caused the elderly to live alone. This analysis should therefore be considered provisional. In the absence of credible evidence to the contrary, however, it appears that the changes in the living arrangements of the elderly during the second half of the twentieth century had more to do with the changing characteristics of the younger generation than with the changing characteristics of the elderly.

CONCLUSION

The finding of Peter Laslett (1965) that nuclear family composition was preferred in the West before the industrial revolution is an artifact of demography. Only a minority of households in the United States in 1850 contained multiple generations; as we have seen, however, the great majority of multigenerational households that could have existed did exist. Early death, late marriage and high fertility meant that few multigenerational households were possible.[26] If we measure multigenerational family structure from the perspective of those elderly who had surviving children, it becomes apparent that multigenerational co-residence was essentially universal in the mid-nineteenth century.

Did the co-residence of the elderly and their children result from "nuclear reincorporation" as a form of old-age assistance before the advent of Social Security? The evidence strongly suggests that it did not. Cross-sectional data are imperfect sources for analysis of the formation of multigenerational families. The evidence on the age and headship patterns of such families, however, suggests that in most cases the elderly did not move in with their children; rather, the younger generation remained in their parental household after they reached adulthood. Nor is there evidence that the elderly preferred co-residence to residing alone but were forced to do so only by dire necessity. The evidence on sickness and socio-economic status clearly indicates that neither sickness nor poverty were associated with multigenerational living.

Although there were far too few elderly in nineteenth-century America to create a majority of multigenerational families, their residence with the younger generation was clearly a social norm.[27] In the twentieth century, the demographic constraints on multigenerational family composition relaxed. Because of declining fertility, increasing life expectancy and shortening generations, by the late twentieth century the opportunities to form multigenerational families had increased dramatically. In 1990, only a small minority of potential multigenerational families existed.

The decline of the multigenerational family made sense for both the older and the younger generations. With the decline of farming and the rise of wage labour, the older generation no longer had need for the labour the younger generation once provided, and the younger generation no longer had need for the assets of the old. The growing education gap in the second half of the century also contributed to the decline in the economic power and authority of the older generation, as it simultaneously expanded opportunities for the young.

Does the American experience apply elsewhere? Many historians argue that the family system of North-western Europe and North America was fundamentally different from that of the rest of the world. Asia and parts of Eastern and Southern Europe, they maintain, were characterized by a joint family system that operated very differently from the nuclear family system of the Western countries (Hajnal, 1982, Kertzer, 1991). It is clear that North-western Europeans married unusually late, and unlike in some other places they seem to have had a strong aversion to the co-residence of married siblings. On the other hand, it is entirely plausible that the basic mechanisms of the decline of the multigenerational family in the United States also underlie the transformation of the living arrangements of the elderly across the globe. The shift to wage labour and the decline in patriarchal authority within the family are worldwide phenomena. Only further research can reveal if there is the same close association between economic opportunity of the younger generation and the simplification of families for the older generation in other countries.

Such research will soon become possible. The author has recently been awarded a large infrastructure grant by the National Science Foundation to make available contemporary and historical census microdata for a wide range of countries. This project will create and disseminate an integrated international census database incorporating 21 countries on six continents. It will be the world's largest public-use demographic database, with multiple samples from each country enabling analyses across time and space. The project entails two complementary tasks: first, the collection of data that will support broad-based investigations in the social and behavioural sciences; secondly, the creation of a system incorporating innovative capabilities for worldwide web-based access to both metadata and microdata. When this project is complete, it will make possible international comparative analyses of change in the living arrangements of the elderly, and we should be able to test whether the American case is in fact exceptional.

NOTES

[1] The IPUMS database and documentation (Ruggles and others, 1998) are available online at www.ipums.umn.edu. Data preparation was supported by NIH grants HD34572, HD34714, HD29015 and HD25839, and NSF grants SBR-9617820, SBR-9422805, SES-9118299 and SBR-9210903.

[2] A few studies — mostly by demographers — attempted long-term comparisons at the national level. These include Kobrin (1976), Smith (1986), Ruggles (1988) and Sweet and Bumpass (1987). Prior to the availability of IPUMS, such studies were plagued by problems of comparability; see Ruggles and Brower (forthcoming).

[3] This estimate is based on examination on the census microfilm of approximately 500 elderly persons residing without children randomly selected from the 1860 sample. It was fairly common for nineteenth-century farmers to build a second house on the property. The second house was usually smaller than the first; it might house a newly married child, and could also serve as a retirement home for the older generation.

[4] The estimate on percentage never-married is based on persons aged 85+ in 1880; the estimate on childlessness is based on persons born before 1820 as reported in the 1900 and 1910 censuses; the estimate on child mortality is based on microsimulation, together with empirical evidence on the clustering of child deaths; see Ruggles (1996b).

[5] The idea of demographic constraints on multigenerational families was first proposed by Levy (1965). The first empirical estimates of the effect were published by Coale (1965) in the same volume. Since then, analysts have used a wide variety of approaches to address the problem, and have obtained a wide variety of results; see Glass (1966), Burch (1970), Wrigley (1969), Bradley and Mendels (1978), Wachter, Hammel and Laslett (1978); Post, and others (1997). The author's own work on the problem, using microsimulation, life-table and demographic decomposition approaches, includes Ruggles (1986, 1987, 1993, 1994, 1996a).

[6] See, for example Smith (1979, 1981, 1986), Costa (1997), Elman (1998), Elman and Uhlenberg (1995), McGarry and Schoeni (1998), Kramarow (1995), Wall (1995), Hammel (1995), Schoeni (1998). The idea that extended families were a refuge for the poor in the nineteenth century is also widespread in the work of the first generation of quantitative social historians, e.g., Anderson (1972), Hareven (1978, 1982), Katz (1975), Foster (1974), and Modell (1978).

[7] This conceptualization owes much to Berkner (1972).

[8] In most states, if the father died without a will, all children and the surviving widow were ordinarily entitled to shares of the inheritance. In some states, the share for sons or for the eldest child was larger than that for other children. A minority of adult decedents — perhaps a quarter to a third — left wills, but among elderly men with multiple children, the proportion was much higher (Shammas, Salmon and Dahlin, 1987).

[9] This difference is significant at the 0.001 level.

[10] About two thirds of elderly individuals and couples responded to these questions. The elderly without property listed cannot be assumed to be poor; many had owned property, but had apparently already transferred their property to their children: most of the elderly without property listed were living with a child who had property. The elderly without listed property were almost identical to the propertied elderly with respect to the percentage residing with children. This results from two countervailing factors. Some elderly had no property because they had already transferred their property to their children; these elderly ordinarily resided with their children. Other elderly had no property listed because they were truly impoverished, and this group rarely resided with their children.

[11] Since self-employment was first explicitly asked beginning in 1910, for earlier years it was estimated by extrapolating the trend in self-employment backwards within each occupational title.

[12] That is, states with at least 100 elderly whites in every census year. These states represent about 90 per cent of the United States population.

[13] It should be noted that this is not identical to the overall percentage decline in residence with children, which was 24 percentage points, because this is the average of the 17 states represented in all census years.

[14] Ninety per cent of the people in the "self-employed" category are listed with one of the following occupational titles (in order of frequency): proprietors (n.e.c.); carpenters; painters; blacksmiths; tailors and tailoresses; brickmasons, stonemasons and tile setters;

physicians and surgeons; plumbers and pipe fitters; real estate agents and brokers; lawyers; insurance agents and brokers; and tinsmiths, coppersmiths and sheet metal workers. The remaining 10 per cent are divided among 33 additional minor occupational titles.

[15] For a discussion of the implications of state fixed-effect models, see Ellwood and Bane (1985).

[16] This measure does not capture within-state migration, which would have formed a more substantial obstacle to co-residence in the nineteenth century than it does today.

[17] For a useful discussion of the problem, see Goldscheider and Lawton (1998).

[18] The data in the graph ignores income for married women. This is because total income is not available for husbands and wives simultaneously in 1950, since income was a "sample line" characteristic asked on only one individual in each household. If the analysis is done including income of married women for the period 1960 onward, the results are unchanged. These data also include the group-quarters population, which have been excluded from many other studies. The group-quarters population tends to have lower income than the rest of the elderly, and of course they do not reside with their children. Therefore, the relationship is a bit stronger if the group-quarters population is excluded.

[19] In reality, of course, there are a myriad of other factors that could create such a relationship. For example, the key factor might really be the income of the children, which is no doubt correlated with the income of the elderly.

[20] The graph uses direct standardization, controlling only for changes in the income distribution. Virtually identical results are obtained through logistic regression.

[21] This result was obtained by decomposing the effects of changing income distribution using the method proposed by Das Gupta (1978), controlling for age in five-year groups, the income categories delineated in figure XVIII, sex and currently married status. The decomposition table is as follows:

	Components of change, 1950-1990	Index of change
Total population difference	0.2052	100.0
Effect of age	-0.0006	-0.3
Effect of sex and marital status	-0.0020	-1.0
Effect of income category	0.0542	26.4
Combined effect of factors	0.0517	25.2
Rate effect	0.1535	74.8

The income effect — 26.4 per cent — in this analysis is generally a bit lower than has been found by other investigators; although there is some disagreement, most studies suggest that about half of the recent shift towards living alone can be explained by rising income (see Beresford and Rivlin (1966); Chevan and Korson (1972); Carliner (1975); Davis and van den Oever (1981); Michael, Fuchs and Scott (1980); Pampel (1983); Ruggles (1988, 1996a, 1996b); also relevant are Anderson (1977), Angel and Tienda (1982), Troll (1971), King (1988)).

[22] Social security might also affect the income of the elderly by influencing retirement decisions.

[23] Using 1990 dollars. In this analysis, elderly married couples are treated as a single observation and their combined income is divided equally between them.

[24] To estimate the effect of Social Security on the family structure of the elderly, an additional assumption must be made. It should be assumed that the reason high-income elderly were less likely to reside with children than were low-income elderly was

simply because they could afford to live alone, and not the result of some other characteristic of high-income elderly. Again, this assumption makes the estimates conservative.

[25] On the impact of education, the interpretation of Caldwell (1982) is relevant.

[26] This statement assumes the context of a residence rule that prohibited joint families. The author does not argue, as Kertzer (1989, 1991) has implied, that a high frequency of extended families is impossible under such demographic conditions. Kertzer, who maintains that the notion of severe demographic constraints has been hard to kill, argues that demographic constraints on family structure are unimportant on the grounds that there was a high frequency of laterally extended joint families in a central Italian village at the turn of the century. But no one, as far as the author knows, has argued that such families would necessarily be infrequent under any demographic conditions; from Levy (1965) onward, the argument of demographic constraints has always referred to multigenerational extended families.

[27] In pre-industrial North-western Europe, with substantially earlier death and later marriage, the demographic constraints on multigenerational families were even more severe. We can be reasonably confident that only a small minority of the eighteenth-century English population had the opportunity to reside in a multigenerational family (see Ruggles (1987)).

REFERENCES

Alter, George, Lisa Cliggett and Alex Urbiel (1996). Household patterns of the elderly and the proximity of children in a nineteenth century city: Verviers, Belgium, 1831-1846. In *Aging and Generational Relations over the Life Course: A Historical and Cross-Cultural Perspective*, T. K. Hareven, ed. Berlin: de Gruyter, pp. 30-42.

Anderson, Michael (1972). Family Structure in Nineteenth Century Lancashire. Cambridge: Cambridge University Press.

_____ (1977). The impact on family relationships of the elderly of changes since Victorian times in governmental income maintenance provisions. In *Family, Bureaucracy, and the Elderly*, E. Shanas and M. B. Sussman, eds. Durham, North Carolina: Duke University Press.

Andorka, Rudolf (1995). Household systems and the lives of the old in eighteenth and nineteenth century Hungary. In *Aging in the Past: Demography, Society and Old Age*, David I. Kertzer and Peter Laslett, eds. Berkeley: University of California Press, pp. 129-155.

Angel, R., and M. Tienda (1982). Determinants of extended family structure: cultural pattern or economic need? *American Journal of Sociology*, 87, pp. 1360-1383.

Bane, Mary Jo (1976). *Here to Stay: American Families in the Twentieth Century*. New York: Basic Books.

Beresford, John C., and Alice M. Rivlin (1966). Privacy, poverty, and old age. *Demography*, vol. 3, pp. 247-258.

Berkner, Lutz (1972). The stem family and the developmental cycle of the peasant household: an eighteenth century Austrian example. *American Historical Review*, 77, pp. 398-418.

_____ (1975). The use and misuse of census data in the historical study of family structure. *Journal of Interdisciplinary History*, 4, pp. 721-738.

Bradley, Brian, and Franklin Mendels (1978). Can the hypothesis of a nuclear family be tested empirically? *Population Studies*, 32, pp. 381-394.

Brown, J. Douglas (1969). *The Genesis of Social Security in America*. Princeton: Princeton University, Industrial Relations Section. Available at www.ssa.gov/history/officials.html.

Burch, Thomas K. (1970). Some demographic determinants of average household size: an analytic approach. *Demography*, vol. 7, pp. 61-70.

Caldwell, John (1982). *Theory of Fertility Decline*. London: Academic Press.

Carliner, Geoffrey (1975). Determinants of household headship. *Journal of Marriage and the Family*, 37, pp. 28-38.

Chevan, A., and J. H. Korson (1972). The widowed who live alone: an examination of social and demographic factors. *Social Forces*, 51, pp. 45-53.

Clague, Ewan (1961). Factors contributing to the passage of the Social Security Act. Lecture delivered at a general staff meeting at the Social Security Administration Headquarters, Baltimore, Maryland, on 20 July. Available at www.ssa.gov/history/officials.html.

Coale, Ansley J. (1965). Estimates of average size of household. In *Aspects of the Analysis of Family Structure*, Marion Levy and others, eds. Princeton: Princeton University Press.

Costa, Dora (1997). Displacing the family: Union Army pensions and elderly living arrangements. *Journal of Political Economy*, 6, pp. 1269-1292.

Cruikshank, Nelson (1978). A philosophy for Social Security. Third Robert M. Ball Lecture, Baltimore, 12 December. Available at www.ssa.gov/history/officials.html.

Das Gupta, Prithwis (1978). A general method for decomposing a difference between two rates into components. *Demography*, vol. 15, pp. 99-112.

Davis, Kingsley, and P. van den Oever (1981). Age relations and policy in advanced industrial societies. *Population and Development Review*, vol. 7, pp. 1-18.

De Vos, Susan (1995). *Household Composition in Latin America*. New York: Plenum Press.

Dillon, Lisa Y. (1997). Between generations and across borders: living arrangements of the elderly and their children in Victorian Canada and the United States. Minneapolis: University of Minnesota. Ph.D. dissertation.

Eliot, Thomas H. (n.d.). The legal background of the Social Security Act. Available at www.ssa.gov/history/eliot2.html; soon to be reprinted in an SSA publication.

Elman, Cheryl (1998). Intergenerational household structure and economic change at the turn of the twentieth century. *Journal of Family History*, 4, pp. 417-440.

Elman, Cheryl, and Peter Uhlenberg (1995). Co-residence in the early twentieth century: elderly women in the United States and their children. *Population Studies*, vol. 49, No. 3, pp. 501-517.

Ellwood, David T., and Jo Bane (1985). The impact of AFDC on family structure and living arrangements. *Research in Labor Economics*, vol. 7, R. Ehrenberg, ed. Greenwich, Connecticut: JAI Press, pp. 137-207.

Fauve-Chamoux, Antoinette (1996). Aging in a never-empty nest: the elasticity of the stem family. In *Aging and Generational Relations over the Life Course: A Historical and Cross-Cultural Perspective*, T. K. Hareven, ed. Berlin: de Gruyter, pp. 75-99.

Foster, John O. (1974). *Class Struggle and the Industrial Revolution: Early Industrial Capitalism in Three English Towns*. London: Weidenfeld.

Glass, David V. (1966). London inhabitants within the walls, 1695. *London Record Society*, 2, introduction.

Goldscheider, Frances K., and L. Lawton (1998). Family experiences and the erosion of support for intergenerational coresidence. *Journal of marriage and the family*, 60, pp. 623-632.

Gross, Stephen (1993). Family, property, community: persistence and accommodation among German Americans in rural Stearns County, Minnesota, 1860-1920. Minneapolis: University of Minnesota. Ph.D. dissertation.

Guinnane, Timothy W. (1996). The family, State support, and generational relations in rural Ireland at the turn of the twentieth century. In *Aging and Generational Relations over the Life Course: A Historical and Cross-Cultural Perspective*, T. K. Hareven, ed. Berlin: de Gruyter, pp. 100-119.

Hajnal, John (1965). European marriage patterns in perspective. In *Population in History*, D. V. Glass and D. E. C. Eversley, eds. Chicago: Aldine, pp. 101-138.

_____ (1982). Two kinds of preindustrial household formation systems. *Population and Development Review*, vol. 8, No. 3, pp. 449-494.

Hammel, E. A. (1995). The elderly in the bosom of the family: La famille souche and hardship reincorporation. In *Aging in the Past: Demography, Society and Old Age*, David I. Kertzer and Peter Laslett, eds. Berkeley: University of California Press, pp. 107-127.

Hareven, Tamara K. (1978). The dynamics of kin in an industrial community. In *Turning Points: Historical and Sociological Essays on the Family*, John Demos and S. S. Boocock, eds. Chicago: University of Chicago Press.

_____ (1982). Family Time and Industrial Time: The Relationship between the Family and Work in a New England Industrial Community. Cambridge: Cambridge University Press.

_____ (1994). Aging and generational relations: intergenerational supports for the old in the United States: a historical life course perspective. *Annual Review of Sociology*, 20, p. 442.

_____ (1996). Introduction: Aging and generational relations over the life course. In *Aging and Generational Relations over the Life Course: A Historical and Cross-Cultural Perspective*, T. K. Hareven, ed. Berlin: de Gruyter, pp. 1-12.

Hermalin, Albert I., and Mary Beth Ofstedal (1996). Types of support for the aged and their providers in Taiwan. In *Aging and Generational Relations over the Life Course: A Historical and Cross-Cultural Perspective*, T. K. Hareven, ed. Berlin: de Gruyter, pp. 400-437.

Katz, Michael B. (1975). The People of Hamilton, Canada West. Cambridge, Massachusetts: Harvard University Press.

Kertzer, David I. (1989). The joint family revisited: demographic constraints and household complexity in the European past. *Journal of Family History*, 14, pp. 1-15.

_____ (1991). Household history and sociological theory. *Annual Review of Sociology*, 17, pp. 155-179.

_____ (1995). Toward a historical demography of aging. In *Aging in the Past: Demography, Society and Old Age*, David I. Kertzer and Peter Laslett, eds. Berkeley: University of California Press, pp. 363-383.

King, Miriam L. (1988). *Changes in the Living Arrangements of the Elderly: 1960-2030*. Congressional Budget Office, special study. Washington, D.C.: Government Printing Office.

Kobrin, Frances (1976). The fall in household size and the rise of the primary individual in the United States. *Demography*, vol. 13, pp. 127-138.

Kramarow, Ellen (1995). The elderly who live alone in the United States: historical perspectives on household change. *Demography*, vol. 32, pp. 335-352.

Laslett, Peter (1965). *The World We Have Lost*. London: Cambridge University Press.

_____ (1972). Introduction. In *Household and Family in Past Time*, Peter Laslett and Richard Wall, eds. London: Cambridge University Press.

_____, and John Harrison (1963). Clayworth and Cogenhoe. In *Historical Essays 1600-1750: Presented to Davis Ogg*, H. E. Bell and R. L. Ollard, eds. London: Barnes and Noble.

Lebergott, Stanley (1964). *Manpower in Economic Growth: the American Record Since 1800*. New York: McGraw-Hill.

Levy, Marion (1965). Aspects of the analysis of family structure. In *Aspects of the Analysis of Family Structure*, Marion Levy and others, eds. Princeton: Princeton University Press.

Martin, Linda G. (1989). Living arrangements of the elderly in Fiji, Korea, Malaysia, and the Philippines. *Demography*, vol. 26, No. 4, pp. 627-643.

McGarry, Kathleen, and Robert F. Shoeni (1998). Social Security, economic growth, and the rise in independence of elderly widows in the 20th century. Santa Monica, California: Rand Corporation, Labor and Population Program. Working paper, series, 98-01.

Michael, R. T., V. R. Fuchs and S. R. Scott (1980). Changes in the propensity to live alone, 1950-1976. *Demography*, vol. 17, pp. 39-53.

Modell, John (1978). Patterns of consumption, acculturation, and family income strategies: late nineteenth-century America. In *Family and Population in Nineteenth Century America*, T. K. Hareven and M. Vinovskis, eds. Princeton: Princeton University Press.

Pampel, Fred C. (1983). Changes in the propensity to live alone: evidence from consecutive cross-sectional surveys. *Demography*, vol. 20, pp. 433-447.

Post, W., and others (1997). Reconstructing the extended kin-network in the Netherlands with genealogical data: methods, problems, and results. *Population Studies*, 51.

Ruggles, Steven (1986). Availability of kin and the demography of historical family structure. *Historical Methods*, vol. 19, No. 3, pp. 93-102.

_____ (1987). *Prolonged Connections: The Rise of the Extended Family in Nineteenth Century England and America*. Madison: University of Wisconsin Press.

_____ (1988). The demography of unrelated individuals, 1900-1950. *Demography*, vol. 25, pp. 521-536.

_____ (1993). Confessions of a microsimulator: problems in modeling the demography of kinship. *Historical Methods*, vol. 26, No. 4, pp. 161-169.

_____ (1994). The transformation of American family structure. *American Historical Review*, 99, pp. 103-128.

_____ (1996a). The effects of demographic change on multigenerational family structure: United States whites, 1880-1980. In *Les systèmes demographiques du passé*, Alain Bideau and others, eds. Lyons: Centre Jacques Cartier, pp. 21-40.

_____ (1996b). Living arrangements of the elderly in America, 1880-1980. In *Aging and Generational Relations Over the Life Course: A Historical and Cross-Cultural Perspective*, T. K. Hareven, ed. Berlin: de Gruyter, pp. 254-271.

_____, and Susan Brower (forthcoming). New estimates of household composition in the United States, 1850-1990. In *Historical Statistics of the United States: Millennial Edition*, Michael Haines, Richard Sutch and Susan Carter, eds. New York and Cambridge: Cambridge University Press.

_____ and others (1998). *Integrated Public Use Microdata Series: Version 2.0.* Minneapolis: University of Minnesota, Historical Census Projects.

Schoeni, Robert (1998). Reassessing the decline in parent-child old-age coresidence during the twentieth century. *Demography*, vol. 35, pp. 307-313.

Shammas, Carole, Marylynn Salmon and Michel Dahlin (1987). *Inheritance in America from Colonial Times to the Present.* Rutgers, New Jersey: Rutgers University Press.

Shanas, Ethel (1962). *The Health of Older People, a Social Survey.* Cambridge, Massachusetts: Harvard University Press.

_____ (1968). *Old People in Three Industrial Societies.* New York: Atherton Press.

Smith, Daniel Scott (1979). Life course, norms, and the family system of older Americans in 1900. *Journal of Family History*, 4, pp. 285-298.

_____ (1981). Historical change in the household structure of the elderly in economically developed countries. In *Aging: Stability and Change in the Family*, R. W. Fogel, S. B. Keisler and E. Shanas, eds. New York: Academic Press.

_____ (1986). Accounting for change in the families of the elderly in the United States, 1900-present. In *Old Age in a Bureaucratic Society: The Elderly, the Experts, and the State in American History*, David Van Tassel and Peter N. Stearns, eds. Westport, Connecticut: Greenwood Press.

_____ (1993). The curious history of theorizing about the history of the Western nuclear family. *Social Science History*, 17, pp. 325-353.

Social Security Administration (1996). *Income of the Population 55 or Older, 1996.* Washington, D.C.: Government Printing Office.

Survey of Current Business (1998). October.

Sweet, James A., and Larry Bumpass (1987). *American Families and Households.* New York: Russell Sage.

Troll, L. E. (1971). The family of later life: a decade review. *Journal of Marriage and the Family*, 33, pp. 263-290.

Uhlenberg, Peter (1996). Intergenerational support in Sri Lanka: the elderly and their children. In *Aging and Generational Relations over the Life Course: A Historical and Cross-Cultural Perspective*, T. K. Hareven, ed. Berlin: de Gruyter, pp. 462-482.

Verdon, Michel (1998). *Rethinking Households: An Atomistic Perspective on European Living Arrangements.* London and New York: Routledge.

Wachter, Kenneth, Eugene Hammel and Peter Laslett (1978). *Statistical Studies of Historical Social Structure.* New York: Academic Press.

Wall, Richard (1995). Elderly persons and members of their households in England and Wales from preindustrial times to the present. In *Aging in the Past: Demography, Society and Old Age*, David I. Kertzer and Peter Laslett, eds. Berkeley: University of California Press, pp. 81-106.

Wrigley, E. A. (1969). *Population and History.* London: McGraw-Hill.

LIVING ARRANGEMENTS OF OLDER PERSONS AND FAMILY SUPPORT IN LESS DEVELOPED COUNTRIES[1]

*Jay Sokolovsky**

Now here is a story to show you how things have changed and what the young think of the old these days. After they married, 35-year-old Slobodan and his wife moved into the small house of his parents near the centre of Belgrade, the capital city of Yugoslavia. When the younger couple started having children they began taking over more of the limited space in the dwelling. By the time Slobodan's wife had their third child, his mother was dead and his 74-year-old father, Zvonko, was becoming frail. Slobodan requested that his father give up his larger bedroom to him and his wife. As his children grew, Slobodan haphazardly built a tiny room onto the house and "encouraged" the father to move into this new space, which he did. Eventually, although he was still able to take care of himself, Zvonko was asked by the son to move into a large, new residential complex for pensioners on the outskirts of the city. Two years passed and the father died. A month later, Slobodan receives a call from the director of the residence for the elderly, asking when he and his family are moving out of the house. Puzzled, Slobodan enquired why the director should ask such a crazy question. He was then informed that Zvonko had been so appreciative of how he was treated at the residence that he had deeded his house to the facility for its use.

Story told to Jay Sokolovsky while studying residential homes for the elderly in Croatia and Serbia from 1983 to 1985.

INTRODUCTION

Discourses of neglect

It was intriguing to hear this story in a country where care of the elderly by their children is constitutionally mandated. Interestingly enough, similar tales of forsaking the aged can be found in such divergent places as Japan, among foraging peoples of Botswana, rural villagers in Kenya and both rural and urban populations in India. These "discourses of neglect", as some have labelled them (Cattell, 1997b; Rosenberg, 1997), act as powerful narratives of

---

* University of South Florida, Bayboro Campus, Florida, United States of America.

caution which can have deep cultural roots. In India, which maintains one of the highest levels of elderly co-residence in the world, Linda Martin notes that as early as the ninth century, the Hindu philosopher Shankaracharya spoke of the harsh dilemma of very late adulthood. In stressing the need for material detachment during the last phase of adult life, he said: "Your family is attached to you as long as you can earn. With frail body and no income, no one in the house will care for you" (Martin, 1990, p. 108).

At the beginning of this new millennium, in countries such as Croatia, India, China, Thailand, Ghana and Mexico, only a small fraction of the elderly population resides in the kind of non-familial residential setting described above. However, the existence of such places combines with specific discourses about ageing to reveal pervasive anxiety about becoming an unwanted burden or of families being unable to sustain growing cohorts of persons living past their sixth and seventh decades of life (Vatuk, 1990). These countries are facing transformations in generational population dynamics and arrangements at a pace more rapid than that experienced in the industrial West. It is easy to sympathize with the assessment of the West African Temne peoples of Sierra Leone, who refer to themselves as the "short-changed generation". As Nana Apt puts it, "They have paid their dues when they were young but, because of social change, their time for the pay-off was begrudged" (Apt, 1998, pp. 13-14). Similarly, in India during the 1990s, Sarah Lamb encountered the following everyday reality while studying a West Bengal village:

> The young girl who worked cleaning my home, Beli Bagdi, responded when I asked her what would happen to her when she became old, "Either my sons will feed me rice or they won't; there's no certainty". In Bengal's villages and cities, wandering beggars, mostly aged, do drift from house to house in search of rice, a cup of hot tea, or a few coins. Old widows dressed in white crowd around the temples in pilgrimage spots waiting for a handful of rice doled out once a day. The powerful documentary film, "Moksha" (Salvation), directed by Pankaj Butalia (1993), portrays destitute Bengali widows at a Vrindavan ashram, who recall poignantly the fights and rejections they experienced in the homes of their sons and daughters-in-law, and their utter loneliness in the world of kin (Lamb, in press).

Nana Apt (1996) elucidates this perception of "caring in crisis" in her recent book on Ghana's elderly. In contrast, however, survey-grounded data show that throughout much of the developing world, especially in Africa and East Asia, the aged are, for the most part, still entwined in multigenerational living arrangements, most often with an adult child. In certain contexts, the discourse of neglect is part of a traditional pattern of reminding community members about expected ideals of support; in other cases, it is a window through which one can see how the modern world has profoundly altered the accepted social contract between generations. Among the most common processes to provoke this reaction in the developing world is the delocalization of economic resources that sustain and connect families with their natal communities. Throughout Africa, Latin America and Asia, increasing numbers of a family's young adults must seek employment far from their natal home (Vatuk, 1996; Kalache, 1995). Viewing this process in Africa, Weisner (1997) uses a construct of "multilocal" families to think more realistically about the support of children. This social pattern, the contours of which are still emerging, has great applicability to an analysis of how the old are sustained in most developing countries.

The present paper focuses on how families are trying to adapt traditional patterns of living arrangements to the powerful changes encountered in less developed countries. In examining this issue, some of the basic data on living arrangements and support in developing countries in the light of urbanizing change are reviewed. Finally, the author uses his own long-term research in a village in central Mexico to show the need to go beyond the surface structure of living arrangements to understand the changing circumstances in which the third world aged find themselves.

THE DEMOGRAPHIC AND SOCIAL BASIS OF FAMILY SUPPORT

There has been a recent and quite dramatic demographic revolution in the developing countries. At the beginning of the 1990s, these countries, for the first time, contained a majority of the world's elders (Kinsella, 1997). By 2015, most will still not have reached the level of "societal ageing" now faced by North America, much of Europe, and Japan, but they will have to contend with an extraordinary increase of 78 per cent in actual numbers, from 214 million to 380 million aged. And, over the coming three decades, currently "young or youthful" countries such as Brazil, Indonesia and Mexico will witness the oldest part of their population (over age 65) at least double — and, in the case of Indonesia, quadruple.

Despite the oncoming rapidity of ageing in many developing countries, their demographic profile, especially for the least developed ones, will still show a relatively youthful population by 2050 (see table 1) and maintain a moderately high potential support ratio (8 younger adults for each person over age 65). It is of more demographic concern that the middle-range countries ("less developed regions") will see a near doubling of the portion of the elderly over age 80, occurring at the same time as a threefold drop in the potential support ratio. By mid-century, countries in this category, especially those in Latin America and industrializing Asia, will present a demographic ageing profile that is similar to the one shown by the more developed countries today.

TABLE 1. SOME DEMOGRAPHIC COMPARISONS BETWEEN MORE,
LESS AND LEAST DEVELOPED REGIONS

Region	Population aged 60 years or older (percentage of total population)		Percentage 80 years or older among those 60 years or older		Potential support ratio (number of persons aged 15-64 years per population aged 65 years or older)	
	1999	2050	1999	2050	1999	2050
More developed regions	19	33	16	27	5	2
Less developed regions	8	21	9	17	12	4
Least developed regions	5	12	7	10	18	8

Source: United Nations (1999a).

While in most of Africa the population will remain quite young, unprecedented demographic changes are occurring in other parts of the developing world. Within 20 years, for example, China will equal Japan's world ageing record — making the transition from a "young" (7 per cent over age 65) to a "mature" (14 per cent over age 65) population in just a quarter of a century (Kinsella, 1997). Most countries have taken two to five times longer to alter their demographic make-up so profoundly. People in such third world countries are not only living longer; overall fertility rates are plummeting. In Asia and Latin America, these rates have fallen about 50 per cent during the period from 1965 to 1995, from six to three children per woman (Kinsella and Gist, 1995). Over the next two decades, countries such as China, Mexico, Ghana, India and Indonesia and most of the Caribbean countries will reverse the dramatic demographic thrust of the past century by actually having minimal or even negative annual growth among the age group 0-14, while those over age 65 will grow at rates between 2.1 and 3.2 each year (World Bank, 1999).

At the extreme edge of these kinds of changes is China, which began a one-family/one-child policy during the 1970s. There has ensued a great public worry around the "4-2-1" dilemma, premised on one child taking care of two parents and four grandparents. Since 1978, the country has sought, in the process of decollectivization, to restore the family as the main local economic unit and reassign to that unit much of the care of the elderly that had previously come from the public sector. However, the dislocations of the economic transformations of the socialist economy are clearly seen among the urban elderly. During the late 1990s, in some areas, pensions were lost when state-sponsored enterprises folded, and, increasingly, as housing is privatized, the urban aged are being moved out of long-familiar neighbourhoods to the outer fringes of cities.[2] Municipal governments have tried to assume some of the pension debt of defunct state-owned businesses, but a persistent question keeps arising: in the market economy, will children have time to care for parents? The 1992 National Survey on Support Systems for the Elderly indicated that in both rural and urban areas social and financial support tend to be need-based, with familial support attempting to compensate for inequalities in elderly persons' access to public resources (Lee and Xiao, 1998). However, in discussing the Chinese intergenerational contract of support by sons, Ikels talks about the changes wrought by the economic transformations of the 1980s and 1990s and how they are challenging some of the presumptions of the 1992 survey:

> Material and psychological incentives along with the threat of social and supernatural sanctions usually made living up to the contract more attractive to the younger generation than reneging on it. In the reform era the strength of these forces has been weakened as the young take advantage of the new opportunities to live and work in communities other than the ones in which they were raised. Nowhere is this more apparent than in the rural area, where the shift from the collective to the individual household as the unit of production has undermined the power of the village (formerly team or brigade) head to penalize neglectful adult children by withholding their wages (Ikels, 1993, p. 332).

In China, throughout the 1990s, there have been strong official expressions of concern about both the desire of adult children to sustain their parents and the need to prevent abuse. Ikels notes that a 1990 report in the Chinese Legal Daily makes note of abuse and neglect being associated with 187 deaths among the elderly between 1989 and 1990. The report states that "these abnormal deaths", of which many were suicides, were the result of being denied medical treatment, being coerced into turning over property, and being bullied and tortured. Local authorities were accused of not paying much attention to these cases and of failing to prosecute the persons responsible (Ikels, 1993, p. 332).

Women and the dilemma of widowhood

Perhaps the greatest challenge over the coming decades will be support of elderly women, especially widows. As can be seen in table 2, throughout the developing world, typically half or more of women over age 60 are widowed. This is dramatic in comparison to men. In Africa, for example, fewer than 1 in 10 are widowers and elsewhere this figure is typically lower than 20 per cent (Cattell, 1997a). Even where the incidence of widowhood dips below half, in Brazil and Mexico, men still had rates three times lower than did women.

The consequences of differential rates of widowed status are no less dramatic in the numbers than in the typical cultural consequences. Older males are more likely to receive social and material support within extended family networks owing to their status as older males, greater access to economic resources, and the much higher likelihood of becoming remarried and having the personal support of a spouse. In many areas of India, there are strong cultural prohibitions against widow remarriage, and even as old age brings some measure of prestige, such women are still considered inauspicious (Lamb, forthcoming). More concretely, work by Jean Dreze (1990) shows that households headed by widows have 70 per cent less spending power than the national average. She identifies five factors creating constraints on widows in India: their inability to return to the parental home; restrictions on remarriage; very limited access to self-employment outside of agricultural wage labour; difficulty in inheriting property in a patrilineal system; and lack of access to credit. These factors will become increasingly important as the size of local close family networks continues to shrink with decreasing fertility and migration.

TABLE 2. PERCENTAGE OF MEN AND WOMEN AGED 60+ WHO ARE WIDOWED, SELECTED COUNTRIES

	Per cent widowed	
	Men	Women
Selected countries in sub-Saharan Africa		
Cameroon	10	62
Sudan	6	54
Botswana	9	53
Kenya	7	50
Uganda	9	48
Mali	5	46
Other developing countries		
Indonesia	17	68
India	19	64
Republic of Korea	13	64
Egypt	12	60
China	27	58
Brazil	12	47
Mexico	12	38

Source: Adapted from Cattell (1997a), p. 73.

Moreover, there are substantial numbers of widows who have no sons, or any biological children for that matter. In the 1980s, Hugo found that in five countries of Central Africa (Cameroon, Central African Republic, Gabon, the Sudan and Zaire) there were regions where 20 to 50 per cent of females over age 50 had never borne children (Hugo, 1985). Similarly, in Indonesia's West Java region, he found childlessness to exceed 15 per cent. In Mexico and Chile, De Vos (forthcoming) found that 18 to 19 per cent of elderly women were also childless. These figures are much higher than in either China or Thailand, with figures under 5 per cent.

In Africa and elsewhere, this dilemma is moderated by high levels of fostering and adoption, as well as the support of collateral kin such as siblings and sometimes nieces and nephews. Within the Mexican village where the author worked, widows, if they were living alone after the death of a spouse, would usually be assigned a teenage grandchild to live with them. This person might remain in the household and eventually inherit the house and agricultural lands assigned to it. Some countries such as China have also begun to encourage older widowed men and women to remarry, relieving some of the pressure on the broader kinship network for support.

RECENT DATA ON LIVING ARRANGEMENTS IN THE THIRD WORLD

Over the past three decades, a great deal of survey data has accumulated on living arrangements and support of the elderly in third world countries. Some of the most important demographic and structural sources of information have been provided by projects such as the Collaborative Study on Social and Health Aspects of Ageing in the Western Pacific Region (Andrews and others, 1986); the Comparative Study in Four Asian Countries: Rapid Demographic Change and the Welfare of the Elderly, in East Asia (Ofstedal, Knodel and Chayovan, 1999); the seven-country study, Social Support Systems in Transition, within Asia, Africa and the Middle East (Hashimoto, 1991; Kendig, Hashimoto and Coppard, 1992); and the United Nations Fertility Survey among Six Latin American Countries (De Vos, 1990).[3] This survey work has been complemented by more focused sociological research in Africa, which has begun to detail how these family structures are adapting to dramatic global changes (Apt, 1996; Okharedia, 1999), in Asia (Hermalin, 1995; Knodel and Saengtienchai, 1999) and in Latin America (de Lehr, 1992; Ramos, 1992; Lloyd-Sherlock, 1997).[4]

On a more local level, a voluminous body of anthropological work now exists on the cultural dynamics of ageing within family networks for most regions of the world (Foner, 1984; Albert and Cattell, 1994; Keith and others, 1994; Rhoads and Holmes, 1995; Sokolovsky, 1997a; Aguilar, 1998; Putnam-Dickerson and Brown, 1998; Ikels and Beall, forthcoming). Such community-based and culturally focused studies are crucial for helping us to understand the dynamic context that is now testing the capacity of families in developing countries to sustain the elderly. Throughout this paper, an attempt is made to integrate this largely qualitative research with the quantitative data sources mentioned above.

Patterns of living arrangements and support

Leo Simmons, in his classic examination of the role of the aged in 71 non-industrial societies, observed that "throughout human history the family has been the safest haven for the aged. Its ties have been the most intimate and long-lasting, and on them the aged have relied for greatest security" (Simmons, 1945, p. 176). If the survey data collected over the past two decades is any judge, Simmons' simplistic axiom about the aged and family living still holds in much of the third world, even in urban areas where a majority of older adults still reside with younger relatives and must rely exclusively on familial resources for survival (Hashimoto, 1991). In the Western Pacific survey, for example, it was found that in Fiji, the Republic of Korea, Malaysia and the Philippines, between 75 and 85 per cent of the elderly reside in extended family settings. Importantly, within each country, variables such as gender, age of elder or marital status had little impact on the likelihood of co-residence. As Albert and Cattell (1994, p. 99) suggest, there seems to be a strong cultural prescription at work in this region. Similar findings from surveys carried out in the mid-1990s show a continuing pattern of high co-residence in the Philippines, Singapore, Taiwan Province of China and Thailand (Ofstedal, Knodel and Chayovan, 1999).

In table 3, which is based on surveys carried out during the 1980s, we see two notable differences between the middle-income countries of Central and South America and the low-income countries drawn almost exclusively from Asia. First, during the 1980s, in the middle-income group, barely a majority of the elderly were residing with adult children or other family (the exception is Argentina), versus more than three quarters in the latter group. Secondly, for all countries, except Costa Rica, over 10 per cent of elders lived alone in middle-income countries compared to typically 5 per cent or less among the lower-income group.

More variation was seen in the United Nations University study of seven countries (table 4), although in all sampled countries, except Brazil and Egypt, a majority of elders lived in multigenerational settings, with the highest percentages occurring in India, Zimbabwe and Thailand (Hashimoto, 1991). One of the significant differences is seen in both Zimbabwe and Thailand, which had the highest percentages of skipped-generation households, where elders resided with their grandchildren or other young relatives.[5] In the Zimbabwean rural community of Manguwende, the study found that the grandparent/grandchild household was the most frequent living arrangement for older adults. The especially high figures of skipped-generation households for Zimbabwe reflect not only heavy migration patterns but also a cultural pattern whereby married sons often reside in another house compound or area of the locality.

Additionally, in Zimbabwe, economic dislocation and one of the world's highest rates of HIV infection (United Nations, 1999b) have conspired to force reformulation of local support systems. One result of the AIDS pandemic is the loss of young and middle-aged adult caregivers, compelling the elderly to work much harder to support themselves and their grandchildren. The Government has asked local headmen to set aside a plot of land to help support stressed grandparents. Non-governmental organizations such as HelpAge International are trying to establish small businesses and collective farms to bolster the economic efforts of destitute seniors.

TABLE 3. LIVING ARRANGEMENTS OF OLDER PERSONS IN THE 1980S: PERCENTAGE OF PERSONS OVER 60 LIVING WITH CHILDREN OR FAMILY, LIVING ALONE OR IN OTHER ARRANGEMENTS

	With children or family	Alone	Other[a]
Middle-income countries			
Argentina	25	11	64
Chile	59	10	31
Costa Rica	56	7	37
Panama	76	10	14
Trinidad and Tobago	41	13	46
Uruguay	53	16	31
Average	**52**	**11**	**37**
Low-income countries			
China	83	3	14
Urban	74	5	22
Rural	89	1	10
Côte d'Ivoire	96	2	2
Guyana	61	2	38
Honduras	90	5	5
Indonesia	76	8	17
Malaysia	82	6	12
Philippines	92	3	5
Thailand	92	5	4
Average	**84**	**4**	**13**

Source: Adapted from World Bank (1994), p. 63.

Note: Averages are unweighted.

[a] Includes persons living with spouse.

TABLE 4. HOUSEHOLD COMPOSITION OF THE AGED IN SEVEN COUNTRIES
(*Percentage*)

Households	Singa-pore	Repub-lic of Korea	Brazil	Thai-land	Zim-babwe	Egypt	India
Single	1.7	7.3	25.8	3.6	5.3	9.1	3.0
Conjugal[a]	2.3	11.3	19.0	8.1	2.7	13.2	1.0
Nuclear[b]	36.3	24.8	28.8	17.8	9.7	42.9	10.0
Multigenera-tional[c]	56.3	53.6	16.3	67.6	75.7	30.8	85.1
2-generation	12.0	3.3	1.4	4.5	5.0	4.1	8.7
3-4-generation	43.3	46.0	14.2	50.2	35.0	24.0	73.7
Skipped-generation	1.0	4.3	0.7	12.9	35.7	2.7	2.7
Other	3.3	3.0	10.2	2.9	6.7	4.1	1.0
	n=300	n=302	n=295	n=309	n=300	n=296	n=300

Source: Adapted from Hashimoto (1991), p. 364.

Notes: n = number of observations.

[a] Elderly couple only.

[b] Elderly parent(s) and unmarried child(ren).

[c] The multigenerational category is the total of 2-generation, 3-4-generation and skipped-generation households. It includes married children and/or grandchildren, along with the elderly parent(s).

More subtle but equally profound changes can be seen in the indigenous belief system. One noted example is the loss of traditional ancestor worship associated with conversion to Christianity. Previously, there was a widespread ritual of ancestor pleasing — *kupira mudzimu*. It was believed that if people did not care for their parents, the ancestors would curse them. This seems now to have lost its effectiveness in an era when cross-generational interdependence is seldom a mainstay of gaining economic maturity for young adults.

The limited survey research on living arrangements in Africa, such as that carried out by Peil (1985) during the 1980s, shows consistently high levels of co-residence and family-based support in both rural and urban areas. She reported that about 80 per cent of her respondents over age 60 were receiving help from children, grandchildren or siblings. However, it is important to note that there is an enormous variation in family and descent systems in Africa, as well as some basic and important differences in informal support systems compared with other regions of the world. Typically, one finds that family-based systems of support tend to encompass a broader definition of kin support than is usually found in many regions of Asia or Latin America (Cattell, 1997a). Especially in West Africa, widespread matrilineal descent systems, coupled with the traditional importance of women in local market economies, appear to provide older women with a more secure late life support network. Support in old age from siblings is also more a part of caregiving than it is in Asia and cultural traditions of child fostering and adoption potentially expand the number of persons one can "claim" as his or her child (Apt, 1996; Cattell, 1993). In some matrilineal systems, where marriage pulled women to the homesteads of their spouses, after menopause they will be reintegrated into their natal households, where they will be supported for the remainder of their lives.

Stability in the face of change?

On the surface, survey measures in a number of regions show relative stability for elders living in extended families. Kolenda's 1987 longitudinal analysis of family structure in a village of India shows joint family formations actually increasing from 29 per cent in 1819 to 45.6 per cent in 1967. In the same country, a regional study of 13 rural communities shows the proportion of those past age 60 residing with sons to have remained at about 80 per cent from 1960 to 1982 (Biswas, 1985). In Martin's (1990) analysis of this data set, she concludes that these patterns reflect relatively stable attitudes towards generationally shared households during a period of increased longevity connected to decreased late life and younger adult mortality. This kind of residential stability is supported by two new community-based studies, one in a New Delhi middle-class neighbourhood (van Willigen and Chadha, 1999) and another in rural West Bengal (Lamb, in press).

Elsewhere in Asia, the work in Thailand by Knodel and others (1999) (see table 5) shows a similar general stability in living arrangements among the elderly during a period of rapid socio-economic changes during the past decade. Importantly, this team's work on the non-co-resident networks of family support finds that those not living with adult children are, nevertheless, in "living arrangements which can be construed as consistent with the prevailing normative mandate assigning family responsibility for support and care of the elderly" (Siriboon and Knodel, 1994, p. 32).

TABLE 5. LIVING ARRANGEMENTS AMONG PERSONS AGED 60+, THAILAND

	1986	1994	1995
Per cent living alone	4.3	3.6	4.3
Per cent living with spouse only	6.7	11.6	11.9
Per cent living with a child (among elderly with at least one child)	79.7	75.4	74.2

Source: Adapted from Knodel and others (1999).

Among the important research indicators emerging from the recent work on living arrangements and ageing in Asia is the need for attention to regional variation, even within relatively small countries. For example, research in Viet Nam (Anh and others, 1997) shows a variation between the Red River Delta area — with an extreme preference for residing with married sons — and Ho Chi Minh City and its surrounding regions, where this preference was much less pronounced. In looking at these types of variation, one should always expect both context and culture to shape the reality of household formation. For example, data from the senior sample of the Second Malaysian Family Life Survey show that more than two thirds of Malaysians aged 60 or older co-reside with an adult child.[6] Analysis by Chan and DaVanzo (1994, 1996) indicates that co-residence is influenced by the opportunities and costs of co-residence versus separate living arrangements. Married seniors were found to be more likely to co-reside with adult children when housing costs were greater in their area or when an elderly spouse was in poor health. This work suggests that married parents and children live together to economize on living costs or to receive help with household services.[7]

In the same study, Chan and DaVanzo found that ethnic and cultural factors strongly influenced co-residence. Chinese and Indian seniors with at least a son and a daughter were more likely than were Malay age peers to live with adult children. Chinese elders, however, were more likely to reside with a son than with a daughter, whereas Malay and Indian elders were about equally likely to live with a child of either sex. This diversity points to two distinct family systems at work in the region. In East Asia and the northern sector of South Asia, cultures based on either Confucian, Hindu or Muslim philosophies and an authoritarian, patrilineal system stress co-residence and care by sons and their spouses. In South-East Asia and the southern zone of South Asia, Buddhist spiritual orders within a less rigid, bilateral kin system push adult daughters to play equal and sometimes more important support roles in elder care than sons (Mason, 1992).

An important variant of this second pattern occurs in Thailand where there is a decided preference for elder parents residing with daughters. This example is particularly important in showing that, despite steep drops in family size during the 1990s, the number of children in a family network has only a modest impact on an elder's chances for co-residence and support. In fact, those elders with only one or two children reported that they felt as well cared for as those with five or six (Knodel, Saengtienchai and Obiero, 1995). Focus group interviews throughout the country showed that Thai parents saw strong benefits in small families. They felt this permitted more investment in the educational future of children, resulting in increased material potential for support and even feeling that this enhanced the chance of developing a stronger sense of gratitude to bolster future caretaking.

In another part of the world, the analysis by Solis (1999) of national census data from Mexico (see table 6) for the period from 1976 to 1994 shows strong consistency in the moderately high percentage of elders residing in complex multigenerational households and a low percentage of seniors living alone. There is little comparable longitudinal data for other countries in Latin

America (Palloni, De Vos and Pelaez, 1999), although Agree's (1993) work in Brazil indicates a sharp increase in living alone, especially among unmarried older adults.

TABLE 6. LIVING ARRANGEMENTS OF THE ELDERLY IN MEXICO, 1976-1994

	1976	1987	1990	1992	1994
Solitary	6.9	5.6	7.8	8.5	7.2
No family	1.4	0.8	1.7	0.8	0.6
Simple	**39.9**	**39.0**	**41.2**	**39.2**	**39.7**
Couple only	15.6	15.5	14.4	15.6	17.2
Couple with children	19.0	18.1	20.9	18.5	16.6
Single parent with children	5.3	5.4	5.9	5.1	5.9
Complex	**51.9**	**54.6**	**49.2**	**51.5**	**52.5**
Single parent, married children and their family					
Couple, married children and their family					
Other complex[a]					
N[b]	4 118	2 568	49 345	18 853	5 159

Source: Solis (1999).

[a] "Other complex" households cover all the elderly living with at least one relative other than their spouse, children, in-laws and grandchildren.

[b] Number of households.

A factor in understanding how the situation in this region differs from that in much of Asia and Africa is that in a majority of Latin American countries, seniors are now primarily city dwellers, and within two decades it is projected that in all but a few countries, two thirds or more will live in such settings. In Mexico, both limited ethnographic information (Velez, 1978) and the analysis of Solis (1999) strongly indicate that, while there may not be a significant drop in the percentage of urban multigenerational households, there are likely to be high numbers of fluid and amalgamated family formations. This is reflected in the statistics Solis analysed for the 1990 Mexican census, which showed that of the "complex" households, the largest subcategory was "other complex", in which, with a wide variety of younger kin other than children, in-laws or grandchildren were incorporated into the home (Solis, 1999).

What can one make of this kind of stability in the face of the rapid change going on in places like India and Mexico. Martin argues that, while a shifting away from massive joint extended families can be seen, the transition from a high to a low mortality and fertility demographic picture can actually maintain a high level of multigenerational "stem" families (Martin, 1990,

p. 106). As will be seen in section V below, this is what the author has observed in his work over the past 26 years in rural Mexico.

THE MODERN URBANIZING CONTEXT OF FAMILY LIFE IN DEVELOPING COUNTRIES

Tradition unbound

The dramatic upsurge in the longevity of older citizens in third world countries is a legacy of the past two decades. This demographic change has been intertwined with powerful modernizing events. These include alterations in economic production and wealth distribution, an explosion of super-sized cities and the often violent devolution of large States into smaller successor nations. The primary model for considering the impact of major worldwide changes on the elderly has been the "modernization" theory. Third world countries are said to develop or progress as they adopt, through cultural diffusion, the modernized model of rational and efficient societal organization. While such a transformation is often viewed as an overall advance for such countries, a strong inverse relationship is suggested between the elements of modernization as an independent variable and the status of the aged as a dependent variable. Validation of this paradigm has been uneven and has spurred a small industry of gerontological writings that debate the proposed articulation of modernization and ageing (see Rhoads and Holmes, 1995, pp. 251-285, for an excellent review). Historians in particular have sharply questioned the model, saying it is not only a historical but that, by idealizing the past, an inappropriate "world we lost syndrome" has been created (Laslett, 1976; Kertzer and Laslett, 1994). For example, summing up research on the elderly living in Western Europe several hundred years ago, historian Andrejs Plakans states: "There is something like a consensus that the treatment of the old was harsh and decidedly pragmatic: dislike and suspicion, it is said, characterized the attitudes of both sides" (Plakans, 1989).

Goldstein and Beall (1981) argue that the concept of "status of the aged" must be constructed as a multidimensional variable with no necessary assumption of co-variance between the different dimensions of status. The ethnographic evidence shows that the impact of change on the elderly is quite varied and depends on such factors as gender, class, social organization of the local community and how the nation-State's political economy transfers modernizing changes into the local region.

A good example of the complexity of this issue is seen in a study of three untouchable communities in the South Tamil Nadu area of India (Vincentnathan and Vincentnathan, 1994). The authors show how in the poorest communities, the assumption of respect and high status as a prior condition does not hold. Here, the elders had no resources to pass on. Modernization programmes that included providing material resources for the elders became a new basis for binding together the young and the old. However, increased education of the young led many children and young adults to feel superior to their parents. This fostered a distinct negative change in generational relations — sometimes involving high levels of abuse and even gericide — closer to the predictions of the modernization theory.

In India, increasingly since the 1980s, there has been much public discussion of the "problem of ageing", evoked in emerging protective legislation, new gerontological societies, popular magazines, and other forms of popular culture. In the Indian State of Himachal Pradish, the Maintenance of Parents and Dependants Bill was passed in 1997 making it mandatory to provide for ageing parents. In the preface to the bill a Himachal Pradish minister proclaims: "Aged and infirm parents are now left beggared and destitute on the scrap heap of society. It has become necessary to provide compassionate and speedy remedy to alleviate their sufferings" (Lamb, forthcoming). Sarah Lamb notes that in some sectors of Indian society (especially urban areas and more prosperous rural zones) a "bad old age" is viewed as a paradigmatic sign of the evils brought by modernization, urbanization and the changing attitudes and behaviour of young women. In the West Bengal community where she lived, she heard people constantly talking about how these modern changes provoked families to break up, old people to be left alone and society in general to be undergoing a general deterioration. Working elsewhere in India during the early 1990s, a lower-caste Nagwa slum of Varanasi, Lawrence Cohen found that the problems of the elderly were discussed in quite different terms. Old-age afflictions set in the context of family conflict were perceived as neither new nor unusual (Cohen, 1998, pp. 223-248). They were blamed on the caste order, impoverishment, the debilities of old age itself and the splitting of joint families through conflict between co-resident brothers.

An urbanizing developing world

As the new millennium begins, we find, for the first time, that a majority of the world's citizens will soon be living in urban places (United Nations, 1998). Those who reside in rural zones still feel the effects of urban cultural desires, witness the outflow of those seeking city-based jobs, and experience the impact of huge portions of national resources being gobbled up by megalopolises and unpayable international debt. Incredibly, only 4 of the top 15 largest cities in the world are in developed countries; all the rest are found in countries like Mexico, India, Brazil and the Republic of South Korea. Mexico City, estimated to house more than 25 million people in its metropolitan area, looms as a dramatic example. At mid-century, Mexico was three quarters rural. Now, the same ratio of its citizens live in cities, with almost one quarter of the entire population living in Mexico City alone (World Bank, 1999). Recently, the country has endured very difficult economic times, for example, in the 1990s, when the value of wages dropped by one half. For the urban elderly, especially females, there has been increasing destitution. This is reflected in Bialik's study of 1,000 older women from Mexican cities and their high degree of impoverishment: a third had no personal income and 12 per cent earned only $5 per month (Bialik, 1992).[8] At the same time, as will be discussed below, the author's own work in an indigenous village 65 miles east of Mexico City indicates that elderly villagers and their families have, in fact, improved their quality of life by exploiting the metropolitan expansion visible from its mountain reaches.

Since the 1980s, a new residential pattern has been emerging in some third world countries as a result of rapid urbanization. For example, in Malaysia, the Philippines and South Africa, Kinsella (1988, p. 28) found that rural households were smaller and less likely than urban households to include elderly persons living with their offspring. Three quarters of urban Filipino households with one or more persons aged 60 and over had at least four members, compared with slightly more than half of similar rural households. A similar pattern was found in a recent study of the living arrangements of the aged in Viet Nam (The Cuong and others, n.d.). Two major factors linked to this unexpected variation are the greater tendency of younger rather than older adults to migrate to cities and the scarcity of urban housing.

Although strong support can be provided by children and other close relatives not living in the household, rapid out-migration can mortally disrupt the fabric of intergenerational caring and reciprocity. This can be an especially hard blow to the life satisfaction of the rural aged, who spent much of their life caring for their own aged parents in the prescribed manner and now find that they are often on their own. Rural surveys in Kenya have found that almost all respondents felt that their children did less than they had done for their parents; a large majority were experiencing severe poverty and 50 per cent of the poor attributed their condition to neglect by the immediate family (Kinsella, 1988, p. 29). Interestingly, historical research has found a similar pattern during the process of industrialization in nineteenth century New England (Gratton and Haber, 1993).

In the paper in the present volume by Yi and George, they found that there was only a modest difference between the degree of co-residence of rural versus urban elders, although among the very old men, somewhat more lived with their families in the urban zones than did their rural counterparts. Another important trend they noticed in the urban families was the growing tendency for the elderly to reside with their daughter's family. In the 1998 Health Longevity Survey, it was found that just over one fourth of the urban aged lived in this kind of arrangement compared to about 1 in 10 in the rural areas.

Generations unbound: what surveys miss

The work of Knodel and Saengtienchai (1999) in rural Thailand is instructive in demonstrating the limitations of survey instruments and the importance of a case-study approach in delineating the dynamics of intergenerational care. Indeed, among the worst mistakes policy makers can make is the assumption that the social status and well-being of elders can be inferred from the residential structure of households. Looking at four South Asian countries (India, Pakistan, Bangladesh and Sri Lanka), Linda Martin cautions not to place inordinate import on younger and older generations living together. She suggests that "status of the elderly ... appears not to be guaranteed by virtue of their co-residence with offspring. Rather, status more likely is a function of sex, health and economic resources" (Martin, 1990,

p. 110). Martin concludes that modernization itself has not dramatically altered the status of the elderly in the family; the largest factor influencing this is the control of economic assets. In another context, Ramos, in his work on the elderly in Brazil, notes that "contrary to some prevailing beliefs, it might be the elderly living in multigenerational households who will first require formal support" (Ramos, 1995, p. 6). In fact, Ramos (1992) found that elderly persons living in multigenerational households had the lowest scores for physical and mental health. This part of the population was predominantly very poor, aged and female, and had few alternatives but to live with relatives.

The consistent survey reports on the living arrangements of the elderly in East Asia must be balanced against the impact of extremely rapid industrialization, which can mimic the dislocations families suffered throughout Europe during its industrial growth in the first half of the nineteenth century. For example, in the early 1990s, Australian epidemiologist John McCallum was reviewing a programme seeking to create awareness of ageing in Indonesia, the Philippines, Singapore and Thailand. National experts from those countries consistently told him that despite rapidly increasing geographic family mobility, families were still very effective in providing for the day-to-day needs of the aged. However, contrary data were obtained when he ventured outside the information network of predominantly male public analysts and spokespersons. McCallum (1993, p. 2) gives as an example the situation in a fast-growing urban fringe settlement that provides workers for new industries at one of the research sites. The pressures of work and getting children to school were such that "a majority of families were placing their elderly early each day, sometimes with little sustenance, in an open field without shade and collecting them in the evening".

Even where the structure of the extended family persists in "traditional societies", policy makers should not harbour unqualified optimism about intergenerational kindness or the capacity of family systems to ensure the well-being of aged relatives (Levine, 1965; Nydegger, 1983). This was powerfully illustrated by the results of an anthropological study of Hindu households in Kathmandu, where 61 per cent of all aged individuals lived with at least one son. It was noted that, while the "ideal" form of the patrilineal extended family existed, not only did it give a false picture of intergenerational relations, but the material and psychological foundations of filial support were rapidly disintegrating. For example, in about 50 per cent of the households in which elders lived with married sons, the aged were essentially supporting themselves and not getting support from their resident son. The authors found it particularly ironic that, given the Hindu ideal value of depending on a male child in old age, "the most truly miserable elderly parents were the very ones who objectively were completely dependent upon a son" (Goldstein, Schuler and Ross, 1983, p. 722).

Some Asian scholars are beginning to strongly question the continued reliance on family support systems as the best cultural medium to sustain the aged. For example, Yow-Hwey Hu (1995) shows that in East Asian industrial societies such as Japan, Singapore, Taiwan Province and Hong Kong Special Administrative Region of China, the high level of three-generation families, even in urban areas, is found in conjunction with exceedingly high rates of suicide by those over age 65. The difference between East and West is particularly noteworthy for older women. Prior to their mid-40s, women in Japan and Taiwan Province kill themselves at about the same rate (11.6 and 10.4 per 100,000) as their counterparts in the United States and France (8.8 and 13.9 per 100,000). Yet, past age 65, women in Japan and Taiwan Province end their own lives at a dramatically higher rate (39.3 and 34.6) compared to the United States and France, where the level of female suicide actually drops (6.6 and 9.7). Yow-Hwey Hu also finds that there is a subtle bias in the questionnaires that such countries use in order to find continued support for elders preferring three-generation residential life. He argues that more objective questions would change the results dramatically, towards a preference for separate but nearby residences.

CASE STUDY, MEXICAN ELDERS AND FAMILIES FACE THE MILLENIUM[9]

A paradox of tradition promoting change

In 1972/73, the author conducted anthropological Ph.D. research in the central Mexican village of Amatango, about 65 miles east of Mexico City (Sokolovsky, 1995). This rural community is one of 27 pueblos (rural villages) in a municipal unit politically led by the city of Texcoco, about 12 miles away.[10] In 1972, Texcoco was a sleepy municipal capital of 25,000, but by the mid-1990s, its population had swelled to about 140,000. Its old market had acquired a wide array of electronic gear, with accompanying audio and video tapes, allowing families from Amatango to become consumers of North American-inspired global popular culture.

When the author first lived in Amatango, the village economy centred around subsistence corn farming combined with occasional wage labour, playing music in traditional fiesta bands and the sale of decorative flowers and wooden crates in Texcoco or Mexico City. Travel to Texcoco was hampered by a very rough dirt road, strewn with large boulders and often impassable to bus traffic. The roughly 2,000 villagers of Amatango, who identified themselves as *indios* (Indians), were thought to be the most ardent followers of indigenous traditions in the region. Close relatives, especially elders, were greeted by a distinctive bowing and hand-kissing gesture of respect, and they continued a regular system of communal labour and a very traditional fiesta complex of activities in which families took on time-consuming and costly responsibilities for ritually celebrating the lives of various Catholic saints. In return visits to the village in 1977/78, 1989, 1993 and 1998, it was possible to examine how household arrangements, reproductive strategies and cross-generational authority patterns have been altered in the light of dramatic modernization (Sokolovsky, 1997b). The author's work illustrates how local control over vital economic resources can become the catalyst for very traditional cultural systems to initiate modernizing change in ways that support the interests of their oldest citizens.

Today, newly installed speed bumps mildly beset the drive to Amatango on a relatively smooth, paved road. The village itself boasts satellite broadcast

179

reruns of "Bonanza", several fledgling teenage street gangs, six popular music bands, adolescents wearing "Metalica" tee-shirts, and microbuses running every 10 minutes to Texcoco. However, one can still hear and see the face of tradition holding a very tenuous sway against the hurricane winds of modern urban culture sweeping rural Mexico. It is reflected in the eyes of young children as they cautiously approach an older relative, gently bowed to plant a ritual kiss on the uplifted hand as they whisper in classic Aztec, *nocultzin* (revered grandparent). It can also be observed in the public fiesta dances, where a child of eight shares the same dance platform and ritual significance with a man or woman of 40, or even 70. So far, such symbolic acts are still embedded in familial and public domains that give ageing adults a place in their society that transcends simple platitudes such as "show respect to your elders".

What originally drew the author to study Amatango was a seeming paradox. How could its strong traditional cultural features coexist with a series of locally initiated "modernizing" changes that also made the village the most rapidly transforming of the indio communities in its region? Some changes, such as village electrification and the building of a new elementary school, had begun a few years earlier. Others were transpiring during and within five years of the author's initial research stay. These changes included construction of a passable road, a medical clinic building and a high school, plus the creation of a potable water system. Amatango was not a passive receptor of these changes, but initiated them through the collective efforts of the local civil-religious hierarchy. In doing so, it has sought to recast itself in terms of local concepts of a "civilized" place. Fortunately for the elderly, Amatango has resolved this paradox of remaining the most traditional while also being the most changing community by relying upon its most customary aspects of belief and village organization to pursue the goal of community transformation.

This was possible because of the community's continuous access to vital economic resources such as agricultural land, mountain forests and pastures, and a still functioning irrigation system that their ancestors helped build in the mid-fifteenth century. When population began to explode in the 1970s and early 1980s, villagers were able to use these resources to intensify traditional agricultural pursuits and to employ extended family labour in the production of items for urban markets. The community-wide cooperative labour system was also employed to plant and harvest communal fields, with the proceeds going to maintain the new school and other village projects.

Fortuitously, it was in the late 1960s and early 1970s that the State Government, with Mexican federal assistance, began to selectively invest in improving the rural infrastructure through electrification, road building and eventually the expansion of rural health-care services. As a start, the community combined its traditional communal labour system with State Government-provided materials and engineers to improve the irrigation system and build a small bridge over a ravine, which had been a serious obstacle to motorized vehicles entering the community. With these initial successes in the 1960s, Amatango's leaders began to petition for the other "modernizing" changes mentioned previously.

Demographic transitions

Between 1972 and 1993, the population of Amatango had almost doubled, from 2,100 to about 3,800, while the percentage of persons over age 65 remained low and unchanged, at 3.5 per cent.[11] The birth rate, averaging 9.39 per family in 1975 (Millard, 1980), had declined by more than half to about 3.5 in 1995 (estimate of local nurse). Early childhood mortality, 390 per 1,000 in 1960, had plummeted to 53.5 by 1990 (Mindek, 1994), along with a similar decline in general mortality, from 33 per 1,000 to 6.5 over the same period.

Yet, the general way elders fit into the household structure has remained quite stable. In 1973, a clear majority (60 per cent) of persons 60 years of age or older (see table 7) lived in three-generational settings, with 90 per cent of such households having no more than one married son in residence. This statistic alone does not give a true picture of family life, then or now. More often than not, at least one other married son resided in a physically independent house, a moment's walk from his elderly parents' dwelling — just across a courtyard or down a dirt path. In only four instances did aged individuals live alone. One third of the aged lived with unmarried children or other single kin, most typically a grandson. In 1993, a survey of 45 households that included a person over age 60 showed that almost two thirds were organized around extended family settings. The other living arrangements did not show significant structural alterations since the 1970s. It should be noted that in 1998 the only elder villager considered abandoned was one widower, aged 68. Even though he resided with an adult son, and two other married sons lived next door, they refused to provide any support as the father was a serious alcoholic, who had not only sold away most of the family land but had severely beaten his wife when she was alive.

Behind this strong statistical consistency lay some important changes related to the position of the elderly in Amatango's families. From the 1920s to the early 1970s, a major shift has involved the significant reduction of very large extended households, where two or more married sons stayed in the house compound to work with and eventually care for their parents. By the early 1970s, reductions in per capita land holdings and the rise of new money-making activities outside the village had stimulated a shift from "joint" to "stem" patrilineal groupings, where only one married son would remain with the parents.[12] At that time, the proportion of joint, patrilineal households with more than one married son living under the parents' domain had been reduced by about half. The more recent practice is the formation of extended households by incorporating an adult daughter's family into her parents' residence, either by themselves or along with a married son.

	Extended households		Nuclear households	
	Elderly parents with		Elderly parent(s) with unmarried children/or other kin	Living alone
	1 married son/daughter	2 married sons/daughters		
1973[a]	44 (54.3%)	5 (6.2%)	28 (34.5%)	4 (5%)
n = 81	(60.5%)			
1993[b]	25 (55.6%)	6 (13.3%)	11 (24.4%)	3 (6.7%)
n = 45	(68.8%)			

Notes: n = number of observations.
[a] Total household survey by author.
[b] Limited household survey by author.

In 1973, only two women and their families lived with parents and, in each case, their married brothers also resided with them. In 1993, five of the regular extended families were being formed with married daughters exclusively; in another four households, married daughters or single daughters with children joined their married brother in living with their elderly parents.

Despite the dominance of patrilineal descent, kinship ties generated through one's mother are also acknowledged by hand-kissing *respeto* behaviour and have great practical importance. Maternal relatives comprise a significant portion of a household's total personal network of support. It is through the exchange of labour, tangible goods and money that families are able to carry out costly and time-consuming public rituals.

"Pero cuatro es el máximo!"

The sharp drop in birth rates noted above came about when Amatango's young women adopted new reproductive strategies despite strong initial resistance from their husbands and mothers-in-law. Birth control was introduced slowly in 1983 by a locally born nurse who worked at the village clinic; by 1993, some form of birth control was used by about a third of the almost 900 women still in their reproductive years. In 1973, when young men and women were asked what the ideal family size was, the standard response was "only God knows". At that time, couples almost universally sought to have as many children as they could. By the 1990s, attitudes had changed dramatically. Almost like a Greek chorus, adults in their 20s would repeat the maxim, *"dos hijos es mejor, pero cuatro es el máximo!"* (two kids is ideal, but the maximum is four). Of the women who were practising some form of birth control, the majority would only begin after they had given birth to three or four children. This shift in reproductive behaviour was influenced by plummeting infant mortality rates, noted previously, and the rising costs of supporting children, especially in the area of education.

In the early 1970s, the emotional structure of family systems was quite authoritarian, dominated by the elder couple, especially the male. Following Aztec legal tradition, parents could take disobedient children to the community judges for punishment in the form of hard labour for the community or a fine. Several such cases were witnessed during 1973.[13] Yet, since the author's first fieldwork stay, indelible change has clearly occurred in generational dynamics. Most notable has been the reduced control of senior kin over the actions of junior relatives. For example, the last public trial for disobeying one's parents was held a decade ago. On a more subtle level, in the early 1970s, when aged parents were asked about divergence from customary behaviour, they accepted that such things were possible but adamantly insisted that the *costumbres* (traditions) would be enforced. Now, in the late 1990s, when confronted with a daughter-in-law who uses birth control or a son who prefers urban factory work to cultivating corn fields, they are likely to respond with a shrug, saying *cada quien* or "to each his own". This is strongly mediated by the fact that about 60 per cent of young adults who are living in the house of their elder parents get a majority of their income from work outside the village.

Elders in the family

Significant changes in village life have not altered the fact that the lives of the aged remain thoroughly embedded in the social matrix of surrounding households, headed by adult children, siblings and cousins. Elders are in constant contact with children, if not with a resident grandchild then with a wide range of very young kin and godchildren living within a few hundred yards.[14] As has been noted in other parts of the developing world, the child-minding aspect of grandparenting has, in fact, increased over the past decade, as in many households at least one parent is working in the city during the day.

Most marriages (about 75 per cent) take place within the village, imparting a particularly intense geographic density to the social networks of the aged, especially for males. While a woman's kin group is more physically dispersed from her abode than is a male's, this does not imply that females are more isolated in old age. In fact, owing to their greater role continuity, women past age 65 will typically maintain reciprocal support networks with more personnel and have greater frequency of exchange than their male age peers.

The public realm of ageing

Beyond the family, the most important source of prestige, respect and power during middle and old age derives from the carrying out of community rituals and civil responsibilities. In Amatango, community roles are loosely ranked, with the higher ones generally requiring more money and/or time but yielding more prestige and authority. There is an expectation that over a lifetime, men and their wives will have undertaken at least one important ritual sponsorship of a major fiesta and thereby be worthy of public esteem.[15]

To a certain degree, wealth conditions the extent of public prestige and power men and their families will garner as they age.[16] Nevertheless, virtually all older men from Catholic families carry out, at least once, the sacred burden of ritual fiesta sponsorship, which gives them lasting honour in the eyes of the community and the saints.[17] By the time most males reach age 60, even those who are relatively poor will also have shouldered at least some local political responsibility.

Besides ritual sponsorship, the fiesta system affords other opportunities to enhance public esteem in old age. All of the fiestas involve dance troops and elaborate processions. Elderly men, and to a lesser extent women can volunteer to take roles as dance leaders, instructors, special musicians or simply as participants.[18] Such activities proclaim not only moral uprightness and continuing prestige, but also that one is still actively involved in the life of the community.

Although the fiesta system performs an implicit age-grading function, it also provides one of the only community-wide arenas where males and females of all ages can participate as relative equals. This occurs in the large dance groups that perform at most fiestas as part of the community's "folk" version of Roman Catholic pageantry. Even in the case where teenagers introduced a new dance formation based on an urban model, middle-aged villagers eagerly volunteered to dress up and perform as *caballeros y caballeras* (cowboys and cowgirls). Such groups have provided the social and psychological model for the public cooperation between young adults and their elders. This was essential in developing the community consensus for initiating and accomplishing the transformation of Amatango.

Although women participate in the Masses, processions and dancing associated with each fiesta, they assume no overt public leadership position in these activities. Yet, during major public ceremonies, older women operate behind the scenes, directing the production and serving huge quantities of the special foods required for successful ritual sponsorship. In accomplishing this, they rely on, and in turn support, a wide circle of female age peers and younger women drawn from their bilateral kin network. The reciprocal flow of assistance stimulated by the annual cycle of fiestas provides a regular source of extrahousehold engagement for all but the most frail women.

Why is Amatango different?

The information gathered about the aged in Amatango seems at variance with some of the modernization theory's predicted dire consequences for the elderly. This is particularly unusual as, under similar conditions of "modernizing" change, the aged of Amatango have fared better than those in many other Latin American peasant communities studied in earlier decades. One reads, for example, that in the Colombian highland village of Aritama: "There is no room and no use for them. Old people are not respected, feared or loved. Their advice is not sought by the younger generation, nor are they thought to possess any special knowledge which might be useful" (Reichel-Dolmatoff and Reichel-Dolmatoff, 1961).

This is an extreme case but, judging from other ethnographic studies, the situation of the aged in rural communities of the region seems, unfortunately, closer to the conditions in Aritama than in Amatango. All too commonly, one finds a despairing elderly population rapidly becoming bereft of support. The elderly are caught in a demographic vacuum caused by departing young adults, and in a cultural lacunae epitomized by the withering away of fiesta systems (Kagan, 1980).

Why is the situation of the aged more favourable in Amatango? Ironically, its isolated location and the mediocre quality of its agricultural lands protected the community from severe exploitation by a landed gentry in pre-revolutionary times. Substantial land and irrigation resources were retained and eventually expanded upon in the early twentieth century. While the onset of economic pressures caused the demise of indigenous institutions and beliefs in similar villages, Amatango's economic strength helped sustain cultural features through which the aged have maintained societal value in the light of rapid change. In fact, when a rising population provoked the need for new sources of revenue and the development of village capital infrastructure, some of those very patterns of traditional life have been used to carry out ongoing economic development projects. An interesting comparison of the creative use of family and community resources to support the elderly can be made with the recent work of Alun and Phillips (1999) in rural China.

In Amatango, the familial and village niches providing roles for elder individuals have not been dramatically altered. Particularly crucial has been the vitality of the civil-religious hierarchy, which not only serves as a bulwark of indigenous identity but also provides the organizational basis for community transformation. In other Latin American peasant communities, either the total collapse of this system or the sharp separation of political and ritual components has severely limited the possibilities of maintaining public esteem in old age (Moore, 1973).

For Amatango, community solidarity bolstered by an economic base has enabled the village to transform itself largely on its own terms. This is the answer to the paradox of how the village could be both the most traditional and the most changing community in the region. While many of the aged are ambivalent about such things as the new schools, which downplay the use of the Aztec language, they are still vitally engaged in the system that brought about those changes.

CONCLUSIONS

Beginning in the 1990s, neo-liberal economists began to expand their catastrophic view of the "ageing crisis" to the global arena (Peterson, 1999). The basic argument, as put forth by the World Bank (1994) in *Averting the Old Age Crisis*, is that informal and public sector programmes are incapable of handling the impending demographic imperatives brought about by ageing in the developing world. Their stress is on allowing the private and voluntary sectors to fill the coming needs in social welfare and reducing state provision of support to only the most extreme cases of need. A presumption in such a model is that universal public pensions and other public support programmes undercut "informal", family-based systems of support for the elderly. The work of Lloyd Sherlock (1997) provides a strong critique of this perspective based on his work in Latin America. Another important examination of this issue was carried out by Briller (2000) during the mid-1990s in rural Mongolia. She showed that pensions can have a positive effect in reinforcing the pre-existing family-centred sentiments and practical support of the aged and do not "crowd out" traditional systems of filial devotion and assistance.

The reality of how living arrangements can continue to sustain elders in the developing world has been succinctly described by African sociologist Nana Apt. In a recent keynote address, she chided international donor organizations, including the United Nations, for operating in a policy void that ignores the workings of traditional welfare systems in favour of modern forms. She observed:

> It is not enough to talk about the bind of tradition, and it's not enough to talk about its disintegration. We must find ways and means of transforming it into a modern form that will make multigenerational relationships much more viable (Apt, 1998, p. 14).

It should be added that, as found in Mexico, these traditional systems will only be sustained if they blend local meaning with regionally based economic systems to give both youth and elders reason to support one another.

NOTES

[1] Parts of this chapter are adapted from the introductory materials in Sokolovsky (1997b).

[2] As at 1 January 2000, all housing construction by state industries for workers was stopped.

[3] For a comprehensive guide to comparative gerontology research up until 1994, see Nusberg and Sokolovsky (1994). There are a good number of other data sets that are now available, especially for demographic analysis in East Asia. These include: Philippine Elderly Survey, 1996; National Survey of Senior Citizens in Singapore, 1995; Survey of the Middle Aged and Elderly in Taiwan, 1996; Survey of the Welfare of the Elderly in Thailand, 1995.

[4] To date, the best academic summaries of these materials are found in two books, Old Age in Global Perspective (Albert and Cattell, 1994) and Averting the Old Age Crisis (World Bank, 1994).

[5] For a discussion of the role of grandparents in Thailand, see Hermalin, Roan, and Perez (1998).

[6] These materials are drawn from "The social and economic functioning of the elderly: highlights of program research", Rand Corporation. Available at http://info.rand.org/organization/drd/labor/Areas/elderly.html.

[7] The Government of Malaysia provides adult children with various economic incentives to have parents live with them — e.g., priority in low-cost housing. The work of DaVanzo and Chan (1994) suggests that such policies are likely to succeed

with families who need to economize on living costs: the higher housing costs are in an area, the study found, the more likely seniors and adult children are to co-reside. However, seniors who are better off economically are less likely to co-reside, a result suggesting that they value privacy and independence.

[8] For other discussion of older women in Mexico, see Robles (1987); Contreras de Lehr (1989, 1992). For a broader view of older women in Latin America, see Pan American Health Organization (1989).

[9] This discussion of ageing in a Mexican village is adapted from Sokolovsky (1997a).

[10] A *municipio* is a Mexican political subdivision similar to the American township. A *pueblo* is a politically dependent rural community. However, the *pueblos* in the *municipio* of Texcoco are comparatively independent, owning their own lands and forming distinct socio-political organizations.

[11] The 1972 figures are based on a house-to-house survey conducted by the author early in 1973; the 1993 data are based on a similar survey conducted by the local nurse who grew up in the village.

[12] In 1994, there were still some huge joint households. The two largest in the village had 24 and 22 persons, respectively, living within single-bounded house compounds, where four to six nuclear families lived under the direction of the elder parents. In both cases, the households were among the more prosperous and entrepreneurial in the village.

[13] In the most traditional families, all money earned by the sons would be given to the parents, who would then decide how best to spend the collective resources. This could be the source of simmering conflict, especially in those families where the sons started to work for salaries in factories in Texcoco or Mexico City.

[14] As in most Latin American rural communities, there is an elaborate system of personal ritual sponsorship, whereby a couple will be asked to be godparent for a specific event such as baptism or marriage. Accepting this responsibility in Amatango forges a very strong bond not only between the godparents and godchild, but also the godchild's parent who will be called *compadre* (co-parent).

[15] Since the early 1970s, the fiesta complex in Amatango has changed in two important ways. First, the number of annual celebrations has been reduced from eight to four and the number of ritual sponsorship positions from 32 to 20, eliminating low-level positions such as bell-ringers. Secondly, whereas previously each charge for a particular fiesta had a variable cost to the individual, now the expenses for a particular saint's celebration are shared equally by its ritual sponsors. This reduction in the number of fiestas is happening throughout Mexican peasant villages. In the case of Amatango, this is related to several factors. In 1992, Amatango became the centre for a new Catholic parish serving the Indian-speaking communities in the mountains and, as such, has had a parish priest residing there since that time. He has worked to concentrate on the fiestas that are least "Indian" and more connected to rituals recognized by the Catholic church. Also, during the period since the author's first fieldwork, there has been a significant increase in households practising religions other than Catholicism. In 1994, there were about 100 households practising either Protestantism or some form of spiritualist religion. Finally, with more adult men working outside the village and becoming dependent on wage labour, it has become more difficult to recruit men to take on their ritual responsibilities.

[16] Unlike other peasant areas of the world, such as rural India or Africa, where distinct class formations are completely embedded in the local social order, Amatango's rich and poor share a common ideology and lifestyle. Men from the wealthier families did not form any permanent landlord-tenant relations with poorer village members. Not

only did they all work in the typical round of agrarian tasks, but they also made an attempt to avoid giving the appearance through dramatically different clothing or house styles of being a class apart from poorer neighbours. However, during his research in the 1970s, the author showed that men from wealthier families had a significantly higher chance of being selected to the highest political posts.

[17] It should be noted that, since the 1950s, there has been a gradual growth in the number of Protestant families in the community. In 1994, at least 70 families were non-Catholic and did not participate in the fiesta system.

[18] A special honour is bestowed each year to several men over age 50 who will guide sacred processions dressed as particular saints.

REFERENCES

Agree, Emily (1993). Effects of demographic change on the living arrangements of the elderly in Brazil: 1960-1980. Durham, North Carolina: Duke University. Ph.D. dissertation.

Aguilar, Mario, ed. (1998). *The Politics of Age and Gerontocracy in Africa.* Lawrenceville, New Jersey: Africa World Press.

Albert, Stephen, and Maria Cattell (1994). *Old Age in Global Perspective: Cross-Cultural and Cross-National Views.* New York: G. K. Hall.

Alun, Joseph, and David Phillips (1999). Ageing in rural China: impacts of increasing diversity in family and community resources. *Journal of Cross-Cultural Gerontology*, vol. 14, No. 2, pp. 153-168.

Andrews, Gary, and others (1986). *Aging in the Western Pacific. A Four-Country Study.* Geneva, Switzerland: World Health Organization.

Anh, Throung S., and others (1997). Living arrangements, patrilineality and sources of support among elderly Vietnamese. *Asia-Pacific Population Journal*, vol. 12, No. 4, pp. 69-88.

Apt, Nana (1996). *Coping with Old Age in a Changing Africa.* Aldershot, United Kingdom: Avebury.

_____ (1998). Keynote address. *Bulletin on Aging*, No. 1-2, pp. 13-15.

Bialik, R. (1992). Family care of the elderly in Mexico. In *Family Care of the Elderly*, J. Kosberg, ed. Newbury Park, California: Sage.

Biswas, S. K. (1985). Dependency and family care of the aged: a case study. *Journal of the Indian Anthropological Society*, vol. 20, pp. 238-257.

Briller, Sherylyn (2000). Crowding out: an anthropological examination of an economic paradigm. Cleveland, Ohio: Case Western Reserve University. Ph.D. dissertation.

Cattell, Maria (1993). Caring for the elderly in sub-Saharan Africa. *Ageing International*, vol. 20, No. 2, pp. 13-19.

_____ (1997a). African widows, culture and social change: case studies from Kenya. In *The Cultural Context of Aging*, 2nd edition, Jay Sokolovsky, ed. Westport, Connecticut: Bergin and Garvey, pp. 71-98.

_____ (1997b). The discourse of neglect: family support for the elderly in Samia. In *African Families and the Crisis of Social Change*, Thomas Weisner, Candice Bradley and Phillip Kilbride, eds. Westport, Connecticut: Bergin and Garvey, pp. 157-183.

Chan, Angelique, and Julie DaVanzo (1996). Ethnic differences in parents' co-residence with adult children in peninsular Malaysia. *Journal of Cross-Cultural Gerontology*, vol. 11, No. 1, pp. 29-59.

Cohen, Lawrence (1998). *No Aging in India*. Berkeley, California: University of California Press.

Contreras de Lehr, E. (1989). Women and old age: status of the elderly women in Mexico. In *Mid-life and Older Women in Latin America and the Caribbean*. Washington, D. C.: Pan American Health Organization.

_____ (1992). Ageing and family support in Mexico. In *Family Support for the Elderly: the International Experience*, H. Kendig, A. Hashimoto and L. Coppard, eds. New York: Oxford University Press.

DaVanzo, Julie, and Angelique Chan (1994). Living arrangements of older Malaysians: who co-resides with their adult children? *Demography*, vol. 31, No. 1, pp. 95-113.

De Vos, Susan (1990). Extended family living among older people in six Latin American countries. *Journal of Gerontology*, vol. 45, No. 3, pp. 87-94.

_____ (forthcoming). Kinship ties and solitary living among unmarried elderly women: evidence from Chile and Mexico. *Research on Aging*.

Dreze, Jean (1990). *Widows in Rural India*. London: Development Economics Research Programme.

Foner, N. (1984). *Ages in Conflict: A Cross-Cultural Perspective on Inequality between Old and Young*. New York: Columbia University Press.

Goldstein, M., and C. Beall (1981). Modernization and aging in the third and fourth world: views from the rural hinterland in Nepal. *Human Organization*, vol. 40, No. 1, pp. 48-55.

Goldstein, M., S. Schuler and J. Ross (1983). Social and economic forces affecting intergenerational relations in extended families in a third world country: a cautionary tale from South Asia. *Journal of Gerontology*, vol. 38, No. 6, pp. 716-724.

Gratton, B., and C. Haber (1993). Rethinking industrialization: old age and the family economy. In *Voices and Visions of Aging*, T. R. Cole and others, eds. New York: Springer.

Hashimoto, Akiko (1991). Living arrangements of the aged in seven developing countries: a preliminary analysis. *Journal of Cross-Cultural Gerontology*, vol. 6, No. 4, pp. 359-382.

Hermalin, Albert I. (1995). Setting the research agenda on Latin America: lessons from Asia. *Elderly in Asia Research Report*, No. 95-33. November.

_____, Carol Roan and Aurora Perez (1998). The emerging role of grandparents in Asia. *Elderly in Asia Research Report*, No. 98-52. Available at www.psc.lsa.umich.edu/pubs.

Hu, Yow-Hwey (1995). Elderly suicide risk in family contexts: a critique of the Asian family care model. *Journal of Cross-Cultural Gerontology*, vol. 10, No. 3, pp. 199-217.

Hugo, G. J. (1985). Population aging: some demographics in developing countries. Paper presented at the thirteenth Congress of the International Association on Gerontology, New York.

Ikels, Charlotte, and Cynthia Beall (1993). Settling accounts: the intergenerational contract in an age of reform. In *Chinese Families in the Post-Mao Era*, Deborah David and Stevan Harrell, eds. Berkeley: University of California Press.

_____ (forthcoming). Age, aging and anthropology, *Handbook of Aging and the Social Sciences*, fifth edition, Robert Binstock and Linda George, eds. San Diego, California: Academic Press.

Kagan, D. (1980). Activity and aging in a Colombian peasant village. In *Aging in Culture and Society*, Christine Fry, ed. New York: Bergin.

Kalache, Alexandre (1995). Migration and aging. *World Health*, vol. 48, No. 6, pp. 23-24.

Keith, Jennie, and others (1994). *The Aging Experience: Diversity and Commonality Across Cultures.* Thousand Oaks, California: Sage.

Kendig, Hal, Akiko Hashimoto and Larry Coppard, eds. (1992). *Family Support for the Elderly: The International Experience.* New York: Oxford University Press.

Kertzer, D., and P. Laslett, eds. (1994). *Demography, Society and Age.* Berkeley: University of California Press.

Kinsella, Kevin (1988). Aging in the Third World. Staff paper, No. 35. Washington, D.C.: United States Bureau of the Census, Center for International Research.

_____ (1997). The demography of an aging world. In *The Cultural Context of Aging*, 2nd edition, Jay Sokolovsky, ed. Westport, Connecticut: Bergin and Garvey, pp. 17-33.

Kinsella, Kevin, and Y. Gist (1995). *Older Workers, Retirement, and Pensions: A Comparative International Chartbook.* Washington, D.C.: United States Bureau of the Census.

Knodel, John, Chanpen Saengtienchai and Walter Obiero (1995). Do small families jeopardize old-age security? Evidence from Thailand. *Bold*, vol. 5, No. 4, pp. 15-19.

Knodel, John, and Chanpen Saengtienchai (1999). Studying living arrangements of the elderly: lessons from a quasi-qualitative case study approach in Thailand. *Journal of Cross-Cultural Gerontology*, vol. 14, No. 3, pp. 197-220.

Knodel, John, and others (1999). Aging in Thailand: an overview of formal and informal support. *Elderly in Asia Research Report*, No. 99-53. January.

Kolenda, Pauline (1987). *Regional Differences in Family Structure in India.* Jaipur: Rawat Publications.

Lamb, Sarah (2000). *White Saris and Sweet Mangoes: Aging, Gender, and Body in North India.* Berkeley: University of California Press.

_____ (forthcoming). Aging, gender and widowhood: perspectives from rural West Bengal. *Contributions in Indian Sociology*, vol. 33, No. 3, pp. 541-570.

Laslett, P. (1976). Social development and aging. In *Handbook of Aging and the Social Sciences*, R. Binstock and E. Shanas, eds. New York: Van Nostrand Reinhold.

Lee, Yean-Ju, and Zhenya Xiao (1998). Children's support for elderly parents in urban and rural China. *Journal of Cross-Cultural Gerontology*, vol. 13, No. 1, pp. 39-62.

Levine, R. (1965). Intergenerational tensions and extended family structures in Africa. In *Social Structure and the Family*, Ethel Shanas and Gordon Strieb, eds. Englewood Cliffs, New Jersey: Prentice-Hall.

Lloyd-Sherlock, Peter (1997). *Old Age and Urban Poverty in the Developing World.* New York: St. Martin's Press.

Martin, Linda (1990). The status of South Asia's growing elderly population. *Journal of Cross-Cultural Gerontology*, vol. 5, No. 2, pp. 93-117.

Mason, Karen (1992). Family change and support for the elderly in Thailand: what do we know? *Asia Pacific Population Journal*, vol. 7, No. 3, pp. 13-32.

McCallum, J. (1993). Foreword: "De-constructing" family care policy for the elderly: a note. *Journal of Aging and Social Policy*, vol. 5, No. 1/2, pp. 1-5.

190

Millard, A. (1980). Corn, cash and population genetics: family demography in Rural Mexico. Austin: University of Texas. Ph.D. dissertation.

Mindek, D. (1994). *"No nos sobra, pero gracias a Dios, tampoco nos falta." Crecimiento Demográphico y Modernización en San Jerónimo Amanalco*. Mexico City: Iberoaméricana University. Master's thesis.

Moore, A. (1973). *Life Cycles in Atchalan*. New York: Teachers College Press.

Nusberg, Charlotte, and Jay Sokolovsky, eds. (1994). *The International Directory of Research and Researchers in Comparative Gerontology*. Washington, D.C.: American Association of Retired Persons.

Nydegger, Corinne (1983). Family ties of the aged in cross-cultural perspective. *The Gerontologist*, vol. 23, No. 1, pp. 26-32.

Ofstedal, Mary Beth, John Knodel and Napaporn Chayovan (1999). Intergenerational support and gender: a comparison of four Asian countries. *Elderly in Asia Research Report*, No. 99-54.

Okharedia, Akhabue (1999). A sociological survey of the socio-economic dilemma of the aged in less developed countries. *Ageing International* (summer), pp. 17-30.

Palloni, Alberto, Susan De Vos and Martha Pelaez (1999). Aging in Latin America. Madison: University of Wisconsin, Center for Demography and Ecology. Working paper 99-02.

Pan American Health Organization (1989). *Mid-life and Older Women in Latin America and the Caribbean*. Washington, D. C.

Peil, M. (1985). Old age in West Africa: social support and quality of life. In *Aging in Developing Societies: A Reader in Third World Gerontology*, John Morgan, ed. Bristol, Indiana: Wyndham Hall, pp. 1-22.

Peterson, Peter (1999). Gray dawn: the global aging crisis. *Foreign Affairs*, vol. 78, No. 1, pp. 42-55.

Plakans, A. (1989). Stepping down in former times: a comparative assessment of retirement in traditional Europe. In *Age Structuring in Comparative Perspective*, D. Kertzer and K. W. Schaie, eds. Hillsdale, New Jersey: Lawrence Erlbaum.

Putnam-Dickerson, Jeanette, and Judith Brown (1998). Women among women: Anthropological Perspectives on Female Age-Hierarchies. Champaign, Illinois: University of Illinois Press.

Ramos, Luis (1992). Family support for old people in São Paulo, Brazil. In *Family Support for the Elderly: the International Experience*, H. Kendig, A. Hashimoto and L. Coppard, eds. New York: Oxford University Press.

_____ (1995). The elderly and the family in developing countries. *Bold*, vol. 5, No. 2, pp. 2-5.

Reichel-Dolmatoff, G., and A. Reichel-Dolmatoff (1961). *The People of Aritama*. Chicago, Illinois: University of Chicago Press.

Rhoads, E., and L. D. Holmes (1995). *Other Cultures, Elder Years*, 2nd edition. Thousand Oaks, California: Sage.

Robles, S. (1987). Widowhood in Los Robles: parent-child relations and economic survival in old age in urban Mexico. *Journal of Cross-Cultural Gerontology*, vol. 1, No. 3, pp. 223-237.

Rosenberg, Harriet (1997). Complaint discourse, aging and caregiving among the Ju'hoansi of Botswana. In *The Cultural Context of Aging*, 2nd edition, Jay Sokolovsky, ed. Westport, Connecticut: Bergin and Garvey, pp. 33-55.

Simmons, L. (1945). *The Role of the Aged in Primitive Society*. New Haven, Connecticut: Archon Books.

Siriboon, Siriwan, and John Knodel (1994). Thai elderly who do not co-reside with their children. *Journal of Cross-Cultural Gerontology*, vol. 9, No. 1, pp. 21-38.

Sokolovsky, J. (1995). *San Jerónimo Amanalco: un Pueblo Indígena en Transición*. Mexico City: Iberoaméricana University Press.

_____ (1997a). Aging, families and community development in an indigenous Mexican community. In *The Cultural Context of Aging: World-Wide Perspectives*, 2nd edition. Westport, Connecticut: Bergin and Garvey, pp. 191-217.

_____ (1997b). *The Cultural Context of Aging: World-Wide Perspectives*, 2nd edition. Westport, Connecticut: Bergin and Garvey.

Solís, Patricio (1999). Living arrangements of the elderly in Mexico. Paper presented at the meeting of the Population Association of America. New York City.

The Cuong, Bui, and others (n.d.). Vietnamese elderly amidst transformations. *Social Welfare Policy Report*, No. 99-436. Ann Arbor: University of Michigan, Population Studies Center.

United Nations (1998). *The State of World Population, 1998: The New Generations*. New York: United Nations Population Fund.

_____ (1999a). *Population Ageing, 1999*. Sales No. E.99.XIII.11.

_____ (1999b). The demographic impact of HIV/AIDS. Report of the Technical Meeting, New York, 10 November 1998. Department of Economic and Social Affairs, Population Division. ESA/P/WP.152.

van Willigen, John, and Narender Chadha (1999). *Social Aging in a Delhi Neighborhood*. Westport, Connecticut: Greenwood.

Vatuk, Sylvia (1990). To be a burden on others: dependency anxiety among the elderly in India. In *Divine Passions: The Social Construction of Emotion in India*, Owen Lynch, ed. Berkeley: University of California Press, pp. 64-88.

_____ (1996). Migration and the elderly in developing countries. In *Meeting the Challenges of Ageing Population in the Developing World*, James Calleja, ed. Proceedings of an experts' group meeting, 23-25 October 1995.

Velez, Carlos (1978). Youth and aging in Central Mexico. In *Life's Career Aging*, Barbara Myerhoff and Andre Simic, eds. Beverly Hills, California: Sage, pp. 107-162.

Vincentnathan, S. G., and Lynn Vincentnathan (1994). Equality and hierarchy in untouchable intergenerational relations and conflict resolutions. *Journal of Cross-Cultural Gerontology*, vol. 9, No. 1, pp. 1-19.

Weisner, Thomas (1997). Support for children and the African family crisis. In *African Families and the Crisis of Social Change*, Candice Bradley and Phillip Kilbride, eds. Westport, Connecticut: Bergin and Garvey, pp. 20-44.

World Bank (1994). *Averting the Old Age Crisis*. New York: Oxford University Press.

_____ (1999). *Entering the 21st Century: World Development Report 1999-2000*. Washington, D.C. Available at www.worldbank.org/wdr/2000/fullreport.html.

LIVING ARRANGEMENTS OF OLDER PERSONS AND FAMILY SUPPORT IN MORE DEVELOPED COUNTRIES

*Jenny de Jong Gierveld, Helga de Valk and Marieke Blommesteijn**

INTRODUCTION

Promoting an age-integrated society that encourages the participation of older persons is one of the main elements of the set of recommendations on Ageing for the Year 2001 as proposed by the United Nations General Assembly. In the present paper, two important avenues to social integration of older persons[1] will be addressed, namely, living arrangements, that is, the composition of the households in which older persons live, and familial embeddedness, more in particular the familial support given and received by older women and men, respectively. The two are directly and reciprocally interrelated: living arrangements, in particular the relationships available within the household, are of crucial importance as determinants of older adults' financial and social situation, the social support arrangements available to them, and the realized level of well-being or loneliness.

Life expectancy continues to increase throughout the world, with top-scoring countries in the European region, Japan, the United States of America and Canada. This increase in life expectancy and the falling birth rate underlie the sharp increase in the number and percentages of persons in the older age brackets. Even more noteworthy is the rate of growth of people aged 80 and over, so-called "double ageing", with an over-representation of older women over older men. According to Myers (1986), the increase in life expectancy, for those in first marriage, results in a longer duration of the partner bond through "ageing together". However, for those individuals who are confronted with a break-up of their partner relationship (either by widowhood or divorce), it may mean very long periods of absence of a partner relationship. Some of the ever-widowed and ever-divorced remarry; many do not. It is well known from country statistics that the probability of remarriage is strongly related to — among other things — sex (women have a higher risk of not remarrying than do men) and age (older persons have a smaller chance of remarrying than do younger people) (Bumpass, Sweet and Martin, 1990). Consequently, living arrangements in later life differ strongly between women and men. In all age

* Netherlands Interdisciplinary Demographic Institute, The Hague, Netherlands.

categories, widowed and divorced women outnumber widowed and divorced men. And, especially at ages above 70, widowed women outnumber married women in many countries.

In investigating the living arrangements as realized in later life, one needs to keep in mind that characteristics of household composition at this time are directly related to the life histories of older persons, including, above all, their marital and partner histories. The marital status characteristics of older adults have undergone constant change since the first half of the century. New cohorts of older persons have dramatically different marital and partner histories that set them apart from previous generations. Thus, heterogeneity and growing complexity is introduced in the spectrum of marital and partner experiences: marriage and remarriage, cohabitation and, perhaps, a "living apart but together" (LAT) relationship — having a partner outside the household — alternated with periods of living alone or as a lone parent with children. These changes in marital histories are reflected in changing living arrangements. On the one hand, households incorporating other family members or non-family members are on the decline. On the other hand, besides living as a couple with children, the periods lived as a couple without children, or as a person alone, may alternate during the course of people's lives.

Older person's types of living arrangements and the familial support given and received will also be affected by country-based differences in socio-structural opportunities. The economic and financial situation, standard of living, and quality of social security and health care systems affect the opportunities and restrictions experienced by older persons in their efforts to realize independence and well-being in later life. Whether support is available when deteriorating health makes help necessary is another important factor that sets apart older inhabitants of different countries. These country differences are based on varying attitudes and good practices towards informal support provided by children and other family members, or by the community.

In the present paper, the living arrangements of older persons will be addressed, taking into account a selection of factors behind the total array of heterogeneity. We shall first look into sex, age groups and marital status. Then, regional differences in Europe will be dealt with.

Data for this study are from the database of the Dynamics of Ageing project, initiated and executed by the Population Activities Unit of the Economic Commission for Europe in Geneva. The data consist of cross-nationally comparable microdata samples based on the 1990 round of population and housing censuses in countries of Europe and North America. In the present paper, data about the following countries will be presented: Finland, representing the Northern European countries; the United Kingdom of Great Britain and Northern Ireland, as a representative of the Western European countries; Italy as a representative of Southern Europe; and Hungary, as a representative of the European countries in transition.[2]

An in-depth investigation of the major national differences in living arrangements and familial support of older adults needs to focus on a large set of determinants behind the country-specific outcomes. In the context of this study, we will briefly indicate some of these factors.

There are major differences in attitudes and beliefs about marriage (versus unmarried cohabitation and living alone as a never-married person) and marriage dissolution (especially as far as social acceptance of divorce is concerned). These differences, together with gender-specific discrepancies in life expectancy, affect the patterns of marital status as realized by older persons. Life expectancies at birth differ significantly for men and women in the four countries studied here; women live an additional 7.7 years in Finland, 5.4 years in the United Kingdom, 6.5 years in Italy and 9.1 years in Hungary (United Nations, 1999).

Older person's financial possibilities and the quality of housing (basic housing as well as specific equipment for physically handicapped older persons) are directly related to and part of the very different national systems of social security, including prevailing ideas and practices with regard to old-age pension schemes. There are major differences in the welfare state, both in ideas about its functioning for public support and in the institutional arrangements available to older persons in need of care. The welfare systems of the Scandinavian countries, including Finland, can be characterized as driven by generous rights to social security and wide acceptance of community solidarity. This is in contrast to the situation in the United Kingdom, with minor rights to social security and less solidarity. The situation in Italy is described as a moderate system of social security and solidarity (Esping-Andersen, 1990). Countries in Central and Eastern Europe have until now not been included in welfare systems research.

When investigating determinants of differences in living arrangements, one needs to take into account a complex set of interrelated fields, such as marital situation and marital history, the availability of living children, the housing market situation, educational level, labour market history and level of income (and/or pension), age, health and, last but not least, gender-based differences in opportunities and restrictions with respect to realizing one's preferences and intentions in the field of living arrangements and social embeddedness.

We shall first discuss the marital status characteristics of older persons. We then address living arrangements and related guarantees for familial support, and, finally, social embeddedness and familial support outside the household.

MARITAL STATUS OF OLDER PERSONS

Facts

Data about the marital status of older men and women are provided in table 1.

TABLE 1. MARITAL STATUS OF PERSONS AGED 50 AND OVER ACCORDING TO AGE AND SEX, IN PERCENTAGES

Age	Never-married men				Never-married women			
	Finland	United Kingdom	Italy	Hungary	Finland	United Kingdom	Italy	Hungary
50-54	13	8	9	5	9	4	7	3
55-59	12	8	8	4	10	5	8	3
60-64	11	8	8	3	10	6	9	4
65-69	9	8	8	3	11	7	10	4
70-74	7	7	7	2	11	7	10	5
75-79	6	6	6	3	12	8	10	5
80-84	6	6	6	3	14	11	11	6
85+	6	5	5	3	17	12	11	6

Age	Married men				Married women			
	Finland	United Kingdom	Italy	Hungary	Finland	United Kingdom	Italy	Hungary
50-54	73	82	87	83	70	80	82	73
55-59	75	83	87	85	66	76	76	67
60-64	76	82	86	84	59	70	67	59
65-69	77	79	84	83	49	59	57	47
70-74	76	77	81	79	36	47	44	33
75-79	70	71	75	71	24	33	30	22
80-84	60	62	66	59	14	21	19	12
85+	42	47	49	41	6	12	9	4

Age	Widowed men				Widowed women			
	Finland	United Kingdom	Italy	Hungary	Finland	United Kingdom	Italy	Hungary
50-54	1	2	1	3	7	6	8	13
55-59	2	3	3	4	12	10	14	20
60-64	4	5	4	7	20	18	22	30
65-69	7	9	7	10	32	29	31	43
70-74	12	14	10	15	46	43	45	57
75-79	20	21	18	24	58	57	60	69
80-84	31	31	27	36	66	66	69	80
85+	49	47	45	55	73	76	80	88

Age	Divorced/separated men				Divorced/separated women			
	Fin-land	United Kingdom	Italy	Hun-gary	Fin-land	United Kingdom	Italy	Hun-gary
50-54	13	8	3	9	14	10	3	10
55-59	11	7	2	7	12	8	3	9
60-64	9	5	2	6	10	6	2	8
65-69	7	4	2	4	8	5	2	6
70-74	5	3	1	3	7	4	1	5
75-79	4	2	1	2	6	3	1	4
80-84	3	2	1	2	5	2	1	3
85+	3	1	1	1	4	1	1	2

Source: Collection of census-based microdata samples of the Population Activities Unit of the Economic Commission for Europe: Finland, 1990 census; United Kingdom, 1991 census; Italy, 1991 census; Hungary, 1990 census.

The distribution of marital status characteristics over the elderly population is directly related to the nuptiality patterns of the populations under study. "What percentage of the population has ever been married?" is one of the crucial questions in this context. For men, table 1 indicates a more or less stable percentage of never-married as far as the older age groups are concerned, followed, especially in Finland and to a lesser extent in the United Kingdom and Italy, by a remarkably higher percentage among the younger elderly. The data in table 1 show that the proportions of never-married women in the oldest age groups are significantly higher than in the young old age groups, indicating that for each of these countries the ultimate proportions of never-married women at age 50 and above will be lower in the future.

Divorce and separation is also found among older persons, especially among the younger old. The percentages are highest in Finland, followed by Hungary and the United Kingdom. In these three countries, the percentages by age category are higher for women than for men, indicating differences in remarriage patterns for divorced men and women.

Most important, however, is the striking difference between older men and older women in the proportion married versus the proportion widowed. By far the majority of older men are still married, while the majority of older women are widowed.

Explanations for differences in marital status

Period changes

We will first address differences in the characteristics of successive cohorts entering the population of older adults. In the field of European demography, changing behavioural patterns, including marital status patterns, have been studied using the concepts of the first and second demographic transition (Van de Kaa, 1987, 1994). Central to the ideas of the second demographic transition is the paradigm that the replacement of older norms, values and behavioural patterns by new ones is caused and supported by in-depth socio-structural, socio-cultural and technical changes that are taking place at the broader national and international levels. The multiple set of causes includes economic growth, an improved standard of living, better quality of social security and health-care systems, a rise in female educational levels and female labour force participation, and cultural changes such as secularization, the shift towards individualization, and post-materialism (Van de Kaa, 1987, 1994; Lesthaeghe and Surkyn, 1988). Incorporated in the concept of the second demographic transition are the differences between regions and countries in their pace of accepting and realizing new behavioural patterns. In this respect, according to Van de Kaa (1987), the Northern European countries are at the forefront of the process, followed directly by the Western European countries. The second group, with a time lag, are countries in Southern Europe, the third group is the Eastern European cluster, and Ireland and Iceland trail behind. Research into these regional European patterns has focused on changes in fertility patterns and family formation, including divorce patterns (Bosveld, 1996). Empirical research concentrates on persons between about 18 and 48 years of age. Research into the acceptance of, and participation in, new behavioural patterns among persons aged 48 and over is, de facto, absent. Now that younger cohorts, raised and educated in the 1960s, are entering the ages of 50 and above, new norms and behavioural patterns are taking shape among younger cohorts of older persons. The relatively large proportion of men who never married in the younger old age groups (see table 1) is thought to be a result of the trend away from marriage and towards long-term, lifelong variations of unmarried cohabitation. The same conclusion can be drawn for the higher percentages of divorced men and women, a phenomenon affected by increased divorce rates among the youngest cohorts entering older ages. In the near future, the proportion of divorced elderly is expected to rise tremendously as this phenomenon, which is widespread among the middle age groups (40-49 years) in Finland, Hungary and the United Kingdom, will reach the elderly population, the more so because remarriage rates do not appear to be keeping pace with divorce rates.

Transitions in marital status among older persons

The transition from marriage to widowhood is one that is broadly expected to happen in this phase of life. However, the age at which the transition is experienced is rising rapidly, more or less parallel to the rise in life expectancy. "Many of the present oldest old never expected to reach their current age, because when they started life's journey early in this century, interrupted lives and broken ties were common, due to infectious disease, famine, and life's dangers. The changes in survival patterns have been so rapid that they have created 'surprised survivors'" (Hagestad, 1998). The percentage of older persons experiencing the transition from married status to divorced status after the age of 50 is low, but still on the rise (Cooney, 1993). Older women, especially wives in dual-career marriages, are well aware of the negative implications of retirement on marital relationships. They foresee implications for emotional harmony, for balance of power and for the maintenance of their own personal space and independence in the home (Hilbourne, 1999).

Selective mortality at older ages

The excess mortality rates of men, at younger and at older ages, is resulting in lower absolute numbers of men and higher absolute numbers of women for each of the 50-and-over age categories in each of the countries under study. As a result, ageing is a female experience. And ageing as a female experience differs significantly from ageing as a male experience. This is apparent first and foremost in the economic and financial domains of life, as well as in the area of social participation in intimate relationships and in the community, more particularly after becoming widowed.

Trends in several Western European countries indicate a decrease in differences in gender-specific life expectancies, in contrast to the situation in Hungary and other countries in transition. This trend will affect the percentage of couples ageing together.

Thus, in conclusion, in the first half of the twentieth century, older cohorts of men and women and their life courses could still fruitfully be described by referring to the "standard biography" or "semi-standard biography". This biography consisted of leaving the parental home to marry (or followed by marriage), followed by the birth of the first child. Included in these standard biographies is the unwritten rule that women have the primary responsibility for taking care of the children and the household. Parents stayed together until death. Usually, the widower remarried, while the widow continued life as a widow living with her children or in a one-person household. This situation has changed remarkably. Instead of standard biographies, more and more adults realize a so-called choice biography (Beck and Beck-Gernsheim, 1996). Transitions no longer follow a strict sequence; a large variety of pathways through the life course are possible, and are followed. Reconsidering transitions of the past and returning to former positions is now accepted. Starting the life course with unmarried cohabitation, followed by marriage, followed by divorce, living alone or as a parent without a partner, followed by unmarried cohabitation with another partner is broadly accepted.

Consequently, investigating the current marital status of older persons provides no more than a partial picture. Those currently married include, for example, older adults in first marriage, as well as men and women involved in a second or higher number of marriages after widowhood or divorce. The effects of different partner histories on the financial and social resources and the well-being of currently married older persons have to be taken into account (Peters and Liefbroer, 1997). Information about marital history and, preferably, also about partner history (including periods of unmarried cohabitation), is urgently needed to fully understand the life courses of older men and women who today face an extension of their lives.

LIVING ARRANGEMENTS OF OLDER PERSONS AND RELATED GUARANTEES FOR FAMILIAL SUPPORT

Facts

Living arrangements are of crucial importance as determinants of the social and financial position of older adults, the social support arrangements available to them, and the realized level of well-being. As a result of the transitions that have already taken place in their long lives — with or without explicit decision-making — heterogeneity and growing complexity are introduced in the marital histories of older persons, and also in their living arrangements. Investigating the household situation could, in the past, comfortably start with the registration of the marital status of the couple, as the core persons, adding the characteristics of other persons who happened to be in the household, such as children, other family members, servants or lodgers. Investigating the marital status of older adult persons as the basic characteristic of households is no longer sufficient or adequate when addressing the determinants and outcomes of household types and family relationships. However, in the absence of detailed information about partner and marital histories in census data, we have to use the current marital status position as the first determinant of differences in living arrangements.

Figures I to IV provide information about living arrangements by age category and country, subdivided for married, widowed and divorced men and women.

The data for married men indicate a high percentage living with a spouse and without others in each of the four countries. Even in the oldest age categories, living with a spouse and without others is the most characteristic living arrangement of older married men. Going from the younger towards the older age groups, living with a spouse and young adult children decreases and is replaced — to a certain extent — by co-residence with adult children. Living with one's spouse, children and grandchildren is uncommon in the United Kingdom, but more prominent in the other countries, especially in Italy and Hungary. Insofar as older women are still married, their living arrangements — to a large extent — resemble those of their spouses. There is one exception: in the oldest age groups, married women more frequently live alone than do married men, especially in the United Kingdom. This might be related to the institutionalization or hospitalization of their spouses.

A large proportion of the older population consists of widows. Figures I to IV provide information about their living arrangements. Among widows, the proportions living alone are highest in Finland and the United Kingdom, considerably lower in Italy, and much lower in Hungary. This is in line with the ideas of the second demographic transition, namely, that living alone as an indicator of individualistic living arrangements will become more and more prominent, starting in the Northern and Western European countries, followed by the Southern European countries. In Finland, older widows, for the most part, continue living alone until the age of 85 and over. In the United Kingdom and in Italy, a decrease in living alone is registered for those aged 85 and over and 75 and over, respectively. The proportion of older widows living alone in

Hungary lags behind those in other countries, gradually decreasing from the age category 70-74 years. Nevertheless, living alone is the most common living arrangement among older widows in each of the four countries. During the second half of the twentieth century, a dramatic increase in the proportions of the widowed population living alone across the more highly developed world has been documented (de Jong Gierveld and van Solinge, 1995; Cherlin, 1983; Clarke and Neidert, 1992; Spitze, Logan and Robinson, 1992).

Living in a two- or three-generation household without others, that is, living with children and/or children-in-law, grandchildren, parents and/or parents-in-law, is common among older widows too. Going from younger to older age groups, living with children first decreases as a result of the nest-leaving process and is replaced by co-residence of older widows with their adult children (and grandchildren). The latter phenomenon is particularly common in Hungary and Italy. In Hungary, and to a lesser extent in Finland, living arrangements of "one generation with others", for example, with a lifelong acquaintance, is also found among widows. For older women, being widowed means either that they live alone (the most widespread living arrangement among older women in Western and Northern Europe) or that they co-reside with their children (and, perhaps, also a parent or grandchildren).

The living arrangements of widowers aged 50 and over in the United Kingdom, Finland and Italy closely resemble those of their female peers. The same parallel is found between the living arrangements of widows and widowers in Hungary, with the following exception: older widows more frequently live as "one generation with others", while older men live both as "one generation with others" and as "one generation without others", the latter indicating living together, for example, with sisters and/or brothers.

In describing the living arrangements of older divorced men, a number of specific characteristics stand out. First, the living arrangements of "one generation with others" and "one generation without others" are more frequently found among divorced men than among divorced women in Finland, the United Kingdom and Italy. Co-residence in two- or three-generation households without others, that is with children (and/or a parent and grandchildren), is significantly less common among divorced men than among divorced women. Living alone is less widespread among older divorced men than among divorced women in Finland, but is more frequently reported by divorced men than by women in Italy and Hungary.

Older divorced women tend to live alone. The proportion of those living alone in Finland is even somewhat higher than among older widows, especially among the oldest old. In contrast, the proportion living in two- or three-generation households, that is, with children (and/or a parent and grandchildren), is lower than among widows in the same age groups.

Figure I. Living arrangements by age category and marital status, Finland, 1990

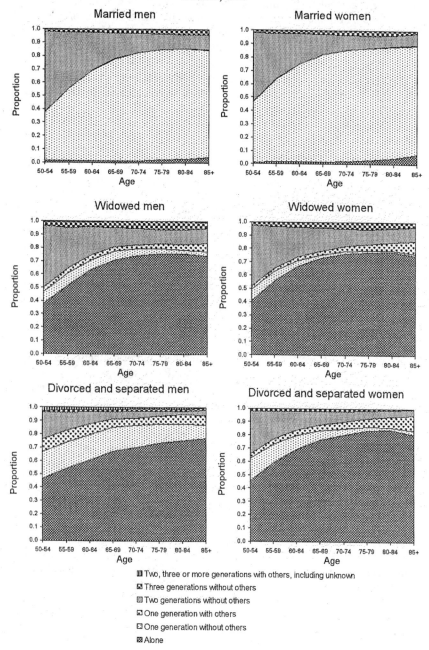

Source: PAU collection of census-based microdata samples.

Figure II. Living arrangements by age category and marital status, United Kingdom, 1991

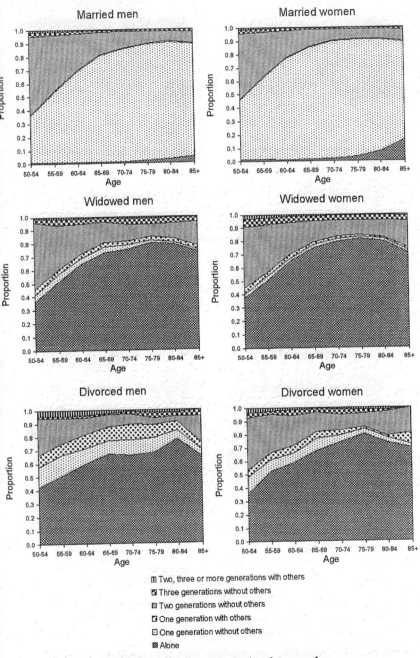

Married men

Married women

Widowed men

Widowed women

Divorced men

Divorced women

⊞ Two, three or more generations with others

▨ Three generations without others

▦ Two generations without others

◨ One generation with others

☐ One generation without others

▩ Alone

Source: PAU collection of census-based microdata samples.

Figure III. Living arrangements by age category and marital status, Italy, 1991

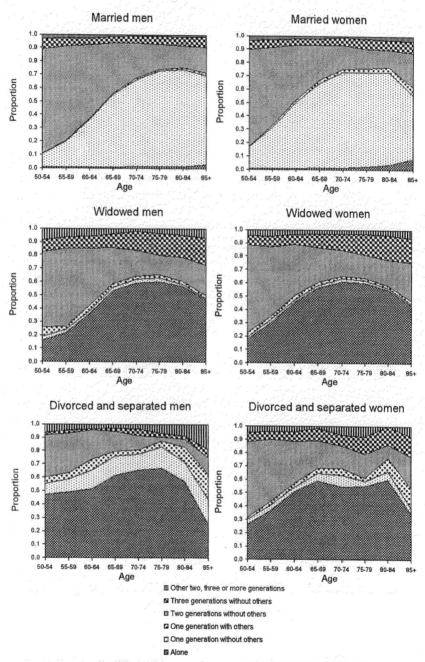

Source: PAU collection of census-based microdata samples.

Figure IV. Living arrangements by age category and marital status, Hungary, 1990

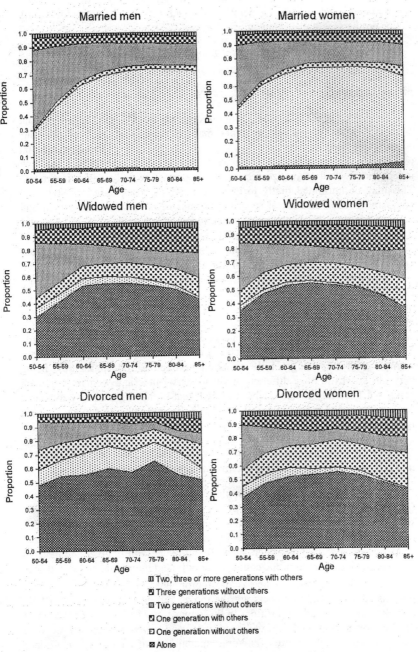

Two, three or more generations with others
Three generations without others
Two generations without others
One generation with others
One generation without others
Alone

Source: PAU collection of census-based microdata samples.

Furthermore, in Finland, the United Kingdom, Italy and Hungary, the proportion of older divorced women in "one generation with others", indicating, for example, unmarried cohabitation or living with a lifelong acquaintance, and in "one generation without others" (living with sisters and/or brothers) is higher than among widows.

Living arrangements of older people and related guarantees for familial support

Living as a couple and reciprocal support

Living together as a couple without others is the living arrangement that is most frequently realized by older married persons in each of the four countries studied (see figures I-IV). It is also the living arrangement that provides older men and women with the greatest possibilities to live independently and to realize reciprocal support on a daily basis, if needed. This may be attributed firstly to their financial situation, based on state and company pension and social security schemes of at least a male person and perhaps additionally of women's past earnings, which tends to be much better than the situation of those living alone, especially women. If household incomes allow, paid helpers to clean the house, wash clothes and dishes, and perhaps cook meals are an option for those who wish to continue living independently. Secondly, one's spouse can and will serve as the optimal long-term provider of emotional as well as instrumental support. Nearly all husbands and three quarters of the wives rely on their spouses (Kendig and others, 1999). Spouses have the proximity, the long-term commitment and the similarity of interests and values that underlie this type of support (Dykstra, 1993). Now that older men are much more likely to be married than are older women, with surprisingly little variation between European regions, being very old proves to have different implications for men and women. For men, being old generally means being attached, that is, having a spouse available for assistance and care. For women, it generally means being spouseless, that is having to turn to others when they are no longer able to cope by themselves.

Living — with or without a spouse — with children (and/or grandchildren and parents): co-residence and reciprocal support

The microdata set of the Population Activities Unit of the Economic Commission for Europe allows us to reliably compare the co-residence situation of older persons in the four countries under study. Assuming that persons aged 69 and under are generally not frail or totally support-dependent, our focus is on men and women aged 70 and over. Table 2 gives the patterns of co-residence for each of the countries, subdivided by marital status and sex.

As expected, co-residence is most prominent under formerly married persons. Widows and widowers are the top scorers in this respect, with Italy and Hungary in a leading position. In these two countries, 30 per cent or more of the non-institutionalized widowed men and women aged 70 or over co-reside with their children (and/or grandchildren and parents). In Finland and the United Kingdom, the percentages are significantly lower, in line with the idea of the second demographic transition that traditional patterns of living arrangements will be less prominent in the Northern and Western European countries.

TABLE 2. PERSONS AGED 70 AND OVER LIVING IN TWO- OR
THREE-GENERATION HOUSEHOLDS WITHOUT OTHERS,[a]
BY SEX AND MARITAL STATUS, IN PERCENTAGES OF
NON-INSTITUTIONALIZED POPULATION

	Finland 1990	United Kingdom 1991	Italy 1991	Hungary 1990
Males				
Married	15.9	11.4	27.1	21.8
Widowed	16.8	16.6	35.1	29.8
Divorced	6.1	9.7	11.8	12.6
Females				
Married	13.4	8.9	23.1	20.7
Widowed	16.2	17.3	36.4	30.8
Divorced	7.9	15.5	27.7	20.3

Source: PAU collection of census-based microdata samples.

[a] Households including spouse and/or children, children-in-law, grandchildren, parents, parents-in-law.

Divorced and widowed parents are treated differently. The children of divorced parents appear to be less frequently involved in co-residence with their parents than are the children of widows and widowers. The risk of not being involved in co-residence with children is highest for divorced fathers, followed by divorced mothers, aged 70 or over. These differences may be explained by the better health situation of divorced parents, who tend to be somewhat younger than widowed parents, and the lower mean number of children born to them. Another explanation refers to disturbed relationships between children and divorced parents, especially with non-custodian fathers (de Jong Gierveld and Dykstra, 1997).

In accordance with the data in table 2, the option of co-residence still seems to be a welcome one in several countries of Southern Europe, but it is evaluated as a less favourable option in the Scandinavian countries as well as in the Netherlands (Mengani and Lamura, 1995). This finding is also in agreement with the data provided by the Eurobarometer Survey (European Commission, 1993). This indicates that patterns in Southern Europe are still more oriented towards traditional family patterns and the idea that children are obliged to support their parents. Younger and older adults in Italy are convinced that the best thing children can do is support their parents, as indicated by the data from the Population Policy Acceptance Surveys (Palomba, 1995).

As far as the oldest old are concerned, co-residence with children can be triggered by deteriorating health and other physical or psychological handicaps that force the elderly to give up independent living. We have to bear in mind that the prevalence of disabilities is strongly age-related and reaches high rates at the more advanced ages.

However, the need to support frail parents is not the only possible trigger to start, or continue, co-residence. The pathways to co-residence are much more diverse and complex, as indicated by Grundy (1992): it is not only the older adults' need for support, but also the needs (socially or financially) of the children that have to be taken into account. This includes situations such as having a disabled child, a specific situation after divorce, the case of single parenthood, and the need for support and comfort of grandchildren when parents are involved in labour market activities. In all these situations, it is the older adult who provides rather than receives support. Home ownership by the older adults can also contribute to co-residence, either because the children lack suitable housing or because they have low levels of income. In general, a low-income situation, either among the children or among the older persons, increases the probability that parents and adult children will co-reside. Societies in Central and Eastern Europe have traditionally been considered to have a high prevalence of extended families. This has been intensified by the fact that the income security of many older persons has been eroded as a result of economic decline. This, combined with the poor housing situation of the younger generation, has forced older and younger persons to co-reside and to give up independent living either as a couple or alone (Botev, 1999). Thus, irrespective of the norms and values prevailing in the Eastern European countries about family responsibilities towards older persons, the socio-economic and housing situation in these countries may force family members to start and continue co-residence.

Today, many older people in Europe and the United States prefer not to live with their children, but to continue living independently either as a couple or alone as long as possible. The oldest old are least likely to emphasize adult children's obligations to their parents. However, Logan and Spitze admit that this pattern may have many sources. The social norms evinced by older people may reflect their desire for autonomy and self-reliance, their sense that the proper role of parents is to be givers rather than receivers, and their wish not to become a burden on the younger generation (Logan and Spitze, 1995, p. 362). In this context, Burch (1985) emphasized the effects of changes in the normative aspects of age and age roles that took place in the second half of the twentieth century: household members attach greater importance to goods such as privacy. As a result, households tend to be less willing to accommodate non-nuclear family members such as their parents. On the other hand, potential household members, such as older parents, may be less interested in entering the households of their adult children, feeling that their niche in the household would not be a favourable one.

Moreover, co-residence may include not only reciprocal support possibilities, but also cost elements. Crowding in co-residence living arrangements, measured in terms of persons per room, is related to poor mental health, poor physical health and poor social relationships in the home, and it has a detrimental effect on childcare (Gove, Hughes and Galle, 1983, p. 184). Other researchers (Townsend and Tunstall, 1973) point to the fact that co-residence of adult children and their parents is a threat to well-being, and is correlated with higher feelings of loneliness among elderly persons, primarily because they see less of their contemporaries, feel obliged to take up a lot of responsibilities and feel a loss of privacy and self-determination.

Included in modern ideas about care, support and services for older persons, taking into account their desire for self-determination and privacy, is the availability of privately or publicly financed institutional care for older persons. The old idea of institutionalization as a "last resort" has to be updated and revised. Feelings of boredom and loneliness, as well as feelings of being a burden on caring family members, frequently characterize older people's lives at home. Thus, many older persons will have made a positive decision to opt for residential care (Oldman and Quilgars, 1999). Table 3 gives the data for men and women aged 70 and over living in institutions, by country. Table 3 clearly shows that, relatively speaking, more persons in the United Kingdom are institutionalized than in Finland, with Hungary lagging behind. No data are available for Italy, but the phenomenon of institutions for the elderly appears to have been almost absent until now. As expected, the percentage of older persons involved in institutional care increases sharply with age, and is higher among women than among men in each of the three countries studied. The higher percentage of older persons in institutional care compensates, to a certain extent, for the lower proportions of co-residing older people in Finland and in the United Kingdom as compared with Italy and Hungary.

TABLE 3. PERSONS AGED 70 AND OVER LIVING IN INSTITUTIONS, BY SEX AND AGE, IN PERCENTAGES OF THE POPULATION[a]

	Finland 1990	United Kingdom 1991	Hungary 1990
Males			
70-74	1.5	1.9	0.9
75-79	2.8	3.0	1.5
80-84	5.7	6.7	2.2
85+	13.5	15.6	3.7
70 years and older	3.7	4.2	1.6
Females			
70-74	1.6	1.8	1.1
75-79	4.0	4.1	1.8
80-84	9.0	10.9	3.3
85+	21.2	27.6	5.8
70 years and older	6.5	7.8	2.4

Source: PAU collection of census-based microdata samples.

[a] No data available for Italy.

Major changes appear to have occurred in the past few decades. A declining proportion of elderly persons live with their children. Statistical data for several European countries and for the United States show that a decreasing proportion of older persons live together with kin in a multigeneration household and that years lived in old-age co-residence have declined substantially. In Europe, more and more elderly — after the death of the spouse — tend to choose to live independently for as long as possible. They appreciate good relationships with their children, but they prefer "intimacy at a distance" (Cherlin and Furstenberg, 1986). As a result, among older adults, family relationships are only indirectly related to household composition.

Living alone

As mentioned earlier, living alone is the most frequently registered living arrangement among older widowed and divorced women and men, according to the 1990/91 census round in each of the four countries studied. Table 4 presents data about living in a one-person household for persons aged 70 and over in the four countries under investigation. An overwhelming majority of older widowed and divorced persons in each of the countries live in a one-person household. The highest proportions living alone are found in Finland and the United Kingdom. This is in accordance with the ideas formulated about trends in the demographic behavioural patterns of the second demographic transition. Italy lags behind, but even in Italy, more than 53 per cent of persons aged 70 and over live independently and alone. In Hungary, the percentages of elderly aged 70 and over who live alone are significantly lower, varying between 48 and 59 per cent.

TABLE 4. PERSONS AGED 70 AND OVER LIVING IN A ONE-PERSON
HOUSEHOLD, BY SEX AND MARITAL STATUS, IN PERCENTAGES
OF THE NON-INSTITUTIONALIZED POPULATION

	Finland 1990	United Kingdom 1991	Italy 1991	Hungary 1990
Males				
Widowed	74.8	77.3	55.9	50.6
Divorced	72.1	67.9	61.8	58.9
Females				
Widowed	76.9	78.5	56.0	47.9
Divorced	81.9	75.6	53.8	52.4

Source: PAU collection of census-based microdata samples.

These recent trends have resulted in an increase in the number of households and a decrease in the number of persons per household in each of the European countries.

As economic welfare increases in more and more countries in the Western world, there is less need for people to share their homes and become part of the same household. At the same time, ongoing improvements in social security are enabling growing numbers of older and younger people to embark on independent living arrangements and lifestyles. These developments go hand in hand with the aforementioned trend towards greater privacy and individualization, resulting in higher percentages of divorce, living alone or living as a parent without a partner. And, as mentioned above, the preferences of older adults in the more developed countries are increasingly moving towards a continuation of independence, by living in a one-person household.

Intentions that today shape specific decisions about future behaviour have been viewed as being part of people's more encompassing ideas about how they want their lives to evolve. Giddens (1991, p. 85) suggests that life planning constitutes a general feature of modern life. In a world of alternative lifestyle options, strategic life planning is of special importance. Through life planning, people can prepare a course of future actions. The concept of individual-level strategic behaviour covers decision-making in a wide variety of domains of life, including partner selection, the start and continuation of a specific type of living arrangement, and other personal relationships. In opting for either "living alone" or sharing a household with adult others, one has to weigh the pros and cons of both options. Sharing a household may provide people with personal care, reciprocal attention and support, solidarity, division of household tasks and other positive goods. Possible negative outcomes include a bias in solidarity costs, whereby one of the partners invests less time, money and effort in the cooperative undertaking than the other, and than laid down in informal contracts between the partners (Lindenberg, 1998). Thus, strategic life planning takes into consideration the specific positive and negative aspects of sharing or not sharing a household.

Older adults (age 50 and over) might hesitate to remarry and restart a two-person household as a married couple. A new marriage bond at older ages involves, by definition, two persons, both of whom are characterized by specific life histories and have evolved into persons with unique personalities and lifelong personality traits. Can these personalities and life histories still be patterned, remodelled and harmonized as they could at young ages? Nowadays, more and more older divorced and widowed persons (starting in the Western and Northern European countries, the United States of America and Canada) are explicitly opting for flexible partner bonds such as unmarried cohabitation (Wu and Balakrishnan, 1994) and LAT relationships — where partners do not actually live together — rather than remarrying. In-depth interviews with persons aged 55 to 89 years involved in an LAT relationship (de Jong Gierveld, forthcoming) showed that for older widows, widowers and divorcees the strong desire to continue living in their own private homes and being able to make independent decisions about their day-to-day activities, in combination with a desire to share time with a partner to avoid loneliness and to be comforted by mutual solidarity, has led them to start an LAT relationship. Among the responses were the following:

"After a period of living alone, you have fixed habits ... It is difficult to adjust ... If you are very old, you are a whole person, and it is difficult to change your habits ..."

"Since we both have a life behind us ... it's much more difficult than starting a relationship from scratch ... He is an authoritarian type of person ... He is always trying to fix things for me ..."

"I know many elderly who start an LAT relationship, simply for the sake of companionship. Most of them drink a cup of coffee together, share meals ... to avoid feeling lonely. Weekends are awful for people who live alone ..."

In doing so, they are realizing the benefits of combining a partner relationship with a one-person household: guaranteeing a certain amount of independence and privacy, time to be alone and to fulfil their private wishes, while at the same time enjoying part-time companionship, friendship, intimacy, love and opportunities for reciprocal care. This has given rise to new questions. Will LAT partners de facto support one another; is the bond strong enough to guarantee ongoing support? And, what responsibilities do children have towards the new partners of their parents?

THE BROADER SOCIAL EMBEDDEDNESS OF OLDER PEOPLE: GUARANTEES FOR FAMILIAL SUPPORT OUTSIDE THE HOUSEHOLD

Social participation of older persons as volunteers and carers in all kinds of community activities is widespread. Many organizations, including religious groups, are dependent on the time budgets and investments of older persons. Within the realm of the family, older parents perform specific activities too, such as supporting young parents in raising their children, either financially or by participating in childcare. Older parents maintain these intergenerational support ties — independent of processes of family change on the part of the parents and/or the children. Older parents speak of a continued link as they adjust to new relationships with their children's generation and to new extended families following divorce (Bornat and others, 1999). Of course, intergenerational contacts are bounded by geographical distance and influenced by country-specific values and infrastructures.

It must be stated that older persons in general, including the oldest old, should not be characterized as a "problem group". While some are unable to remain independent, a majority are able to do so. It cannot be denied, however, that with advancing age, older adults are increasingly confronted with ill health and physical and mental handicaps. Many studies show that if health deteriorates and help is needed, the elderly continue to rely primarily on family members, firstly on their partners, but in the absence of a partner, other family members will step in. The first ones to substitute for the bereaved intimate relationship with the partner will be the children, daughters more specifically (Kendig and others, 1999). Studies carried out in developed countries have repeatedly shown that adult children are more supportive, either providing time or money, of parents living alone than of parents who are still together (Dykstra, 1990; Wenger, 1984). Children provide all kinds of support, such as health care, social companionship and housekeeping assistance, for disabled old people who continue to live independently. This informal, private-sector support still prevails across the more developed world, despite the availability of institutional care and other types of social services. Families still provide most of the support needed. Within the realm of the present paper it is not possible to provide an in-depth overview of all the data available about children who are involved in the changing networks of ageing individuals, as well as information about care given to non-co-resident older parents in need of support. More information about this phenomenon can be found in, among others, Grundy (1999) and Van Tilburg (1998).

In today's developed world, the decision to start giving informal support to frail older parents is not a matter of course. The decision depends on the ongoing quality of social relationships between parents and children, on voluntary principles and on individual agreement (Keith, 1992). As pointed out earlier in the present paper, within each of the countries studied, co-residence is more frequently reported by older widows and widowers and less frequently by older divorced women and men. The same pattern has been found for informal support provided to non-co-resident older parents. Research has shown that about half of the older widowed persons who live independently, with children alive, and who are in need of support, mentioned that one (or more) of the children were active in the support network, compared with less than a quarter of all the ever-divorced older persons (de Jong Gierveld and Dykstra, 1997). In such a situation, those most likely to be at risk are fathers who did not maintain a high-quality relationship with their children following divorce (Bornat and others, 1999). The latter have to rely more heavily on support from community volunteers ("meals on wheels"), as well as on support that has to be paid for, or formal support arrangements.

However, national surveys from several countries indicate that a majority of older persons can rely on, and receive assistance from, informal helpers. This enables the elderly to continue living independently, which is welcomed by many older persons.

AN AGENDA FOR FUTURE POLICY-MAKING AND RESEARCH

The present paper provides a comprehensive picture of some characteristics of the living arrangements of older persons in four countries in Europe. We can conclude that new ideas, attitudes and demographic behaviour are not restricted to young adult persons, but are also found in the lives of persons aged 50 and over. New behavioural patterns such as divorce and living alone, unmarried cohabitation and LAT relationships are becoming more widespread among the elderly in Europe. In accordance with the central ideas of the second demographic transition, these trends started in the countries of North-western Europe, followed at some distance by the Southern European countries. The data provided by the Population Unit Activities in the

Dynamics of Ageing project served as a reliable and valid tool to investigate the first, general outcomes of this trend. Data from the 2000/01 round of national censuses are needed to further investigate the trend. Will co-residence in Italy and Hungary continue to decrease? Will higher percentages of older persons opt for new types of living arrangements? Ideally, one needs cohort data to investigate changing patterns of living arrangements, and the determinants of these developments. The present paper contains data about four countries. In total, more than 12 countries were involved in the Unit's undertaking. Most of the countries involved are located in Central and Eastern Europe; many Western European countries were not included. A new programme elaborating on this initiative is urgently needed. The new initiative should preferably include more detailed information about the important themes under investigation. In particular, and in conclusion, we shall identify some areas in which more detailed information and more research are needed. This could serve as a basis for the improvement of existing policies and for ideas about new avenues for policy-making in the field of ageing.

There is an urgent need for improved statistical information about

- Marital status, including partner and marital history;
- New types of living arrangements among older people (e.g., unmarried cohabitation, "living apart but together");
- Determinants of multigeneration households (including information about the timing, and motives for starting such households, and support given and received).

Research is needed on how and why decisions are made to live alone, to start a couple relationship, to enter the household of one of the children, and so on. More research is needed on the effects of types of living arrangements on independence and self-reliance, and on personal and social well-being (of each of the household members of each of the generations involved).

NOTES

[1] When we refer to older persons or elderly persons, we address a category that is not clearly defined. Not only does the minimum age fluctuate — 55, 60 or 65 — but various classifications are used within the group as well.

[2] Data of national censuses have been recoded ex post to harmonize answer categories as accurately as possible in order to facilitate comparative analysis. This ex post data manipulation cannot compensate for intrinsic discrepancies in census question-and-answer categories between national censuses. In particular in the area of complex types of living arrangements and of housing equipment, intrinsic differences still exist, making between-country comparisons difficult. In other fields, comparisons are difficult because not all national censuses include questions about specific themes, such as older persons' institutionalization in Italy, and housing equipment in the United Kingdom.

Beck, U., and E. Beck-Gernsheim (1996). Individualization and "precarious freedoms": perspectives and controversies of a subject-orientated sociology. In *Detraditionalization: Critical Reflections of Authority and Identity*, P. Heelas, S. Lash and P. Morris, eds. Oxford, United Kingdom: Blackwell, pp. 22-48.

Bornat, J., and others (1999). Stepfamilies and older people: evaluating the implications of family change for an ageing population. *Ageing and Society*, vol. 19, pp. 239-262.

Bosveld, W. (1996). *The Ageing of Fertility in Europe. A Comparative Demographic-analytic Study*. Amsterdam: Thesis Publications.

Botev, N. (1999). Older persons in countries with economies in transition. In *Population Ageing, Challenges for Policies and Programmes in Developed and Developing Countries*. New York and Brussels: United Nations Population Fund and CBGS, pp. 85-100.

Bumpass, L., J. Sweet and T. C. Martin (1990). Changing patterns of remarriage. *Journal of Marriage and the Family*, vol. 52, pp. 747-756.

Burch, T. K. (1985). Changing age-sex roles and household crowding: a theoretical note. *Proceedings, International Population Conference, Florence, 1985*, vol. 3. Liège, Belgium: International Union for the Scientific Study of Population, pp. 253-261.

Cherlin, A. (1983). Changing family and household: contemporary lessons from historical research. *Annual Review of Sociology*, vol. 9, pp. 51-66.

_____, and F. F. Furstenberg (1986). *The New American Grandparent: A Place in the Family, A Life Apart*. New York: Basic Books.

Clarke, C. J., and L. J. Neidert (1992). Living arrangements of the elderly: an examination of differences according to ancestry and generation. *The Gerontologist*, vol. 32, No. 6, pp. 796-804.

Cooney, T. M. (1993). Recent demographic change: implications for families planning for the future. *Marriage and Family Review*, vol. 18, No. 3/4, pp. 37-55.

De Jong Gierveld, Jenny (forthcoming). Older adults between kin solidarity and independence. In *Ménages, comportements démographiques et sociétés en mutation. Households, Demographic Behaviour and Changing Societies*. Chaire Quételet 1998, Institut de Démographie, Université Catholique de Louvain. Louvain-la-Neuve, Belgium: Academia-Bruylant/l'Harmattan.

_____, and Pearl A. Dykstra (1997). The long-term consequences of divorce for fathers. *Proceedings, International Population Conference, Beijing, 1997*, vol. 2. Liège, Belgium: International Union for the Scientific Study of Population, pp. 849-866.

De Jong Gierveld, Jenny, and Hanna Van Solinge (1995). *Ageing and its Consequences for the Socio-medical System*. Population Studies No. 29. Strasbourg, France: Council of Europe Press.

Dykstra, Pearl A. (1990). Disentangling direct and indirect gender effects on the supportive network. In *Social Network Research: Substantive Issues and Methodological Questions*, C. P. M. Knipscheer and T. C. Antonucci, eds. Lisse, Netherlands: Swets and Zeitlinger, pp. 55-65.

_____ (1993). The differential availability of relationships and the provision and effectiveness of support to older adults. *Journal of Social and Personal Relationships*, vol. 10, No. 3, pp. 355-370.

Esping-Andersen, G. (1990). *The Three Worlds of Welfare Capitalism*. Cambridge, United Kingdom: Polity Press.

European Commission (1993). *Age and Attitudes: Main Results from a Eurobarometer Survey.* Brussels.

Giddens, A. (1991). *Modernity and Self-identity: Self and Society in the Late Modern Age.* Cambridge, United Kingdom: Polity Press.

Gove, W. R., M. Hughes and O. R. Galle (1983). *Overcrowding in the Household: An Analysis of Determinants and Effects.* New York: Academic Press.

Grundy, Emily (1992). The living arrangements of elderly people. *Reviews in Clinical Gerontology*, vol. 2, pp. 353-361.

_____ (1999). Changing role of the family and community in providing support for the elderly. In *Population Ageing, Challenges for Policies and Programmes in Developed and Developing Countries.* New York and Brussels: United Nations Population Fund and CBGS, pp. 103-122.

Hagestad, G. (1998). Towards a society for all ages: new thinking, new language, new conversations. Keynote address, United Nations, 1 October.

Hilbourne, M. (1999). Living together full time? Middle-class couples approaching retirement. *Ageing and Society*, vol. 19, pp. 161-185.

Keith, J. (1992). Caretaking in cultural context: anthropologized queries. In *Family Support for the Elderly. The International Experience*, H. L. Kendig, A. Hashimoto and L. C. Coppard, eds. Oxford, United Kingdom: Oxford University Press.

Kendig, H., and others (1999). Social support of older people in Australia and Japan. *Ageing and Society*, vol. 19, pp. 185-208.

Lesthaeghe, R., and J. Surkyn (1988). Cultural dynamics and economics of fertility change. *Population and Development Review*, vol. 14, pp. 1-45.

Lindenberg, S. (1998). Solidarity: its microfoundations and macrodependence. A framing approach. In *The Problem of Solidarity: Theories and Models*, P. Doreian and T. Fararo, eds. Australia: Gordon and Breach Publishers, pp. 61-112.

Logan, J. R., and G. D. Spitze (1995). Self-interest and altruism in intergenerational relations. *Demography*, vol. 32, No. 3, pp. 353-364.

Mengani, M., and G. Lamura (1995). Elderly women, family structure and care patterns in Italy. In *The Elderly Women in Europe: Choices and Challenges*, G. Dooghe and N. Appleton, eds. Brussels: CBGS.

Myers, G. C. (1986). Cross-national patterns and trends in marital status among the elderly. In *Populations agées et révolution grise.* Chaire quételet 1986, M. Loriaux, D. Remy and E. Vilquin, eds. Louvain-la-Neuve, Belgium: Institut de démographie.

Oldman, C., and D. Quilgars (1999). The last resort? Revisiting ideas about older people's living arrangements. *Ageing and Society*, vol. 19, pp. 363-384.

Palomba, R. (1995). Italy, the invisible change. In *Population, Family and Welfare: A Comparative Survey of European Attitudes*, H. Moors and R. Palomba, eds. Oxford, United Kingdom: Clarendon Press, pp. 158-176.

Peters, A., and A. C. Liefbroer (1997). Beyond marital status: partner history and well-being in old age. *Journal of Marriage and the Family*, vol. 59, pp. 687-699.

Spitze, G., J. R. Logan and J. Robinson (1992). Family structure and changes in living arrangements among elderly non-married parents. *Journal of Gerontology: Social Sciences*, vol. 47, No. 6, pp. S289-S296.

Townsend, P., and S. Tunstall (1973). Sociological explanations of the lonely. In *The Social Minority*, P. Townsend, ed. London, Lane: pp. 240-266.

United Nations (1999). *World Population Prospects: The 1998 Revision*, vol. 1, Comprehensive Tables. Sales No. E.99.XIII.9.

Van de Kaa, D. J. (1987). Europe's second demographic transition. *Population Bulletin*, vol. 42, No. 1, 57 pp.

_____ (1994). The second demographic transition revisited: theories and expectations. In *Population and Family in the Low Countries, 1993: Late Fertility and Other Current Issues*, G. C. N. Beets and others, eds. Lisse, Netherlands: Swets and Zeitlinger, pp. 81-126.

Van Tilburg, T. (1998). Losing and gaining in old age: changes in personal network size and social support in a four-year longitudinal study. *Journal of Gerontology: Social Sciences*, vol. 53B, No. 6, pp. S313-S323.

Wenger, G. C. (1984). *The Supportive Network. Coping with Old Age*. London: Allen and Unwin.

Wu, Z., and T. R. Balakrishnan (1994). Cohabitation after marital disruption in Canada. *Journal of Marriage and the Family*, vol. 56, pp. 723-734.

IMPACT OF PENSION REFORM ON THE LIVING ARRANGEMENTS OF OLDER PERSONS IN LATIN AMERICA

*Paulo Murad Saad**

INTRODUCTION

Social security systems have become major elements of social development in the twentieth century, with particularly important effects on the well-being of the older groups of society. The past 25 years alone have witnessed dramatic improvements in living standards among the elderly in Europe and the United States of America, combined with similar shifts in pension payments and the maturing of pension plans. In fact, in those countries, there has been a substantial decline in the proportion of those covered by social assistance who are elderly (Laczco, 1990). Although less markedly than in the more developed countries, social security has also played an important role in the development process of many Latin American countries (Nitsch and Schwarzer, 1995).

More recently, however, Governments in developed as well as developing countries have come to view changes to the regulation and laws of their social security systems as key factors in the reform of the State. In truth, the social security crisis, which includes the reform of the pension system, has become one of the world's most debated social policy issues at the end of the twentieth century.

The reasons for the crisis seem to differ between the more developed and the less developed regions. With respect to developed economies, the rising affluence of the elderly has prompted a debate over what constitutes an equitable distribution of income and wealth between age cohorts (Duncan and Smith, 1989). Among the member countries of the Organisation for Economic Cooperation and Development, benefit obligations for which funding does not yet exist are on the order of US$ 30 trillion (Quin and Burkhauser, 1994). Despite this observation, most industrialized countries have instituted retirement policies that discourage the elderly from working. Between the 1960s and the 1980s, the average retirement age in developed countries decreased by five years (Médici, 1997). During this same period, spending on retirement and pension payments increased threefold, resulting from the

---

* Population Division, United Nations Secretariat.

increase in the number of senior citizens, the expectation of longer lives after retiring, and the average amount paid out in benefits.

In the past decade, however, these policies have begun to change in several countries. Recent legislation in the United States, for instance, has outlawed mandatory retirement, banned the cessation of service year credits in pension calculations after a particular age, and increased the social security credit for delayed retirement after the age of 65 (Quin and Burkhauser, 1994). Several other countries have also already implemented changes in their primary retirement pension systems, designed to raise the normal retirement age within the next few years (Morrison, 1986).

In Latin America, on the other hand, the recent past has been characterized by persistent external imbalances, declining levels of income per capita, growing unemployment, an expanding informal sector, and an ever-increasing number of people living below the poverty line (Durán, 1996). Within this framework of increasingly severe socio-economic problems, countries have been forced to adopt structural adjustment programmes and to question their own retirement and pension systems, particularly in the light of unfavourable economic conditions, rapidly moving demographic transformations and their own errors and limitations.

Several countries of the region have already experienced structural reforms in their pension systems, following the pioneer experience in Chile at the beginning of the 1980s. In general, these reform movements have cast doubt on all aspects of the previous regimes, and given rise to a confrontation between the polarized positions of collective versus individual, immediate versus lasting, public versus private, and financial techniques versus actuarial techniques (Mesa-Lago, 1997). The major difference between the initial and the reform movements, however, is the existence among the latter of a contingent of beneficiaries with legally acquired rights who demand the creation of acceptable and viable transition alternatives.

Since pension reforms in Latin America have represented the imposition of a new paradigm — the complementation or even substitution of the public allocation system by a private system of individual funds — we can expect not only an important impact in the macroeconomy of the region, but also important effects on the population's living conditions, especially in the case of the elderly, who are the main beneficiaries of the system.

The purpose of this study is to present a brief analysis of the pension reforms conducted in Latin American countries, emphasizing those aspects that could, at least in theory, influence the living arrangements of the elderly. It is not an easy task to measure the success of pension reform — whose effects are felt only in the long run — especially when it involves changes in the objectives that gave rise to the institution itself, and where previous experience is practically non-existent.

Therefore, rather than present a conclusive analysis of the consequences of pension reforms on the household structure of the elderly in Latin America, the intention is to provide insights for future research concerned with the relationships between transformations in the pension systems and the well-being of the Latin American elderly population.

Determinants of living arrangements of the elderly

Multivariate analyses of the living arrangements of the elderly have emphasized benefits and costs associated with different arrangements (DaVanzo and Chan, 1994; Knodel and others, 1991; Martin, 1989), pointing out "the apparent interplay of constraints and preferences" (Casterline and others, 1991). In these analyses, the living arrangement of an elderly individual is assumed to be the outcome of a series of decisions taken by a number of people over a considerable period of time, which is heavily influenced by factors such as changes in marital status, employment history, savings and investment, migration, housing, and health-related behaviour. At a given moment in time, an individual is subject to various constraints with respect to the range of living arrangements available; she or he will have a set of preferences as to which arrangements are better than others, and these, in turn, will be juxtaposed with the constraints, resources and preferences of the members of the elderly person's family network.

Preferences for different living arrangements result from the balance between costs and benefits of cohabitation, and may be influenced by cultural standards and values. The benefits of cohabitation for both the elderly and the other household members may vary from companionship and emotional support to physical and financial support. Among the costs, the literature emphasizes the loss of privacy, the decline in social status of the elderly after losing control of financial resources, and the burden that physically or mentally impaired seniors would represent for live-in caregivers — typically a daughter.

The primary constraint on the choice of living arrangements refers to the size and composition of one's kinship network. A second set of factors that constrain living arrangements are those related to financial and physical feasibility. Many studies have found a positive relationship between economic resources and independent living, suggesting that, whenever feasible, elderly people prefer to purchase goods and services that otherwise live-in children may provide. At the same time, research has shown that disability, illness and advanced age are often associated with a reduced likelihood of living on one's own. In any case, some basic conditions are clearly required for the elderly to live independently.

How pension reforms can influence the living arrangements of the elderly

The most direct effect of pension reform on the household structure of the elderly refers to the influence it may exert on their financial autonomy. Should the benefits increase in value, and if the proportion of the older population who are covered increases, a greater share of elderly individuals would have better conditions for exerting their preferences in terms of household structure, which would probably increase the tendency for independent arrangements (living alone or with a spouse only) among the elderly. On the contrary, if the benefits situation does not significantly improve, the majority of the elderly will remain financially dependent on their family, and living arrangements in which they cohabit with relatives will persist or even become more prevalent.

When considering the effects of pension reform on the living arrangements of the elderly, however, it is important to analyse the elderly's situation vis-à-vis the situation of the remaining population groups. There are cases in which the possibilities of the elderly who are financially independent to opt for independent living arrangements are constrained by the less favourable situation of their immediate family.

Saad (1996, 1998), for instance, found that while higher income of the elderly in the most affluent region of Brazil splits generations into different households, it stimulates co-residence between generations in the poorest region. According to the author, the exercise by the elderly of their preference for independent living arrangements is overridden, in the latter region, by the needs of their adult children. In this case, the modifications brought about by the 1988 Brazilian Constitution, which included the rural population in the retirement pension system and increased the pension value from one half to one minimum wage, has transformed the income of the elderly into an important family asset in that region, particularly if compared with the poorer conditions of the younger generations (Souza, 1998).

THE LATIN AMERICAN PENSION SYSTEMS CRISIS

In Latin America, the first retirement and pension systems began at the turn of the century in Brazil, Argentina, Cuba, Chile and Uruguay, and were implemented gradually in the remaining countries over a 50-year period. The majority of them were originally based on European models, relying on hypothetical full employment and continued economic growth. Overall, the region's systems expanded within national development contexts characterized by protectionist economic models, high demographic growth rates and increasing employment opportunities.

Since their inception, these systems have been organized primarily under pay-as-you-go schemes. These are in fact social contracts calling for the unrestricted, mandatory transfer of funds from the active workforce to retirees and pensioners. This transfer has been backed by an implicit commitment by the Government that on reaching retirement age, today's workers would benefit from the contributions of future generations of workers.

From a financial standpoint, these plans are fine as long as benefit payments are matched by contributions. While these payments initially represent a surplus of capital, they are subsequently subject to actuarial adjustments. This capital must be invested in the form of reserve funds to be deployed for benefit payments when the system reaches maturity. Increases in the beneficiary/contributor ratio lead to losses in the system, forcing corrections to the value of both variables (Uthoff, 1997).

As put forward by Lo Vuolo (1996), those in favour of reform in the Latin American case argue that traditional systems have been economically inefficient and socially unfair, leading to:

(a)   Inequitable impacts such as reduced benefit payments, separation between the level of contributions paid and benefits received, exclusion of the poorest members of society, and unequal protection between the various age cohorts;

(b)   Poor management evidenced by high administrative costs and negative revenues from funds managed by public agencies;

(c)   Economic distortions such as increased use of capital-intensive technologies and tax evasion, a result of the growing tax load placed on labour, and the lack of long-term financial sustainability owing to the greying of the population.

The worsening ratio between active contributors and inactive beneficiaries, which at first glance seems due to an increasingly ageing population base structure, also owes something to the adverse economic situations that predominate in the region. These economic woes impact negatively on the system's contribution base, reflected in declining job creation and salary mass. The social security dependency ratio in Brazil, for example, went from 31 contributors per beneficiary in 1940 to the current 1.7, a figure even lower than that in countries such as Germany, the United States of America, Uruguay and Japan, which have much more mature systems (Oliveira Beltrão and Ferreira, 1997). Explanations for this decline include the inarguable prevalence of very early retirement, the high unemployment rate and the size of the informal economy, which robs the Government of about 25 per cent of its potential tax revenues.

The informal economy and its related labour market is one of the most important Latin American phenomena of the 1990s. The region seems to have lost its vitality for creation of jobs in the formal sector, and this has led to an increase in the level of informal work. Between 1980 and 1990, the numbers of Latin American workers active in the informal sector grew from 25.6 per cent to 30.8 per cent, meaning that practically one in every three workers in the region is employed in an informal capacity (Durán, 1996).

It is estimated that in the next 30 years the population of Latin America will increase by approximately 221 million inhabitants. In addition, the current number of senior citizens (65 years and older) will grow by 40 million to 55 million people. Under existing conditions, which vary considerably among the region's countries, at least one third of these senior citizens will not be entitled to formal pension benefits, meaning that after 2025, nearly 18 million senior citizens will find themselves without any form of guaranteed income replacement (Durán, 1996).

In addition to declining income levels and the lack of social coverage faced by workers, one of the informal labour market's worst consequences is tax evasion, as very few of these workers contribute voluntarily to social security (Pinheiro, 1999). As this aspect is vital to the reform of the region's social welfare institutions, the first comprehensive effort conducted by the

Governments should be a full-scale drive to incorporate the informal sector into the formal economy.

Another factor responsible for Latin America's social security crisis is the existence of an anomalous set of benefits that translates into undeserved special retirement packages, characterized by lower contribution values, higher benefit payments and an early legal retirement age.

PENSION REFORMS IN LATIN AMERICA

The position of international organizations

Social security reform has long occupied centre stage in debates over social policy. However, it was not until the release of position papers by both the International Labour Organization (ILO) and the World Bank, published in 1993 and 1994, respectively, that international financial and technical agencies finally tabled detailed proposals on dealing with the issue (Mesa-Lago, 1996).

The two documents presented similar diagnoses of the problems associated with traditional pension systems, namely, contributions well in excess of salary levels; high incidences of tax evasion and contribution payments in arrears; inadequate application of tax funds and poorly performing investments. There was also common ground over their recommendations, with each set based on three distinct elements. In both cases, the first element consisted of a minimum benefit guaranteed through a mandatory and universal allocation plan financed by taxes and managed by the public sector. There was also agreement over the third element, which offered supplementary pensions based on defined contributions and non-defined benefits, and state-regulated, privately managed individual funds.

Where the two proposals differed, however, was in their treatment of the second element. Here, strategies for reforming the system disagree over a number of variables, including the legal nature of the proposed reform, the financial plan, contributions, benefits and how the assets are to be managed. Although the importance of this second element is not in question, the ILO position is based on a system of partially harmonized funds, with defined benefits financed through contributions from workers and employers, to be managed by social security. Conversely, the World Bank favours an individual savings plan, with non-defined benefits being managed by the private sector, subject to state regulation.

The ILO proposal, whose views are also shared by the International Association of Social Security, seeks to improve the current systems by adopting such non-structural measures as increasing the legal retirement age, eliminating special privilege plans, administrative cost-cutting and better control over tax evasion and contributions in arrears. While the World Bank agrees with the need for these measures, it considers them insufficient to resolve longer-term problems, and instead proposes radical structural reform based on an overhaul of the political system.

223

With the exception of Chile, whose social welfare reform pre-dates the publication of these two proposals, many Latin American countries brought about reforms to their retirement systems that were either too flexible or at odds with the World Bank and ILO recommendations. While the reforms in the majority of these countries have been structural — meaning the incorporation of a privately managed, individually funded system — there are important differences between their approaches. In Mexico, Bolivia and El Salvador, whose reforms were conducted between 1995 and 1996, the public system was totally abolished. In Argentina (1993) and in Uruguay (1995), mixed systems were adopted that incorporated a reworked public component. In Peru (1992) and in Colombia (1993), parallel alternative systems were implemented, combining private management with a reorganized public mandate (Mesa-Lago, 1997).

The Chilean reforms, conducted from 1979 to 1981, represent a model of transferring government control to private management, which has had a strong influence on other reforms in the region. However, the drastic Chilean reforms were only possible owing to a powerful authoritarian Government that dissolved Congress, banned political parties and trade unions, controlled the media, and eliminated and/or weakened any type of opposition to the reforms (Mesa-Lago, 1997). Given this unique set of conditions, a "pure" duplication of the Chilean reforms could not be implemented elsewhere in the region. With the re-emergence of democracy throughout the region, the chances of an occurrence similar to what transpired in Chile have also become much less likely. In countries that are still discussing social security reform, the proposals most similar to the ILO recommendations are those most likely to be adopted.

PRELIMINARY RESULTS OF THE CHILEAN REFORM

Even though the Chilean reforms are the oldest in Latin America, it is still too early to evaluate their impact definitively, as the effects they generated will continue to be felt for a long time to come. However, considerable efforts have been made by social welfare specialists to analyse the partial results of the Chilean reforms vis-à-vis their initial intents and expectations.

In 1996, 15 years after reforms to the social welfare system were implemented in Chile, 15 private companies were managing the accounts of 5.5 million Chileans, or approximately 99 per cent of the economically active population. The assets managed by these companies were on the order of $28 billion, or about 40 per cent of Chile's gross national product (Nitsch and Schwarzer, 1998). Despite these impressive figures, the overall evaluation has been a negative one, particularly in terms of the social impact.

One reform originally sought to enhance the level of social coverage, while at the same time reducing tax evasion and increasing the amount of benefit payments. Data from 1997, however, point to a reduction in the scope of the new system in relation to the previous one, as only about 45 per cent of the workforce were contributing regularly (Nitsch and Schwarzer, 1998). In addition, this disparity was even more apparent among the management companies representing low-income workers, meaning that the poorest members of the workforce, who most need assistance, were being left unprotected by the system.

With respect to tax evasion, no significant improvement was noted. Among self-employed workers, about 95 per cent still do not contribute regularly. For regular employees, most pay only the minimum required amounts (Azeredo, 1994). Regarding benefit payments, the situation appears no better. A study assuming 45 years of uninterrupted contributions being made in individual accounts, at profits of 3 per cent a year, would mean the contributor would receive back only 44 per cent of his or her contribution salary over this same period (Ruiz-Tagle, 1994).

Other attempts were made to bring more transparency and efficiency to the system by allowing the public to choose among the management companies. In theory, these institutions would then be forced to continue improving their service to maintain their market share. Studies have shown, however, that administrative costs for the privatized system are even higher than those of the previous system. About half of the contributors are unable to understand their account statements, while the three largest management companies — representing about two thirds of qualified contributors and 55 per cent of the assets under administration — feature neither the best levels of profitability nor charge the lowest commission rates, and in fact have the highest advertising budgets (Nitsch and Schwarzer, 1998).

One of the main objectives in privatizing the social security system was to remove the expenses of retirement payments and pensions from the public treasury. But contrary to that expectation, one of the consequences was a marked loss of income for the public sector. While the State took on the financial onus of privatization, remaining as manager for the old system, it lost immediate revenue sources from the new social security contributions now being made to the pension funds.

Consequently, the difficulties faced by the extant public system — which continues to address the majority of retirees and pensioners — have grown considerably, resulting in a dramatic drop in the amount of benefit payments. In addition to this, the regulations of the private fund managers stipulate that widows cannot receive any pension following the death of the retired beneficiary. The flaws in the private system can already be seen on the streets, where it has become more common to see an elderly person begging than a child (Alves, 1997). If the situation has reached such dramatic proportions in the urban areas, it tends to be even worse for rural workers, the majority of whom do not contribute to the private social security system.

FINAL REMARKS

Living arrangements constitute one of the most important dimensions of the well-being of the elderly. As previously stated, they depend on a set of strongly interacting factors, among which the financial autonomy of the elderly plays a crucial role. Thus, by affecting the income conditions of the

225

elderly through the payment of retirement benefits under new regulations, pension reforms in Latin America are expected to have an important impact on the household structure of the elderly population, either by increasing or decreasing their decision power for choosing living arrangements of their preference.

Pension reforms in the region are still too recent for a better evaluation regarding their consequences. Only after a relatively long period of time will it be possible to know the real impact of these reforms on the living conditions of the elderly, and particularly on their living arrangements. Up to now, however, the results seem not to favour an increase in the financial autonomy of the elderly in the future, especially if pension reforms are not accompanied by a broader set of other socio-economic reforms.

In fact, there has been a long-held belief that structural reforms resulting from a social security crisis could somehow solve all the problems of previous systems. This would hold even when someone's work history included several periods of unemployment or informal employment, and salary levels continued to be precarious, such as in Latin America. The effectiveness of the private system, however, is based on regular contributions of sufficient levels of funds over the worker's professional life. This means the system will only function satisfactorily for those whose income already affords the ability to save. For lower-income workers, who typically have a less stable presence in the formal economy, chances are low they might set aside enough money in a fund to allow them to survive periods of unemployment or inactivity.

The issue, therefore, does not boil down to defining ways of extracting compulsory savings from workers, but rather is a fundamental matter of creating conditions for workers to generate those savings. Such an environment, though, can only be derived through higher levels of work-related revenue or other forms of remuneration. Thus, the need to link reform of the social security system to a set of more encompassing reforms, including those of the health and employment systems, becomes more apparent.

In a way similar to what happened with the previous systems, the reformed systems seem to place emphasis on vertical growth to the detriment of horizontal expansion, which would allow a sustainable development phase. Until now, efforts targeting transfers from contributors have been much more significant than those focused on increasing the actual numbers of contributors. In reality, certain groups such as agricultural workers, the informal sector, the self-employed and so on, who have little political representation and who have traditionally been excluded from the pension and retirement systems, remain practically marginalized by the reformed systems, depending almost exclusively on the minimum pension guaranteed by the State (Lo Vuolo, 1996).

Accordingly, the mere substitution of a public system by a private one would not be enough to solve today's major social welfare problems. In fact, such a transfer of administration might even further aggravate the problems of segmentation and social exclusion in Latin America, and lead to an even more severe impact on the public purse. The region's social heterogeneity and the narrowness of the formal economy make it difficult to solve the problem of guaranteeing income for retirees and the unemployed through a privately operated, individually funded investment model. In other words, the majority of the population cannot manage without a social welfare programme, or a public vehicle designed for the redistribution of income and wealth.

If it is true that pension reforms in Latin America have been primarily motivated by the desire to improve benefits and augment the national treasury, the success of such reforms will depend on the ability of the region's policy makers to harmonize their strategies in terms of social security. Thus, they are expected to continually modernize and adapt the pension systems to current socio-economic conditions, to achieve a suitable and sustainable equilibrium between social and economic objectives.

REFERENCES

Alves, Paulo (1997). *Aposentadoria privada no Chile exclui pobres. A Tribuna de Santos (16 de novembro)*.

Azeredo, Beatriz (1994). *A previdência privada do Chile: um modelo para a reforma do sistema brasileiro? Indicadores Econômicos FEE: Análise Conjuntural (Porto Alegre-RS)*, vol. 22, No. 2, (2° semestre), pp. 132-139.

Casterline, J. B., and others (1991). Differences in the living arrangements of the elderly in four Asian countries: the interplay of constraints and preferences. Paper presented at the annual meeting of the Population Association of America, Washington, D. C., March.

DaVanzo, J., and A. Chan (1994). Living arrangements of older Malaysians: who co-resides with their adult children? *Demography*, vol. 31, No. 1, pp. 95-113.

Duncan, G. J., and K. R. Smith (1989). The rising affluence of the elderly: how far, how fair, and how frail? *American Review of Sociology* (Annual Reviews Inc.), vol. 15, pp. 261-289.

Durán, Clemente R. (1996). *Hacia una reforma de la seguridad social con visión ciudadana. Comercio Exterior* (Mexico-DF), vol. 46, No. 9 (septiembre), pp. 717-721.

Knodel, J., and others (1991). Familial support and the life course of Thai elderly and their children. Comparative Study of the Elderly in Asia Research Reports. Ann Arbor: University of Michigan, Population Studies Center.

Laczco, F. (1990). New poverty and the old poor: pensioners' incomes in the European Community. Ageing and Society, vol. 10, pp. 261-277.

Lo Vuolo, Rubén M. (1996). *Reformas previsionales en América Latina: una visión crítica en base al caso argentino. Economia e Sociedade* (Unicamp: *Campinas-SP*), vol. 6 (junho), pp. 153-181.

Martin, L. G. (1989). Living arrangements of the elderly in Fiji, Korea, Malaysia and the Philippines. *Demography*, vol. 26, No. 4, pp. 627-643.

Médici, André C. (1997). *A saúde e o custo de envelhecer. Como Vai? População Brasileira* (Brasilia, DF), ano 2, vol. 2 (setembro).

Mesa-Lago, Carmelo (1996). *Las reformas de las pensiones en América Latina y la posición de los organismos internacionales. Revista de la CEPAL (Naciones Unidas)*, vol. 60 (diciembre), pp. 73-94.

_____ (1997). *Análise comparativa da reforma estrutural do sistema previdenciário realizada em oito países latino-americanos; descrição, avaliação e lições.* Paper presented at the Seminário Internacional sobre Reforma no Sistema Previdenciário, Universidade de Miami, 12 de maio.

Morrison, Malcolm H. (1986). Work and retirement in older society. In *Our Aging Society, Paradox and Promise,* A. Pifer and L. Bronte, eds. New York: Carnegie Corporation, pp. 341-365.

Nitsch, Manfred, and Helmut Schwarzer (1995). Recent developments in financing social security in Latin America. Discussion Paper, *Lateinamerika-Institut,* Berlin, August.

_____ (1998). *De paradigmas e mitos: notas sobre os fundos de pensão chilenos.* Revista de Economia Política (São Paulo-SP), vol. 18, No. 2 (abril-junho), pp. 96-105.

Oliveira, Francisco B., Kaisô I. Beltrão and Mônica G. Ferreira (1997). *Texto para discussão,* No. 508. Rio de Janeiro: IPEA.

Pinheiro, Liliana (1999). *Informalidade é uma bomba para a Previdência. O Estado de São Paulo* (29 de agosto).

Quin, J. F., and R. V. Burkhauser (1994). Retirement and labor force behavior of the elderly. In *Demography of Aging,* Linda G. Martin and Samuel H. Preston, eds. Washington, D. C.: National Academy Press, pp. 50-101.

Ruiz-Tagle, Jaime (1994). *La evolución del nuevo sistema de pensiones en Chile.* In *Economia y Trabajo en Chile,* Jaime Ruiz-Tagle and Mario Velázquez, eds. Santiago de Chile: PET — Fourth Annual Report.

Saad, Paulo M. (1996). Living arrangements of the elderly in north-east and south-east Brazil, 1980. *Anais do X Encontro Nacional de Estudos Populacionais,* Caxambu, MG: ABEP.

_____ (1998). Support transfers between the elderly and the family in north-east and south-east Brazil. Austin: University of Texas, Ph.D. dissertation.

Souza, Marcelo M. (1998). *A importância dos rendimentos dos idosos nos rendimentos das famílias. Como Vai? População Brasileira* (Brasília, DF), ano 3, vol. 3 (dezembro).

Uthoff, Andras (1997). *Reformas a los sistemas de pensiones, mercado de capitales y ahorro. Revista de la CEPAL (Naciones Unidas),* vol. 63 (diciembre), pp. 29-50.

POLITICAL, SOCIAL AND ECONOMIC CRISES AND LIVING ARRANGEMENTS OF OLDER PERSONS: THE CASE OF UKRAINE

*Vladislav V. Bezrukov and Natalia A. Foigt**

In some countries of the former Soviet Union, the transition from centrally planned to market-oriented economies is progressing more or less smoothly, in others it appears to be shock therapy, and in still others, shock without therapy. Political instability, economic recession or even crisis in the post-communist countries have led to changes in the priorities of social programmes and to the impaired functioning of existing institutions responsible for the welfare of vulnerable groups of population.

Decentralization of control over social protection and delegation by the central Governments of their responsibilities to local governments and non-governmental and private sectors have brought additional hardships to the social protection and well-being of the elderly.

In other words, the introduction of welfare programmes in the countries of the former Soviet Union is taking place in very unfavourable social and economic conditions. The elderly population groups find themselves extremely unprotected in all spheres of life, including income security, health care and living arrangements.

THE SOCIO-ECONOMIC SITUATION AND THE POPULATION AGEING PROFILE

The present economic status of Ukraine, like that of other republics of the former Soviet Union, is characterized by further declines in production, a drop in the gross domestic product (GDP) and a decline in the living standards of the people. According to data of the State Statistical Committee, in 1998 GDP fell by 40.9 per cent compared to 1990 (Ukraine, State Statistical Committee, 1999b). Goods and services output fell by 31.8 and 22.6 per cent, respectively (see figure I). Although the number of people who could not afford a basket of the 22 most important food items decreased from 22.2 per cent in 1995 to 15.7 per cent in 1998, it is still very large.

---

* Institute of Gerontology, Academy of Medical Science, Kiev, Ukraine.

Figure I. Changes in basic economic indices, 1990-1998

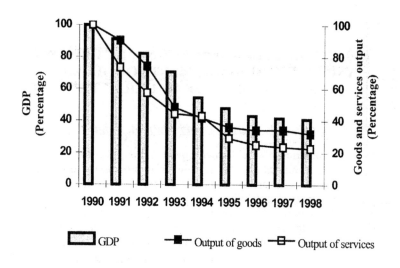

Sources: Ukraine, Ministry for Statistics (1996a); Ukraine, State Statistical Committee (1998b, 1999b).

Under such conditions, population growth in Ukraine has become negative: birth rates have fallen, death rates have risen, rates of natural increase are negative, and the depopulation process has become protracted (see figures II and III). During the past decade, the life expectancy of the population of Ukraine as a whole, and particularly the elderly population, has declined at a rapid pace: by 1997, the life expectancy at birth had dropped to 68.1 years, a decrease of 2.6 years in comparison with 1989, and life expectancy at age 65 declined from 14.96 years in 1989/90 to 13.69 years in 1997/98 (Ukraine, State Statistical Committee, 1998a) (see tables 1-3). All of these changes have occurred against a background of progressive population ageing.

Within a nine-year period, from 1989 to 1998, the number of persons aged 60 and over increased from 18.3 per cent to 19.5 per cent. Women typically outnumber men. At the same time, the sex ratios of older age groups have decreased during the past decade owing to a greater increase in female mortality, especially at very old age. In the 60+ age group, there were 49 men for every 100 women in 1989 and 55 men for every 100 women in 1998. The trends in dependency ratios indicate a substantial dependency shift from children to persons aged 60+ during the period of transition. The youth-dependency burden decreased from 40 dependants for every 100 workers in 1989 to 35 in 1998, while the elderly-dependency burden increased from 31 to 33 dependants, respectively.

**Figure II. Birth rate, death rate and rate of natural increase,
1989-1998**

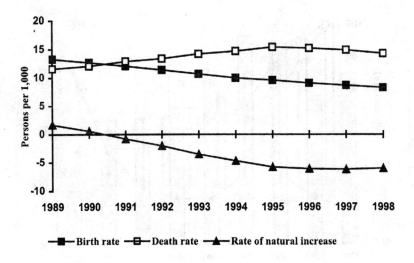

Source: Ukraine, State Statistical Committee (1999b).

Figure III. Changes in population size and ageing indices, 1989-1998

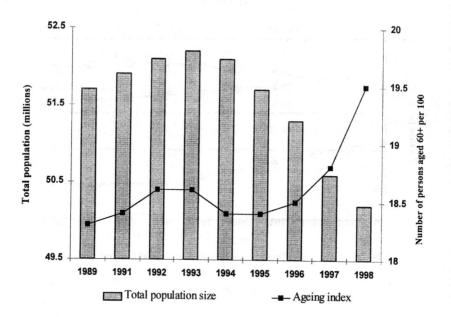

Source: Ukraine Ministry for Statistics (1996a); Ukraine, State Statistical Committee (1996b).

TABLE 1. DEATH RATE BY AGE, 1985-1998
(Per 1,000)

	1985/86	1990/91	1994/95	1996/97	1998
Total population	11.6	12.6	15.1	15.0	14.4
60-64	18.9	20.7	26.1	25.3	23.5
65-69	29.4	29.0	35.5	36.0	34.6
70+	80.9	87.6	95.4	88.2	84.4

Source: Ukraine, State Statistical Committee (1999b).

TABLE 2. LIFE EXPECTANCY AT BIRTH, 1985-1998
(Years)

	Total population	Male	Female
1985/86	70.5	65.9	74.5
1989/90	70.7	65.9	75.0
1992/93	69.3	64.2	74.2
1993/94	68.7	63.5	73.7
1994/95	67.2	61.8	72.7
1995/96	66.9	61.4	72.7
1996/97	67.4	61.9	73.0
1997/98	68.1	62.7	73.5

Source: Ukraine, State Statistical Committee (1999b).

TABLE 3. LIFE EXPECTANCY AT BIRTH AND AT AGE 65, 1989-1998
(Years)

	Life expectancy at birth	Life expectancy at age 65
1989/90	70.7	14.96
1991/92	69.3	14.42
1992/93	68.7	14.27
1994/95	67.2	13.62
1995/96	66.9	13.54
1996/97	67.4	13.67
1997/98	68.1	13.69

Source: Ukraine, State Statistical Committee (1998a, 1999b).

As to changes occurring in the demographic basis of family support, it is necessary to note the decrease in the absolute and relative numbers of kin supporters. The potential support ratio (number of persons aged 15-64 per those aged 65+) declined from 5.7 supporters per one supportee in 1989 to 4.8 supporters per one supportee in 1998. Taking into account the average length of one generation, which was roughly 26 years in Ukraine at the end of the twentieth century and tended to change very slowly, the contemporary changes in the number of generations of children (0-26 years of age), parents (27-52 years), grandparents (53-78 years) and great grandparents (79+) in the entire population indicate a decrease in the proportion of younger generations in favour of older ones (see table 4). Between 1989 and 1998, the caregivers/care-receivers ratio dropped among the young cohorts and increased markedly between grandparents and great-grandparents. This has created a big problem for those elderly who receive limited assistance from their children and who, simultaneously, have to take care of very old dependent parents. This situation is expected to become much more acute in the future.

TABLE 4. POPULATION AGE STRUCTURE AND POTENTIAL SUPPORT RATIO PER GENERATION, 1989 AND 1998

Generation[a]	Age structure (percentage)		Potential support ratio per generation (number of supporters per 100 supportees)		
	1989	1998		1989	1998
Children (age 0-26)	38.0	36.6	Children/parents	105	102
Parents (age 27-52)	36.1	35.8	Parents/grandparents	155	143
Grandparents (age 53-78)	23.3	25.0			
Great-grandparents (age 79+)	2.7	2.6	Grandparents/ great-grandparents	868	961

Sources: Ukrainian Soviet Socialist Republic, Ministry for Statistics (1991); Ukraine, State Statistical Committee (1999a).

[a] Average length of generation = 26 years.

PATTERNS OF LIVING ARRANGEMENTS

At the beginning of the twentieth century, the extended family in Ukraine was not the true, classical pattern of the patriarchal family. It represented a conglomeration of nuclear family members, unmarried siblings of the nuclear couple, lodgers, hired hands and older kin who managed to survive infections, ailments, accidents and the like (Ponomaryov, 1989). During the course of socio-economic development, family transformation occurred, with a breakdown of families into separate generations, keeping their own households. The current household composition indicates a high level of family nuclearization and a weakening of traditional family bonds. According to 1989 census data, a married couple with or without children under age 18 constituted the major part (58.0 per cent) of total households (see table 5). Male and female households with children and without a spouse constituted 12.1 per cent of all households. At the same time, the proportion of households where one or two younger generations co-resided with their parents constituted 18.1 per cent. In accordance with the 1989 census data, the majority of people aged 60+ (more often men than women) lived with one or several persons (see table 6). Some 13.0 per cent of men and 46.0 per cent of women of this age group lived alone. Older men living alone were more than three times outnumbered by older women living alone. In the study sample, the proportion of urban elderly living in multigenerational families was higher than the proportion of those living alone or with a spouse (see table 7). Men are more likely to live independently with a spouse. Women mostly live in three-generation families. Also, the proportion of women living alone outnumbers by more than two times the corresponding group of men.

TABLE 5. FAMILY LIVING ARRANGEMENTS, 1989

Household type	Per cent of all households
Family households	
One married couple with/without children	58.0
One married couple with/without children, with parents	11.5
Two or more married couples with/without children, with parents	4.8
Female householder (no spouse present) with children	9.4
Female householder (no spouse present) with children and parents	1.6
Male householder (no spouse present) with children	0.9
Male householder (no spouse present) with children and parents	0.2
Non-family households	
Female householder, living alone	9.7
Male householder, living alone	1.4
Others	2.5

Source: Ukraine, Ministry for Statistics (1992a).

TABLE 6. ABSOLUTE AND RELATIVE NUMBERS OF PERSONS LIVING ALONE, 1989, BY AGE AND SEX

Age	Absolute number (thousands)		Per cent of population	
	Male	Female	Male	Female
Below 15	11.3	8.9	0.3	0.2
15-19	28.8	52.0	2.3	4.0
20-29	167.2	127.2	6.5	4.8
30-39	129.0	81.6	4.7	2.8
40-49	126.7	138.8	6.5	6.5
50-54	81.3	151.4	7.3	11.9
55-59	60.1	202.5	7.7	21.4
60 and over	226.7	1 540.1	13.0	46.0

Source: Ukraine, Ministry for Statistics (1992a).

TABLE 7. LIVING ARRANGEMENTS OF URBAN POPULATION AT AGE 60 AND OVER IN UKRAINE IN 1995, BY SEX OF SAMPLED PERSONS (Percentage)

Household composition	Male (N=305)[a]	Female (N=363)[a]
Living alone	7.6	17.3
Living with a spouse	36.8	22.0
Living with or without a spouse with children	20.5	18.8
Living with or without a spouse with children and grandchildren	35.1	41.9

Source: Natalia Foigt (forthcoming).
[a] Number of observations.

As is evident from the data (Chuiko, 1996), reduced rates of marriage and increased rates of divorce and widowhood represent the most acute transformation and structural shifts that occur as a result of socio-economic crisis in the marital/familial sphere. In view of the general control over birth rates and family planning, there is an increasing trend towards childlessness and unmarried motherhood, the prevalence of informal sexual partnerships, a rise in the proportion of incomplete families and an increased number of orphaned children. Nevertheless, in accordance with matrimonial/familial traditions, 38.6 per cent of the Ukrainian population live in families, the number of which is more than 14 million.

Based on the data of the State Statistical Committee, the number of marriages per 1,000 population dropped from 9.5 in 1989 and 1991 to 7.6 in 1992, 7.7 in 1994 and 6.2 in 1998. At the same time, the number of divorces grew from 3.7 per 1,000 population in 1989 to 4.3 in 1992, and then decreased to 3.6 in 1998 (see figure IV). It is noteworthy that divorces are more widespread in towns, especially in large towns. One of the consequences of divorce, which may be encountered by the divorced couple, is difficulty in supporting ageing parents. Familial relations between grandparents and grandchildren are also affected.

Compared to 1989, when, according to census data, the average size of a household was 3.2 persons, the results of the sociological study "Health 1996", carried out by the Kiev International Institute of Sociology, show that, in 1996, the average size of a household increased to 3.8 persons, with 3.7 persons in towns and 4.3 persons in villages (Ukraine, Cabinet of Ministers, 1997). By contrast, the number of two-person households decreased from 35.1 per cent in 1989 to 12.1 per cent in 1996, indicating that a large number of young families cannot live separately from their parents, owing to economic constraints or lack of housing.

Figure IV. Marriages and divorces, 1990-1998

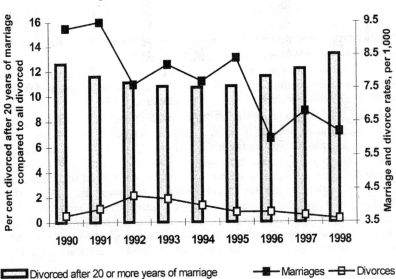

Sources: Ukraine, Ministry for Statistics (1996a); Ukraine, State Statistical Committee (1999b).

Social, economic, ethnic and interpersonal relationships have been transformed during the course of the transition in Ukraine. The family continues to play a major role in providing informal care for the elderly, but the role of the family is weakening. This particularly holds true in the rural areas, where there are more intensive concentrations of elderly people living alone. Problems related to worsening health become even more acute against a background of low income, price increases and inadequate medical services. There are more hardships for the elderly living alone, which they cannot resolve by themselves, namely, the absence of daily living services, maintenance and repair of their houses, and a lack of conveniences, including transport.

Based on the data of a longitudinal study (carried out jointly with the World Health Organization) of the residents of Kiev aged 60 and over (1,364 subjects), it was found that, with age, there is an increase in the correlation between the degree of worsening health and family composition: the number of persons with pronounced physical limitations rises almost three-fold in the 75 and over age group compared to those aged 60-74 years. The relative number of elderly persons who have lost the ability to take care of themselves and who live with family was 1.1 to 1.8 times the number living alone.

Concerning family composition, among the oldest old versus the younger old living alone, there was a smaller increase in the number of persons with marked physical limitations compared to those living with family. The difference varied from 2.5 to 4.0 times, respectively.

Despite the fact that persons living alone versus those living with family have fewer health problems, the former appear to have greater needs for medical and social services.

The Kiev Institute of Gerontology has developed a new method for assessing the health needs of the elderly for various types of medical service, a so-called automated expert system for quantifying dependency on medical, social and psychological assistance (AESKOZ). Using this method, researchers have conducted a selective socio-medical study of the population in different regions of Ukraine (8,574 persons of retirement age). The results obtained have permitted researchers to assess, promptly and with very high accuracy, not only the needs of people beyond retirement age for various kinds of medical service, but also its tentative costs. It is noteworthy that these costs are equal to the size of all budget expenses allocated by the State for public health care.

According to the data from the above study, in the sample aged 70 years and over, who were living alone, there were subgroups of persons with different degrees of dependency. Thus, the percentage of those needing constant social and medical care (for whom in-home service could not be provided) was 13.8 per cent in towns and 2.7 per cent in villages (Chaikovskaya, 1998). Among village residents, it was predominantly found that one elderly spouse was still able to look after the other. Among urban residents, 69.6 per cent of the elderly were referred to special departments of community social centres, the remainder were taken care of by their spouses, relatives or others. Of the latter group, 10 per cent were looked after in accordance with an agreement concerning housing inheritance.

Some 13.2 per cent of town residents and 6.6 per cent of village residents needed partial assistance in daily living from other people or needed placement in boarding houses or shelters.

Among town residents, 43.13 per cent expressed the need to bring commercial and daily living services closer to the residential areas of the elderly; the figure for village residents was 36.6 per cent. These services include home-delivery of food products and help in the performance of heavy household work (e.g., gardening, cleaning, washing windows, and laundry).

A representative study of changes in the system of non-formal support for the elderly during a period of political and socio-economic crisis was carried out in Kiev in 1995 (Foigt, forthcoming). In this study, the data from interviews of 663 citizens of Kiev aged 60 and over were examined. The main findings indicate that the new socio-economic conditions tend to encourage a transformation of the elderly person's family: intergenerational cooperation has undergone changes in terms of level, structure and trends, and the breakdown of multigenerational families has slowed down.

In comparison with 1980, when 5 per cent of the working elderly and 10 per cent of the non-working elderly received material support from their adult children (Shapiro, 1980), in 1995 such support was received by almost 30 per cent of the elderly living separately from their children (Foigt, forthcoming). At the same time, in 1980, 64 per cent of the working elderly and 26 per cent of the non-working elderly provided economic support to their adult children, while in 1995, the number of elderly parents giving assistance in money or in kind to their children's families declined to 15 per cent. It should also be noted that the character of interrelationships within the elderly person's family also changed: according to the 1995 data, during the process of socio-economic transformation, about 80 per cent of elderly people reported a reduction in family contacts and, on average, 12 per cent of them reported an increase in intrafamilial tension and frequency of family conflicts.

SOCIO-ECONOMIC STATUS OF OLDER PERSONS' FAMILIES

The worsening economic situation affects the level and living conditions of the entire population and, in particular, the elderly as its most vulnerable segment. The growing cost of living owing to soaring retail prices, inflation and low pensions (the size of pensions has long been unchanged) has led to a bigger gap between the economic provision of pensioners and the changing living standards of the working population.

The normal process of population ageing has acquired some negative aspects under conditions of economic crisis. Production restructuring, accompanied by a growing unemployment, has pushed out from the labour market those citizens who, in accordance with existing legislation, are entitled to receive a pension after retirement. As a result, they have been deprived of any opportunity to improve their material well-being. In other words, there has been an increase in the number of ageing people who are fully dependent on the level and quality of social security in the country. Simultaneously, the number of working individuals among the population able to work has decreased. Thus, a vicious circle has occurred; a fall of production, an imperfect taxation system, and so on have reduced revenues, whereas an intensive growth of population groups who are in need of social support is consuming the social funds of the State.

Within a short period of time there has been a marked increase in the gap in incomes between the working population and non-working pensioners. Thus, while in 1985/86, the average monthly old-age pension was more than 40 per cent of the average wage of workers, in 1998, that number fell to 27.7 per cent (Ukraine, State Statistical Committee, 1999b) (see figure V). Although the ratio between old-age pensions and wages tending to level off, pensioners are being pushed into the so-called low-income population group.

The growing differentiation in incomes has become a source of population stratification, increasing social discomfort and tension in society. According to the data contained in the report of the President of Ukraine to Parliament on the economic and social development of Ukraine in 1995, the average earnings of 10 per cent of the well-to-do citizens surpassed the earnings of 10 per cent of the low-income population by 6.7 times in 1993, by 9 times in 1994, and by 12 times in 1995.

Analysis of the income structure of families with a varying level of per capita income shows differences in the degree of ability to adapt under market economy conditions in some population groups. With a gradually reducing share of wages and social transfers (pensions, stipends, etc.) in the budgets of all groups of families, the proportion of these income sources in low-income families appears to be highest (see tables 8 and 9).

As living standards decline, the share of necessary expenditures (for foodstuffs, services, etc.) within the income-spending structure of disadvantaged families increases sharply, while the income share devoted to buying non-food products, particularly those of long-term usage, decreases. It is noteworthy that the share of income for savings was negative for the low-income population in 1995 and 1998 (more money was withdrawn than deposited).

With the declining income of pensioners, the volume and structure of consumption in this group is shifted towards limiting expenditures on non-essential goods and services. Thus, their purchasing capacity for non-food products becomes limited and access to most vital services difficult.

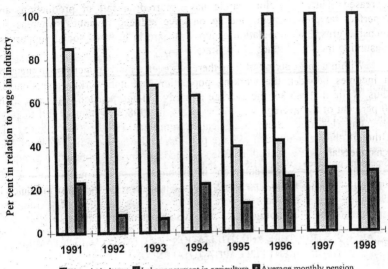

Figure V. Ratio of average monthly wages to pension,
1991-1998

■ Wage in industry ■ Labour payment in agriculture ■ Average monthly pension

Sources: Ukraine, Ministry for Statistics (1996a); Ukraine, State Statistical Committee (1999b).

TABLE 8. AVERAGE PER CAPITA TOTAL INCOME DISTRIBUTION, 1995 AND 1998, BY FAMILY COMPOSITION

	1995			1998		
	Below subsistence level	Middle income	High income	Below subsistence level	Middle income	High income
Small families (1-2 persons)	42.8	26.4	34.8	20.9	50.7	28.4
Middle-sized families (3-4 persons)	50.6	37.8	11.6	46.7	46.6	6.7
Large families (5 persons or more)	71.5	25.6	2.9	70.6	28.0	1.4

Sources: Ukraine, Ministry for Statistics (1996a); Ukraine, State Statistical Committee (1999b).

TABLE 9. STRUCTURE AND UTILIZATION OF TOTAL INCOME IN FAMILIES WITH DIFFERENT PER CAPITA TOTAL INCOME, 1995 AND 1998

	1995			1998		
	Low income	Middle income	High income	Low income	Middle income	High income
Income sources						
Labour payment	46.6	45.3	41.5	38.6	46.0	53.3
Pensions and social transfers	11.6	9.1	8.1	32.2	10.5	9.6
Self-employment earnings	21.6	28.4	35.1	22.8	26.3	23.0
Others	20.2	17.2	15.3	6.4	17.2	14.1
Utilization						
Foodstuff	68.7	59.8	53.2	79.4	56.5	46.5
Goods	16.2	17.5	17.0	14.4	16.2	16.8
Services	9.4	8.9	7.9	10.0	13.6	14.6
Taxes	2.7	3.6	4.2	2.5	4.6	7.0
Others	6.1	7.3	11.3	5.8	8.9	11.0
Savings	-3.1	2.9	6.4	-12.1	0.2	4.1

Sources: Ukraine, Ministry for Statistics (1996a); Ukraine, State Statistical Committee (1999b).

Because of the economic crisis, the consumption of food products is reduced and the structure of their consumption is changed. In the low-income families of pensioners, the consumption of essential products, such as meat, eggs, fish and fruits, is rapidly decreasing. Judging by changes in the consumption structure, they are being replaced by cheaper foodstuffs — milk, sugar, bread and potatoes — although their amounts in the diet of low-income families have decreased more rapidly in comparison with other population groups. To support the disadvantaged and marginalized groups, particularly pensioners, the Government provides monetary assistance. Also, local authorities are making efforts to provide non-cash (partial payment of food products and commodities, spa and resort vouchers, community services, fuel, etc.) and cash assistance (see figure VI). But with the growing number of low-income citizens against a background of chronic budget deficits, the number of persons receiving such assistance has declined.

The total amount of assistance has been reduced as well. Thus, while in 1993 the average size of non-cash assistance was 17.1 per cent and of cash assistance was 31.4 per cent of the average monthly pension, in 1998 those numbers fell to 6.5 per cent and 5.9 per cent, respectively. Some shifts have occurred in providing non-cash assistance. In 1992, government expenditures were channelled to pay partially for food products and industrial commodities, while in 1994, the main portion was spent on providing food for the low-income elderly population. In 1995, the number of specialized dining rooms and daily living services for low-income citizens declined. Thus, impoverished pensioners, encountering difficulties in taking care of themselves, have been marginalized.

ECONOMIC ACTIVITY OF SENIOR CITIZENS

The living standards of the population are in large measure determined by the level of employment. According to data from the State Statistical Committee, between 1990 and 1997 the percentage of people who were engaged in all areas of production reduced by 8.6 per cent (Ukraine, State Statistical Committee, 1999b). In accordance with the data on the economic activity of the population (carried out by the same Committee), in October 1996 the level of employment among the population aged 15-70 was 64.0 per cent (68.7 per cent for males and 59.9 per cent for females), a figure much lower than in the pre-crisis period. The level of registered unemployment during 1992-1994 was 0.3 per cent, at the beginning of 1995 and 1996 it was 0.5 per cent, and at the beginning of 1997 it was 1.3 per cent of the population of working age, who are able to work. The main component of unemployment in Ukraine is a so-called "hidden unemployment", that is, forced unpaid leave and part-time workdays.

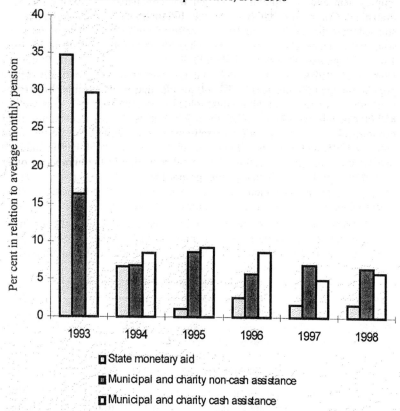

Figure VI. Provision of monthly monetary aid, cash and non-cash assistance for low-income pensioners, 1993-1998

☐ State monetary aid

■ Municipal and charity non-cash assistance

☐ Municipal and charity cash assistance

Sources: Ukraine, Ministry for Statistics (1994, 1995, 1996a); Ukraine, State Statistical Committee (1998b, 1999b).

A large-scale survey of households with respect to economic activity, employment and unemployment, which was conducted in 1995 by the State Statistical Committee jointly with the International Labour Organization, showed that the absolute number of post-working age population (60 plus) who were engaged in various branches of the economy declined from 1,027,300 people in 1989 to 643,300 in 1995 (Ukraine, State Statistical Committee, 1996b). In 1995, the total number of the economically active population aged 60 plus was 1,496,100 people, that is, the number of persons working in private agricultural households or the industrial sector, as well as 852,000 people who had applied for a job, that is, 57 per cent of the total economically active population of retirement age. During the period from 1989 to 1995, a shift in the structure of older workers employed in industry occurred. Against the background of a total reduction in the number of older workers employed in industry, the proportion of old employees reduced sharply in the non-production sector (culture, education, medicine, etc.), where white-collar personnel are most prevalent (see figure VII).

Workers of retirement age are mainly concentrated in industry and in the public sector. At the same time, their numbers are few in joint and private ventures, which, in accordance with their personnel policies, avoid employing elderly workers.

In 1995, unemployed persons aged 60 and over accounted for 4 per cent of the total unemployed population. The percentage of persons registering themselves as unemployed among the economically active population aged 60 plus is much lower than among young people but is slightly higher than among the middle-aged group. In other words, the working potential of the older population, who are able and willing to work, is insufficiently utilized in comparison with the middle-aged group of the economically active population.

HOUSING CONDITIONS

During the past decade, there has been a slow increase in housing provisions for Ukrainians: on average from 17.8 square metres of living space per one inhabitant in 1990 to 21.0 sq m in 1997, that is 18.0 per cent (Ukraine, State Statistical Committee, 1999b). In towns, the increase has been from 16.5 to 20.8 sq m (26.1 per cent) and in rural areas, from 20.6 to 22.7 sq m (10.2 per cent).

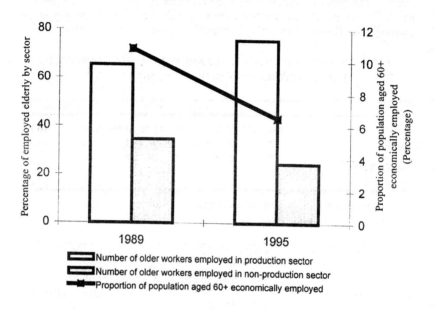

Figure VII. Changes in number and structure of employees aged 60+, 1989 and 1995

Number of older workers employed in production sector
Number of older workers employed in non-production sector
Proportion of population aged 60+ economically employed

Sources: Ukraine, Ministry for Statistics (1992b, 1996b).

With the declining possibility of receiving a new flat, the prospect for people of retirement age to obtain one from the state housing fund is a little better than from the community housing department fund: in 1997, the index of housing provision from the state fund was 2.7 per cent against 0.5 per cent from the community housing department fund. However, when analysing the dynamics of the average size of flats, which have been built from the state fund during the period from 1990 to 1997, it is possible to conclude that housing construction preferences are given to flats with large metric areas, that is, flats that are designed for large families. One- and two-room apartments, which are generally needed by the pensioners' families, are being constructed mainly at the expense of the community housing departments; under the conditions of growing construction costs, such flats have become unaffordable for the elderly.

According to the 1989 population census, less than half of the families in Ukraine live in flats that have central heating (42.3 per cent), cold water (46.8 per cent), hot water (31.9 per cent) and a sewage system (41.6 per cent) (Ukrainian Soviet Socialist Republic, Ministry for Statistics, 1991) (see table 10). Only 38.4 per cent of families had a bath or a shower in their houses. The population best provided with conveniences were families living in multi-storey apartment houses: almost two thirds of those inhabitants had cold and hot running water, a bath or a shower, an electric or gas stove and central heating. At the same time, the availability of modern conveniences in individually constructed houses remained low: only 40 per cent of families living in this type of dwelling used a central water supply, of those 24 per cent had hot water and 20 per cent had central heating. There is a huge gap in the housing amenities of urban and rural elderly persons (see figure VIII).

TABLE 10. PERCENTAGE OF FAMILY AND NON-FAMILY HOUSEHOLDS LACKING COMMON HOUSEHOLD AMENITIES, 1989

	Family households	Non-family households
Toilet	51.1	59.1
Bath	54.5	63.2
Water supply	45.1	54.4
Hot water	61.9	67.3

Source: Ukraine, Ministry for Statistics (1992a).

Figure VIII. Provision of communal services and distribution of older population by type of settlement, 1998

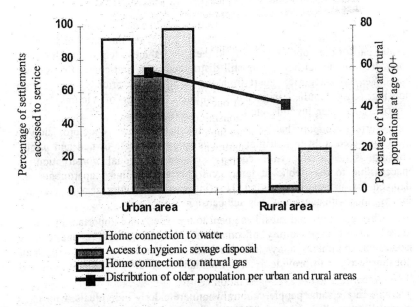

Source: Ukraine, State Statistical Committee (1999b).

The results of studies on the relationship between the life expectancy of people aged 60 and over and their housing conditions, which had been conducted by the Institute of Gerontology in 1998-1999, show that favourable housing has a positive influence on the life expectancy of the elderly (Foigt, unpublished). At the same time, unfavourable housing, with a lack of amenities, thus making it impossible to meet the specific needs of the elderly, reduces their life expectancy. Because of the lack of amenities of individual constructions in the rural areas, the proportion of 85-plus individuals among residents of specialized boarding houses for the aged is higher than among residents of other types of residential dwellings.

Under the conditions of a growing housing market, when comfortable living accommodations are practically unavailable to the low-income population, the State is trying to take appropriate measures to lessen the acute shortage of well-equipped adequate housing for the elderly. Policies for the provision of senior citizens with new housing and the improvement of existing ones are being implemented. One strategy is to relieve the financial pressure on the elderly in view of the necessity to cover their housing expenses.

Thus, for certain categories of pensioners, among them war and labour veterans, a number of legislative acts envisage partial or complete exemption from paying rent and some community services. For some groups of senior citizens, living in houses without central heating, it is envisaged to provide fuel on a free or partially paid basis.

Another type of state assistance in the area of housing provision for the elderly is to accord them priority on waiting lists for new housing. Under the existing conditions of a shortage in new housing, on the one hand, and a greater part of the population being in the low-income category, on the other hand, free municipal housing is still distributed on a first-come, first-served basis. Several categories, apart from the elderly, have priority in receiving housing (e.g., families with many children, families of victims of the Chernobyl disaster, invalids, etc.).

Current economic hardships in Ukraine do not allow a wide provision of the guaranteed right to housing: the development of state-owned and public housing is at a standstill, cooperative and individual construction is inaccessible to the public at large, and contracts to finish apartments are delayed for an indefinite period. Housing and community service fees are incongruous with average wages and pensions.

The privileges and subsidies given to the elderly are important in paying these costs. The possibility of privatizing, inheriting, selling and buying houses or apartments allow the elderly to manipulate, in some way, their housing in order to provide a certain amount of security for themselves and their relatives.

There are some people, among whom are elderly individuals, who have no dwelling at all. In a special investigation on the spread of beggarliness in Ukraine, carried out by members of the School of Social Work of the National University, Kiev Mohyla Academy, it was found that the average age of those who beg in Kiev is 64-65 years (Nevtjuk, 1997). Two thirds of the people who have no roof over their head and live by begging are persons over 60 years of age.

HEALTH AND HEALTH SERVICES

The health status of the elderly in the countries of Eastern Europe and the former Soviet Union is much worse than in the Western countries. It is reflected in a shortening of the lifespan and lower survival to retirement age, and increased morbidity and mortality rates, etc.

According to recent data, negative morbidity trends were noted in many Eastern European countries, including Ukraine. For example, in Ukraine between 1990 and 1998, total morbidity increased owing to, in particular, diseases of the nervous system, and infectious and parasitic diseases (see table 11). Among the latter group of diseases, tuberculosis is the main one. As pulmonary diseases occur most commonly at very old age, and as the absolute number of this population segment has been markedly reduced during the past decade, the morbidity indices for this class of disease tend to decrease.

TABLE 11. MORBIDITY RATE, 1990-1998, BY CATEGORY OF ILLNESS

Category of illness	Cases of illness registered for the first time, per 10,000 population		
	1990	1995	1998
Infectious and parasitic diseases	257	292	304
Malignant tumours	60	64	74
Diseases of nervous system	509	590	663
Cardiovascular diseases	222	270	336
Pulmonary diseases	3 283	3 051	2 762
Diseases of musculo-skeletal system	265	275	318
Other diseases	1 613	1 781	1 906
Total	**6 209**	**6 323**	**6 364**

Source: Ukraine, State Statistical Committee (1999b).

Many factors contribute to these negative trends. They include a polluted environment, bad working conditions and exhausting work, widespread unhealthy habits (smoking, alcohol consumption, etc.), malnutrition, and inadequate health-care systems.

The public health-care system of Ukraine was formed during the time of the former Soviet Union, when the prevention of diseases was the priority of the medical institutions and socio-epidemiological services. Despite steadily increasing spending on various health-care aspects, cost-effectiveness has never been a priority.

The high priority given to public health care and the efforts towards its socialization, during 1970s, brought about a 75 per cent coverage of health care from public funds in the 1980s. In subsequent years, when the demand for resources began to exceed the state's capacity, the share of public spending on overall health-care expenditures began to decline. At the same time, an approach was taken to use patients' and other private resources in order to resolve the public health-care problems in the country. At first, this approach seemed to create a system of equal medical services for all. But, in reality, the well-to-do patients were able to pay informally to get better-quality medical service.

During the transition to a market-based economy, the amount of state expenditure on public health care has declined considerably. State-owned medical institutions face many difficulties, which are associated with the acute lack of medicine and equipment and the non-payment of wages of medical personnel. As a consequence, the quality of treatment has worsened considerably.

Considering the low level of income of elderly patients, who represent the main consumers of public health-care services, the Government has tried to assist them by proposing several social programmes:

- Free or partially paid medicines, prostheses, spa and resort treatments;
- Advantages in using specialized health-care institutions;
- Material and personnel for medical examinations of certain elderly population groups.

SOCIAL WELFARE SERVICE

The functioning of the state social welfare system, which is supposed to provide formal socio-medical services for the elderly, depends on the condition of the state budget. In the case of the newly independent countries of Europe, in which budget spending is greater than real revenues, it is difficult to expect efficient provision of the state social services. At the same time, the generally observable trend in Europe to shift the emphasis from a policy of full state responsibility for these services to a policy of encouraging the use of an ageing person's individual resources leads to the necessity of developing a formal social support network to keep the elderly in their natural environment.

The social protection of elderly citizens in Ukraine is undertaken by organizing social and daily living services and a medical service through a network of boarding houses, community centres and social welfare departments. At the present time, there are 57 boarding houses for aged citizens and the disabled, 14 nursing homes and 147 psycho-neurological boarding houses, accommodating 47,800 persons. These institutions are provided free of charge. The residents receive 10 per cent of their pensions as pocket money.

During the period of economic crisis, the financing of institutions for the aged from state resources has been reduced. Thus, in 1998, expenditures for the maintenance of boarding houses in Ukraine amounted to, on average, only 79 per cent of the needed amount. As of 1 February 1999, the credit debt of these institutions amounted to 19 hryvnias.

The state-supported system of formal social welfare services for the elderly living beyond the reach of a domiciliary service is funded from the federal and municipal budgets. Currently, services for the elderly who live alone and are disabled are carried out by 631 community centres and 130 social welfare units. Some 38,000 social workers provide domiciliary assistance for 500,000 needy persons. Scarce resources do not permit an increase in the volume or the development of a structure of provided services. Municipal and local social welfare bodies ensure services to only some categories of the elderly (those who live alone, low-income persons and disabled individuals), providing a limited number of services to them (mainly "meals-on-wheels" and home help). There are certain daily living services (laundry, hairdressing and dry cleaning) that are provided by local authorities based on a contract with a given institution. However, these services are not commonly used, and are particularly lacking in rural areas.

Non-governmental organizations are becoming more involved in providing social services for the elderly. These include religious and veterans' organizations, voluntary youth organizations and others. Efforts will be made to develop a voluntary movement, to arrange for its entry into the system of formal support for the elderly, and to create a cooperative environment that encourages an exchange of experience between volunteers and professionals. These are the main activities in this area.

CONCLUSION

The socio-economic crisis in Ukraine has seriously affected the elderly in relation to income provision, health status, living arrangements, accessibility to medical and social services, and their quality of life.

The change in income of older persons has noticeably weakened their financial autonomy and reduced their choice of preferences in terms of household structure. Low income encourages co-residence between the elderly and their relatives, mainly adult married children.

The transition to new property and ancestral relationships has led to structural changes in behavioural patterns, reducing the number of elderly living alone, increasing the number of divorces in advanced age, and encouraging unmarried cohabitation among elderly couples.

The old stereotype of the formation of family relations is broken; the balance between the level of assistance that elderly people expect to receive from their children and other relatives and the amount of assistance that a younger generation is ready to give them has been disturbed. Thus, the level of material support and emotional and psychological solidarity has been reduced, while the traditional basis for the social integration of an elderly person has eroded.

Under such conditions, appropriate social policy measures should be taken to encourage intergenerational integration and the more active participation of older persons in intrafamilial construction. The major goal of this policy is to ensure the continuous and consecutive development of family traditions, adding to the general ethnic culture, as well as strengthening solidarity among generations.

Mutual self-realization of young and old generations within a family brings about economic benefits. It promotes the replacement of older workers with their young counterparts, on the one hand, and leads to reducing the need for a number of social services (caring for children, sick family members, etc.), on the other. Economic evaluation of the share and structure of social services, the consumption of which is substituted by an intrafamilial division of labour, a rational redistribution of the released resources for purposes of developing multigenerational families in the form of legal payments to the family and additional pension payments will raise the status of the elderly in the family and consolidate relationships among generations.

Unemployment and low and irregular earnings in the formal economy seriously affect the quality of life of older generations. More acute problems relating to income security at old age arise for those workers who work in agriculture, the informal sector or are self-employed. This group is doomed to be marginalized and exclusively dependent on the minimum pension guaranteed by the State.

One of the ways of solving the problems of a sharp drop in income and unemployment among the population of retirement age is the development of a unified state strategy of support for elderly workers in a tight labour market.

Special attention should be paid to searching for ways to ensure effective economic and social self-realization of elderly people. This primarily implies the development of self-employment and entrepreneurship. The creation of an expanded network of profession-oriented institutions, adequate state financial support for self-employment and the provision of markets represent an effective means of stimulating the physical, occupational, economic and social resources of the pensioners.

The reduction of state support for the elderly and the lack of private and voluntary sectors has created a huge deficit in meeting their future needs for health care and social welfare. Under such conditions, it is especially important to develop a policy that is aimed at maintaining elderly people's health, preventing declining health and avoiding an increase in disability.

To solve the above problems, there is a need to develop a unified state strategy for older citizens that would be based on a mobilization of all societal efforts to support socially unprotected elderly persons, on the one hand, and creating conditions for the maximum realization of individual potential of this population group, on the other. The possibility of realizing such a strategy is determined by the prospects for resolving the economic crisis and improving the life of the people.

REFERENCES

Bezrukov, Vladislav V., Vera V. Chaikovskaya, and Elena I. Konshina (1999). A new method for evaluating the needs of elderly people in medico-social service. *Proceedings of the Conference on Organization of the System of Quality of Medical Care and Medical Services for the Population with the Use of Information Technologies.* Kiev: Scientific Information-Analytical Centre for Medical Statistics, pp. 126-129.

Bezrukov, Vladislav V., and Natalia N. Lakiza-Sachuk (1995). Status and conditions of the elderly within the family in Ukraine and other countries of Eastern and Central Europe (ECE). *Bold,* vol. 5, No. 2, pp. 23-35.

Bezrukov, Vladislav V., and others (1991). An automated system for quantifying the risk of the loss of self-servicing abilities as a new approach to assessing needs of elderly people in various kinds of medico-social service. *Problems of Aging and Longevity,* No. 1, pp. 63-69.

Bezrukov, Vladislav V., Nina V. Verzhykovskaya, and Vera V. Chaikovskaya (in press). The problems of health of elderly people and provision of medical care in Ukraine. *Zhurnal of the Academy of Medical Science of Ukraine.*

Chaikovskaya, Vera V. (1998). An informational support for decisions concerning the organization of medico-social service for the older population beyond working age. *Proceedings of the Conference on Informational Provision for Health Care as Part of Medical Service Network in Kiev.* Kiev, December 1998, pp. 85-89.

_____ (1999). The needs of elderly people in medico-social services: challenges and methodology of assessment. *Social Policy and Social Work. The Ukrainian Chronicle,* No. 3, pp. 53-61.

Chuiko, Lyubov V. (1996). Social and economic factors of the families' demographic transformation. In *Demographic Advances. Interdepartmental Book Collection of Scientific Works.* Issue 18. Valentina Steshenko, ed. Kiev: Institute of Economics of the National Academy of Sciences of Ukraine, pp. 86-98.

Foigt, Natalia A. (forthcoming). Simulation of discomfort occurring in the elderly, representing various demographic types of families, in new socio-economic conditions. *Problems of Aging and Longevity.*

_____ (unpublished). Life expectancies at old age: reality, factors, perspectives.

Nevtjuk, Fedir L. (1997). Beggary in Kiev. *Social Policy and Social Work,* Kiev, No. 2-3, pp. 50-59.

Ponomaryov, A. P. (1989). *Development of family and marital family relations in Ukraine.* Kiev: Naukova Dumka.

Shapiro, V. D. (1980). *Man on Pension. Social Problems and Life Style.* Moscow: Nauka.

Ukraine, Cabinet of Ministers (1997). *Health of Children and Women in Ukraine.* Kiev: United Nations Office in Ukraine.

_____, Ministry for Statistics (1992a). Family in Ukraine. Data from the 1989 population census. Kiev. Unpublished.

_____ (1992b). Social and professional structure of population in Ukraine per branches of economy. Data from the 1989 population census. Kiev. Unpublished.

_____ (1994). *National Economy of Ukraine in 1993.* Kiev: Tekhnika.

_____ (1995). *1994 Statistical Yearbook for Ukraine.* Kiev: Tekhnika.

_____ (1996a). *1995 Statistical Yearbook for Ukraine.* Kiev: Tekhnika.

_____ (1996b). *Economic Activities of the Population in Ukraine in 1995.* Kiev: Tekhnika.

_____, State Statistical Committee (1998a). Life tables for population of Ukraine, 1990-1998. Kiev. Unpublished.

_____ (1998b). *1997 Statistical Yearbook for Ukraine*. Kiev: Ukrainian Encyclopedia.

_____ (1999a). Composition of population in Ukraine by sex and age at 1 January 1999. Kiev. Unpublished.

_____ (1999b). *1998 Statistical Yearbook for Ukraine*. Kiev: Tekhnika.

Ukrainian Soviet Socialist Republic, Ministry for Statistics (1991). Composition of population in Ukrainian SSR by sex and age at 12 January 1989. Data from the 1989 All-Union population census. Kiev. Unpublished.

EXTREMELY RAPID AGEING AND THE LIVING ARRANGEMENTS OF THE ELDERLY: THE CASE OF CHINA

*Zeng Yi and Linda George**

Populations are ageing, with changes in the living arrangements of the elderly occurring in most countries, as a result of lower fertility, higher mobility, changing attitudes about family structure and function, and increasing life expectancy, especially mortality declines in later life. The population of China, which consists of more than two fifths of the world total, is ageing at an extraordinarily rapid pace. There are important interactions between population ageing, changes in the living arrangements of the elderly and the need for long-term-care service. Such interactions are directly related to community and family support systems and public policies. The present paper reviews the extremely rapid ageing process and the current status and trends in the living arrangements of the elderly in China. Some policy recommendations are also proposed based on our analysis.

EXTREMELY RAPID PROCESS OF POPULATION AGEING

Fastest increase in proportion of elderly persons

Previous studies (e.g., Liang, Tu and Chen, 1986; Ogawa, 1988; Zeng, 1989; Grigsby and Olshansky, 1989; Zeng and Vaupel, 1989; Banister, 1990; Vaupel and Zeng, 1991; Zeng, 1994) show that, although the proportion of the elderly aged 65 and above of the Chinese population is not very high at the present time (5.6 per cent in 1990), the speed of population ageing will be extremely fast in the first half of the twenty-first century. Under medium fertility[1] and medium mortality[2] assumptions, the Chinese elderly aged 65 and

* Zeng Yi is Senior Research Scientist at the Center for Demographic Studies and the Department of Sociology of Duke University, United States of America, Professor at the Institute for Population Research of Peking University, and Distinguished Research Scholar at the Max Planck Institute for Demographic Research. Linda George is Professor in the Department of Sociology and Associate Director of the Center for the Study of Aging and Human Development at Duke University. A longer version of this paper (including not only population projection but also family household projection) appeared in the online journal Demographic Research (Rostock, Germany), vol. 2/5 (May 2000). It is available at www.demographic-research.org.

older will account for 15.8 and 23.1 per cent of the total population by 2030 and 2050, respectively (Zeng and Vaupel, 1989; Zeng, 1994). The 1998 projections of the United Nations under medium fertility and medium mortality assumptions show that the Chinese elderly aged 65 and older would comprise 15.7 and 22.6 per cent of the total population in 2030 and 2050, respectively (United Nations, 1999b, p. 273). The medium variant of the United Nations projection is almost the same as our medium projection 10 years ago, which was performed independently and based on substantially different methodologies and base populations in various years.[3] Such consistency confirms that extremely rapid population ageing in China in the first half of the twenty-first century is definite — the proportion of the elderly population aged 65+ in 2050 will be more than four times higher than in 1990. The annual rate of increase in the proportion of the elderly population between 1990 and 2050 is 2.3 per cent.

In European societies, the ageing transition has been spread over one century or more. In China, however, this change will take place within a few decades and will reach more or less the same level of population ageing as in most of the developed countries by the middle of the twenty-first century. The proportion of the elderly in China will increase much faster than in almost all other countries in the world. It will take about 20 years for the elderly population to increase from 10 to 20 per cent in China (2017-2037), compared to 23 years in Japan (1984-2007), 61 years in Germany (1951-2012), 64 years in Sweden (1947-2011) and 57 years in the United States of America (1971-2028) (United Nations, 1999b). Japan is regarded as a country with very rapid population ageing, but the ageing process of the Chinese population will be even faster than that for Japan (Ogawa, 1988). Table 1 gives the percentage of elderly persons aged 65 and above in 1990, 2030 and 2050 in selected countries. Figure 1 shows the average annual growth rates of the proportion of elderly persons between 1990 and 2050 in China and in selected developing and developed countries with large population sizes. By the middle of the twenty-first century, the proportion of elderly persons in China will be higher than that in the United States by 0.9 percentage points, and the average annual increase between 1970 and 2050 in China will be 2.6 times as high as in the United States. The anticipated proportion of the elderly population in China in 2050 is somewhat lower than in Canada, France, and the United Kingdom of Great Britain and Northern Ireland, and substantially lower than in Germany, Italy and Japan. But the annual increase of the percentage of the elderly population between 1990 and 2050 in China will be much higher than in the above-mentioned European countries and 44 per cent higher than in Japan.

TABLE 1. INTERNATIONAL COMPARISON OF INDICATORS OF POPULATION AGEING

| | Percentage of elderly aged 65+ | | | | Number of elderly persons (millions) | | | |
	1990	2030	2050		Aged 65+ 1990	Aged 65+ 2050	Aged 80+ 1990	Aged 80+ 2050
China	5.6	15.7	22.6		63.0	334.0	7.839	99.602
India	4.3	9.7	15.1		37.0	230.9	4.017	46.999
Mexico	4.0	10.9	18.6		3.3	27.3	0.644	5.979
Republic of Korea	5.0	18.1	24.7		2.1	12.6	0.276	3.763
Canada	11.2	22.6	23.8		3.1	10.1	0.643	3.759
France	14.0	23.2	25.5		7.9	15.3	2.136	5.696
Germany	15.0	26.1	28.4		11.9	20.8	2.985	8.299
Italy	15.3	29.1	34.9		8.7	14.4	1.963	5.787
Japan	12.0	27.3	31.8		14.8	33.4	2.922	12.090
United Kingdom	15.7	23.1	24.9		8.1	14.1	2.092	5.287
United States of America	12.4	20.6	21.7		31.5	75.8	7.213	26.914

Source: United Nations (1999a, 1999b).

257

Figure I. International comparison of average annual increase rates of elderly populations, 1990-2050

(*Percentage*)

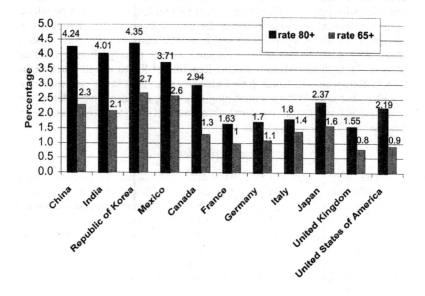

It is interesting to note that China is not alone with respect to extremely rapid population ageing among the developing countries. The proportion of elderly persons in the Republic of Korea will climb to a higher level with a larger annual increase rate than in China. Mexico and India, two developing countries with large population sizes, will also undergo very rapid population ageing at annual increase rates of 2.6 and 2.1 per cent, although their proportion of elderly persons in 2050 will be substantially lower than in China. The annual increases in the proportion of the elderly between 1990 and 2050 in China, India, Mexico and the Republic of Korea are all much higher than in European and North American countries. This fact deserves serious attention, not only in those developing countries, but also from international organizations and developed countries as well (Kinsella, 1988; Kinsella and Suzman, 1992; Martin and Kinsella, 1994).

Huge numbers of elderly persons

The very large size of the elderly population is another unique characteristic of population ageing in China. In 1990, there were 63 million elderly persons aged 65 and over. By 2030 and 2050, there will be 232 million and 331 million elderly people in China, respectively, under the medium mortality assumption, based on our projection (Zeng and Vaupel, 1989; Zeng, 1994). The most recent revision of the United Nations population projection forecasts that there will be 234.5 million and 333.6 million elderly persons in China in 2030 and 2050, respectively, under the medium mortality assumption (United Nations, 1999b, p. 273). Again, the surprising consistency of the projected total numbers of the elderly in China in the twenty-first century, produced independently by different scholars at different times, 10 years apart, following substantially different approaches, confirms the anticipated huge number of elderly persons in China in the twenty-first century.

Table 1 also gives the numbers of elderly persons in other selected countries, projected by the Population Division of the United Nations Secretariat (1999a, 1999b) under the medium variant. Under the medium mortality assumption, China's elderly population will be fairly close to the total population size of the United States, and 4.4 times as large as the United States elderly population by the middle of the twenty-first century. China's elderly population will outnumber India's by 103 million in 2050, while its total population size will be smaller than that of India by 51 million.

Even more extremely rapid increase of oldest old persons after 2020

Most younger elderly persons (less than 80 years old) are relatively healthy, but the oldest old usually need help. The oldest old consume amounts of services, benefits and transfers far out of proportion with their numbers. For example, in 1988, about a quarter of the Medicare payments to hospitals in New York City were on behalf of the oldest old patients (Suzman, Manton and Willis, 1992, p. 6). According to a German study, 1.7, 3.2, 6.2, 10.7 and 26.3 per cent of the elderly aged 65-69, 70-74, 75-79, 80-84 and 85+, respectively, regularly need health-care services (Schneekloth and others, 1996). It is the oldest old who are most likely to need help. However, in China and in almost all other developing countries, very little is known about the oldest old, and almost all published statistics, based on census data, are truncated at age 65 or so. The Population Division of the United Nations Secretariat has taken a groundbreaking step forward by revising the United Nations population estimates and projections to extend the open-ended age interval from 80+ to 100+ (United Nations, 1999b). In the present paper, we examine the projected oldest old population in China in the twenty-first century based on our study and compare it to the most recent projections by the United Nations Population Division.

Table 2 provides the projected numbers and percentage distributions by various age groups for the elderly population in China. There were about 8 million oldest old (aged 80 and over) in 1990. As compared with the increase of all elderly persons aged 65 and above, the number of the oldest old will climb much faster, to about 13 million, 32 million, 76 million and 114 million in 2000, 2020, 2040 and 2050, respectively, under the medium mortality assumption. The average annual increase rate of the oldest old between 1990 and 2050 will be 4.2 per cent. The percentage of the oldest old among the elderly population will be nearly tripled from 1990 to 2050. From 1990 to 2040, the share increases by approximately 2.5 percentage points per 10 years. But in the 10 years from 2040 to 2050, the share increases by 10.6 percentage points. The main reason for the number of oldest old to climb so quickly after 2040 is that the population born during China's baby booms in the 1950s and the 1960s will fall into the category of oldest old at that time.

As shown in table 2, the numbers of elderly persons aged 65+ projected by Zeng and Vaupel (1989) are fairly close to those projected by the United Nations Population Division (1999b). However, the United Nations projected number of oldest old in 2050 (99.6 million) is considerably smaller than that projected by Zeng and Vaupel (114.4 million), and the projected age distributions of the elderly population differ (see table 2). This discrepancy is mainly attributable to the different approaches for interpolating age-specific death rates in future years. We believe that our projected larger numbers and higher proportion of the oldest old may be closer to the reality of the future trend, although subject to a lot of uncertainties (see the annex below for an explanation). Despite the discrepancy and uncertainties in accurately forecasting the oldest old population, it is certain that the oldest old will increase tremendously in the twenty-first century in China (see, also, Mayer, Torrey and Kinsella, 1992, pp. 81-82). The middle of the twenty-first century will be a difficult time for China owing to the serious problems of population ageing.

TABLE 2. AGE DISTRIBUTION AMONG ELDERLY PERSONS AGED 65+ IN CHINA

Age		Projection using the model developed by Zeng and Vaupel					Projection by United Nations Population Division			
		1990	2000	2020	2040	2050	2000	2020	2040	2050
65-74	(millions)	44.4	62.1	111.3	188.0	150.1	60.2	114.3	194.3	158.7
	(per cent)	70.5	66.3	65.8	59.2	45.4	68.8	68.4	60.5	47.6
75-84	(millions)	16.3	26.4	44.0	96.5	131.6	23.6	42.3	97.8	132.6
	(per cent)	25.9	28.2	26.0	30.4	39.8	27.0	25.3	30.5	39.7
85+	(millions)	2.3	5.2	13.9	33.0	48.9	3.7	10.5	29.0	42.3
	(per cent)	3.7	5.5	8.2	10.4	14.8	4.2	6.3	9.0	12.7
80+	(millions)	7.7	13.1	32.2	76.1	114.4	11.5	26.6	64.3	99.6
	(per cent)	12.2	14.0	19.0	24.0	34.6	13.2	15.9	20.0	29.9
75+	(millions)	18.6	31.6	57.9	129.5	180.5	27.3	52.9	126.8	174.9
	(per cent)	29.5	33.7	34.2	40.8	54.6	31.2	31.6	39.5	52.4
65+	(millions)	63.0	93.7	169.2	317.5	330.6	87.5	167.2	321.1	333.6
	(per cent)	100.0	100.0	100.0	100.0	100.0	100.0	100.0	100.0	100.0

Sources: Projections using the model developed by Zeng and Vaupel (1989) are from Zeng (1994, p. 77); projections by the United Nations Population Division are from United Nations (1999b).

Extraordinarily rapid population ageing under the low mortality scenario

The extremely rapid population ageing discussed above is based on the medium mortality variant assumed by the United Nations Population Division (1999a) and by us. The underlying assumption of the medium mortality variant is that there will be slow progress in reducing mortality in China during the twenty-first century — from a life expectancy of 68.4 years for both sexes combined in 1990 to 78.8 years in 2050. This is quite conservative, given the fact that life expectancy in Japan in 1995 was already 80 years. Some recent research indicates that there may be a significant improvement in mortality in the twenty-first century, because of biomedical advances and breakthroughs and better personal health practices, such as healthy diets, not smoking and exercise. We therefore have made another optimistic scenario, namely, life expectancy for both sexes combined is assumed to approach 84.9 years by 2050 (Ogawa, 1988), a level that is about 4.5 years higher than in Japan today. This low mortality scenario is subject to uncertainty, but we believe that it is not impossible. For example, male and female life expectancies in Japan in 1950 were 7.7 and 10 years lower than in the United States, respectively, but the difference disappeared in the 1960s (Ogawa, 1988, p. 32). Rapid socio-economic development in China, plus the East Asian style of healthy diets and habits, may narrow the gap between Chinese and Japanese mortality levels in the twenty-first century. Some scholars believed that a life expectancy of 85 years represented the limit of human life expectancy (e.g., Fries, Green and Levine, 1989; Olshansky, Carnes and Cassel, 1990). However, most scholars now believe that human beings can, on average, live much longer than 85 years (e.g., Manton, Stallard and Tolley, 1991; Vaupel and Gowan, 1986; Guralnik, Yanagishita and Schneider, 1988). Despite uncertainty, the medium and low mortality scenarios contain an informative range of possibilities in China during the first half of the twenty-first century.

Under the low mortality scenario, the elderly will comprise 17.4 and 26.5 per cent of the total Chinese population in 2030 and 2050, respectively. The annual increase rate of the proportion of the elderly population aged 65+ between 1990 and 2050 is 2.6 per cent. By 2020, 2030, 2040 and 2050, there will be 187 million, 264 million, 370 million and 407 million elderly people, respectively, in China. Under the low mortality scenario, the oldest old will number 38 million, 58 million, 100 million and 161 million in 2020, 2030, 2040 and 2050, respectively (Zeng and Vaupel, 1989; Zeng, 1994).[4] If biomedical breakthroughs and improved health practices make the low mortality scenario a reality, population ageing problems in China will be much more serious in the twenty-first century.

More serious ageing problems in rural areas than in urban areas[5]

Although fertility in rural areas of China is much higher than in urban areas, ageing problems will be more serious in rural areas because of the continuing massive rural-to-urban migration, the large majority of which are young people. Under the medium fertility and medium mortality assumptions,

262

the proportion of the elderly will be 26 and 22 per cent in rural and urban areas, respectively, by the middle of the twenty-first century. The proportions will be 31 per cent in rural areas in contrast to 26 per cent in urban areas under the medium fertility and low mortality assumptions (Zeng and Vaupel, 1989).

While the percentage of the elderly in rural areas in the twenty-first century will be substantially higher than in urban areas, the rural elderly are much less able to obtain the necessary social support and services. According to a survey of the elderly carried out in 1992 in 12 provinces (Beijing, Tianjing, Shanghai, Zhejiang, Jiangsu, Heilongjiang, Shanxi, Shananxi, Shichun, Guangxi, Guizhou and Hubei), only 5.9 per cent of the rural elderly aged 60 and over were pension recipients, in contrast to 73.7 per cent in the urban areas. Some 66.6 per cent of the urban elderly had their medical expenses paid entirely or in part by the Government or collective enterprises in 1991. However, this figure was only 9.5 per cent for the rural elderly. In another survey, carried out in 1987, a relatively small proportion (32.5 per cent) of the elderly in urban areas reported that they had difficulties in obtaining medical care, while a large majority (94.8 per cent) of the rural elderly had such difficulties. About 21.3 per cent of the urban elderly reported that their nutrition status was poor; for the rural elderly, the percentage was as high as 53.3 (Population Research Institute of China Academy of Social Sciences, 1988).

It is also important to note that the extremely rapid and large-scale population ageing in China is accompanied by a per capita gross national product that is considerably lower than that of many other developing countries, especially in rural areas. Thus, resources for addressing the serious problems caused by rapid population ageing are very limited.

LIVING ARRANGEMENTS OF ELDERLY PERSONS

It is clear that Chinese population ageing will be extremely rapid and the size of the elderly population will be exceptionally large in the first half of the twenty-first century. Population ageing is accompanied by changes in family household structure (see, e.g., Wolf, 1994, for a review). Elderly persons depend on spouses and children for emotional and physical support, as well as financial aid, especially in rural areas. Past research has shown that family care is an important part of long-term care, and has substantial impact on caregiving arrangements for the elderly (e.g., Soldo, Wolf and Agree, 1990). In particular, the use of institutional long-term care has been shown to vary by family status (Freedman, 1996). Cohorts who will become the elderly in the twenty-first century have been on the leading edge of family changes, with rapid decreases in fertility and quick rises in divorce (Zeng and Wu, forthcoming), and changes in attitudes about co-residence between parents and married children (Zeng, Li and Liang, 1992). Long-term-care costs in the United States have doubled during each decade since 1970, reaching an annual level of $106.5 billion in 1995. Home health-care costs grew 90.7 per cent from 1990 to 1995, in contrast to 33.4 per cent for institutional care costs (Stallard, 1999). Thus, the combination of home-based and institutional care has been rapidly shifting towards home health care, especially for the oldest old (Cutler and Meara, 1999). Clearly, changes in family structure strongly affect caregiving needs, the long-term health-care service system, and health-related policy-making (Doty, 1986; Himes, 1992).

How may demographic and socio-economic changes alter family households and the living arrangements of the Chinese elderly population? How many elderly persons live alone, or with a spouse only, or with children or grandchildren or other relatives, or in an institution? How many elderly live with a son or a daughter and his or her spouse? What are the gender and rural-urban differences? What are the changes in living arrangements in the recent past? What are the implications of those changes on future trends? Based mainly on the data from the one-per-thousand microdata files of the 1990 and 1982 censuses, the present section addresses questions such as these, which are important for elderly caregiving and health-related policy-making.

Living arrangements of elderly persons in 1990

Table 3 and figure II present detailed and simplified percentage distributions of the living arrangements of elderly persons in mainland China, comparing rural and urban areas, based on the 1990 census data. We classify the elderly into three age groups: modest old (persons aged 65-79), very old (persons aged 80-89), and extremely old (persons aged 90+). The broader age category oldest old is a combination of the very old (aged 80-89) and the extremely old (aged 90+). We will employ this terminology in the following discussion.

Co-residence with children

A large majority of the modest old women (73.9 per cent) and men (68.7 per cent) live with their children (hereafter, children include grandchildren, unless otherwise specified). A higher proportion (79.9 per cent of females and 69.1 per cent of males) of the very old live with their children. The corresponding figures for the extremely old are the highest, 82.4 per cent for women and 76.7 per cent for men (see table 3). It is clear that a large majority of the Chinese elderly live with their children, and the higher the age, the higher the proportion living with their children. Female elderly persons of all age groups are more likely to live with their children, because elderly women are more likely to be economically dependent and widowed.

TABLE 3. PERCENTAGE DISTRIBUTION OF LIVING ARRANGEMENTS OF THE ELDERLY IN CHINA (ALL 30 PROVINCES), 1990, COMPARING RURAL AND URBAN AREAS

| | | Alone | Spouse | Living with spouse and child/grandchild or others | | | | | No spouse, living with child/grandchild or others | | | | | Institution | Total number |
				Child	Grandchild	Child and grandchild	Others only	Subtotal	Child	Grandchild	Child and grandchild	Others only	Subtotal		
Ages 65–79															
Males	Rural	8.3	20.8	16.6	1.2	24.9	0.2	42.9	4.2	0.4	22.4	0.2	27.2	0.8	205 269
	Urban	7.1	23.9	15.8	3.6	26.1	0.5	46.0	3.7	0.9	15.8	0.4	20.8	2.1	69 595
	Total	8.0	21.6	16.4	1.8	25.2	0.3	43.7	4.1	0.5	20.7	0.3	25.6	1.1	274 864
Females	Rural	9.9	15.1	5.4	0.8	16.2	0.1	22.6	7.8	0.6	43.9	0.1	52.3	0.2	237 923
	Urban	11.4	15.5	5.1	2.5	15.0	0.3	22.8	6.6	2.5	40.1	0.4	49.7	0.7	75 686
	Total	10.2	15.2	5.3	1.2	15.9	0.2	22.6	7.5	1.0	42.9	0.1	51.6	0.3	313 609
Ages 80–89															
Males	Rural	13.8	15.3	4.0	0.5	15.7	0.1	20.3	5.8	0.6	43.1	0.2	49.7	0.9	20 227
	Urban	11.4	18.0	4.4	2.9	16.7	0.3	24.3	6.2	2.0	35.4	0.6	44.2	2.0	6 966
	Total	13.2	16.0	4.1	1.1	16.0	0.2	21.3	5.9	1.0	41.1	0.3	48.3	1.2	27 193
Females	Rural	15.5	4.1	0.7	0.1	3.5	0.0	4.4	11.1	0.6	63.8	0.1	75.6	0.4	36 334
	Urban	14.2	3.8	0.6	0.6	3.0	0.0	4.2	11.6	3.4	61.1	0.5	76.6	1.3	12 543
	Total	15.2	4.0	0.7	0.2	3.4	0.0	4.3	11.3	1.3	63.1	0.2	75.8	0.7	48 877

		Alone	Spouse	Living with spouse and child/grandchild or others					No spouse, living with child/grandchild or others					Insti-tution	Total number
				Child	Grand-child	Child and grand-child	Others only	Sub-total	Child	Grand-child	Child and grand-child	Others only	Sub-total		
Ages 90+															
Males	Rural	13.5	8.6	4.4	0.9	9.8	0.0	15.1	8.6	1.2	51.4	0.1	61.3	1.5	777
	Urban	12.3	6.7	2.5	1.7	10.1	0.0	14.3	10.4	2.5	50.7	0.3	63.9	2.8	357
	Total	13.1	8.0	3.8	1.1	9.9	0.0	14.8	9.2	1.6	51.1	0.2	62.1	1.9	1 134
Females	Rural	18.2	0.4	0.2	0.0	0.7	0.0	0.8	16.1	0.5	63.4	0.1	80.1	0.5	2 261
	Urban	10.8	0.8	0.0	0.0	0.9	0.0	0.9	20.0	3.3	61.6	0.3	85.2	2.4	1 011
	Total	15.9	0.5	0.1	0.0	0.7	0.0	0.9	17.3	1.3	62.8	0.2	81.7	1.1	3 272
Ages 80+															
Males	Rural	13.8	15.0	4.0	0.5	15.5	0.1	20.1	5.9	0.6	43.4	0.2	50.1	0.9	21 004
	Urban	11.5	17.5	4.3	2.8	16.4	0.3	23.8	6.4	2.0	36.1	0.6	45.2	2.0	7 323
	Total	13.2	15.7	4.1	1.1	15.7	0.1	21.1	6.0	1.0	41.5	0.3	48.9	1.2	28 327
Females	Rural	15.7	3.9	0.7	0.1	3.4	0.0	4.2	11.4	0.6	63.8	0.1	75.8	0.5	38 595
	Urban	13.9	3.6	0.6	0.5	2.8	0.0	3.9	12.2	3.4	61.2	0.5	77.2	1.4	13 554
	Total	15.2	3.8	0.6	0.2	3.2	0.0	4.1	11.6	1.3	63.1	0.2	76.2	0.7	52 149

| | | Living with spouse and child/grandchild or others | | | | | | No spouse, living with child/grandchild or others | | | | | | |
	Alone	Spouse	Child	Grand-child	Child and grand-child	Others only	Sub-total	Child	Grand-child	Child and grand-child	Others only	Sub-total	Insti-tution	Total number
Ages 65+														
Males														
Rural	8.9	20.3	15.4	1.1	24.1	0.2	40.8	4.4	0.4	24.3	0.2	29.4	0.8	226 273
Urban	7.5	23.3	14.7	3.6	25.2	0.5	43.9	4.0	1.0	17.8	0.4	23.2	2.1	76 918
Total	8.5	21.0	15.2	1.7	24.3	0.3	41.6	4.3	0.6	22.7	0.3	27.8	1.1	303 191
Females														
Rural	10.7	13.5	4.8	0.7	14.4	0.1	20.0	8.3	0.6	46.6	0.1	55.6	0.2	276 518
Urban	11.8	13.7	4.4	2.2	13.1	0.3	20.0	7.5	2.7	43.3	0.4	53.8	0.8	89 240
Total	10.9	13.5	4.7	1.1	14.1	0.1	20.0	8.1	1.1	45.8	0.2	55.1	0.4	365 758

Figure II. Living arrangements of elderly persons in 1990, comparing between rural and urban areas

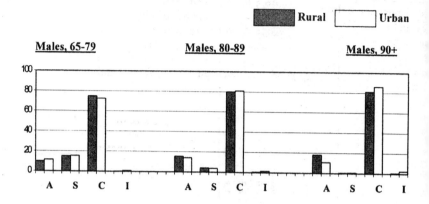

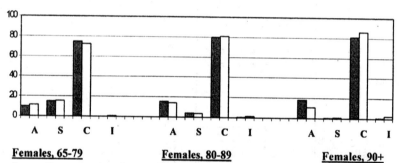

Females, 65-79   Females, 80-89   Females, 90+

A: alone;   S: spouse only;   C: combination of with children and spouse,   I: institution.
with children only and with other
relatives or non-relatives only;

In the Chinese censuses, householders' children and children's spouse were coded as one category, "children", so that it is impossible to distinguish between married sons and married daughters who live with their parents. Thus, we have to rely on other data sources to examine the living arrangements with sons versus daughters. According to the 1998 health and longevity survey, which sampled elders aged 80+ in 22 provinces,[6] the percentage living with a daughter (among those living with children) was 17.3, 17.7 and 17.7 for men aged 80-89, 90-99 and 100+, respectively. The corresponding figures for women aged 80-89, 90-99 and 100+ are 15.4, 18.8 and 18.1, respectively. These figures show that, on the one hand, most of the oldest old live with adult sons and, on the other hand, a considerable portion of them live with adult daughters.

Based on 1990 census data, among the modest old who live with offspring, a majority (66.8 per cent of men and 79.6 per cent of women) live with both children and grandchildren. A larger majority (82.6 per cent of men and 83.2 per cent of women) of the very old who live with offspring live with both children and grandchildren. The corresponding figures for the extremely old men and women are 79.5 per cent and 77.1 per cent, respectively (see table 3). In the cultural context of Chinese society, multigeneration family households are one of the main living arrangements for the elderly, especially for the oldest old.

Slightly more than 2 per cent of the modest old men and women live with grandchildren without a son or a daughter present. The corresponding figures are 2.1 and 1.5 per cent for very old men and women, and 2.7 and 1.3 per cent for extremely old men and women (see table 3). This kind of two-generation household, consisting of grandparents and grandchildren, indicates that, in Chinese society grandchildren may care for their grandparents when the middle generation is not available (perhaps owing to job location or death); another scenario is that not very old grandparents may take care of young grandchildren.

Living with a spouse

Among the modest old men and women living with children, 36.8 and 69.7 per cent do not have a spouse present. Among the very old who live with children, a large majority (69.5 per cent of men and 94.6 per cent of women) do not live with a spouse. The corresponding figures are 80.7 and 98.9 per cent for the extremely old men and women. The proportion of elderly men who live with a spouse only is 21.6, 16.0 and 8.0 per cent at ages 65-69, 80-89 and 90+, respectively, in contrast to 15.2, 4.0 and 0.5 per cent for their female counterparts (see table 3). The proportion of the elderly not living with a spouse increases tremendously with age, owing to high rates of widowhood at old ages (divorce rate in China is extremely low). Many more elderly women are widowed than are men because of the gender differential in mortality at advanced ages.

Living alone or with other relatives or non-relatives

The proportion of the modest old men and women living alone is 8.0 and 10.2 per cent, in contrast to 13.2 and 15.2 for the oldest old men and women, respectively (the difference in the proportion living alone between ages 80-89 and 90+ is very small) (see table 3). It should be noted that elderly women are much more likely to be widowed and thus live alone. On the other hand, elderly women are economically more dependent. Therefore, the disadvantages of women in marital life and living arrangements are substantially more serious than are those of men at advanced ages.

A small proportion (0.6 and 0.3 per cent of the modest old men and women; 0.4 and 0.2 per cent of the oldest old men and women, respectively) of the Chinese elderly lives with other relatives or non-relatives, without children present (see table 3). This fact demonstrates that Chinese elderly rarely live with people other than offspring and spouse.

Living in institutional households

The proportions of the modest old, very old and extremely old men living in institutional households in 1990 were 1.1, 1.2 and 1.9 per cent, respectively.[7] The corresponding figures for the modest old, very old and extremely old women were 0.3, 0.7 and 1.1 per cent, respectively (see table 3). Given the extremely limited facilities available for institutional care for the elderly, perhaps the major cause of institutionalization of elderly persons in China in 1990 was childlessness (or absence of children). Therefore, the percentage of institutionalized elderly persons was extremely low as compared to that in developed countries, where the most important reason for an elderly person being placed in an institution was disability. It should be noted that the lower social and economic status of elderly Chinese women made them less likely to be able to access long-term-care facilities. This is another social disadvantage faced by elderly women in Chinese society, which merits attention by the Government and society.

Rural-urban differentials in 1990

Table 3 and figure II present detailed and simplified percentage distributions of the living arrangements of elderly persons in 1990, with a comparison between rural and urban areas. The proportion of the modest old men who live with children in rural and urban areas in 1990 was 69.7 and 65.9, respectively, and the corresponding figures for women were 74.7 and 71.8 (see table 3). Thus, rural modest old persons are more likely to live with their children than are their urban counterparts. However, the proportion of the very old and extremely old persons who live with their children in the rural areas is slightly lower than that in the urban areas, except for men aged 80-89. More studies are needed to explain this phenomenon.

An interesting finding is that many more urban oldest old persons live with daughters than do their rural counterparts. Among the oldest old men and women aged 80+ who live with children in urban areas, 26.6 and 28.8 per cent live with a daughter, while the corresponding figures are 11.8 and 9.5 per cent in the rural areas, based on data from the 1998 health and longevity survey. Such striking rural-urban differentials of proportions living with daughters among the oldest old also exist at age groups 80-89, 90-99 and 100+. This shows the traditional idea of relying on sons for old-age care is less popular in urban areas, and is changing with modernization. Old people in urban areas accept, or even prefer, to live with a daughter, if possible, since daughters are more likely to provide better care to old parents than are sons. This gives us hope that the traditional son preference in China may be reversed if urbanization is accompanied by appropriate social programmes that aim at increasing women's status and encouraging old persons to live with their daughters.

The proportion of those modest old, very old and extremely old men and women who live with both children and grandchildren is higher in rural than in urban areas (see table 3). This confirms the fact that the multigeneration family household is more popular in rural areas than in urban areas in contemporary China.

The proportion of the modest old, very old and extremely old who live with grandchildren, without a son or a daughter present, is about two to five times higher in urban areas than in rural areas (see table 3). This suggests that job location (rather than death) of the middle generation is the main reason for these special two-generation households, consisting of grandparents and grandchildren.

Slightly more of the modest old men and women in urban areas than in rural areas live with a spouse only. However, among the very old and extremely old, there is no clear pattern of rural-urban differences in living with a spouse only (see figure II and table 3).

There is no clear pattern of rural-urban differences in the proportion of the modest old who live alone, but it is evident that the proportion of the very old and extremely old who live alone is higher in rural areas than in urban areas (see figure II and table 3). People generally speculate that the urban elderly are more likely to prefer privacy and independent living arrangements, and thus are more likely to live alone than are their rural counterparts. But Chinese census data do not support this hypothesis. Perhaps, other factors such as higher widowhood rates, lower remarriage rates and fewer long-term-care facilities in rural areas than in urban areas offset the effects of rural-urban attitude differences. One may also speculate that the preference for privacy and independent living arrangements, even among Chinese elderly in urban areas, is still not strong. More in-depth studies are needed.

The proportions of institutionalized modest old, very old and extremely old men and women were two to four times higher among the urban population than for rural residents in 1990 (see figure II and table 3). This is not surprising since very few institutional facilities for the elderly are available in rural areas. The rural oldest old living in institutional households are there because of childlessness rather than disability. Chinese policies in rural areas allow only those elderly who have no close relatives to stay in government-subsidized institutional households. In urban areas, facility limitation and institutional policies are relatively less restrictive, permitting more elderly to live in institutional households.

Changes between 1982 and 1990

Table 4 and figure III contain detailed and simplified percentage distributions of the living arrangements of elderly persons (rural and urban areas combined),[8] with a comparison between 1990 and 1982, based on the census data collected in those two years. The proportion of the elderly living with children decreased slightly, from 69.6 per cent in 1982 to 68.7 per cent in 1990, for the modest old men and remained virtually unchanged for the modest old women (74.1 per cent in 1982 and 73.9 per cent in 1990). The proportions of the very old and extremely old men and women who live with children increased by two to four percentage points between 1982 and 1990 (see table 4). The proportion of elderly men and women aged 65-79, 80-89 and 90+ who live with both children and grandchildren also increased between 1982 and 1990 (see table 4). Furthermore, the proportion living alone declined considerably at all ages (see figure III and table 4). Were the living arrangements of Chinese elderly in 1990 more traditional than in 1982? This seems unlikely, given the rapid socio-economic development and opening door to the outside world that occurred in China during the 1980s. How, then, can we interpret this phenomenon, which is contradictory to general and theoretical expectations? We believe that the following factors may have contributed to this situation. First, the elimination of the previous food rationing system and changes in the function of household register booklets around 1990 may have played a role. In the 1970s and early 1980s, low efficiency in the collective agriculture production system resulted in severe food shortages. In addition to the main food rationing, other foodstuffs such as meat, fish, and eggs were primarily supplied on the basis of the household register booklet. Each household could periodically purchase certain amounts of low-priced subsidiary foods, and the household register booklet was used as identification. This led some young and old people, who actually lived with family members, to register as a separate household. The number of one-person households, including elderly persons living alone, was overenumerated and the number of the elderly living with children was underenumerated. Such biases resulted in the State Statistical Bureau adjusting the urban average family household size enumerated in the 1982 census from 3.84 to 3.95 through a post-census sample check. The rural household size was not adjusted, but a similar bias (possibly smaller) existed in the rural areas in the 1982 census. Such biases were much less serious in 1990 because the food rationing system was basically eliminated and the incentive for having more household register booklets was greatly reduced. Secondly, increases in remarriage rates and decreases in death rates at old ages may also partly explain why the proportion of the elderly who lived alone declined between 1982 and 1990. The increase in remarriage rates among elderly persons was a result of the social reform and the success of match-making services in the late 1980s. The reform aimed at protecting elders' rights, including the right to remarry, which were often violated by the intervention of children and other family members in traditional Chinese society. Rapid economic development, accompanied by substantial improvements in the standard of living, may have decreased the death rate at old ages. Although these explanations are speculative owing to the lack of empirical data, we believe that the living arrangements of the Chinese elderly in the 1980s were not a return to tradition. We also believe that the custom of Chinese elderly living with their children has changed little, if at all, between 1982 and 1990.

The proportion of the elderly living with spouses (including with spouse only and with spouse and children) increased considerably between 1982 and 1990 among the modest old and very old men and women, but remained almost unchanged among women aged 90+ and decreased by three percentage points among men aged 90+ (see table 4). Similar changes in the proportion of the elderly living with spouse only between 1982 and 1990 among the modest old, very old and extremely old persons were also observed (see figure III and table 4). We believe that possible explanatory factors for this interesting phenomenon are increases in remarriage rates among the elderly aged 65-89 and decreased death rates in the 1980s, as discussed above. Another possible explanation is a decrease in divorce rates among the modest old persons. However, this factor can be ruled out, since divorce rates among elderly persons are extremely low in China, and there is no evidence of a further decline. In fact, the general divorce rates for the entire population have substantially increased in China since 1980 (Zeng and Wu, forthcoming).

As compared to 1982, the proportion of the elderly living in institutional households increased in 1990 among women aged 80-89 and men and women aged 90+, remained unchanged among men aged 80-89 and women aged 65-79, and decreased among men aged 65-79 (see figure III and table 4). Socio-economic development in the 1980s may have contributed to an improvement in long-term-care facilities, which facilitated the increase in the proportion of those living in institutional households, although it is still very low. Commercial nursing home facilities for the elderly have been growing at a fast pace since 1990 owing to rapid economic development. Based on the data from the 1998 survey conducted in 22 provinces, the percentage of the institutionalized oldest old is 6.1 for men and 6.7 for women aged 80+. These figures are still low when compared with Western countries but have increased tremendously since 1990. Modernization in China may further increase the proportion of the elderly living in long-term-care institutions in the future.

TABLE 4. PERCENTAGE DISTRIBUTION OF LIVING ARRANGEMENTS OF THE ELDERLY IN CHINA (ALL 30 PROVINCES), RURAL AND URBAN AREAS COMBINED, COMPARISON BETWEEN 1990 AND 1982

			Living with spouse and child/grandchild or others						No spouse, living with child/grandchild or others						
	Alone	Spouse	Child	Grand-child	Child and grand-child	Others only	Sub-total	Child	Grand-child	Child and grand-child	Others only	Sub-total	Insti-tution	Total number
Ages 65-79														
Males														
1990	8.0	21.6	16.4	1.8	25.2	0.3	43.7	4.1	0.5	20.7	0.3	25.6	1.1	274 864
1982	10.5	17.5	19.2	1.7	21.7	0.4	43.0	5.2	0.6	21.2	0.5	27.5	1.5	186 530
Females														
1990	10.2	15.2	5.3	1.2	15.9	0.2	22.6	7.5	1.0	42.9	0.1	51.6	0.3	313 609
1982	13.1	11.9	5.0	1.1	12.2	0.3	18.5	9.2	1.3	45.5	0.3	56.2	0.3	226 812
Ages 80-89														
Males														
1990	13.2	16.0	4.1	1.1	16.0	0.2	21.3	5.9	1.0	41.1	0.3	48.3	1.2	27 193
1982	16.5	14.2	4.7	1.4	14.1	0.4	20.4	4.7	1.2	41.2	0.5	47.6	1.2	15 584
Females														
1990	15.2	4.0	0.7	0.2	3.4	0.0	4.3	11.3	1.3	63.1	0.2	75.8	0.7	48 877
1982	18.5	3.0	0.4	0.2	2.5	0.1	3.2	8.5	1.6	64.5	0.4	75.0	0.3	29 653
Ages 90+														
Males														
1990	13.1	8.0	3.8	1.1	9.9	0.0	14.8	9.2	1.6	51.1	0.2	62.1	1.9	1 134
1982	16.5	8.7	6.3	3.3	7.1	0.5	17.1	6.9	0.8	47.8	0.6	56.1	1.5	665
Females														
1990	15.9	0.5	0.1	0.0	0.7	0.0	0.9	17.3	1.3	62.8	0.2	81.7	1.1	3 272
1982	20.2	0.7	0.1	0.1	0.6	0.0	0.8	13.0	1.9	62.6	0.2	77.7	0.5	1 767

		Alone	Spouse	Living with spouse and child/grandchild or others					No spouse, living with child/grandchild or others					Insti-tution	Total number
				Child	Grand-child	Child and grand-child	Others only	Sub-total	Child	Grand-child	Child and grand-child	Others only	Sub-total		
Ages 80+															
Males	1990	13.2	15.7	4.1	1.1	15.7	0.1	21.1	6.0	1.0	41.5	0.3	48.9	1.2	28 327
	1982	16.5	14.0	4.7	1.4	13.8	0.4	20.3	4.8	1.2	41.4	0.5	48.0	1.2	16 249
Females	1990	15.2	3.8	0.6	0.2	3.2	0.0	4.1	11.6	1.3	63.1	0.2	76.2	0.7	52 149
	1982	18.6	2.9	0.4	0.2	2.4	0.0	3.1	8.8	1.6	64.3	0.3	75.1	0.3	31 420
Ages 65+															
Males	1990	8.5	21.0	15.2	1.7	24.3	0.3	41.6	4.3	0.6	22.7	0.3	27.8	1.1	303 191
	1982	10.9	17.2	18.1	1.7	21.0	0.4	41.2	5.2	0.7	22.8	0.5	29.1	1.5	202 779
Females	1990	10.9	13.5	4.7	1.1	14.1	0.1	20.0	8.1	1.1	45.8	0.2	55.1	0.4	365 758
	1982	13.8	10.8	4.4	1.0	11.0	0.3	16.7	9.2	1.3	47.8	0.3	58.5	0.3	258 232

Figure III. Living arrangements of elderly persons, rural and urban areas combined, comparison between 1990 and 1982

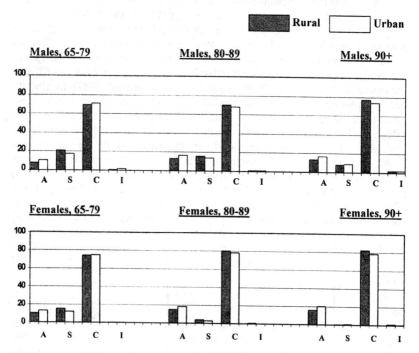

A: alone;   S: spouse only;   C: combination of with children and spouse,   I: institution.
                                                         with children only and with other
                                                         relatives or non-relatives only;

A combination of rapid fertility decline since 1970, continued decrease in mortality and the large baby-boom cohorts born in the 1950s, 1960s and early 1970s is the demographic basis for the extremely rapid ageing of the population in China. Total fertility rates have declined tremendously, from about 6 children per woman before 1970 to about 2.6 children by the end of the 1970s, more than a 50 per cent reduction in a decade. Chinese fertility has continued to fall steadily (with some fluctuation around 1987) to slightly below replacement level at the present time. While the lower fertility rate since 1970 has resulted in smaller cohorts of young persons, the large number of cohorts born during the first and second baby booms in the 1950s, 1960s and early 1970s will become elderly in the first half of the twenty-first century. There were 172 million persons aged 35-44 (born in 1950-1959) in 1995, and they will be aged 65+ after 2015-2024. There were 355 million persons aged 20-34 (born in 1960-1974) in 1995, and they will be aged 65+ after 2025-2039. Continued mortality decline will enable more members of those huge baby boom cohorts to survive to old ages. As indicated by Grigsby and Olshansky (1989, p. 328), at least 50 per cent of the projected increase in population ageing between 1980 and 2050 in China is a product of the momentum for ageing that is already built into the present age structure and vital rates.

The trend of Chinese population ageing is not avoidable, and further declines in mortality and fertility will accelerate this trend. What can we do to respond to such extremely rapid ageing of the population in China? In the present paper it has been suggested that strengthening family support for the elderly is one policy strategy that needs to be investigated and adopted. As discussed above, a large majority of Chinese elderly, especially the oldest old, live with their children, including grandchildren. The strong cultural preference of the Chinese elderly for living with children has lasted for thousands of years. The benefits of co-residence with children for the majority of the Chinese elderly are not only financial and material support, but also psychological satisfaction (Lin, 1995, p. 141). The Government of China needs to consider a series of policies that aim at strengthening family support for the elderly. For example, adequate tax exemption and favourable housing policies may be awarded to persons living with old parents. To encourage family support for the elderly and to satisfy the increasing needs for privacy and independence in daily life, the so-called parent-child proximity apartment units need to be promoted through governmental subsidies. The basic idea is to have two kitchens, two living rooms and at least two bathrooms in one apartment unit. The unit is structured so that old parents and one of their adult children and his or her family live in the same housing unit, with both generations also enjoying their own privacy and independence. The elderly can easily receive assistance from their children and they can conveniently provide help in caring for grandchildren, while at the same time, generation differences with respect to preferences regarding eating, watching television and time schedules of daily activities can be preserved.

Population ageing in China will lead to a heavy burden of support of a mass of elderly people, and ageing problems will be more serious in rural areas than in urban areas. Responding to the problems of population ageing in rural areas is an urgent issue on China's agenda for the twenty-first century. Given the strong cultural preference of the Chinese elderly for living with children and the possibility of maintaining or even strengthening family support in China, should the Government give all or a major part of the responsibility for old-age care to families? Because there are very few social insurance programmes in the rural areas and limits on government resources, some people, including some policy makers propose an official statement that old-age support in rural areas should rely mainly on the family. We think that this policy is inappropriate for several reasons. First, mainly relying on the family for old-age support in rural areas may not be feasible in the twenty-first century, because ageing problems will be more serious in rural areas than in urban areas. The future rural elderly will have, on average two children, and many of the children may migrate to urban areas (in contrast to the rural elderly of the past and present who had about six children staying in rural areas). The joint survival of parents and children will increase substantially in the future, so that the burden of caring for old parents, per child, will be much larger than at present (Tu, Liang and Li, 1989). Secondly, relying mainly on family support without social security would largely limit the independence of the elderly in decision-making concerning their own lives. Family support plus social security would place the elderly in a much better position for happiness. Thirdly, couples in many less developed rural areas still bear three or more children. A popular idea and practical need for having more children, especially sons, is expressed in the old Chinese saying "having sons for old-age care" (*yang er fang lao*). When fertility is greatly reduced, the practical need for "having sons for old-age care" has led people to try to determine the sex of the child prenatally, by ultrasound and other techniques, and to have sex-selective abortions (Zeng and others, 1993). The reported sex ratio at birth reached 117.0 boys per 100 girls in 1997 (China, State Statistical Bureau, 1998), in contrast to the normal value of about 106. If the Government officially states that old-age supports rely mainly on the family in rural areas, peasants may ask "if we do not have more children, and at least one son, how can the elderly be supported?" Such a policy will not be good for family planning and reversing the dangerous trend of a rising sex ratio at birth. The establishment of an old-age insurance system in rural areas is therefore an extremely important response to population ageing, family planning and reversing the sex ratio at birth in China. However, is it practical and how can peasants who have just been lifted out of poverty be mobilized to pay the premium for old-age insurance? Is it feasible and how can an old-age insurance programme be implemented in the less developed rural areas? With such questions in mind, the first author went to Shandong and Shichuan Provinces, which are the experimental areas for the old-age insurance programme in rural areas, to conduct field studies in 1993 and 1996. The evidence gathered in this and other studies shows a promising trend towards establishing old-age insurance programmes in rural areas. However, the momentum has just started and it is facing and will continue to face many problems and difficulties. The Government of China and all levels of society should pay more attention and make greater efforts in this area (Zeng, 1995).

The old pension system in China, which was implemented in state-owned enterprises in urban areas, was established in the 1950s and was based on the former Soviet Union's model at that time. Many Chinese reformers have recognized the urgent need for reforming the old pension system in urban areas. Moreover, the new system should also cover citizens who are not working in state-owned enterprises. Chinese policy makers should continue to act effectively to establish and reform old-age insurance systems in both rural and urban areas. This may be regarded as building a new Great Wall to prevent the possible crises that may be caused by extremely rapid population ageing in China in the twenty-first century.

In addition to an old-age insurance programme, which is critical to respond to the ageing challenges and to reduce son preference, another important policy recommendation is to encourage the elderly to live with their daughters. The present study has shown that this policy option is highly feasible, given the fact that nearly 30 per cent of the elderly in urban areas lived with their daughters in 1990, and the figure was nearly 18 per cent for rural and urban areas combined. If the Government provides economic incentives and the public media give more publicity to families with old parents and daughters living together, the traditional preference for sons may gradually become weaker. Since daughters and their spouses are usually more willing and able to provide better physical and psychological care to their old parents, a policy for promoting living with daughters may be beneficial for the elderly as well.

Data analyses presented in this paper have shown that elderly women are much more likely to be widowed and more likely to live alone. Elderly women are economically more dependent and less likely to use long-term-care facilities. The disadvantages that older women face in marital status and living arrangements are substantially more serious at advanced ages and in rural areas. This is another important issue that needs serious attention from society and the Government. Any type of long-term-care services sponsored by the Government should take into account the disadvantaged status of elderly women and provide them with favourable policies. Careful attention should be given to ensure that any old-age insurance programmes being developed or reformed benefit older women and men equally.

Numerous studies have shown that the elderly are not only consumers and care receivers, but are also producers and care providers, especially when they are still healthy. Based on a survey carried out in the Wuhan area of China (Liang, Gu and Krause, 1992, p. 58), it was found that elderly persons usually provide a substantial amount of help to others while they receive care, and they are satisfied with such interpersonal supportive ties. In addition to helping their children with housework and caring for grandchildren, the younger and healthier elderly can provide supplementary assistance in caring for the older and more frail elderly, either within or outside their own families. For example, the success of care services organized by the neighbourhood committee in Shanghai illustrates the value of fostering community programmes that mobilize the younger and healthier elderly to provide accessible services for the dependent elderly (Lin, 1995, p. 145). It was estimated that one fourth to one third of China's elderly continue to be employed in paid or volunteer work. Many retired professionals, for example, provide technical consulting services to small firms located in towns or villages (Nusberg, 1987, p. 19). Properly mobilizing and organizing the elderly to participate in community services and interpersonal exchange programmes will also improve the elderly person's spiritual well-being, in particular to continue to feel needed and productive. This is one of the important policy actions that should be considered in order to resolve the serious ageing problems in the twenty-first century.

Facing extremely rapid population ageing, we believe that China needs to embark on a smooth transition to a "two-child plus spacing" policy. This policy would promote later marriage, later first birth and appropriate spacing (four to five years) between the first and second child. Couples who voluntarily choose to have only one child should be rewarded. As shown in some limited experimental areas discussed elsewhere (Zeng, 1997), the two-child plus spacing policy can help reduce the still high fertility rate in many rural areas, because it better meets the practical needs of peasants and is thus more acceptable to rural couples. Couples who follows the current one-child policy in urban areas and the 1.5-child policy (e.g., if the first child is a girl, the couple is allowed to have a second child) in rural areas will have much less family support when they become old, as compared to those who have more children by ignoring the policy. This is unfair, but difficult to change because the one-child and the 1.5-child policy do not meet peasants' practical needs. The universal two-child plus spacing policy will better realize the principles of equality among citizens. Later birth and longer spacing will enable future elderly persons to enjoy a longer period of support from their young and middle-aged children, as compared to the usual practice of early childbearing under the current policy. The current 1.5-child policy in the rural areas implicitly gives more value to a boy child. The two-child plus spacing policy can help eliminate such a bias and equalize the familial position of sons and daughters, thus reversing the increasing sex ratio at birth. There are many reasons to believe that the two-child plus spacing policy is better for China in the twenty-first century, especially in dealing with extremely rapid ageing. However, we also realize that any sudden relaxation in the population policy without appropriate operational preparations in such a large country, which has many poor and backward rural areas, may cause a new baby boom. China needs carefully designed scientific research to convince policy makers to move towards the two-child plus spacing policy. China also needs solid operational studies, including establishing more experimental areas in different parts of the country, to ensure a successful transition of policy.

ANNEX

Note on the discrepancy in the projected number of oldest old persons aged 80+

As discussed in the text, the United Nations projected number of oldest old persons (aged 80+) in 2050 (99.6 million) is considerably smaller than our projection (114.4 million), and the projected age distributions among the elderly population differ notably (see table 2). This discrepancy is partly attributable to differences in model specification and slightly different assumptions about future life expectancy. We classified the population into rural and urban sectors; the United Nations did not. The starting years of our projections and those of the United Nations differ. The United Nations used a constant −0.1 per thousand net international migration rate; we did not. In our current research for preparing this paper, we performed a new exercise in which we combine rural and urban sectors, start our projection from 1995 and use the same life expectancy assumption and constant net international migration rate as the one used by the United Nations. In this new exercise, the only difference is the method for interpolating age-specific death rates. The United Nations Population Division used model life tables to interpolate the five-year age-specific death rates in future years. We followed an iterative procedure to alter the death rates proportionally at the same rate at all ages of single-year specifics, and the iterative procedure stops when the projected life expectancy at birth in the particular year is achieved (Wade, 1989; Ahlburg and Vaupel, 1990). The discrepancy between the results of our new exercise and the United Nations projection becomes even larger: our new exercise projected 125 million oldest old persons in 2050, in contrast to the 99.6 million projected by the United Nations. We therefore concluded that the discrepancy is mainly attributable to the different approaches in interpolating age-specific death rates in future years. The United Nations model life-table approach assumes that the age pattern of changes in death rates in the future is the same as what was observed in the past, namely, death rates decline faster at younger ages than at older ages. This approach has led to implausible values (almost zero) of projected death rates at some young ages when mortality level is very low (Buettner, 1999, p. 8; United Nations, 1998, pp. 7-8; Lee and Carter, 1992, p. 666). The approach we employed assumes that changes in death rates at each age are proportional to the age-specific death rates, which implies a faster decline of mortality at advanced ages than at young ages when mortality level is low, and does not produce too low death rates at young ages. We compare the projected life tables with the same assumptions of life expectancies at birth but following the United Nations model life-table approach and our approach of proportionally reducing death rates, respectively. The shapes of the curves of the two sets of life-table survival probabilities look plausible, but the United Nations model life-table survival probabilities are slightly higher before age 75 and significantly lower after age 80.

Since the early 1970s, female death rates in Japan have declined at annual rates of about 3 per cent for the elderly aged 80-89 and 2 per cent for those aged 90-99 (Vaupel and others, 1998, p. 856), which is substantially higher than the rate of decline at younger ages. Rates of progress in reducing mortality rates among the elderly aged 60 and above in Sweden have accelerated over the course of the century, and from the 1960s to the 1980s ran at an average rate of 1 to 2 per cent for females and half a per cent for males (Vaupel and Lundstrom, 1994, p. 303, table 12.1). In most developed countries, the rate of reduction of death rates at older ages has been accelerated, especially since 1970 (Kannisto and others, 1994; Vaupel and others, 1998, p. 855). If the recent trend of an accelerated reduction in mortality rates at advanced ages observed in several European countries persists in the future, our projected larger numbers and higher proportion of oldest old persons may be closer to reality. We also realize that proportionally reducing death rates at all ages is not ideal either, and further research on how to forecast age-specific rates of changes in mortality is imperative. Such research will be very useful to improve the accuracy of population projection, which may have major implications in ageing studies and socio-economic policy-making.

NOTES

[1] The medium fertility variant assumes that the rural total fertility rate (TFR) would gradually decrease from 2.65 observed in the late 1980s to 2.23 in 2000, and reach the replacement level of 2.15 by the middle of the twenty-first century. The urban sector would have a total fertility rate of 1.64 in 2000 and 1.70 in 2050 (Zeng and Vaupel, 1989). These assumptions were made by us 10 years ago and seem quite plausible based on current information. The latest official figure of Chinese TFR in 1998 is 1.84 (*People's Daily*, 12 October 1999). But we believe that it is a substantial underestimation. Our estimates are that current TFR in rural areas is about 2.2, and urban TFR is about 1.6 (see Zeng, 1996, for a detailed discussion). We estimate that the weighted average of TFR for all of China is about 2.0 at the present time (with an estimated 60 per cent and 40 per cent rural and urban population, respectively). As stated above, we assume that TFR in rural and urban areas of China in 2050 would be 2.15 and 1.7, respectively. The weighted average for the entire country would be 1.8 in 2050 (with assumed weights of 20 per cent and 80 per cent of rural and urban sectors, respectively).

[2] These projected figures are all under the medium fertility variant, which assumes that rural fertility will gradually reach the level of replacement by the middle of the twenty-first century, and the urban sector will have a total fertility rate of 1.7 in 2000 and remain constant thereafter.

Life expectancies at birth under the medium and low mortality assumptions are listed as follows:

		Medium mortality			Low mortality		
Year		Male	Female	Both sexes	Male	Female	Both sexes
2000	Rural	69.0	72.0	70.5	71.0	74.0	72.5
	Urban	72.0	76.0	74.0	74.0	78.0	76.0
	Total	70.5	74.0	72.3	72.5	76.0	74.3
2050	Rural	75.0	77.5	76.3	79.4	85.6	82.5
	Urban	78.0	81.0	79.5	81.9	89.1	85.5
	Total	77.4	80.3	78.8	81.4	88.4	84.9

[3] Given the evidence that urbanization is under way and the likelihood that substantial rural-urban fertility differences will persist, the model developed by Zeng and Vaupel (1989) incorporates the disaggregation of the population according to the rural-urban dichotomy and a net migration flow from rural to urban areas by single year of age. The dynamics of the model are based on the calculation procedures of multiregional population projection (Rogers, 1975; Rogers and Willekens, 1986; Schoeni, 1988; Land and Rogers, 1982). The United Nations 1998 revision follows a classical approach of population projection with five-year age classifications, without consideration to rural-urban differentials and dynamics (United Nations, 1999a, 1999b).

[4] The United Nations 1998 projections do not include the low mortality variant for China and any other countries, so that no comparisons are available under the low mortality assumption between our projections and those of the United Nations for China and between China and other countries.

[5] The United Nations Population Division did not classify population projections by rural and urban sectors. We were therefore unable to make a comparison with the United Nations projection for the rural-urban differentials of population ageing.

[6] The 1998 health and longevity survey was carried out in 22 provinces: Liaoning, Jilin, Heilongjiang, Hebei, Beijing, Tianjing, Shanxi, Shananxi, Shanghai, Jiangsu, Zhejiang, Anhui, Fujian, Jiangxi, Shangdong, Henan, Hubei, Hunan, Guangdong, Guangxi, Sichuan and Chongqing, covering 985 million people, 85.3 per cent of the total population of China. The survey interviewed 9,073 oldest old individuals aged 80 and above (see Zeng and others, forthcoming, for a more detailed description of the survey and data-quality evaluation).

[7] The Chinese censuses define nursing homes or other type of long-term care institutions for the elderly, as well as other households consisting of young or middle-aged persons who have no familial relationships, as *ji ti hu*. *Ji ti hu* can be literally translated into English as "collective households" or, based on its substantive meaning for the elderly, as "institutional households". We use the term "institutional households" in this paper.

283

[8] It is almost impossible to compare the rural and urban differentials between 1990 and 1982 owing to large changes in the rural-urban administrative boundaries in 1990, which included substantial portions of rural people into the urban boundary and did not reflect the truth of urbanization (Ma, 1988).

REFERENCES

Ahlburg, Dennis A., and James W. Vaupel (1990). Alternative projections of the U.S. population. *Demography*, vol. 27, pp. 639-652.

Banister, J. (1990). Implications of aging of China's population. In *Changing Family Structure and Population Aging in China: A Comparative Approach*, Zeng Yi, Zhang Chunyuan and Peng Shongjian, eds. Beijing: Peking University Press. Also in *The Population of Modern China*, Dudley L. Poston, Jr. and David Yaukey, eds. New York: Plenum Press, 1992.

Buettner, Thomas (1999). Approaches and experiences in projecting mortality patterns for the oldest old in low mortality countries. Working paper No. 31. Statistical Commission and Economic Commission for Europe. Conference of European Statisticians. Joint ECE-Eurostat work session on demographic projections.

China, State Statistical Bureau (1998). *1997 National Population Sample Survey Data*. Beijing: Statistical Press of China.

Cutler, David M., and Ellen Meara (1999). The concentration of medical spending: an update. Working paper No. W7279 (August). Cambridge, Massachusetts: National Bureau of Economic Research.

Doty, Pamela (1986). Family care of the elderly: the role of public policy. *Milbank Memorial Fund Quarterly*, 64, pp. 34-75.

Freedman, Vicki A. (1996). Family structure and the risk of nursing home admission. *Journal of Gerontology: B. Psychological Science and Social Science*, vol. 51, pp. S61-69.

Fries, J. F., L. W. Green and S. Levine (1989). Health promotion and the compression of morbidity. *The Lancet*, vol. I, pp. 481-483.

Grigsby J. S., and S. J. Olshansky (1989). The demographic components of population aging in China. *Journal of Cross-Cultural Gerontology*, 4, pp. 307-334.

Guralnik, J. M., M. Yanagishita and E. L. Schneider (1988). Projecting the older population of the United States: lessons from the past and prospects for the future. *Milbank Memorial Fund Quarterly*, 66, pp. 283-308.

Himes, Christine L. (1992). Future caregivers: projected family structures of older persons. *Journal of Gerontology: Social Sciences*, vol. 47, pp. S17-26.

Kannisto, V., and others (1994). Reductions in mortality at advanced ages: several decades of evidence from 27 countries. *Population and Development Review*, vol. 20, pp. 793-810.

Kinsella, Kevin G. (1988). Aging in the third world. Staff paper, No. 35. Washington, D. C.: United States Bureau of the Census, Center for International Research.

_____, and Richard Suzman (1992). Demographic dimensions of population aging in developing countries. *American Journal of Human Biology*, 4, pp. 3-8.

Land, K. C., and A. Rogers, eds. (1982). *Multidimensional Mathematical Demography*. New York: Academic Press.

Lee, R. D., and L. Carter (1992). Modeling and forecasting the time-series of U.S. mortality. *Journal of the American Statistical Association*, 76.

Liang, Jersey, Shengzu Gu and Neal Krause (1992). Social support among the aged in Wuhan, China. *Asia-Pacific Population Journal*, 7, pp. 33-62.

Liang, Jersey, Edward Jow-Ching Tu and Xiangming Chen (1986). Population aging in the People's Republic of China. *Social Science and Medicine*, vol. 23, pp. 1353-1362.

Lin, Jiang (1995). Changing kinship structure and its implications for old-age support in urban and rural China. *Population Studies*, 49, pp. 127-145.

Ma, Xia (1988). Criterion for urban-rural classification and the level of urban development. *Population and Economics* (6 November) (in Chinese).

Manton, K. G., E. Stallard and H. D. Tolley (1991). Limits to human life expectancy: evidence, prospects, and implications. *Population and Development Review*, vol. 17, pp. 603-637.

Martin, Linda G., and Kevin Kinsella (1994). Research on the demography of aging in developing countries. In *Demography of Aging*, Linda G. Martin and Samuel H. Preston, eds. Washington, D. C.: National Academy Press, pp. 356-403.

Mayer, George C., Barbara Boyle Torrey and Kevin G. Kinsella (1992). The paradox of the oldest old in the United States: an international comparison. In *The Oldest Old*, Richard M. Suzman, David P. Willis and Kenneth G. Manton, eds. Oxford: Oxford University Press, pp. 58-85.

Nusberg, C. (1987). Aging China — policies in transition. *Aging International* (winter, 19).

Ogawa, Naohiro (1988). Aging in China: demographic alternatives. *Asia-Pacific Population Journal*, 3, pp. 21-64.

Olshansky, S. J., B. A. Carnes and C. Cassel (1990). In search of Methuselah: estimating the upper limits of human longevity. *Science*, 250, pp. 634-640.

Population Research Institute of China Academy of Social Sciences (1988). Population aged over 60 years, sample survey data, China, 1987 (Computer Tabulation). *Population Sciences of China*, special issue, 1 (in Chinese).

Rogers, Andrei (1975). *Introduction to Multiregional Mathematical Demography*. New York: John Wiley and Sons.

_____, and Frans Willekens, eds. (1986). Migration and Settlement: *A Multiregional Comparative Study*. Dordrecht, Netherlands: D. Reidel.

Schneekloth, U., and others (1996). Hilfe- und Pflegebedürftige in privaten Haushalten, Endbericht; Bericht zur Repräsentativerhebung im Forschungsprojekt. Möglichkeiten und Grenzen selbständiger Lebensführung, vol. 111.2, Verlag W. Kohlhammer, ed. Stuttgart/Berlin/Köln: Bundesministerium für Familie, Senioren, Frauen und Jugend.

Schoeni, R. (1988). *Modelling Multi-group Population*. New York: Plenum Press.

Soldo, B. J., D. A. Wolf and E. M. Agree (1990). Family, households, and care arrangements of the frail elderly: a structural analysis. *Journal of Gerontology: Social Sciences*, vol. 45, pp. S238-S249.

Stallard, Eric (1999). Retirement and health: estimates and projections of acute and long-term-care needs and expenditures of the U.S. elderly population. Paper presented at the Society of Actuaries' Retirement Needs Framework Conference, Orlando, Florida, 10-11 December 1998.

Suzman, R. M., K. G. Manton and D. P. Willis (1992). Introducing the oldest old. In *The Oldest Old*, Richard M. Suzman, David P. Willis and Kenneth G. Manton, eds. Oxford: Oxford University Press.

Tu, Edward Jow-Ching, Jersey Liang and Shaomin Li (1989). Mortality decline and Chinese family structure: implications for old-age support. *Journal of Gerontology*, vol. 44, pp. 157-168.

United Nations (1998). Extending population projections to age 100. Statement prepared by the Population Division. Administrative Committee on Coordination Subcommittee on Demographic Estimates and Projections, twentieth session, 23-25 June. New York.

_____ (1999a). World Population Prospects. The 1998 Revision, vol. I, Comprehensive Tables. Sales No. E.99.XIII.9.

_____ (1999b). World Population Prospects. The 1998 Revision, vol. II, Sex and Age. Sales No. E.99.XIII.8.

Vaupel, James W., and A. E. Gowan (1986). Passage to Methuselah: some demographic consequences of continued progress against mortality. *American Journal of Public Health*, 76.

Vaupel, James W., and Hans Lundstrom (1994). The future of mortality at older ages in developed countries. In *The Future Population of the World: What Can We Assume Today?* Wolfgang Lutz, ed. London: Earthscan Publications, pp. 295-315.

Vaupel, James W., and others (1998). Biodemographic trajectories of longevity. *Science*, 280, pp. 855-860.

Vaupel, James W., and Zeng Yi (1991). Population trade-offs in China. *Policy Sciences*, 24, pp. 389-406.

Wade, A. (1989). Social security area population projections: 1989. Actuarial study No. 105. Washington, D. C.: Social Security Administration, Office of the Actuary.

Wolf, D. A. (1994). The elderly and their kin: patterns of availability and access. In *Demography of Aging*, Linda G. Martin and Samuel H. Preston, eds. Washington, D.C.: National Academy Press, pp. 146-194.

Zeng, Yi (1989). Aging of the Chinese population and policy issues: lessons learned from a rural-urban dynamic projection model. Paper selected for publication in the report of the International Union for the Scientific Study of Population, Twenty-first General Conference. Liege, Belgium: IUSSP, pp. 81-101.

_____ (1994). *China's Population Trends and Strategies*. Beijing: Peking University Press.

_____ (1995). China's agenda for an old-age insurance program in rural areas. *Journal of Aging and Social Policy*, 6, pp. 101-114.

_____ (1996). Is fertility in China at the beginning of the 1990s far below replacement level? *Population Studies*, 50, pp. 27-34.

_____ (1997). Dilemmas of family size norms in China. Proceedings of the International Population Conference. Paper selected for publication in the report of the International Union for the Scientific Study of Population, Twenty-third General Conference. Liege, Belgium: IUSSP, pp. 1405-1418.

Zeng, Yi, Li Wei and Liang Zhiwu (1992). The status, regional differences, and trends of Chinese family structure. *Chinese Journal of Population Science*, 4, pp. 263-284. Published in the United States by Allerton Press, Inc.

Zeng, Yi, and others (1993). An analysis of causes and implications of the recent increase in the sex ratio of births in China. *Population and Development Review*, vol. 19, pp. 283-302.

Zeng, Yi, and others (forthcoming). Health and longevity survey and active life expectancy of the oldest old in China. *Population*.

Zeng, Yi, and J. Vaupel (1989). Impact of urbanization and delayed childbearing on population growth and aging in China. *Population and Development Review*, vol. 15, pp. 425-445.

Zeng, Yi, and Wu Deqing (forthcoming). Regional analysis of divorce in China since 1980. *Demography*.

RAPID URBANIZATION AND LIVING ARRANGEMENTS OF OLDER PERSONS IN AFRICA

*Nana Araba Apt**

INTRODUCTION: AGEING AND LONGEVITY

The world's population is ageing and this presents a major policy issue in the developing world (United Nations, 1991). In Asia, the crisis is an immediate one (World Bank, 1994); China stands out as the most rapidly ageing society, and its population structure will be closer to that of the developed regions by 2025 (United Nations, 1999a, 1999b). In Africa, ageing is a crisis that is just beginning to reveal its shape; at present, it is a family crisis (Apt, 1995; Apt and Greico, 1994). In demographic terms, the proportion of Africa's population aged 65 and over stands at 3.1 per cent (United Nations, 1999a, 1999b). Although sub-Saharan Africa's older population is not as large in size as in other regions of the world, it must still be considered as a potential cause for concern since Africa is ageing at a time when its resources are being depleted. Tables 1 and 2 show the growth in the population aged 60+ and 65+ in the regional areas of Africa from 1950 to 1995 and the projected growth in the 60+ and 65+ populations to 2050.

The most rapid growth in the older population is expected in Western and Northern Africa, whose older populations are projected to increase by a factor of nearly five between 1980 and 2050. Of relative importance is the fact that the number of the very old in Africa is also expected to grow at a very fast rate. Between 1980 and 2025, the population aged 75 and over will increase by 434 per cent in Eastern Africa, 385 per cent in Middle Africa, 427 per cent in Northern Africa and 526 per cent in Western Africa. In Western Africa, Nigeria will be among the countries in Africa that will experience large increases in this age group. Another unique feature of Africa's ageing situation is that by 2020, rural segregation of the old will manifest itself and the older segment of the African population will be concentrated primarily in rural areas.

---

* Center for Social Policy Studies, University of Ghana, Legon, Ghana.

TABLE 1. GROWTH OF 60+ POPULATION, 1950-1995: AFRICAN REGION

Region	Indicator (percentage)	Year									
		1950	1955	1960	1965	1970	1975	1980	1985	1990	1995
Africa	60+	5.1	5.0	4.9	4.9	5.0	4.9	5.0	4.9	4.9	4.9
	65+	3.2	3.0	3.0	3.0	3.1	3.1	3.1	3.1	3.1	3.1
East Africa	60+	4.8	4.6	4.5	4.5	4.5	4.5	4.6	4.6	4.5	4.4
	65+	2.9	2.8	2.8	2.7	2.8	2.8	2.9	2.9	2.8	2.8
Middle Africa	60+	5.9	5.4	5.2	5.2	5.1	5.1	5.1	5.1	5.0	4.9
	65+	3.8	3.4	3.2	3.1	3.1	3.1	3.2	3.2	3.2	3.1
North Africa	60+	5.6	5.4	5.3	5.7	6.1	5.7	5.7	5.6	5.7	5.9
	65+	3.5	3.3	3.3	3.6	3.9	3.8	3.7	3.6	3.6	3.8
West Africa	60+	4.6	4.5	4.5	4.4	4.4	4.4	4.5	4.5	4.6	4.7
	65+	2.8	2.7	2.7	2.7	2.7	2.7	2.7	2.8	2.8	2.9
Southern Africa	60+	6.0	6.0	6.0	5.9	5.9	5.5	5.4	5.3	5.3	5.5
	65+	3.6	3.8	3.8	3.8	3.7	3.5	3.4	3.3	3.3	3.4

Source: United Nations (1999a, 1999b).

TABLE 2. MEDIUM VARIANT PROJECTIONS: POPULATION 60+ FOR TWO REGIONS

Region	Indicator (percentage)	Year										
		1995	2000	2005	2010	2015	2020	2025	2030	2040	2050
Southern Africa	60+	5.5	5.7	5.8	5.9	6.2	6.6	7.3	7.9	10.1	13.5
	65+	3.4	3.6	3.6	3.7	3.9	4.3	4.7	5.3	6.6	9.0
Western Region	60+	4.7	4.8	4.8	4.9	4.9	5.1	5.6	6.2	8.2	11.2
	65+	2.9	3.0	3.1	3.2	3.3	3.3	3.5	4.0	5.3	7.4

Source: United Nations (1999a, 1999b).

Ageing and longevity have together occupied the world's platform of popular concerns in the past century. Besides the demographic factors, there are economic and social factors that are bound to impact adversely on older persons during the current process of urbanization and industrialization occurring in the developing regions of the world, including Africa. That process gradually weakens traditional family patterns that provide centrality and social roles for older persons. There is no simple panacea for addressing the problem of meeting the social and economic needs of an ageing world. The orthodoxy of the industrialized world — the welfare state, old-style public pension schemes and public-financed medical provision — are all experiencing major difficulties. The crucial question is whether the cultural norms of African countries will remain strong enough for families to maintain their ties to older members as the dependency burden increases in the twenty-first century.

While ageing has drawn considerable attention in developed societies for a very long time, in many African countries it has thus far barely been perceived as a potential demographic change whose occurrence is only a matter of time. It goes beyond the small proportion of the older population currently projected in the population structure of African countries. Many sub-Saharan African countries have other urgent demographic problems, namely, rapid population growth, high infant and child mortality, excessive rural-urban migration and, most recently, high levels of HIV/AIDS infection.

The present paper looks at a major trend in Africa's modern development — rapid urbanization — and reviews the living arrangements of older persons. This gargantuan task has been attempted in the firm conviction that there are wide regional and even national variations in the living situation of older persons across the African continent. There are, indeed, considerable differences in African living conditions depending on the level of development and the degree of urbanization, modernization and other developmental processes that impact on living conditions. Nevertheless, within the context of urbanization, tradition and cultural change, we can argue that there are some common grounds for discussion, if not in actual individual country details.

The paper is composed of six parts. The first part is devoted to a theoretical discussion of urbanization within the context of migrational trends in Africa and its observed impact on older persons. The second part looks at ageing and the African family in a historical and cultural perspective. The third part reviews the stresses of African families within the constraints of contemporary urbanizational life. The fourth part specifically addresses the issue of urbanization and the living arrangements of older persons in one African country, my own country, Ghana. The fifth part, the conclusion, reviews future options, and the sixth and final part makes recommendations aimed at improving the living standards of older persons in Ghana.

In the present paper, older persons, the elderly and ageing persons are used synonymously.

It is generally accepted that all countries of the world are passing through two fundamental demographic changes, namely, the urbanization of most cities and towns and the rapid ageing of the population. In reviewing the effects of urbanization on older persons, the writer was constrained by the lack of literature in the area of population ageing in the context of urbanization. Urbanization and population ageing have separately received their share of research. They have been severally addressed at the national level as two separate problems but not as a combined area for investigation. The lack of research in these two related areas — urbanization and ageing — has been acknowledged by the Department of Economic and Social Affairs of the United Nations Secretariat (United Nations, 1991).

Migration and urbanization have both separately and jointly been pinpointed as contributing to the de-stabilization of the value that in the past sustained older persons in a closely knit, age-integrated African society. Concern about the well-being of the elderly left behind in rural Africa while the young and able-bodied seek greener pastures in urban centres was first emphasized by African delegations at the World Assembly on Ageing, which was held in Vienna from 26 July to 6 August 1982, in almost all the national reports.[1]

It was repeatedly reported that some older Africans find themselves deprived of their formal family-based resources of support as they become increasingly isolated in rural areas. Zambia, which had experienced a large-scale rural shift in population (according to the 1963 and 1969 population censuses), identified the elderly as those most affected by the shift. According to its national report, the elderly are left behind in rural areas to eke out a living from the land with very limited tools. The situation of the elderly left on their own in villages in Botswana is said to be worsened by periodic droughts that make subsistence farming even more difficult. The delegation of Kenya summed it up as follows:

> The shift from the agrarian economy, which by its very production activities maintained the cohesion and stability of the family, to plantations, mines and factories is now causing physical separation of family members, often by great distance, thus weakening the traditional family ties. The concentration of industry, trade and educational opportunities in cities spurs the migration of young people from their villages.

Should the elderly follow their children to the cities, United Nations studies (1975) indicate that they live in slums and uncontrolled settlements. Africa has a long history of migration within countries and across borders within the continent. What is of consequence with regard to migration in contemporary Africa is the rapidity with which populations, mostly young people, are moving from rural areas to towns and cities. Although sub-Saharan African countries are even now overwhelmingly rural, the continuous depletion in the size of the young population in rural areas surpasses all else in the history of the advanced world and requires serious policy decisions.

Between 1970 and 1982, African urban populations, on average, grew by almost 6 per cent a year, more than twice the overall rate of population growth (Goliber, 1985). In 1960, about 11 per cent of the African population lived in urban areas; 22 years later, in 1982, that population had nearly doubled, to about 21 per cent. In 1960, only seven cities in the African region had more than half a million residents; by 1980, the number was 35, of which nine were in Nigeria alone. Along with the rapid growth of towns and cities, the development of single, dominant metropolitan areas is another characteristic feature of the region's urbanization. Thus, as far back as 1980, in Western Africa, 50 per cent of Togo's urban population was concentrated in the capital, Lomé. In Eastern Africa, 57 per cent of Kenya's urban population could be found in Nairobi, and in Southern Africa, 50 per cent of Zimbabwe's urban population was in Harare, the capital. Africa's cities continue to grow and swell with rural migrants. The city of Accra grew from 16,267 in 1891 to 61,558 in 1931 and reached 964,879 in 1984 (Ahuno, 1992). The city is unplanned and is characterized by shanty suburbs created by the migrant influx into the city. At present, it is estimated to have 2 million inhabitants.

Young people with some education move in numbers from rural areas to towns and cities. Opportunities for earning a good income are greater if one has an education and the facilities for acquiring good education or for earning a better income are definitely not available in the rural areas. In the African context, migration does not necessarily mean a permanent separation of migrants from rural kin left behind. On the contrary, much interaction takes place between urban and rural relations. Remittances from and to immediate kin are a regular feature of African urbanization and, as such, emotional and family ties are maintained with those left behind.

Nevertheless, according to many observers, the ability of modern families in Africa to care for their elderly relatives in the urban context is seriously impaired by crowded housing, limited financial resources and increasing education and employment of women, who are the main caregivers of the elderly. It is further observed that elderly parents have generally become economic appendages to their children's families, instead of, as in the past, integrated members with economic activities revolving around them (Apt, 1995, p. 156). One reason suggested is that the African family structure is increasingly becoming nuclear rather than extended. Especially in urban areas, it is the nuclear rather than the extended family that is common. Western African studies (Little, 1974; Caldwell, 1967; Oppong, 1981; Azu, 1967) support this trend. Almost everywhere, the pattern of marriage has become more footloose than before. The attachment to each other's family house that was found in being married is giving way to the Western style of marriage. The family, which was sanctified by the traditional culture, has virtually degenerated into a profane association of partners who believe more in trial than in permanent marriage.

Consequently, it is argued, traditional family patterns are disintegrating owing to reasons of modernization, industrialization, and urbanization and the resultant complex factors such as education, the introduction of convertible monetary systems, easy travelling, and the establishment of social and economic values and political patterns. These, then, conclusively make up a modern society, with stratifying factors like being rich or poor, being educated or not and having this or that other thing or not. It is important now, in present African society, to be a member of this social stratum or of a professional group or a partner in politics or other interest groups. The current trend is to be recognized, and the values now being accepted by the young, educated, ambitious and urbanized population are a pertinent and also a detrimental factor to the old family pattern, where cash is a scarce commodity.

It is against this background of rapid change that we examine the elderly generation's existence and traditional pattern of support.

THE HISTORICAL AND CULTURAL CONTEXT: AGEING AND THE AFRICAN FAMILY

African values

Historically, African communities had a well-articulated caring structure that preserved the quality of life of older persons, but this was linked to the low probability of survival of large numbers of older persons. The situation is changing, albeit, gradually; early mortality no longer limits the number of surviving elderly persons and traditional respect and caring structures are now facing substantial social challenge (Habte-Gabr, Blum and Smith, 1987; El-Badry, 1988; Adamchak, 1995; AGES, 1995; Vatuk, 1996). The literature on informal support systems characteristic of the African model frequently forewarns of the weakening of African traditional family structures. Much of the literature cites the modern nuclear family's inability to continue its caregiving roles in the context of the current monetized urbanizational life, as women increasingly join the labour force. The impact of world economic trends on family living standards is likewise projected as paving the way for extended family exclusivity (Mosamba, 1984; Shuman, 1991; Apt, 1992, 1996). The family's capacity to cushion older members depends essentially on three variables: its social and economic situation; whether it falls within the ambit of a social security system and the actual nature and structure of the family (Chawla, 1996).

When elderly Nigerians were asked "what sort of things give the most status today" (Ekpenong, Oyeneye and Pell, 1987, pp. 16-17), the general agreement was that money, character and education (in that order) were most important. Only a few respondents mentioned the traditionally accepted norm, namely, children and family. The majority of Nigerian elders are said to be pessimistic about modern circumstances in Nigeria and about the present and future situation of older persons. In the final analysis, the conclusion drawn by the authors was that even though elderly Nigerians continue their traditional roles, those roles are now less important in an increasingly materialistic society. Elderly Temne of Sierra Leone, also in Western Africa, summarize the situation in their reflective assessment of themselves as "a short-changed generation" (Dorjahn, 1989, pp. 272-275). In this reflection, they meant that they had "paid their dues" when they were young but their turn for a pay-off was begrudged by social change. As to the Samia of Kenya, in Eastern Africa,

Cattell (1989, p. 233) observes that the influence of elderly Samians has been "devalued, displaced, replaced and a significant basis of their respect has been eroded". Many elderly Samians identified education as the crucial element in this change and emphasized that it had reduced respect for them, the support and care given them and the seeking of advice from them. Now, one needs new knowledge, which old people, especially women lack (ibid., p. 236).

The writing is already on the wall. In many African countries, neglect and isolation of older persons is increasingly surfacing at two levels: at the family level and at the societal level. A 74-year-old widow, in a Ghanaian urban setting, stated, with deep sorrow, "I did not know life would be so bad" (Apt, 1996, p. 128). Increasingly, the indicators are of a trend away from the traditional perception of an obligation to the elderly and the practice of caring for them:

> When your elders take care of you while you cut your teeth, you must in turn take care of them while they are loosing theirs (a Ghanaian proverb).

Similar value orientations operate in other African countries. In South Africa, *ubuntu* stands for human respect, dignity, trust, equality, togetherness, mutual responsibilities and mutual assistance. A Ubuntu community is built on strong and caring families and neighbourhood. In Kenya, *harambee* stands for togetherness, mutual responsibilities and mutual assistance, pulling resources together to build family and community. In Rwanda, *urukwavu rukaze rwonka abana*, literally meaning "an old hare suckles from the young", expresses the cultural concept of intergenerational support (Marzi, 1994, pp. 3-7).

Traditional inclusivity

By tradition, older people in Africa are not excluded from the process of productive and social participation. In a typical African household, each person has a role to play, whether young or old. The elder plays an important role in the social upbringing of the young and thereby becomes the educator and guiding spirit behind many initiatives of the young, psychologically a very satisfying role. As one entrusted with family land, property and family wealth, the elder is consulted in administrative matters and is always consulted when important decisions are to be made, a role that is linked to their closeness to ancestors. Consequently, the Shona of Zimbabwe refer to the old as "ancestral spirits". In this role, the elders officiate in marriage, birth and death ceremonies, and act as adjudicators to ensure that peace and harmony prevails within the greater family.

This social arrangement enables the young and the old to engage in productive intercourse, and intergenerational experiences are shared; the young have something to learn from the old and the old person is given a helping hand. Daily encounters between generations place the elderly person in a strong position that is useful, challenging and ego-building. This domain of kinship network, within which the older person resides under traditional circumstances, acts as a protective environment, an economic and psychological social security system.

Jomo Kenyatta, in his book *Facing Mount Kenya* (1965, p. 297), stresses the African seniority principle and societal inclusivity of elders:

> As a man grows old, his prestige increases according to the number of age grades he has passed. It is his seniority that makes an elder almost indispensable in the general life of the community. His presence or advice is sought in all functions. In religious ceremonies, the elders hold supreme authority. The custom of the people demands that the elder should be given his due respect and honour.

On the isolation of older persons, Kenyatta (ibid.) makes the following observation, reflecting African moral and political thinking:

> Nobody is an isolated person. First and foremost, he is several people's relative and several people's contemporary.

The seniority principle, however, needs to be qualified. In the African ideology, old age is accompanied by certain roles and responsibilities that are bound to the elder's life experience and accumulated wisdom. Thus, the respect and honour attached to being old continues as long as the elder is responsive to traditional expectations. Accordingly, old age in the Kikuyu society of Kenya is defined functionally as the ability to contribute actively to the labour and leadership obligations of "adulthood" (Cox and Mberia, 1977). In other words, the individual who has learned nothing from his life experience to enhance the life of others younger than himself forfeits the respect and honour reserved for elders. The Akans of Ghana and the Yorubas of Nigeria have many proverbial images describing this type of culturally deficient elder who has nothing of his past to enhance the life of future generations.

URBANIZATION: AFRICAN FAMILIES UNDER STRESS

Support of the elderly in kind was the traditional practice in rural Africa; support of the elderly in cash is increasingly becoming a requirement of urban life in Africa. However, low wages and employment insecurity work against the ability of urban African offspring to meet the income requirements of their parents, as compared to their rural counterparts' ability to meet the need requirements of the rural elderly (Korboe, 1992). Clearly, the domestic separation of the urban elderly from the traditional structure tells us something about the changing image of the traditional family. Conflict of loyalties is evident between the newer urbanized conjugal family and the extended traditional family (Fortes, 1971; Oppong, 1981; Korboe, 1992).

In a study of the views of Ghanaian youth on ageing (Apt, 1991), it was evident that young families would not be living with their elders much longer, as 81 per cent of the respondents were of the opinion that this arrangement was not feasible at the present time. It would, however, be a mistake to think that such separation is simply the outcome of the adoption of modern values and attitudes, as there are obvious infrastructural and structural factors involved in this change of practice. Urban housing conditions provide a good part of the explanation for these changes.

296

In the rural Ghanaian context, the provision of accommodation for all social categories is unproblematic; shortage of land is not a factor and simple additional dwellings are constructed of local materials as the need arises. Urban accommodation typically requires cash payment and is frequently subject to the landowner's limitation on the number of persons entitled to inhabit a property. These factors, taken together, place pressures on families, especially where family size is large, to subdivide into component units (rural/urban). Such subdivision, in turn, adversely affects the internal budgeting arrangements of the conjugal family in respect of its ability to meet traditional welfare obligations.

It is not only the budgeting capabilities of the conjugal family that are affected by subdivision. Such subdivision also has consequences for the arrangement of various personal service and care arrangements within the extended family. For example, the traditional functions performed by older persons in respect of child care are negatively affected by domestic separation. Similarly, the caring services extended to the elderly within the traditional household become more problematic, sporadic and, on occasion, even impossible, when elderly people become geographically separated from kin, even within the same area of a city (Apt, 1993) or are forced to live with caregivers in an unfriendly urban environment. The Kenya case study below illustrates the latter example (Tout, 1989).

Uprooted from a rural area, Mrs. S tells her story:

> *When I was at home, I had a field and managed to do all I wanted, but here in town, I am hardly able to take a walk because I am old and, besides, in town there is a danger of cars. I always tell my son that I want to go home to live the life I am used to. I am, however, too old and sick and no one is prepared to come with me. I have no future but to wait for death.*

The reciprocity that existed between generations in the traditional extended family has thus been disrupted by urban life; in the process, the elderly, who were previously valued for their services, increasingly occupy the unenviable position of being viewed as useless consumers of scarce resources and uncooperative. When old people living in rural areas have no option but to migrate to the city to live with relatives there, it is not an easy situation for either side. It can be quite traumatic for the old person (HAG, 1999) and stressful for the relative.

Nevertheless, although signs of an imminent crisis concerning the social welfare of the old in Africa are already visible, currently, in most sub-Saharan African countries, owing to the lack of a comprehensive social security system for all, the family continues to be the dominant source of care and support for older persons.

THE GHANAIAN EXAMPLE: URBANIZATION AND LIVING ARRANGEMENTS OF OLDER PERSONS

Demographic profile

The demographic profile of Ghana shows that people are living longer and will continue to live longer in the years ahead. The population of Ghana, which is relatively young, is currently estimated to be over 18 million. The population at the last census, in 1984, was 11 million. The next census, to confirm the 18 million estimate, will begin in 2000. The Ghanaian population is not only youthful but is so in every subsection. The median age of a worker is only 30 years and one out of nine members of the labour force is over 50 years of age. Table 3 shows the population of Ghana, projected to 2000, for selected age groups.

The post-independence population censuses carried out in Ghana in 1960, 1970 and 1984 gave total population figures of 6.7 million, 8.5 million and 12.5 million, respectively. The 1970 census shows an increase of 2.4 per cent per year over the population of the first census, while the 1984 census recorded an annual growth rate of 2.6 per cent during the period from 1970 to 1984. Between 1960 and 1970, the population aged 60 and above had increased by 3.2 per cent, the same increase observed for the period from 1970 to 1984 (see table 4). This suggests that Ghana's population is growing older. Table 5 shows the life expectancy of Ghanaians in 1990 at age 60, 65, 70 and 75. Table 6 shows the geographical distribution of the population aged 60 and over and it indicates, for all the computed years, that more older persons live in rural areas. The link between rural-urban migration in Ghana and the ageing of rural areas has been well documented by researchers (Engman, 1986; Caldwell, 1967; Addo, 1972; Nabilla, 1986). The movement from rural areas to towns, is dominated primarily by the youth (15 to 34 years).

Urbanization and migration

Like most of tropical Africa, the growth of Ghana's towns has accelerated over the years and rural-urban migration has increased alarmingly. According to the Central Bureau of Statistics, urban population increased from 23.0 per cent of the total national population in 1960 to 28.6 per cent in 1970 and further to 31.3 per cent in 1984. During the period from 1960 to 1984, the urban population within the greater Accra region, in which Ghana's capital is located, rose from 78.8 per cent to 83.5 per cent. In the northern region, where rural poverty is at its highest, the urban population rose from 13.0 per cent to 24.7 per cent in the same period. The drift away from rural areas to urban centres is not only causing a high rate of unemployment and overcrowding in towns, among other social and economic problems, but it is also contributing to the isolation of the aged in rural areas and the deprivation of their usual sources of social and economic support.

TABLE 3. PROJECTED POPULATION OF GHANA BY SELECTED AGE GROUPS, 1985-2000

Year	Age group 0-14	Age group 15-59	Age group 60+
1960[a]	2 996 506 (44.5%)	3 398 795 (50.6%)	331 516 (4.9%)
1970[a]	4 015 956 (46.9%)	4 085 475 (47.8%)	457 873 (5.3%)
1984[a]	5 535 116 (45.0%)	6 041 830 (49.2%)	719 135 (5.8%)
1985	5 722 605 (45.0%)	6 296 185 (49.5%)	698 913 (5.5%)
1990	6 750 385 (45.8%)	7 249 841 (49.2%)	743 760 (5.0%)
1995	7 973 658 (46.4%)	8 410 459 (48.9%)	813 761 (4.7%)
1998	8 830 414 (46.7%)	9 194 404 (48.7%)	868 966 (4.6%)
2000	9 395 228 (46.7%)	9 782 500 (48.7%)	924 547 (4.6%)

Source: *Analysis of Demographic Data*, vol. 1 (Accra, Ghana Statistical Service).
[a] Data from the population censuses for 1960, 1970 and 1984.

TABLE 4. POPULATION OF GHANA AGED 60 AND ABOVE

Year	Absolute number	As a percentage of total population	Period	Increase
1960	331 516	4.6	1960-1970	3.2
1970	457 873	5.3	1970-1984	3.2
1984	719 135	5.8	1960-1984	3.2

Source: Ghana population censuses 1960, 1970 and 1984.

TABLE 5. LIFE EXPECTANCY FOR AGES 60-75, 1990 FIGURES

Age	Life expectancy		Expected age at death	
	Males	Females	Males	Females
60	16.05	17.69	76.05	77.69
65	13.67	14.97	78.67	79.97
70	11.69	12.81	81.69	82.81
75	10.77	11.82	85.77	86.82

TABLE 6. PROJECTED GEOGRAPHICAL DISTRIBUTION OF 60+ POPULATION

	Age groups					
	60-64	65-69	70-74	75-79	80+	Total
1984						
Urban	58 327	38 658	32 807	18 072	32 062	179 922
Rural	167 449	106 655	96 056	53 741	115 309	539 213
1991						
Urban	82 357	52 412	44 484	24 504	43 474	243 964
Rural	200 874	126 695	115 233	64 468	138 326	646 847
2000						
Urban	120 789	80 048	67 940	37 425	66 397	372 600
Rural	236 957	150 927	135 933	76 048	163 173	763 040
2025						
Urban	262 184	173 752	96 556	81 235	144 121	808 796
Rural	247 240	157 477	141 832	79 348	170 254	796 155

Sources: Computed from the *1984 Population Census of Ghana, Demographic and Economic Characteristics, Total Country*, table 1A, p. 1 (Accra: Ghana, Statistical Service, 1987); projections are based on 1984 census data.

In reviewing the findings of the 1970 and 1984 censuses, the following facts emerge: it is the young age group that is migrating from rural to urban areas and, consequently, rural areas are increasingly inhabited by older people.

It is estimated that at least 50 per cent of the children of the elderly in Ghana migrate to distant places (Apt van Ham, 1989) and personal contact between children and the parents left behind is rather sporadic (Apt, 1971, 1972, 1980, 1986). The question of visits from children to their old parents is of crucial importance in the context of psychological or emotional support. Data collected in Ghana since the 1970s indicate that migrant children's visits to family members left behind average once or twice a year and that older people in rural areas are visited less often by their children than are their counterparts in urban areas (Apt, 1996, pp. 72-76).

Changing family structure: crowding out older persons

In Ghana, as in all Africa in general, the family is undergoing basic structural and functional modifications. It is, however, the type of changes occurring that remains debatable. The introduction of Western-type education, with its built-in ideologies on living, and wage and income-earning jobs, often channels young people's efforts away from their kith and kin and from their home areas; at the same time, it diminishes the value of the authority, knowledge and skills of the senior generation. The strain on traditional family structure that is introduced by distance is compounded by economic stagnation, individualization of the legal contract in the market economy and an increasing emphasis on romantic love as the basis for marriage. These reinforcing elements tend to create for individuals and couples a direction of independence from the larger family. This direction is further reinforced by the imposition of law courts in matters of property rights and so on, and in the nuclear family housing units provided by employers and public authorities for urban residents.

Migration, urbanization, education and wage labour are the main factors within a broad range of socio-economic changes that are affecting the living arrangements and support system of the family. They affect the care and well-being of the elderly at three levels. First, the departure of resourceful persons within the family and household, that is, the able-bodied and the young, whose services are needed in the processing of daily needs. Secondly, the departure of caregivers, mostly women, through modern education and employment, as providers of services within the household and, finally, the inability of the able-bodied to earn needed income as providers owing to increasing unemployment, underemployment and low salary levels even for the fully employed. Added to the above is income security of the elderly themselves, which diminishes with age as a result of the absence of pension and social security schemes for Ghanaian informal sector workers. The majority of older Ghanaians are small-scale farmers and artisans and have no benefits to rely on when they retire from active work.

Family support

Social indicators show an alarming decline in the living standards of Ghanaians in the past two decades. Although the responsibility for old parents is not resented by the young, the ability of families to care for their elderly in the urban context is seriously impaired by limited financial resources. Empirical studies over the years have placed the burden of care of the old on spouses and children (Brown, 1984; Okraku, 1985). Further indications are that children's monetary support to elderly parents are meagre and infrequent. Food, clothing, medical care and housing are part of children's support to elderly parents. The extent of overall economic and social support to older persons in Ghana from their children can be seen in table 7.

TABLE 7. CHILDREN'S SUPPORT TO ELDERLY PARENTS

Type of assistance	Percentage receiving assistance	Percentage not receiving assistance	Number
Pay rent/provide housing	3.4	96.6	1 003
Provide money for food	91.5	8.5	957
Pay medical bills	52.2	47.8	956
Provide clothing	27.2	72.8	957
Provide other things	5.0	95.0	802

Source: Apt (1996), p. 84.

Demographic characteristics of older persons

Old persons in Ghana tend to remain where they have spent most of their adult lives (Apt van Ham, 1989). In spite of increasing urbanization, Ghana is still a rural country, with an economy that relies heavily on agriculture. The heavy out-migration of the young from rural areas to urban areas has contributed to a large proportion of older persons in rural areas being engaged in agricultural work. Older persons in urban areas have greater opportunities for formal employment if they have some education. Most of the elderly persons left behind in rural areas have existing ties to family members who have moved to urban areas. A small but increasing minority have no ties and no support.

Marital status and living arrangements of older persons vary tremendously by locality (urban/rural) and by gender (see tables 8 and 9). Many older men remain married and in family settings as heads of households, whereas many women spend their later years as widows, separated or divorced. Widowhood status among older women is very prominent, as indicated in table 8a. Compared to men, the rate of widowhood is twice as high for urban woman and even higher for rural woman. The proportion of older women in rural areas who are head of household is 51 per cent; in urban areas, the proportion is 29 per cent (Apt, 1994).

TABLE 8a. MARITAL STATUS, ELDERLY FEMALES

	Urban	Rural
Status	(Percentage)	
Married	28.1	39.6
Widowed	51.0	51.7
Separated/divorced	14.6	8.2
Never married	6.3	0.5
Total	**100.0**	**100.0**

Source: Apt (1994).

TABLE 8b. MARITAL STATUS, ELDERLY MALES

	Urban		Rural	
Status	Number	Percentage	Number	Percentage
Married	66	65.3	166	75.1
Widowed	22	21.8	38	17.2
Separated/divorced	9	8.9	16	7.2
Never married	3	3.0	1	0.5
No answer	1	1.0	-	-
Total	**101**	**100.0**	**221**	**100.0**

Source: Apt (1994).

TABLE 9. HOUSING ARRANGEMENTS OF THE ELDERLY, BY RESIDENCE TYPE

	Urban	Rural	Valid responses	
In whose house are you living?	(Percentage)		Number	Percentage
Own house	29.5	8.0	305	28.9
Family house	42.0	40.3	436	41.4
Child's house	10.6	19.0	145	13.8
Renting	12.4	1.5	87	8.3
Spouse's house	1.4	1.3	14	1.3
Father's/mother's house	1.1	0.3	8	0.8
Uncle's house	-	3.5	14	1.3
Brother's house	-	3.3	13	1.2
Other	3.1	3.0	32	3.0
Valid responses	100.0	100.0	1 054	100.0

Source: Apt (1996), p. 68.

While the majority of older persons in Ghana live in their own houses or ancestral family homes (see table 9), they are most likely to live in older homes of lower value. Although age of housing is not necessarily an index of physical condition, it does bear a relationship to functional obsolescence and ease of maintenance. A fair number of older persons, particularly in rural areas, live in dilapidated houses which, at first impression, require maintenance work. Very few older persons live in rented accommodations; those who do are usually in urban areas (Apt, 1994) and the rent is usually paid by children as part of their welfare contribution. Other common living arrangements are in houses belonging to children and, to a lesser extent, in houses belonging to other family members.

In general, it is unusual in Ghana to find older persons living alone. However, living alone is becoming more manifest in both urban and rural areas. The common living arrangement is to live in households with relations. These are most often children not in gainful employment and grandchildren. Other relations likely to be found in the household of older persons, in ranking order, are sisters and brothers, nieces and nephews and, occasionally, cousins (Apt, 1996, p. 74). On average, two children and four grandchildren live in the household of older persons in urban areas and, in rural areas, the average is two children and seven grandchildren (ibid., p. 74). Grandparents, especially grandmothers with diminished resources, are actively involved in the care and nurturing of grandchildren. They provide food, pay school fees and provide health care (Apt, 1985). In return, grandchildren and children assist in daily household activities such as cleaning, washing and laundering (ibid.).

The important role that older persons continue to play in their family and community and their usefulness to the family has been documented by Brown (1984), Okraku (1985), Apt van Ham (1989) and HAG (1999). We can draw three basic conclusions here: first, that older Ghanaians are socially active and contribute to the development of their family and community; secondly, that older Ghanaians feel needed by their family, although the difference between the present urbanized family life and the earlier traditional life lies in the extent and depth of the older person's social interactions with the now mainly nuclear family; and thirdly, that with financial and emotional support, as well as confidence in the older person's ability to be useful to the family and community, the social health of older Ghanaians will be adequately managed.

CONCLUSION: FUTURE POLICY ACTIONS

The structural dependency within the African family has already changed profoundly. The authority and dominance of the elders have been weakened as they have become appendages of nuclear families. Rapid urbanization and migration for reasons of work have significantly altered family relations, especially where changing living conditions and lack of income stretch family capacities to provide for the elderly. An increase in life expectancy in the coming decades will broaden the age spectrum in Africa. At the same time, the family will increasingly lose its protective function (Kilson,

1966; Kinsella, 1996). As we move into the twenty-first century, the care of older, dependent parents will fall on fewer children, and the impact will be greatest on those who have the least material resources.

Africa belongs to the young and this will remain so in the coming decade. Actual increases of older persons, especially the 80+ group, will overtake those in the developed world. Politically and economically, the elderly as an entity have a low priority rating in Africa. If the traditional norm of security in old age cannot be effectively complemented by extra family assistance, a particularly difficult situation for Africa's elderly will occur. This predicament could be offset by a general improvement in the economic situation of the continent as a whole, in consonance with political stability, but above all, indigenous long-term solutions should be the way forward to the future.

What long-term policy options need to be considered to ensure viable and affordable solutions? Africa is striving towards the modern world, where the cornerstones of quality and successful living are considered to be financial security, good living conditions, health care and social integration.

Africa is unlikely, at least in the foreseeable future, to have at its disposal sufficient resources to build a comprehensive welfare state to meet the needs of its newly enfranchised poor. It must therefore find a new approach to social welfare policy, an approach that encourages traditional welfare arrangements rather than dismantles or erodes indigenous self-help forms of support.

Thus far, national Governments in Africa have not tackled head on the issue of how to develop an appropriate social welfare policy for Africa. Social welfare has typically had a low priority and the contribution of the family to welfare has largely been neglected. As a consequence, policy-making on how better to harness the energies and resources of the family and the community to resolve the social needs of individuals and groups has barely commenced.

Traditional domestic arrangements had intergenerational support built into them; modern arrangements are in the process of destroying this key social welfare feature. Recognizing that this is the case raises the question of how to design intergenerational support back into mainstream social relations so that the elderly are not marginalized and put at risk by the urbanization process.

The impoverishment of Africa means a deterioration of living conditions, particularly of women who bear the triple responsibility of raising a family, working to bring home wages and upholding community structures. Africa has the largest number of old people who are forced by economic and family circumstances to work well beyond the age of 65 (International Labour Organization, 1993; Brown, 1984; Okraku, 1985). The problems of survival that they face leave them little opportunity or energy to develop measures of their own for qualitative living. In this respect, tax breaks for those taking care of older relatives, housing designs that permit multigenerational living, and social facilities, for example, day centres that can be used as meeting places or clubs by older persons, are worth considering. Each of these simple measures can play a part in sustaining an environment conducive to inter-generational solidarity.

Most importantly, the resource constraints experienced in Africa make it imperative that networks of policy makers and researchers be formed to develop continental policies on ageing. Networks are key to reducing research costs and to ensuring the efficient and inexpensive transmission of new policy approaches and developments.

RECOMMENDATIONS FOR GHANA

The following recommendations are specially aimed at improving the living standards of older persons in Ghana.

Strengthening the capability of older farmers

Since older people constitute an increasing portion of the rural agriculture labour force, economic policies should aim at enhancing their farming performance. Equitable access to financial resources and services should be provided. They will need credit and extension services and assistance in adopting improved farming practices and technologies that are suited to their capabilities. Such technologies should be simple, operationally safe, labour saving, without requiring expert skills, inexpensive and capable of enhancing the profitability of farming. Training will be a necessary precondition for technological innovation.

Increasing opportunities for employment

There should be an increase of opportunities for continued participation of both urban and rural elderly persons in productive work. Efforts should be made to encourage older persons to engage in self-employment, which would not only enable them to do things at their own pace but would also encourage them to introduce innovations for productivity and profit. In addition, the provision of opportunities for job training and continued education would enhance their self-employability. Retraining programmes should therefore be initiated to re-educate the elderly and update their knowledge of modern techniques and skills so that they can continue in their present occupation or take up a new one.

Promoting rural development

Integrated rural development is seen as the key for alleviating the impact of the ageing population on the rural economy. Its main aims are:

(a)   To improve productivity;

(b)   To stem the flow of youth migration to urban areas;

(c)   To strengthen the capabilities of the rural labour force, including older workers.

In order to achieve these objectives, policy programmes should include: availability of farm loans; revision of price policies for agricultural products; provision of special training in new agricultural techniques and marketing procedures; better utilization of cooperative systems; and higher levels of investment in rural areas.

Reactivating village industries and enterprises

In connection with increasing the job prospects and improving the sources of income of older persons, there is a need to reactivate small-scale village industries and enterprises in which the ageing can be more involved. For example, production centres for traditional handicrafts could be set up to be run and self-managed by the ageing to provide for the manufacture of basket work, pottery and various leather articles. These activities, often involving production at home on a piece-rate basis, could be promoted by improving women's access to simple tools that they can own or rent.

Providing financial assistance for income-generating projects

The establishment of income-generating projects targeted at older persons should be an important element in the employment strategy. The financing of such small economic undertakings can take several forms: (a) a no-interest and no-collateral assistance programme administered by the Government to help older workers; (b) the allocation of a lump sum from social security funds to workers upon retirement to provide the capital necessary for self-employment ventures; and (c) special government-subsidized community funds to finance development projects and assist destitute and disabled older persons to become self-supporting.

Encouraging participation in rural cooperatives

Cooperative ventures can play a key role in strengthening the capacity of the ageing to contribute to rural development by providing equipment, technical assistance, marketing access, and managerial and other inputs for farming and small non-farm activities. However, the successful participation of poor, ageing farmers in cooperative ventures will depend very much on the concurrent implementation of education and training programmes, input of managerial expertise, access to modern production tools and, in some cases, land reform.

Providing education and training

A continuous and progressive education and training programme, aimed at developing older person's awareness, favourable attitudes, leadership skills and management abilities, vocational competence and business management, should receive support from both local and external institutions. The well-being of older people, particularly women, is directly related to social and environmental circumstances and their ability to cope with those circumstances. Older women in general in sub-Saharan Africa face hardships that are directly linked to their economic condition. The main reasons for economic hardship are partly cultural and partly owing to the fact that existing pensions and social security schemes cover a small proportion of the female population. With inadequate and decreasing family support attributable to migration patterns in the region, the vulnerability of older women should become an important matter for technical assistance programmes in the future.

NOTES

[1] The statements cited are representative of those of other African delegations. Statements are on file in the Centre for Social Development and Humanitarian Affairs of the Department of Economic and Social Affairs of the United Nations Secretariat.

REFERENCES

Adamchak, D. J. (1995). Pension and household structure of older persons in Namibia. *Southern African Journal of Gerontology*, vol. 4, No. 2; pp. 11-15.

Addo, N. O. (1972). Urban population and employment in Ghana. In *Population Growth and Economic Development in Africa*, S. Ominde and C. N. Ejiogu, eds. London: Heineman.

AGES (1995). Effective response to aging in Africa by the year 2000: AGES workshop report. Accra: African Gerontological Society.

Ahuno, T. M. (1992). The development of Accra: pattern and processes of growth. Project submitted to the Department of Geography and Resource Development, University of Ghana, Legon, in partial fulfilment of the requirements for the Bachelor of Arts degree.

Apt, N. A. (1971). Socio-economic conditions of the aged in Ghana. Accra: Department of Social Welfare and Community Development.

_____ (1972). The role of the aged in the Ghanaian family: young people's view. Accra: Department of Social Welfare and Community Development.

_____ (1980). Rural aging: The case of Ejisu/Bosomtwe district of Ashanti. Legon: University of Ghana, Department of Sociology.

_____ (1985). The role of grandparents in the care of children. In *Problems and Aspirations of Ghanaian Children: Implications for Policy Planning in Action*, P. A. Twumasi and others, eds. Project report for the Ghana National Commission on Children.

_____ (1986). Grandparenthood role: an example from the eastern region of Ghana. Legon: University of Ghana, Department of Sociology.

_____ (1991). Ghanaian youth on Ageing. *Bold* (Malta), vol. 1, pp 3-11.

_____ (1992). Family support to elderly people in Ghana. In *Family Support for the Elderly: The International Experience*, Hal Kendig, Akiko Hashimoto and Larry Coppard, eds. Oxford: Oxford University Press.

_____ (1993). Care of the elderly in Ghana: an emerging issue. *Journal of Cross-cultural Gerontology*, vol. 8, pp. 301-312.

_____ (1994). The situation of elderly women in Ghana. Report to the United Nations. New York.

_____ (1995). Aging in Africa: toward a redefinition of caring. In *An Aging Population, an Aging Planet and a Sustainable Future*, Stanley Engman and others, eds., vol. 1, chap. 9. Texas Institute for Research and Education on Aging.

_____ (1996). *Coping with Old Age in a Changing Africa*. Aldershot, United Kingdom: Avebury.

_____, and M. Greico (1994). Urbanization, caring for the elderly and the changing African family: the challenge to social welfare and social policy. *International Social Security Review*. Geneva, pp. 111-122.

Apt van Ham, N. A. (1989). Impact and consequences of social change on ageing in Ghana. Legon: University of Ghana. Doctoral dissertation.

Azu, Gladys (1967). The Ga family and social change. Legon: University of Ghana, Institute of African Studies. Master of Arts thesis.

Brown, C. K. (1984). Improving the social protection of the ageing population in Ghana. Legon: University of Ghana, Institute of Statistical, Social and Economic Research.

Caldwell, J. C. (1967). Migration and urbanization. In *A Study of Contemporary Ghana*, W. Birmingham and others, eds., vol. 2. London: Allen and Unwin, pp. 111-144.

Cattell, M. G. (1989). Knowledge and social change in Samia, western Kenya. *Journal of Cross-cultural Gerontology*, vol. 4, No. 3.

Chawla, S. (1996). The eradication of poverty in old age. *United Nations Bulletin on Ageing*, Nos. 2 and 3. New York, pp. 4-8.

Cox, F. M. and N. U. Mberia (1977). Aging in a Changing Society: A Kenyan Experience. New York: International Federation on Aging.

Dorjahn, V. R. (1989). Where do the old folk live? The residence of the elderly among the Temme of Sierra Leone. *Journal of Cross-cultural Gerontology*, vol. 4, No. 3.

Ekpenyong, S., O. Oyeneye and M. Pell (1987). Nigerian elderly: a rural-urban and interstate comparison. *African Gerontology*, No. 5.

El-Badry, M. A. (1988). Aging in developing countries: one more population problem? In *Economic and Social Implications of Aging*. New York: United Nations. Sales No. 90.XIII.18, pp. 389-398.

Engman, E. V. T. (1986). *Population of Ghana 1850-1960*. Accra: Ghana University Press, pp. 207-227.

Fortes, M. (1971). *The Family: Bane or Blessing?* Accra: Ghana University Press.

Goliber, T. J. (1985). Sub-Saharan Africa: population pressures on development. Washington, D. C.: Population Reference Bureau.

Habte-Gabr, E., N. S. Blum and I. Smith (1987). The elder in Africa. *Journal of Applied Gerontology*, vol. 6, No. 2, pp. 163-182.

HAG (1999). The contribution of older persons to development. *HelpAge Ghana Report*. Accra.

International Labour Organization (1993). *World Labour Report, 2*. Geneva.

Kenyatta, J. (1965). *Facing Mount Kenya*. New York: Vintage Books.

Kilson, Marion (1966). Urban tribesmen and social continuity among the Ga of Accra. Cambridge, Massachusetts: Harvard University. Ph.D. thesis.

Kinsella, Kevin (1996). Population ageing in developing countries. In *Meeting the Challenges of Ageing Populations in the Developing World*. Malta: International Institute on Ageing, pp. 24-25.

Korboe, D. (1992). Family houses in Ghanaian cities: to be or not to be. *Urban Studies*, vol. 29, p. 7.

Little, Kenneth (1974). Urbanization as a Social Process: An Essay on Movement and Change in Contemporary Africa. London: Routledge and Kegan Paul.

Mosamba, ma Mpolo (1984). Older persons and their families in a changing village society: a perspective from Zaire. New York: International Federation on Aging. Washington, D. C.: World Council of Churches.

Marzi, H. (1994). Old age in Rwanda: a problem? *Bold* (Malta), vol. 5, No. 1, pp. 3-7.

Nabila, J. S. (1986). Rural-urban migration and its implications for rural development in Ghana. In *Rural Development in Ghana*, C. K. Brown, ed. Accra: Ghana University Press, pp. 75-89.

Okraku, I. O. (1985). A study of Ghanaian public service pensioners. Report presented at the Thirteenth International Congress of Gerontology, New York.

Oppong, C. (1981). Middle Class African Marriage: A Study of Ghanaian Civil Servants. London: Allen and Unwin.

Shuman, T. K. (1991). Support for the elderly: the changing urban family and its implications for the elderly. In *Ageing and Urbanization*. New York: United Nations. Sales No. 91.XIII.12, pp. 279-287.

Tout, K. (1989). *Ageing in Developing Countries*. Oxford, United Kingdom: Oxford University Press.

United Nations (1975). Aging in Slums and Uncontrolled Settlements. New York. Sales No. 77.IV.2.

_____ (1991). *Ageing and Urbanization.* New York. Sales No. 91.XIII.12.

_____ (1999a). World Population Prospects: The 1998 Revision, vol. I, Comprehensive Tables. Sales No. E.99.XIII.9.

_____ (1999b). World Population Prospects: The 1998 Revision, vol. II, Sex and Age. Sales No. E.99.XIII.8.

_____ (1999c). *Population Ageing 1999,* A wall chart. Sales No. E.99.XIII.11.

Vatuk, S. (1996). Meeting the Challenges of Ageing Populations in Developing Countries. Final Report. Malta: International Institute on Ageing.

World Bank (1994). *Averting the Old Age Crisis.* New York: Oxford University Press.

LIVING ARRANGEMENTS AND THE HEALTH OF OLDER PERSONS IN DEVELOPED COUNTRIES

*Emily Grundy**

INTRODUCTION

In 1950/51, only a handful of developed countries had populations in which those aged 65 comprised 10 per cent, or slightly more, of the total. By 1996, virtually all developed countries were in this position, and in most of Northern, Southern and Western Europe those over 65 accounted for 15 per cent or more of the population (Council of Europe, 1998). In much of Europe and North America recent increases in the proportion of very old people have been particularly marked (Grundy, 1996).

The same post-Second World War period has seen substantial changes in the living arrangements of older people. The proportions living alone have increased and the proportions living in complex households with kin other than members of the nuclear family have plummeted (Kobrin, 1976; Pampel, 1983; Murphy and Grundy, 1994; Elman and Uhlenberg, 1995; Weinick, 1995). These trends are illustrated for England and Wales in figures Ia and IIb.

Figures Ia and Ib show that the average size of households in which elderly people lived was considerably lower in 1991 than in 1981 or 1971. It can also be seen that the relationship between age and household size has changed. In 1971, household size initially fell in the younger elderly groups (reflecting the effects of widowhood and the departure of children from the home) but rose at later ages, suggesting movement by some into the households of relatives. By 1991, this latter rise is not apparent at all among men and is only manifest among women among the extreme aged. Indeed, by 1991, as shown in figures IIa and IIb, the proportion of adults living alone increased steadily throughout adult life, reaching very high levels among those aged 85 and over, particularly among women. The changes between 1971 and 1991 do not reflect increases in widowhood — on the contrary, sex differentials in England and Wales and in some developed countries have recently narrowed, with a consequent increase in the proportion of elderly women still living with a spouse (Murphy and Grundy, 1994). However, while living with a spouse has in some (but not all) developed countries become

---

* Centre for Population Studies, London School of Hygiene and Tropical Medicine.

slightly more prevalent at older ages, co-residence with a child in the very old age groups has become much less usual. In England and Wales, as recently as 1971, 41 per cent of women aged 85 or over lived in two- or three-generation households; by 1991, this proportion had fallen to 21 per cent (Grundy, 1999). Trends in other Western populations show similar declines (Börsch-Supan, 1990; Sundstrom, 1994; Kramarow, 1995; Waehrer and Crystal, 1995). In Japan, where co-residence between elderly parents and their children has historically been the norm, rates of co-residence remain much higher than in the West, but declines have been proportionately just as great (Ogawa and Retherford, 1997).

This conjunction of rapid growth in both the number and proportion of older people, particularly very old people, and the proportion living alone has raised a number of concerns among policy makers,[1] particularly with regard to the implications for demand for formal care and support services (Allen and Perkins, 1995).

LIVING ARRANGEMENTS AND USE OF SERVICES

A large share of the research on the relationship between health and household composition among older people has focused on the implications of the choice of living arrangements for the provision of care (Cafferata, 1987; Arber, Gilbert and Evandrou, 1988; Chappell, 1991). Some studies (Arber, Gilbert and Evandrou, 1988) have found that the allocation of formal care (in terms of the provision of statutory services) was influenced more by household composition than by the gender of either the aged person or the caregiver. Thus, in the mid-1980s, older people in the United Kingdom of Great Britain and Northern Ireland who lived alone were five times more likely to receive home help support than those who were married. Associations between living arrangements and the use of medical services (as opposed to support services provided in the home) are less clear-cut. Some studies have found that those living with others are more likely to use such services, as family members facilitate access and encourage medical consultation (Magaziner and others, 1988); however, results from other studies conflict with this finding (Cafferata, 1987). Those living alone do, however, have a much higher rate of entry into long-term institutional care than do those living with others (Dolinsky and Rosenwaike, 1988; Grundy 1992a; Grundy, and Glaser, 1997). However, risks for never-married elderly people tend to be even higher, suggesting that part of this association reflects a possible lack of relatives, rather than living alone per se.

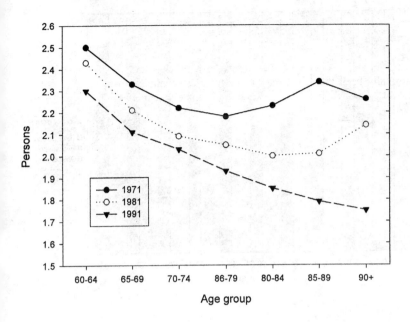

Figure Ia. Average household size lived in, England and Wales, Males

- 1971
- 1981
- 1991

Persons

Age group

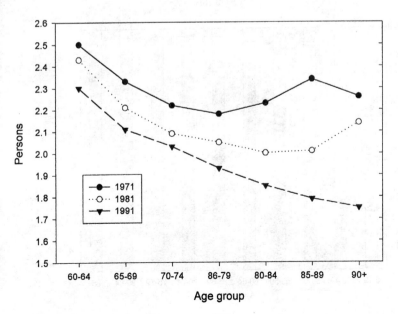

Figure Ib. Average household size lived in, England and Wales Females

- 1971
- 1981
- 1991

Persons

Age group

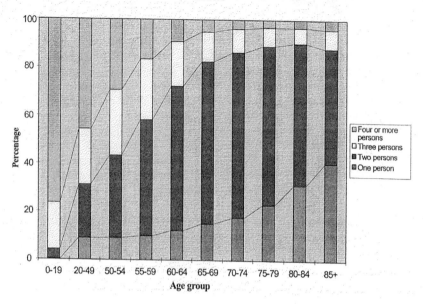

Figure IIa. Household size distribution by age, United Kingdom, 1991
Males

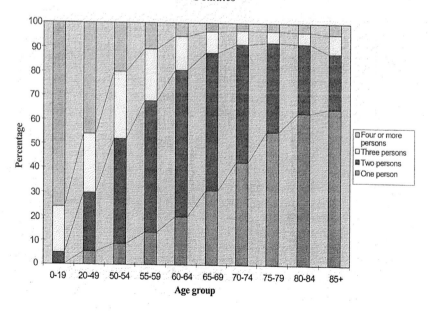

Figure IIb. Household size distribution by age, United Kingdom, 1991
Females

This research suggests that, not surprisingly, a lack of intra-household support has consequences for the demand for extra-household help, including formally provided assistance. A second issue of importance is the possible consequences for the well-being of those in the older age groups. It is well established that selection effects (considered in more detail below) are an important factor in accounting for differences in the health status of marital status groups, but the literature on associations between marital status and health and on links between social ties and health also suggests a number of mechanisms whereby living with others might have beneficial effects on health. These include the provision of services such as meals, nursing care when ill and support and companionship (Verbrugge, 1979; Umberson, 1992; Hahn, 1993; Murphy, Glaser and Grundy, 1997). Marriage or co-residence with other relatives may also bring material advantages, especially for women (Hahn, 1993; Rendall and Speare, 1995). Finally, marriage (or co-residence) may bring control of unhealthy behaviours; unmarried men, for example, have higher rates of alcohol consumption than do married men (Umberson, 1992).

While living with a spouse would seem to confer various health-related benefits, it does not necessarily follow that living with someone other than a spouse (the only likely "choice" for an elderly widow) confers similar advantages over living alone. Evidence on this, reviewed below, is sparse compared with the literature on marital status and even more complicated by the problem of selection effects.

LIVING ARRANGEMENTS AND HEALTH: PREVIOUS STUDIES

There is some rather fragmentary evidence that living alone may be associated with various health-related disadvantages. Davis and others (1990), for example, found a greater prevalence of dietary inadequacy among elderly people living alone in the United States of America. There are also some studies that have found higher rates of poor health among people living alone. Murphy (1997), for example, reported that, in the United Kingdom, rates of long-standing illness were higher among those living alone than among those in other types of household, but only in middle-aged groups. Welin and others (1985), in a large prospective study of middle-aged and elderly Norwegian men, found an inverse relationship between household size and mortality, that is, those with the most co-residents had the lowest risks of death. Mor and others (1989), using data from another longitudinal study, the United States Longitudinal Study of Aging, found that after controlling quite carefully for initial health status, elderly people living alone had a higher risk of functional decline than did others. Sarwari and others (1998), in a prospective study of elderly white women in Baltimore, Maryland, found that among women with severe impairment at the baseline, those who lived alone experienced significantly greater deterioration in functional status than did those living with others, particularly those living with non-spouse others. However, among the women without severe impairment at the baseline, the reverse was the case — those living alone experienced the least deterioration.

A wider range of research has reported relationships between living arrangements and mental health. Harrison and others (1999), in a survey of adults aged 18 and over in the north-west of England, found that those living alone had a 50 per cent higher risk of anxiety and depression (measured by score on the General Health Questionnaire (GHQ)) than did those living with at least one other adult, even after controlling for age and sex. (The risk for adults living only with children was even higher.) However, marital status was not controlled for. Results from the 1984 Health and Lifestyle Survey in the United Kingdom also showed poorer mental health (indicated by GHQ score) among those living alone, including elderly men. In that study, 40 per cent of men aged 65 and over who lived alone were above the threshold indicating probable psychiatric morbidity compared with 26 per cent of those living with a spouse and 29 per cent of those living with people other than a spouse. A slightly higher proportion of elderly women living alone were also above this threshold when compared with women living with persons other than a spouse, but this latter difference was not statistically significant (Grundy, 1989). (These differences, in cross-sectional studies, do not, of course, indicate a causal link; it may be that those prone to depression and anxiety have fewer chances of finding, or remaining with, co-residents.)

The studies referred to above show associations between living alone, or with fewer people, and various indicators of poor health, particularly poor psychological health, although in only a few of them is this relationship apparent in elderly age groups. More numerous are studies of elderly people that show those living alone, at least in the older old age groups, to be healthier than their counterparts living with adults other than a spouse, or in some cases, even than married adults (Fengler and others, 1983; Cafferata, 1987; Dale, Evandrou and Arber, 1987; Arber, Gilbert and Evandrou, 1988; Magaziner and others, 1988; Crimmins and Ingegneri, 1990; Soldo, Wolf and Agree, 1990; Stinner, Byun and Paita, 1990; Spitze, Logan and Robinson, 1992; Prohanska, Mermelstein and Van Nostrand, 1993; Glaser, Murphy and Grundy, 1997; Hebert, Brayne and Spiegelhalter, 1999).

LIVING ARRANGEMENTS AND HEALTH: EVIDENCE
FROM THE UNITED KINGDOM

In the following section, we use data from a microsample drawn from the 1991 census of the United Kingdom (the 1 per cent sample of anonymized records) and from the 1993-1995 health surveys for England to examine variations in indicators of health in the older population. Table 1 shows the prevalence of self-reported limiting long-term illness by age group and gender according to family/household type and relationship to the household "reference person" (roughly equivalent to head of household).

Household type	Men			Women		
	65-74	75-84	85+	65-74	75-84	85+
Couple+children	32	39	60	26	48	-
Couple no children	34	41	55	30	45	58
Lone parent	39	44	63	32	52	74
Not in family, lives with others	38	48	55	33	47	62
Lives alone	38	48	55	33	47	62
Relationship to head of household						
Head or partner	34	43	55	31	46	62
Parent or parent-in-law	39	54	69	38	59	73
Other	35	41	70	29	50	64

Source: Analysis of samples of anonymized records.

It can be seen that, as would be expected, the prevalence of poor health as measured here increases with age; the extent of variation by living arrangement also increases with age. Among men aged 65-74, those living with a partner and a child have the lowest rates of illness, and lone parents and those who are not part of a family the highest. (Families are defined as co-resident couples or single persons living with never-married children.) Among women of this age, those with a spouse and children (who, within the broad age band would be younger on average) also have slightly lower rates of long-term illness than those in other groups. Among older women, lone parents appear to have the worst health. Among both men and women, rates of long-term illness among those living alone and those who, although not part of a family, lived with others (for example, never-married children or siblings) were identical. Looking at variations by relationship to the head of household, it can be seen that rates of poor health are elevated among those who are the parent or parent-in-law of the household head. A similar picture is evident when the prevalence of long-term illness according to the number of generations in the household are examined (see figures IIIa and IIIb). Differences are slight among the younger elderly, but in older groups of women are lowest for those in one-generation households. Among men, those in three-generation households report the highest prevalence of ill health in the age groups 75-79 and 80-84, while at age 85+, living in a two-generation household appears most disadvantageous.

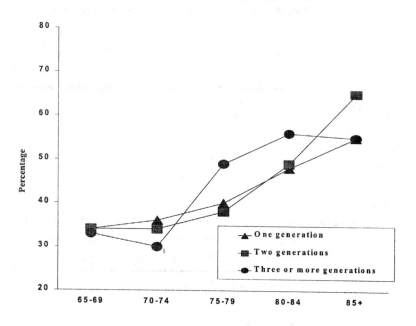

Figure IIIa. Proportion of men with limiting long-term illness by number of generations in the household

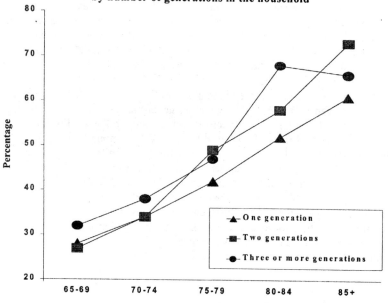

Figure IIIb. Proportion of women with limiting long-term illness by number of generations in the household

The health survey for England (a large, nationally representative survey) includes more detailed information on health status and on health-related behaviours. These data are used below to compare elderly people living alone with those living with a spouse and those not living with a spouse but with at least one other person. Three aspects of health are examined: smoking behaviour, psychiatric morbidity as indicated by GHQ score, and self-rated health status.

Figures IVa and IVb show the prevalence of smoking among men and women, respectively, according to whether they lived alone, with a spouse (with or without others) or in some other type of private household (for example, with a child). Rates of smoking were lower among married persons (except among women aged 85 and over), although variations between those living alone and those living with others were less consistent.

Among men, the prevalence of probable psychiatric morbidity (indicated by a score of 4 or more on the GHQ) was also lowest among the married (see figure Va), although differences between those living alone and those living with others were slight. Among women over 80, however, the lowest rates of morbidity were observed among those living alone.

Results from multivariate analyses of variations in psychiatric morbidity, and of poor self-rated health, are shown in table 2. Among men, psychiatric morbidity was significantly higher among those living alone or with others compared with those living with a spouse, even after control for age, smoking, social class and physical health. However, the difference between those living alone and those living with others was not significant. The proportions rating their health as poor (bad or very bad) were also higher among men living alone and men living with others, compared with those living with a spouse, but these differences were not significant once other factors were controlled for.

These results show lower rates of smoking among people living with a spouse, consistent with social control hypotheses, and that men living with a spouse had a lower prevalence of probable psychiatric morbidity than did other men, even after taking other factors like smoking, social class and physical health into account. However, for those not living with a spouse, there is no apparent advantage in living with others rather than living alone; indeed, among women, the reverse seems to be the case. For women, the odds of psychiatric morbidity were higher for those living with others, both when compared with those living with a spouse and in comparison with those living alone. There were no significant differences in reported poor health.

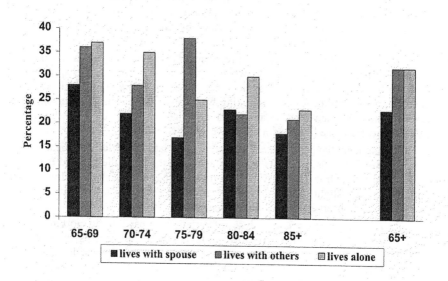

Figure IVa. Prevalence of smoking among elderly men by whether
they are living with a spouse, living with others
or living alone, England, 1993-1995

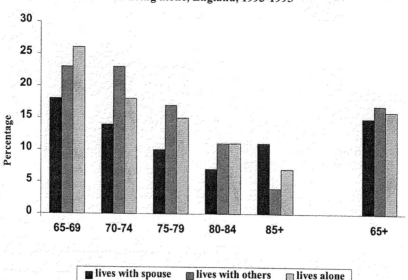

Figure IVb. Prevalence of smoking among elderly women by whether
they are living with a spouse, living with others
or living alone, England, 1993-1995

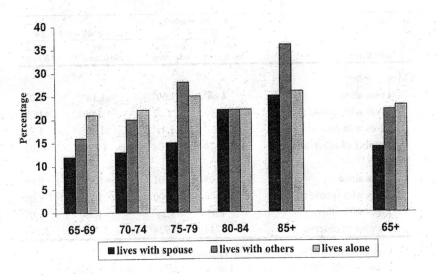

Figure Va. Prevalence of psychiatric morbidity among elderly men by whether they are living with a spouse, living with others or living alone, England, 1993-1995

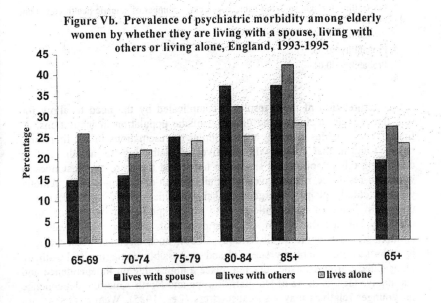

Figure Vb. Prevalence of psychiatric morbidity among elderly women by whether they are living with a spouse, living with others or living alone, England, 1993-1995

TABLE 2. ASSOCIATIONS BETWEEN LIVING ARRANGEMENTS AND HEALTH
AMONG PEOPLE AGED 65 AND OVER IN PRIVATE HOUSEHOLDS,
ENGLAND, 1993-1995

Household type	Psychiatric morbidity (GHQ 4+)		Poor self rated health[a]	
	Model 1[b] odds ratio	Model 2[c] odds ratio	Model 1[b] odds ratio	Model 2[c] odds ratio
Men				
Lives alone	1.68[d]	1.60[d]	1.18[e]	1.07
Lives with spouse (ref)	1.00	1.00	1.00	1.00
Lives with others	1.67[f]	1.47[e]	1.55[f]	1.32
Number of observations	4 124	4 108	4 199	4.103
Women				
Lives alone	1.05	1.01	0.99	0.89
Lives with spouse (ref)	1.00	1.00	1.00	1.00
Lives with others	1.37[f]	1.28[e]	1.19	1.09
Number of observations	5 744	5 724	5 728	5 709

Source: Analysis of health surveys for England, 1993-1995.

[a] Rated health "bad" or "very bad" on five-point scale also including "very good", "good" and "fair".

[b] Controlling for age.

[c] Controlling for age, smoking habit, social class, number of somatic health conditions and year of survey.

[d] Probability <0.001.

[e] Probability <0.05.

[f] Probability <0.01.

Interpretation of these results is complicated by the need to allow for selection effects, including the omission of the population in institutions. A first glance at tables 1 and 2, and at similar representations in the literature, might suggest that living with relatives is damaging to health. Before dismissing this hypothesis, it should be noted that there are circumstances in which co-residence might have potentially health-damaging effects. Among younger elderly people, intergenerational co-residence may arise because of the return home of adult children who have experienced divorce or other adversity, or the failure of health-impaired or otherwise disadvantaged children to leave home at all (Grundy, 2000). Such circumstances, we may hypothesize, are potentially stressful and so possibly damaging to health. In older elderly groups in societies that place a high value on independence and autonomy, such as those of Northern Europe and North America, dependence on younger relatives may also cause stress (Lee, 1985). Wenger (1984), for example, found in a survey of elderly people in Wales that those who lived with their children expressed higher levels of loneliness and dissatisfaction than did those who lived alone. Finally, in a small minority of cases, disabled elderly people may be subject to physical or mental abuse by co-residents (Wolf, 1997). However, these caveats aside, it is clear that a crucial factor underlying observed relationships between living arrangements and health is that of health-related selection in particular types of living arrangements.

HEALTH SELECTION AND LIVING ARRANGEMENTS

The very extensive literature on associations between marital status and health has shown that the married have the best health, followed by the single, the widowed and then the divorced. Apart from the direct benefits of marriage considered earlier on, a major explanation for this pattern is health-related selection in and out of marriage. Ill people are less likely to marry, or remarry (Brown and Giesy, 1986). Those who are widowed, especially at relatively young ages, may also share various characteristics with their deceased spouse, including a common environment, and so may themselves be selected for poor health; additionally, the stress of bereavement or marital breakdown may itself have negative consequences for health (Bowling, 1994). Most studies have found that relationships between indicators of health and marital status are weaker in older age groups. Goldman, Korenman and Weinstein (1995) found that, at older ages, never-married women had better health outcomes than did their married counterparts. However, their analyses were based on data that excluded the population in institutions, a potential source of bias because the likelihood of entering an institution is strongly associated with both marital status and health. Analyses based on the whole population, including those in institutions, have shown a continuing, although weaker, advantage for the married even in the oldest age groups (Murphy, Glaser and Grundy, 1997).

The importance of marriage-related selection effects will vary according to the proportions in different marital status groups. Cross-national studies have shown that the smaller the proportions in the non-married groups, the greater their excess risk, as in these countries single people are more "selected" than in populations that include larger proportions of unmarried individuals (Hu and Goldman, 1990). This is an important point to remember in interpreting associations between marital status and health (or living arrangements and health) in developed countries, as there are considerable variations in marital status distributions between, for example, Western and Eastern Europe, Western Europe and North America and Western countries and Japan and other newly industrialized South-East Asian countries (Grundy, 1996). There are also large variations in the proportions living alone and, conversely, in co-residence with children, with solitary living being most prevalent in Northern Europe and the United States of America and living with children more common in Eastern and Southern Europe and Japan (Wall, 1989; Wolf, 1990; Grundy, 1992b; Sundstrom, 1994).

Whereas in the case of marriage, selective and protective effects are hypothesized to operate in the same direction (both tending to confer advantage on the married), in the case of the association between living arrangements and health in the older age groups, the impact of "protection" and "selection" is likely to operate differentially.

There is considerable evidence to indicate that increases in disability among older people lead to changes in their living arrangements, in particular to moves into institutions or the households of relatives (Wolf and Soldo, 1988; Crimmins and Ingegneri, 1990; Stinner, Byun and Paita, 1990; Speare, Avery and Lawton, 1991; Angel, Angel and Himes, 1992; Grundy, 1993). The health status, and subsequent mortality, of individuals making these kinds of household transitions has been shown to be much worse than that of other elderly people (Speare, Avery and Lawton, 1991; Spitze, Logan and Robinson, 1991; Glaser and Grundy, 1998). Wolf, Burch and Matthews (1990) found that limitations in the ability to undertake very specific tasks (such as meal preparation) were associated with a reduced chance of living alone, suggesting that future studies on the effects of health status on living arrangements would benefit from the use of detailed, rather than global, assessments of health status.

DISCUSSION

The living arrangements of older people have changed dramatically in the recent past, with increases in the proportions living alone, and decreases among those living with others, that is, siblings, parents and children. Hypotheses concerning changes in household structure have examined the impact of demographic, cultural and economic factors (see Grundy, 1992b, and Glaser, 1997, for reviews of this literature). Demographic factors are important, in that changes in kin availability, and the timing of fertility, affect both the feasibility of living with relatives and whether or not children are still likely to be at home when parents reach early old age. Cultural factors may reflect adherence to family norms and values affecting the likelihood of co-residence with an aged parent. Economic factors are believed to determine the extent to which individuals are able to achieve their goals of privacy and independence. A fourth factor that perhaps should be more explicitly considered is the extent to which changes in living arrangements have been facilitated by improvements in the health status of the older population.

Although there are a number of theoretical reasons that suggest that living alone might have adverse effects on the health of at least some older people, the empirical evidence tends not to support this finding, except perhaps in the case of psychiatric morbidity among men. However, in interpreting the data it is essential to take account of the importance of selective moves to institutions and to the households of relatives. Particularly among the very old, living alone may only be an "attractive" or possible option for those in reasonably good health with good support systems. Given that surviving spouses, attentive daughters and personality cannot be randomly allocated, it is unlikely that the "true" effects of living arrangements on the health of elderly adults can ever be quantified. Moreover, these are certain to vary between populations and individuals. The psychological effect of living alone, for example, may be damaging for older people who regard this situation as undesirable or stigmatizing, but beneficial for those who regard it as a positive indication of independence and autonomy. Social consequences will vary according to other social support opportunities available. Most elderly people in developed countries are in frequent contact with relatives, even though they do not live together, and the proportions at risk of isolation may be small (Crimmins and Ingegneri, 1990; Wolf, 1994; Grundy, Murphy and Shelton, 1999). Murphy (1982), in a study of risk factors for clinical depression, found that among elderly people in the United Kingdom, having a close relationship with someone seen only every two or three weeks was just as "protective" as having a confidant in the same household. It was those who had no close relationship — many of whom had never had such a relationship — who were most at risk. Similarly, we could hypothesize that the reduced possibilities of economies of scale in purchasing adequate housing, heating and food may mean that living alone has adverse consequences for elderly people on low incomes, but no similar effect on the well-off. Lack of domestic services, such as cooking and cleaning, may disadvantage those who lack the relevant skills or ability to undertake these tasks themselves, but have no effect on "competent" elderly people. Hypothesized interactions of this kind are illustrated schematically in table 3. It would seem that future research on unravelling the complex relationships between households and health could be fruitfully focused on investigating these kinds of interactions both within and between countries. Finally, it is important to note that many of the co-residents of elderly people with health problems may themselves be in poor health; data from the United Kingdom show that those with a long-term illness are more likely than others to live in households including others with long-term illness (Glaser, Murphy and Grundy, 1997). This suggests that policy makers need to consider household, rather than just individual, characteristics when deciding on the allocation of services.

TABLE 3. POSSIBLE EFFECTS OF LIVING ALONE: INTERACTIONS WITH OTHER DOMAINS AND POPULATIONS IN WHICH THE EFFECT MAY BE OBSERVED

Type of effect	Negative	Positive/neutral
Psychological	If living alone is seen as stigmatizing (lower educated in Japan/S. Europe)	If independence and autonomy are valued (highly educated in N. Europe/USA)
Economic	Low-income elderly lose opportunities for economies of scale (E. Europe, Greece)	No effect on high-income elderly (high-income USA, N. Europe)
Services/care	Elderly lacking domestic skills ("traditional" men; elderly with short-interval care needs)	No effect on "competent" elderly
Social support	If few other social ties (childless widowers/divorced men, especially in Northern Europe/USA; recent migrants; housebound)	No effect on well-supported

NOTES

¹ As one contributory factor to declines in co-residence may be declines in the availability of kin resulting from falls in fertility (and consequent age-structure changes), these two trends are interrelated.

REFERENCES

Allen, I., and E. Perkins, eds. (1995). *The Future of Family Care for Older People.* London: Her Majesty's Stationery Office.

Angel, R. J., J. L. Angel and C. L. Himes (1992). Minority group status, health transitions, and community living arrangements among the elderly. *Research on Aging,* vol. 14, pp. 496-521.

Arber, S., G. N. Gilbert and M. Evandrou (1988). Gender, household composition and receipt of domiciliary services by elderly disabled people. *Journal of Social Policy,* vol. 17, pp. 153-175.

Börsch-Supan, A. H. (1990). A dynamic analysis of household dissolution and living arrangement transitions by elderly Americans. In *Issues in the Economics of Aging,* D. A. Wise, ed. Chicago: National Bureau of Economic Research.

Bowling, A. (1994). Mortality after bereavement: an analysis of mortality rates and associations with mortality 13 years after bereavement. *International Journal of Geriatric Psychiatry,* vol. 9, pp. 445-459.

Brown, J. S., and B. Giesy (1986). Marital status of persons with spinal cord injury. *Social Science and Medicine,* vol. 23, No. 3, pp. 313-322.

Cafferata, G. L. (1987). Marital status, living arrangements, and the use of health services by elderly persons. *Journal of Gerontology,* vol. 42, pp. 613-618.

Chappell, N. L. (1991). Living arrangements and sources of caregiving. *Journal of Gerontology,* vol. 46, No. 1, pp. S1-8.

Council of Europe. (1998). *Recent demographic developments in Europe.* Strasbourg, France: Council of Europe Publishing.

Crimmins, E. N., and D. G. Ingegneri (1990). Interaction and living arrangements of older parents and their children. *Research on Aging,* vol. 12, pp. 3-35.

Dale, A., M. Evandrou and S. Arber (1987). The household structure of the elderly population in Britain. *Ageing and Society,* vol. 7, pp. 37-56.

Davis, M. A., and others (1990). Living arrangements and dietary quality of older U. S. adults. *Journal of the American Dietetic Association,* vol. 90, No. 12, pp. 1667-1672.

Dolinsky, A. L. and I. Rosenwaike (1988). The role of demographic factors in the institutionalization of the elderly. *Research on Aging,* vol. 10, No. 2, pp. 235-257.

Elman, Cheryl, and Peter Uhlenberg (1995). Co-residence in the early twentieth century: elderly women in the United States and their children. *Population Studies,* vol. 49, pp. 501-517.

Fengler, A. P., and others (1983). Later life satisfaction and household structure: living with others and living alone. *Ageing and Society,* vol. 3, No. 3, pp. 357-377.

Glaser, K. (1997). The living arrangements of elderly people. *Reviews in Clinical Gerontology,* vol. 70, No. 1, pp. 63-72.

_____, and E. Grundy (1998). Migration and household change in the population aged 65 and over, 1971-1991. *International Journal of Population Geography*, vol. 4, pp. 323-339.

Glaser, K., M. Murphy and E. Grundy. (1997). Limiting long-term illness and household structure among people aged 45 and over, Great Britain, 1991. *Ageing and Society*, vol. 17, pp. 3-20.

Goldman, N., S. Korenman and R. Weinstein (1995). Marital status and health among the elderly. *Social Science and Medicine*, vol. 40, No. 12, pp. 1717-1730.

Grundy, E. (1989). Longitudinal perspectives on the living arrangements of the elderly. In *Growing Old in the Twentieth Century*, M. Jefferys, ed. London: Routledge, pp. 128-150.

_____ (1992a). Socio-demographic variations in rates of movement into institutions among elderly people in England and Wales: an analysis of linked census and mortality data, 1971-1985. *Population Studies*, vol. 46, pp. 65-84.

_____ (1992b). The living arrangements of elderly people. *Reviews in Clinical Gerontology*, vol. 2, No. 4, pp. 353-361.

_____ (1993). Moves into supported private households among elderly people in England and Wales. *Environment and Planning A*, vol. 25, pp. 1467-1479.

_____ (1996). Population ageing in Europe. In *Europe's Population in the 1990s*, D. Coleman, ed. Oxford: Oxford University Press, pp. 267-296.

_____ (1999). Household and family change in mid-life and later in England and Wales. In *Changing Britain: Families and Households in the 1990s*, S. McRae, ed. Oxford: Oxford University Press, pp. 201-228.

_____ (2000) Co-residence of mid-life children with their elderly parents in England and Wales, changes between 1981 and 1991. *Population Studies*.

_____, and K. Glaser (1997). Trends in, and transitions to, institutional residence among older people in England and Wales: 1971 to 1991. *Journal of Epidemiology and Community Health*, vol. 51, pp. 531-540.

Grundy, E., Mike Murphy and Nicola Shelton (1999). Looking beyond the household: intergenerational perspectives on living with kin and contacts with kin in Great Britain. *Population Trends*, vol. 97, pp. 19-27.

Hahn, B. A. (1993). Marital status and women's health: the effect of economic and marital acquisitions. *Journal of Marriage and the Family*, vol. 55, pp. 495-504.

Harrison, J., and others (1999). Social determinants of GHQ score by postal survey. *Journal of Public Health Medicine*, vol. 21, No. 3, pp. 283-288.

Hebert, R., C. Brayne and D. Spiegelhalter (1999). Factors associated with functional decline and improvement in a very elderly community-dwelling population. *American Journal of Epidemiology*, vol. 150, No. 5, pp. 501-510.

Hu, Y., and N. Goldman (1990). Mortality differentials by marital status: an international comparison. *Demography*, vol. 27, No. 2, pp. 233-250.

Kobrin, F. E. (1976). The primary individual and the family: changes in living arrangements in the United States since 1940. *Journal of Marriage and the Family*, vol. 38, pp. 233-238.

Kramarow, E. A. (1995). The elderly who live alone in the United States: historical perspectives on household change. *Demography*, vol. 32, pp. 335-352.

Lee, G. R. (1985). Kinship and social support of the elderly: the case of the United States. *Ageing and Society*, vol. 5, pp. 19-38.

Magaziner, J., and others (1988). Health and living arrangements among older women: Does living alone increase the risk of illness? *Journal of Gerontology*, vol. 43, No. 5, pp. M127-133.

Mor, V., and others (1989). Risk of functional decline among well elders. *Journal of Clinical Epidemiology*, vol. 42, pp. 895-904.

Murphy, E. (1982). Social origins of depression in old age. *British Journal of Psychiatry*, vol. 141, pp. 135-142.

Murphy, M. (1997). Household and family factors in morbidity and mortality. In *Morbidity and Mortality Data: Problems of Comparability*, Guillaume Wunsch and Attila Hancioglu, eds. Proceedings of the European Association for Population Studies and the Hacettepe Institute of Population Studies Workshop, Urgup, Turkey, 18-20 October 1995. Ankara: Hacettepe Universitesi, Nufus Etutleri Enstitusu, pp. 209-233.

_____, K. Glaser and E. Grundy (1997). Marital status and long-term illness in Great Britain. *Journal of Marriage and the Family*, vol. 59, pp. 156-164.

Murphy, M., and E. Grundy (1994). Co-residence of generations and household structure in Britain: aspects of change in the 1980s. In *Solidarity of Generations, Demographic, Economic and Social Change and Its Consequences*, H. A. Becker and P. L. J. Hermkens, eds. Amsterdam: Thesis Publishers, pp. 551-582.

Ogawa, N., and R. D. Retherford (1997). Shifting the cost of caring for the elderly back to families in Japan: Will it work? *Population and Development Review*, vol. 23, pp. 59-96.

Pampel, F. C. (1983). Changes in the propensity to live alone: evidence from consecutive cross-sectional surveys, 1960-1976. *Demography*, vol. 20, pp. 433-447.

Prohanska, T., R. Mermelstein and J. Van Nostrand (1993). Functional status and living arrangements. In *Health Data on Older Americans: United States, 1992*, J. Van Nostrand, S. Furner and R. Suzman, eds. Hyattsville, Maryland: United States Department of Health and Human Services, pp. 23-39.

Rendall, Michael and Alden Speare (1995). Elderly poverty alleviation through living with family. *Journal of Population Economics*, vol. 8, pp. 383-405.

Sarwari, A. R., and others (1998). Prospective study on the relation between living arrangement and change in functional health status of elderly women. *American Journal of Epidemiology*, vol. 147, No. 4, pp. 370-378.

Soldo, B. J., D. A. Wolf and E. M. Agree (1990). Family, households, and care arrangements of the frail elderly: a structural analysis. *Journal of Gerontology*, vol. 45, pp. S238-249.

Speare, A., R. Avery and L. Lawton (1991). Disability, residential mobility, and changes in living arrangements. *Journal of Gerontology*, vol. 46, pp. S133-142.

Spitze, G., J. R. Logan and J. Robinson (1992). Family structure and changes in living arrangements among elderly non-married parents. *Journal of Gerontology*, vol. 47, pp. S289-296.

Stinner, W. F., Y. Byun and L. Paita (1990). Disability and living arrangements among elderly American men. *Research on Aging*, vol. 12, pp. 339-363.

Sundstrom, G. (1994). Care by families: an overview of trends. In *Caring for Frail Elderly People*. Paris: Organisation for Economic Cooperation and Development.

Umberson, D. (1992). Gender, marital status and the social control of health behavior. *Social Science and Medicine*, vol. 34, No. 8, pp. 907-917.

Verbrugge, L. M. (1979). Marital status and health. *Journal of Marriage and the Family*, vol. 41, pp. 267-285.

Waehrer, K., and S. Crystal (1995). The impact of co-residence on economic well-being of elderly widows. *Journal of Gerontology*, vol. 50, pp. S250-S258.

Wall, R. (1989). The residence patterns of the elderly in Europe in the 1980s. In *Later Phases of the Family Cycle: Demographic Aspects*, E. Grebenik, C. Hohn and R. Mackensen, eds. Oxford: Clarendon Press.

Weinick, R. E. (1995). Sharing a home: the experiences of American women and their parents over the twentieth century. *Demography*, vol. 32, pp. 281-297.

Welin, L., and others. (1985). Prospective study of social influences on mortality. *Lancet*, pp. 915-918.

Wenger, G. C. (1984). *The Supportive Network: Coping with Old Age*. London: Allen and Unwin.

Wolf, D. A. (1990). Household patterns of older women: some international comparisons. *Research on Aging*, vol. 12, No. 4, pp. 463-506.

_____ (1994). The elderly and their kin: patterns of availability and access. In *Demography of Aging*, L. G. Martin and S. H. Preston, eds. Washington, D.C.: National Academy Press.

_____, T. K. Burch and B. Matthews (1990). Kin availability and the living arrangements of older unmarried women. *Canadian Studies in Population*, vol. 17, pp. 49-70.

Wolf, D. A. and B. J. Soldo (1988). Household composition choices of older unmarried women. *Demography*, vol. 25, No. 3, pp. 387-403.

Wolf, R. S. (1997). Elder abuse and neglect: an update. *Reviews in Clinical Gerontology*, vol. 7, No. 2, pp. 177-182.

LIVING ARRANGEMENTS AND THE HEALTH OF OLDER PERSONS IN DEVELOPING COUNTRIES: EVIDENCE FROM RURAL BANGLADESH

*Mohammed O. Rahman**

SUMMARY

Background

There is very little information about the impact of living arrangements on patterns of morbidity for older adults in developing countries. The present study uses newly collected comprehensive data to examine the impact of living arrangements (particularly the presence of various family members) on self-reported general health and limitations in activities of daily living for older adults aged 50 and over in rural Bangladesh.

Methods

In 1996, the Matlab Health and Socio-economic Survey collected data on self-reported general health status and limitations in a variety of self-reported activities of daily living (ADLs) for 1,891 men and women aged 50 and older in the Matlab surveillance area in rural Bangladesh. Logistic regression is used to examine the impact of living arrangements as operationalized by the co-residence of a spouse and, in the case of older women, co-residence of a spouse and sons, on both self-reported general health and self-reported ADLs, controlling for age, education and household assets.

Results

For older men, controlling for age, education and household assets, a co-resident spouse does not have any impact on self-reported general health or on self-reported ADLs. On the other hand, for older women, a co-resident spouse has a significant positive impact on self-reported general health but not on ADLs. The presence of co-resident sons does not seem to have any impact on the self-reported general health or ADLs of older women.

---

* Harvard University, United States of America.

Conclusions

The gender difference in the impact of spouses on self-reported general health is consistent with the notion of spouses being more important for older women than for their male peers in a social setting where women have limited access to resources. These cross-sectional results need to be viewed with some caution because co-resident spouses appear not to impact on ADLs for both older men and women, and earlier longitudinal prospective mortality studies in the same study population show that the impact of spouses is greatest for older men and is mixed for older women in terms of mortality. These discrepancies reflect either differences owing to variations in study design or differences in various dimensions of health status. They help underscore the complex dynamics of the relationship between living arrangements and the health status of older persons in developing countries.

INTRODUCTION

A number of studies in the developed world have demonstrated that living arrangements as primarily operationalized as the presence or absence of a spouse have a significant impact on the mortality of older individuals, with the currently married having a significant survival advantage relative to their non-currently married peers. Moreover, once access to financial resources is controlled for, the absence of a spouse affects older men more than older women (Seeman and others, 1987; Bowling, 1987; Kaplan and others, 1988; Trovato and Lauris, 1989; Hu and Goldman, 1990; Ross, Mirowski and Goldstein, 1990; Lillard and Waite, 1995). In keeping with the mortality studies, there have also been a number of studies in Europe and the United States of America that have by and large documented higher levels of morbidity for non-currently married individuals compared to their currently married peers, with some differences by type of non-marriage (i.e., never married, widowed, divorced or separated) (Wyke and Ford, 1992; Goldman, Korenman and Weinstein, 1995; Glaser and Grundy, 1997). In general, these studies have shown that widowed individuals have poorer health than do the currently married, with differences being greater for men than for women, and at younger ages. Moreover, in these studies, both divorced men and women report poorer health than do the currently married, while for the never married, only single men report worse health than their married counterparts, but not single women. While the overall trend in the literature has been to document greater morbidity for the non-currently married compared to the currently married, with men suffering more than women, as in the case of the mortality studies, a recent report from the United Kingdom (Arber and Cooper, 1999) was unable to demonstrate any significant impact of marital status for either men or women on morbidity as measured by self-reported poor general health or reported limitations in activities of daily living.

In contrast to the developed world, relatively little is known about mortality and morbidity (especially the latter) for the elderly in the developing world, and even less about how they are impacted by living arrangements and gender differences therein (Martin, 1990; Feachem and others, 1992; Rahman,

Menken and Foster, 1992). A priori one could hypothesize that, given differences between the developed and developing world in the nature of social and kin networks (e.g., the importance of patriarchal kin relationships) and in women's access to resources (i.e., the lack of economic opportunities and the greater dependence of women on primary male relatives for economic support in the developing world), the absence of a spouse would have a greater negative impact on the health and survival of older women than men in the developing world (Cain, 1984, 1986; Ellickson, 1988; Martin, 1990; Rahman, Menken and Foster, 1992; Rahman, 1997).

With regard to mortality, a series of well-controlled longitudinal prospective studies from rural Bangladesh have demonstrated somewhat complex and nuanced results. While all of the studies have unequivocally shown that non-married older males have significantly higher mortality than do their married peers (Rahman, 1997, 1999a, 1999b), the picture with respect to older women is less clear-cut. In some of the research, older non-married women do not have higher mortality than their currently married peers (Rahman, 1999a), while in other studies, the level of mortality disadvantage is strongly related to the degree of decline in economic status suffered as a result of widowhood or divorce, with some women suffering a lot and others hardly at all (Rahman, 1997; Rahman, Menken and Foster, 1992). By and large, the older the woman, the less impact the loss of a spouse has on her mortality. In addition to spouses, recent evidence suggests that other family members, such as sons and brothers, play an important but complex role in affecting the survival of older individuals in the developing world, and it is the existence of family members rather than their proximity to the older individual that determines the impact (Rahman, 1999a).

Until recently, owing to the absence of large-scale population-based data on morbidity, parallel analyses of the impact of living arrangements on morbidity in the developing world and gender differences therein have not been readily available. The present analysis uses newly collected comprehensive data from a surveillance population in rural Bangladesh (Rahman and Liu, 1999; Rahman and others, 1999) to examine the impact of living arrangements on self-reported general health and self-reported difficulties in activities of daily living among older adults aged 50 years and over.

DATA, VARIABLES AND METHODS

Study population

The data for the present analysis come from the Matlab Health and Socio-economic Survey, which, in 1996, collected a comprehensive set of health and socio-economic information on approximately 11,190 individuals aged 15 and over in 4,536 households who were part of an ongoing surveillance population in rural Bangladesh (Rahman and others, 1999). The Matlab data have been used extensively in the demographic literature and are considered to be among the few high-quality (i.e., complete, accurate and up to date) data sources in the developing world. In particular, age reporting is considered to be highly accurate, a feature not found in other South Asian data sources (Menken and Phillips, 1990; Rahman, Menken and Foster, 1992; Rahman and others, 1999).

The present analysis focuses on 1,891 respondents aged 50 and above (981 males and 910 females) who answered questions on self-reported general health status and self-reported limitations in activities of daily living. There are three separate clusters of self-reported ADLs (gross mobility limitations, range of motion and personal care, which are described below).[1]

Variable measurement

All respondents to the Survey were asked to rate their general health status ("What is your current health status?") as "excellent", "good" or "poor". This three-level variable has been dichotomized for the purposes of the present analysis into poor general health status (coded as 1) and non-poor general health status (coded as 0). It is worth noting that several studies have shown reported poor general health to be a good predictor of mortality (Mossey and Shapiro, 1982; Idler and Benyamini, 1997).

A number of researchers have suggested that self-reports of limitations in activities of daily living are less subject to reporting bias than are self-reports of general health, and are good indicators of underlying functional disabilities (Rosow and Breslau, 1969; Katz and others, 1970; Nagi, 1976; Guralnik and others, 1989; Elam and others, 1991; Gijsbers van Wijk and others, 1991; Kelly-Hayes and others, 1992; Merrill and others, 1997). In the Survey, information is available on limitations in 13 separate ADL items, which (following Merrill and others, 1997) are divided for the present analysis into three different clusters: (a) limitations in personal care — four items; (b) gross mobility limitations — three items; and (c) range of motion limitations — six items. In the questionnaire, each ADL item has a three-level score: "can do on their own easily" (scored as 1); "can do on their own with difficulty" (scored as 2); and "unable to do on their own" (scored as 3). For the purposes of this analysis, the three-level score for each ADL item has been initially collapsed into a dichotomous measure: (a) can do on their own easily (scored as 1); vs. (b) can do with difficulty or unable to perform the activity (scored as 0).

Limitations in personal care are ascertained using a modified version of the Katz ADL (Katz and others, 1970) and include ability to: (a) bathe; (b) dress; (c) get up and out of bed; and (d) use the toilet. For the present analysis, the dichotomous item measures for each of the four personal care items were summed to construct an aggregate personal care limitation score ranging from 0 to 4. This aggregate score was then dichotomized into: (a) can do all four items easily (scored as 0); vs. (b) can do with difficulty or unable to do one or more items (scored as 1).

Gross mobility limitation items include ability to (a) walk one mile; (b) use a ladder to climb to a storage place at least five feet in height; and (c) sweep the floor or courtyard. These items were adapted to the local conditions of rural Bangladesh from an instrument developed by Rosow and Breslau (1969). For the present analysis, the dichotomous item measures for each of the three gross mobility items were summed to construct a gross mobility limitation summary score ranging from 0 to 3. This summary score was then dichotomized into: (a) able to do all three items easily (scored as 0); vs. (b) able to do with difficulty or unable to do one or more items (scored as 1).

Range of motion limitation items include ability to: (a) carry a 10 kilogram weight for 20 yards; (b) use a hand pump to draw water; (c) stand up from a squatting position on the floor; (d) sit in a squatting position on the floor; (e) get up from a sitting position on a chair or stool without help; (f) crouch or stoop. These items were adapted from an instrument developed by Nagi (1976) and adapted to the local conditions of rural Bangladesh. For the present analysis, the dichotomous item measures for each of the six range of motion items were summed to construct an aggregate range of motion limitation score ranging from 0 to 6. This summary score was then dichotomized into: (a) able to do all six items easily (scored as 0); vs. (b) able to do with difficulty or unable to do one or more items (scored as 1).

Methodology

It is important to note that respondents reported on in the present analysis were selected in a multi-stage sampling scheme (Rahman and others, 1999). In 1996, the Matlab surveillance area consisted of approximately 200,000 individuals living in about 40,000 households, which were clustered in about 7,440 residential compounds known as *baris* varying from 1 to 26 households. From the computerized population lists of the Matlab surveillance area, the Survey in the first stage selected 2,687 *baris* or household clusters randomly. Within each *bari*, one household was selected at random. In *baris* where there were more than one household, a second household was selected purposively on the basis of relationship to the head of the first selected household. Within each selected household, all individuals aged 50 and over were chosen for interview. For those below age 50, a complex set of decision rules was used to choose respondents.

The present analysis is restricted to 1,891 individuals aged 50 and over chosen from the randomly selected first-pick households in 2,687 *baris*. As all individuals aged 50 and over in the households were selected for interview, the only adjustments required are those for the probability of the *bari* and the household being selected. For the bivariate results (see tables 1, 2 and 3), the actual unweighted figures (for the number of respondents and the percentages reporting limitations in general health and ADLs) are reported. It should be noted that weighted bivariate analyses have been done and do not show any differences from the unweighted bivariate analyses. For the multivariate analyses, the binary logistic regression results shown are those estimated after appropriate adjustments were made for the multistage sampling scheme.

Results

Table 1 shows some general descriptive characteristics for older adults in our study population in rural Bangladesh. There are marked gender differences in marital status, educational status and ownership of assets, with older women being much more likely than older men to be not currently married, to have no education and to own less than or equal to $20 worth of assets. In this study, individual access to financial resources was measured by summing the estimated monetized value of a number of assets that were singly or jointly owned (including land, jewellery, bicycle, watch, radio etc.).

With regard to ownership of assets (results not shown in table), among older males aged 50 and over, the non-married are more likely to have less than $20 worth of assets than are their currently married peers (20 per cent or 12/60 vs. 5 per cent or 45/921). However, among older females, there is no difference in asset ownership by marital status (59 per cent or 294/500 vs. 59 per cent or 244/410). With regard to educational attainment, among older males, there is no difference by marital status (45 per cent of each marital group have no education). However, among older females, the non-married are more likely to have no education than are their currently married peers (83 per cent or 341/410 vs. 76 per cent or 378/500).

Table 2 shows differences in self-reported general health status stratified by age group and marital status for men and women aged 50 and over. For both older men and older women, non-married individuals aged 50 and over taken as a group are more likely to report poor general health relative to their married counterparts. However, once one stratifies by age, these marital status differences by and large disappear. Moreover, older women as a whole are more likely to report poor general health than are older men (42 per cent vs. 32 per cent) (results not shown in table 2).

Table 3 shows differences in ADL limitations for men and women stratified by 10-year age intervals. As in the case of self-reported general health, older women are significantly more likely to report limitations than are their male counterparts in each ADL item and each of the three summary ADL categories. For the summary categories, the disparity is greatest for the gross mobility limitation ADL scores (75.9 per cent of women vs. 38.4 per cent of men having difficulty or unable), and the smallest for the personal care ADLs (19.9 per cent of women vs. 10.6 per cent of men having difficulty or unable).

With regard to marital status differences (results not shown in table 3), for both older men and older women aged 50 and over as a group, the non-married report a higher frequency of ADL limitations than do their currently married peers. The relevant figures (non-married vs. currently married) are (a) summary range of motion limitations: males (67 per cent vs. 37 per cent); females (79 per cent vs. 67 per cent); (b) summary gross mobility limitations: males (60 per cent vs. 37 per cent); females (82 per cent vs. 71 per cent); and (c) summary personal care limitations: males (19 per cent vs. 10 per cent); females (29 per cent vs. 13 per cent). It should be noted, however, that once these figures are adjusted for the higher ages of the non-married, the marital status differences in ADL limitations disappear.

TABLE 1. DESCRIPTIVE CHARACTERISTICS OF OLDER ADULTS IN RURAL BANGLADESH

Males				Females			
Percentage with different characteristics				Percentage with different characteristics			
Age category	ncmar[a]	noedu[b]	<=$20 asset[c]	Age category	ncmar[a]	noedu[b]	<=$20 asset[c]
50-59 n=411	1[d]	42[d]	5[d]	50-59 n=520	30	75	56
60-69 n=375	6[d]	49[d]	5[d]	60-69 n=283	55	80	61
70-79 n=162	16[d]	46[d]	6[d]	70-79 n=76	89	93	67
80-95 n=33	21[d]	51[d]	18[d]	80-95 n=31	100	100	74
Total n=981	6[d]	46[d]	6[d]	Total n=910	45	79	59

[a] Not currently married.
[b] Never had formal schooling.
[c] Owns less than or equal to US$ 20 worth of assets, either singly or jointly.
[d] Gender difference significant at the 5 per cent level.

TABLE 2. DIFFERENCES IN SELF-REPORTED POOR GENERAL HEALTH FOR OLDER ADULTS IN RURAL BANGLADESH

Age category	Male		Female	
	Currently married	Not currently married	Currently married	Not currently married
50-59	n=407	n=4	n=364	n=156
	% in ph, 23	% in ph, 25	% in ph, 35	% in ph, 37
60-69	n=352	n=23	n=128	n=155
	% in ph, 33	% in ph, 35	% in ph, 44	% in ph, 50
70-79	n=136	n=26	n=8	n=68
	% in ph, 45	% in ph, 42	% in ph, 50	% in ph, 56
80-95	n=26	n=7	n=0	n=31
	% in ph, 58	% in ph, 100[a]	% in ph, not applicable	% in ph, 74
Total[a]	n=921	n=60	n=500	n=410
	% in ph, 31	% in ph, 45[a]	% in ph, 37	% in ph, 48[a]

Notes: % in ph = percentage in poor general health.
[a] Marital status difference significant at the 5 per cent level.

TABLE 3. SELF-REPORTED ADL LIMITATIONS FOR OLDER ADULTS IN RURAL BANGLADESH

ADL limitations	Men		Women	
	Number	Percent-age	Number	Percent-age
Personal care items (percentage having difficulty or unable) (n=1,811)	937		874	
Bathing	85	9.1	148	16.9[a]
Dressing	52	5.6	93	10.6[a]
Getting up and out of bed	61	6.5	131	14.9[a]
Using the toilet	68	7.3	106	12.1[a]
Percentage having difficulty or unable to do one or more items	99	10.6	175	19.9[a]
Gross mobility items (percentage having difficulty or unable) (n=1,812)	938		874	
Walk one mile	291	31.1	607	69.1[a]
Use a ladder to climb at least five feet in height	251	26.8	479	54.6[a]
Sweep the floor or courtyard	267	28.5	499	56.8[a]
Percentage having difficulty or unable to do one or more items	359	38.4	667	75.9[a]
Range-of-motion items (percentage having difficulty or unable) (n=1,891)	981		910	
Carry 10 kg weight for 20 yards	336	34.4	629	69.1[a]
Use a hand pump to draw water	246	25.2	507	55.7[a]
Stand up from a squatting position on the floor	131	13.4	245	26.9[a]
Sit in a squatting position on the floor	157	16.1	295	32.4[a]
Stand up from sitting on a chair or stool	113	11.6	221	24.3[a]
Crouch or stoop	175	17.9	321	35.3[a]
Percentage having difficulty or unable to do one or more items	378	38.7	660	72.5[a]

[a] P<0.001 in chi-square tests of gender differences.

Table 4 shows results (separately for men and women) from sequential binary logistic regressions examining the impact of marital status on poor general health status, adjusting for the addition of various controls. For older women, in model 1, the results indicate that controlling for age (measured in calendar years), non-currently married women (the vast majority of whom are widowed) in this study population are significantly more likely to report poor general health than are their currently married counterparts (odds ratio of non-married vs. married = 1.5). In models 2 and 3, additional controls for education and household assets do not appreciably change the impact of marital status on poor general health (odds ratio of married vs. non-married changes from 1.5 to 1.49). Finally, in model 4, introducing further controls for number of co-resident sons does not change the impact of marital status on poor general health for older women (odds ratio of married vs. non-married remains at 1.49 (95 per cent C. I. of 1.00-2.22)).

For older men, in model 1, the results indicate that non-currently married men are no more likely to report poor general health than are their currently married peers. This lack of impact of marital status on poor general health is not affected by the addition of controls for education and household assets in models 2 and 3, respectively (odds ratio of married vs. non-married = 0.98 (95 per cent C. I. of 0.48-2.02)).

Table 5 shows results (for men and women separately) from logistic regressions examining the impact of marital status on three different categories of ADL limitations (personal care limitation, gross mobility limitation, and range of motion limitation), controlling for age, education, household assets and (for women, the presence of co-residential sons). In no case is there a statistically significant impact of marital status on any of the ADLs. It should be noted that sequential models were run and no impact was found for marital status on ADL limitations once controls were added for age (results not shown in table 5).

TABLE 4. ODDS RATIOS OF POOR GENERAL HEALTH FOR OLDER MEN AND WOMEN IN RURAL BANGLADESH

Variables	Males			Females			
	Model 1	Model 2	Model 3	Model 1	Model 2	Model 3	Model 4
Not currently married	0.99 ns [0.48–2.01]	0.96 ns [0.47–1.96]	0.98 ns [0.48–2.02]	1.50^a [1.00–2.23]	1.49^a [1.00–2.22]	1.49^a [1.00–2.22]	1.49^a [1.00–2.22]
Age in years	1.05^a [1.03–1.08]	1.05^a [1.03–1.08]	1.05^a [1.03–1.08]	1.03^a [1.01–1.06]	1.03^a [1.00–1.05]	1.03^a [1.01–1.05]	1.03^a [1.01–1.05]
No education	--	1.80^a [1.22–2.67]	1.80^a [1.22–2.67]	--	1.77^a [1.13–2.80]	1.78^a [1.13–2.81]	1.78^a [1.13–2.83]
<=$20 of assets	--	--	0.92 ns [0.42–2.04]	--	--	0.98 ns [0.67–1.43]	0.98 ns [0.67–1.43]
# co-resident sons	not applicable	not applicable	not applicable	--	--	--	1.00 ns [0.85–1.18]
# parameters	2	3	4	2	3	4	5
-2 log likelihood	1 201.9	1 184.1	1 184.0	1 204.28	1 194.6	1 194.6	1 194.6
n	980	980	980	909	909	909	909

Notes: ns = not statistically significant.

[ ] = 95% C.I.

^{a} P<= 0.05.

TABLE 5. ODDS RATIOS OF ACTIVITY OF DAILY LIVING LIMITATION FOR OLDER ADULTS IN RURAL BANGLADESH

Variables	Personal care limitation		Range of motion limitation		Gross mobility limitation	
	Male	Female	Male	Female	Male	Female
Not currently married	0.42 ns [0.16--1.15]	1.40 ns [0.80--2.45]	1.54 ns [0.72--3.33]	0.86 ns [0.54--1.38]	1.55 ns [0.73--3.31]	0.91 ns [0.55--1.52]
Age in years	1.12[a] [1.08--1.16]	1.08[a] [1.05--1.12]	1.12[a] [1.09--1.15]	1.12[a] [1.08--1.17]	1.12[a] [1.08--1.15]	1.12[a] [1.06--1.14]
No education	1.17 ns [0.63--2.17]	0.94 ns [0.44--2.01]	1.40 ns [0.94--2.07]	0.92 ns [0.54--1.58]	1.21 ns [0.81--1.82]	1.19 ns [0.68--2.07]
<=$20 of assets	0.70 ns [0.27--1.82]	1.09 ns [0.63--1.89]	0.63 ns [0.29--1.37]	1.47 ns [0.93--2.31]	0.61 ns [0.27--1.40]	1.29 ns [0.80--2.10]
# co-resident sons	not applicable	0.88 ns [0.71--1.09]	not applicable	0.84 ns [0.93--2.31] [0.70--1.00]	not applicable	0.84 ns [0.70--1.01]
# parameters	4	5	4	5	4	5
-2 log likelihood	538.0	782.2	1 114.1	936.5	1 079.1	853.5
n[b]	936	873	980	909	937	873

Notes: ns = not statistically significant -- P>0.05.
[ ] = 95% C.I.
[a] P<=0.05.
[b] The different figures for the various ADLs reflect the different numbers of respondents aged 50 years and above who had valid responses for the questions.

341

Discussion

The fact that older non-currently married women report worse general health status than do their married peers in rural Bangladesh mirrors the bulk of the findings on this issue from Europe and the United States. These results also fit with earlier longitudinal research in the same study population that shows that non-married older women have higher mortality than do their married peers (Rahman, Menken and Foster, 1992; Rahman, 1997, 1999b). However, these results are somewhat at odds with other longitudinal research that show that the absence of a spouse does not have any impact on mortality for older women (Rahman, 1999a). An explanation for this discrepancy may lie in the fact that cross-sectional differences in health status between married and non-married women reflect health conditions that cause distress but do not affect mortality (e.g., migraine and arthritis). A number of studies have suggested a similar explanation for the paradox of high female morbidity coupled with low female mortality relative to men (Wingard, 1984; Verbrugge and Wingard, 1987; Kandrack, Grant and Segall, 1991). The discrepancy between the self-reported general health results and the ADL results (the latter showing no impact of marital status) also suggests that the different measures of health status are tapping into different dimensions of health and that ADLs may be more reflective of mortality risks than self-reported general health.

There are a number of possible explanations that one can invoke to understand why the presence of a spouse may be associated with better health for older women, even though, as discussed above, it may not lead to better survival. These explanations fall into two conceptually different approaches to understanding the association between marital status and health. The first and most often cited approach posits a so-called "protective effect", that is having a spouse is deemed to directly cause an improvement in one's health, which is mediated through a variety of proximate factors such as increased access to financial resources, improved caregiving, emotional buffering, better diet and less risk-taking behaviour (Bowling, 1987; Ross, Mirowski, Goldstein, 1990). The second explanation posits a "selection effect", whereby one's marital status per se does not have any causative impact on one's health (Goldman, 1993; Rahman and others, 1994; Goldman, Korenman and Weinstein, 1995). Instead, the association between marital status and health status is merely a marker of some underlying process by which intrinsically healthier people, for example, may be more likely to be currently married. This distinction between "protection" and "selection" has bedevilled the interpretation of associations between marital status and health (particularly cross-sectional comparisons) and the resolution of this debate relies at least partially on detailed longitudinal data on early health prior to marriage, which is most often not available.

From the protective effect point of view, as commented on above, one of the more obvious explanations for why non-married older women have worse health than their married peers is that the non-married have decreased access to financial resources. This is thought to be particularly true in a setting such as rural Bangladesh, where women have limited economic mobility and are dependent on their husbands and sons primarily for economic support (Cain, 1984, 1986; Ellickson, 1988). Thus, loss of a husband may result in a decrease in the availability of financial resources. The decrease in financial resources associated with the loss of a husband may come about in two ways, directly and indirectly. The direct consequence would be from the loss of the income-generation capability of the husband. The indirect adverse consequence would be in the diminution of the receipt of resources from other earning household members, typically sons. In the social setting of rural Bangladesh, where sons often live together with parents and contribute financially to the joint household income, the death of a father usually precipitates household splitting and the resultant loss of income from the son who moves away (Aziz, 1979; Foster, 1993). Regardless of how the decrease in financial resources occurs, it is hypothesized to lead to poorer health. The potential mechanisms include decreased access and use of health-care services, worse nutrition and lifestyle and increased environmental and occupational hazards (Ross, Mirowski and Goldstein, 1990; Wyke and Ford, 1992).

In the present study, an individual woman's access to financial resources is proxied in two ways, first by household asset ownership, and second by the presence of co-residential sons. Our results show that, having less than or equal to US$ 20 worth of household assets is not a statistically significant predictor of poor general health (controlling for age and marital status) and, moreover, does not account for any of the marital status difference in health. The fact that asset ownership does not have a significant impact on general health status in this population may be explained by the fact that the measured assets are relatively long term and not very liquid (i.e., they cannot easily be transformed into cash to be used for health services, medication or nutritional needs) and thus do not quite capture the availability of financial resources at the individual level. Moreover, controlling for the number of sons co-resident in the household also does not account for any of the marital status differences in self-reported general health among older women. Parenthetically, it should be noted that the number of co-resident sons does not have any impact on an older woman's health status. The lack of impact of co-resident sons on marital status differences in self-reported general health and, indeed, on the health status of older women is broadly consistent with earlier longitudinal research on mortality that showed that non-co-resident sons may be just as important as co-resident sons and that proximity does not necessarily confer any particular advantage. The lack of impact of proximity is due to two possible reasons: the first is that there may be a selection effect, whereby sick mothers move in with sons and healthy mothers do not. The second reason is that if remittances of income are the mechanism by which sons improve their mother's health, distant sons (for example, living in the city where there are more income-earning opportunities) may be better able to impact their mother's health than co-resident sons in a stagnant village economy.

As discussed above, the association between marital status and health may reflect the possibility that currently married older women in this social setting are intrinsically in better health than are their non-married peers. In this traditional rural society, where near-universal marriage is the norm, and divorce is rare, the essence of this argument is that intrinsically healthier women are less likely to become widowed and the difference in reported health status by marital status among older women reflects differences in underlying early health prior to marriage, which has nothing to do with their current marital status. To test this proposition, one should ideally have some marker for early health, that is, health prior to marriage. In the absence of such data, educational attainment (which is completed prior to marriage) may be a crude but effective proxy to the extent that higher educational attainment prior to marriage reflects better health prior to marriage. While individual educational attainment significantly reduced the risk of mortality, it did not account for any of the marital status differences in health.

Thus, the present study provides little support for either protective effects (e.g., changes in financial resources) or selective effects (early educational attainment) in understanding the mechanism by which the absence of a spouse among older women is associated with poorer general health.

As to the case of older men in the study population, the present analysis shows that, among older men, marital status does not affect self-reported general health status or ADL limitations. This result is somewhat puzzling as it is at odds with earlier longitudinal work in this population (Rahman, 1997, 1999a, 1999b) and in Europe and North America, which clearly demonstrates that older men without spouses are at a significantly increased risk of dying relative to their currently married counterparts (Bowling, 1987; Ross, Mirowski and Goldstein, 1990). It is also at odds with evidence from several studies in the developed world that have documented increased morbidity for older non-married men (particularly widowers) compared to their currently married peers (Wyke and Ford, 1992; Goldman, Korenman and Weinstein, 1995; Glaser and Grundy, 1997). One possible explanation for this disjunction in results between the cross-sectional and the longitudinal studies may be related to differential mortality selection by marital status. The thinking here is that we can only observe individuals who have survived to enter our study. Thus, if sick non-married younger men die earlier than their sick married counterparts (presumably owing to differences in caregiving), one is left with a residual pool of fairly robust non-married older men. In a cross-sectional comparison such as the one reported on in the present study, this differential mortality by marital status would artefactually decrease the morbidity differences between currently married and non-married older men (Rahman and others, 1994; Goldman, Korenman and Weinstein, 1995; Rahman, 1999a). Another possibility (though less likely) is that health conditions that would lead to higher mortality for one group may not be manifested in symptoms that would be differentially reported. Thus, for example, if the bulk of old-age mortality is from conditions that have relatively few preceding symptoms, one may not observe differences in self-reported health.

As the above discussion suggests, there appears to be a complex dynamic relationship between living arrangements and health status, with differences by gender, by the outcome measure of health (morbidity vs. mortality and different measures of morbidity), by various measures of living arrangements (i.e., spouses vs. sons) and by study design (cross-sectional vs.

longitudinal). Moreover, the possible mechanisms by which living arrangements may affect health status remain thus far unelucidated. Further progress in this line of inquiry requires more detailed information on a variety of measures of health status (both self-reported and measured), indicators of early health, the ability to track both changes in living arrangements (e.g., by the presence of various co-residential family members) and health status over time, and better measures of access to financial resources and changes in caregiving.

NOTES

[1] For one of them (gross mobility limitations), the data set has information on nearly the full complement of 1,891 individuals (i.e., 1,887 subjects). For the second (range of motion) and third (personal care), however, owing to interviewer misinterpretation, there is missing information on specific items and complete data are available for only 1,813 of the 1,891 eligible respondents. The 78 individuals for whom ADL data are missing on specific items have been analysed and found to be no different from the rest of the 1,813 in terms of age, gender and other self-reported health status measures.

REFERENCES

Arber, S., and H. Cooper (1999). Gender differences in health in later life: the new paradox? *Social Science and Medicine*, vol. 48, pp. 61-76.

Aziz, K. M. A. (1979). *Kinship in Bangladesh*. Dacca: International Centre for Diarrhoeal Disease Research.

Bowling, A. (1987). Mortality after bereavement. A review of the literature on survival periods and factors affecting survival. *Social Science and Medicine*, vol. 24, pp. 117-124.

Cain, M. (1984). Women's status and fertility in developing countries: son preference and economic security. World Bank Staff Working Papers, No. 682. *Population and Development Series*, No. 7. Washington, D.C.: World Bank.

_____ (1986). The consequences of reproductive failure: dependence, mobility, and mortality among the elderly of rural South Asia. *Population Studies*, vol. 40, pp. 375-388.

Elam, J. T., and others (1991). Comparison of subjective ratings of function with observed functional ability of frail older persons. *American Journal of Public Health*, vol. 81, pp. 1127-1130.

Ellickson, J. (1988). Never the twain shall meet: aging men and women in Bangladesh. *Journal of Cross-Cultural Gerontology*, vol. 3, pp. 53-70.

Feachem, R. G. A., and others (1992). *The Health of Adults in the Developing World*. Washington, D. C.: World Bank.

Foster, A. (1993). Household partition in rural Bangladesh. *Population Studies*, vol. 47, pp. 97-114.

Gijsbers van Wijk, C. M., and others (1991). Symptom sensitivity and sex differences in physical morbidity: a review of health surveys in the United States and the Netherlands. *Women's Health*, vol. 17, pp. 91-124.

Glaser, K., and E. Grundy (1997). Marital status and long-term illness in Great Britain. *Journal of Marriage and the Family*, vol. 59, pp. 156-164.

Goldman, N. (1993). Marriage selection and mortality patterns. *Demography*, vol. 30, No. 2, pp. 189-207.

_____, S. Korenman, and R. Weinstein (1995). Marital status and health among the elderly. *Social Science and Medicine*, vol. 40, No. 12, pp. 1717-1730.

Guralnik, J. M., and others (1989). Physical performance measures in aging research. *Journal of Gerontology: Medical Sciences*, vol. 44, M, pp. 141-146.

Hu, Y., and N. Goldman (1990). Mortality differentials by marital status: an international comparison. *Demography*, vol. 27, pp. 233-250.

Idler, E. L., and Y. Benyamini (1997). Self-rated health and mortality: a review of twenty-seven community studies. *Journal of Health and Social Behavior*, vol. 38, pp. 21-37.

Kandrack, M. A., K. R. Grant, and A. Segall (1991). Gender differences in health-related behavior: some unanswered questions. *Social Science and Medicine*, vol. 32, pp. 579-590.

Kaplan, G. A., and others (1988). Social connections and mortality from all causes and from cardiovascular disease: prospective evidence from eastern Finland. *American Journal of Epidemiology*, vol. 128, pp. 370-380.

Katz, S., and others (1970). Progress in development of the index of ADL. *Gerontologist*, vol. 1, pp. 20-30.

Kelly-Hayes, M., and others (1992). Functional limitations and disability among elders in the Framingham study. *American Journal of Public Health*, vol. 82, pp. 841-845.

Lillard, L. A., and L. J. Waite (1995). Till death do us part: marital disruption and mortality. *American Journal of Sociology*, vol. 100, pp. 1131-1156.

Martin, L. G. (1990). The status of South Asia's growing elderly population. *Journal of Cross-Cultural Gerontology*, vol. 5, pp. 93-117.

Menken, J., and J. F. Phillips (1990). Population change in a rural area of Bangladesh, 1967-1987. *Annals of the American Academy of Political and Social Science*, vol. 510, pp. 87-101.

Merrill, S. S., and others (1997). Gender differences in the comparison of self-reported disability and performance measures. *Journal of Gerontology: A. Biological Sciences, Medical Sciences*, vol. 52, No. 1, M, pp. 19-26.

Mossey, J. M., and E. Shapiro (1982). Self-rated health: a predictor of mortality among the elderly. *American Journal of Public Health*, vol. 72, pp. 800-808.

Nagi, S. Z. (1976). An epidemiology of disability among adults in the United States. *Milbank Memorial Fund Quarterly*, vol. 54, pp. 439-468.

Rahman, O. (1997). The impact of spouses on the mortality of older individuals in rural Bangladesh. *Health Transition Review*, vol. 7, No. 1, pp. 1-12.

_____ (1999a). Family matters. The impact of kin on elderly mortality in rural Bangladesh. *Population Studies*, vol. 53, pp. 227-235.

_____ (1999b). Age and gender variation in the impact of household structure on elderly mortality. *International Journal of Epidemiology*, vol. 28, pp. 485-491.

_____, and J. Liu (1999). Gender differences in functioning for older adults in rural Bangladesh. The impact of differential reporting? *Journal of Gerontology: Medical Sciences* (December).

Rahman, O., J. Menken, and A. Foster (1992). Older widow mortality in rural Bangladesh. *Social Science and Medicine*, vol. 34, No. 1, pp. 89-96.

Rahman, O., and others (1994). Gender differences in adult health: an international comparison. *The Gerontologist*, vol. 34, No. 4, pp. 463-469.

_____ (1999). *The Matlab Health and Socio-economic Survey: Overview and User's Guide, 1999*. Santa Monica, California: Rand Corporation.

Rosow, I., and N. Breslau (1969). A Guttman health scale for the aged. *Journal of Gerontology*, vol. 21, pp. 557-560.

Ross, C. E., J. Mirowski, and K. Goldstein (1990). The impact of the family on health: the decade in review. *Journal of Marriage and Family*, vol. 52, pp. 1059-1078.

Seeman, T. E., and others (1987). Social networks and mortality among the elderly in the Alameda County study. *American Journal of Epidemiology*, vol. 126, pp. 714-723.

Trovato, F., and G. Lauris (1989). Marital status and mortality in Canada, 1951-1981. *Journal of Marriage and the Family*, vol. 51, No. 4, pp. 907-922.

Verbrugge, L. M., and D. L. Wingard (1987). Sex differentials in health and mortality. *Women's Health*, vol. 12, pp. 103-145.

Wingard, D. L. (1984). The sex differential in morbidity, mortality, and life style. *Annual Review of Public Health*, vol. 5, pp. 433-458.

Wyke, S., and G. Ford (1992). Competing explanations for associations between marital status and health. *Social Science and Medicine*, vol. 34, No. 5, pp. 525-532.

LIVING ARRANGEMENTS OF OLDER PERSONS AND POVERTY

*Peter Lloyd-Sherlock**

OLD AGE, POVERTY AND LIVING ARRANGEMENTS: CASE STUDIES FROM LATIN AMERICA

The living arrangements of older people are usually an important determinant of their quality of life. They are particularly significant for poor elders in the developing world, where formal welfare systems are less extensive. Policy debates in developing countries often allege that extended families and cultural mores of respect for elders have been more resilient than in the West (Contreras de Lehr, 1989). However, it is likely that rapid processes of social and economic transformation have had important impacts on household structures and on the positions of elders within them. To date, these issues remain very lightly researched, and empirical data are scant. The present paper provides some insights from a number of microlevel studies of poor communities in Buenos Aires and São Paulo.

The paper briefly explores a number of related issues. First, it considers the extent to which shanty town districts in the cities studied are currently experiencing population ageing, and how much they will do so in the future. This touches on a larger theme: whether population ageing in middle-income countries is largely a phenomenon of relatively privileged groups, or whether the poor are also surviving extended periods of old age. This issue has important implications for equity and policy, but has been largely ignored. The paper goes on to consider how the living arrangements of elderly shanty town residents may differ from those of other groups of older people. This includes the sizes of households containing older people, the economic relations between older people and other household members, and patterns of homeownership.

The paper does not seek to provide conclusive statements about the living arrangements of poor older people in Latin American cities. The heterogeneity of older people as a group and the variety of contexts in which they live preclude generalization. Instead, the paper seeks to explore and map out some relevant issues, to draw attention to their complexity and to emphasize the dangers of facile interpretation.

---

* University of East Anglia, United Kingdom of Great Britain and Northern Ireland.

The conventional view is that Latin American shanty towns are still overrun with children and adolescents, and that older people are few and far between (Hardoy and Satterthwaite, 1989; Bellardi and De Paula, 1986). This, it is claimed, reflects demographic characteristics such as high levels of fertility and low life expectancy at old age. Youthful age structures also result from a supposed tendency for residents to move away before reaching later life, either returning to their regions of origin (given that the great majority were once rural migrants) or moving to a better neighbourhood (on the optimistic premise that the slum is a jumping-off point for upwardly mobile migrants). A survey from São Paulo in 1992 observed that:

> A great many of the slum's elderly population return to their place of origin. Since the family's origin is usually the north-east of the country, where it is very warm, the aged who came with their families return during the first winter in São Paulo because they cannot get used to the climate or because they feel unable to live in the big city (Karsch and Baptista, 1992, p. 51).

The perceptions of local residents and organizations sometimes reinforce this view. A social worker dealing with older people in Buenos Aires shanty towns commented:

> The old person remains hidden inside the home. They scarcely consider themselves as old. One may ask "Are there many old people around here?" and they tell you "No, not very many", and the problems of mothers, children, youths and out-of-work adults come first (Lloyd-Sherlock, 1997, p. 108).

Fragmentary data for Buenos Aires and São Paulo show that concentrations of older people in shanty towns are indeed lower than for the cities as a whole. There are, however, indications that numbers of older people are now growing rapidly, at least in some slum districts. Although fertility levels and adult life expectancy have yet to completely converge with those of more privileged urban groups, considerable progress has been made over the past two decades. Owing to the regional economic slowdown of the 1980s and the persistence of high unemployment rates since then, opportunities for residents to "make good" and move away before reaching old age have been reduced. The author's own surveys have found that return migration is not always a preferred option as people reach old age, since many have spent several decades living in the city and most of their friends and family are based there. He also found that a significant proportion of older residents had migrated when already old, particularly in São Paulo, often to gain access to superior health facilities or to accompany younger relatives (Lloyd-Sherlock, 1999).

There are signs that some shanty towns are now ageing as settlements, and that those dating back 40 or 50 years contain higher concentrations of elders than those established by more recent waves of migration. The district of Villa Jardín, established in Buenos Aires in the 1930s, is a case in point. Here, the population aged 60 or more roughly doubled in both absolute and relative terms (to reach 7.2 per cent) during the 1980s, and the large size of cohorts aged between 50 and 59 suggests that this trend will have continued (Lloyd-Sherlock, 1997, pp. 114-115). Similar trends are identifiable for the Favela de Vila Prudente, one of the oldest shanty towns in São Paulo.

These limited data suggest that quite high concentrations of older people can be found in some shanty towns. The lack of mobility and political status of this group, coupled with the recent nature of population ageing in these settings, has meant that older shanty town residents have largely gone unnoticed as a group by academics, government agencies, non-governmental organizations and even their own neighbours. This increases their vulnerability and explains the lack of policy initiatives directed at their particular needs.

HOUSEHOLD SIZE AND STRUCTURE

Large household size is often positively correlated with poverty (Ahlburg, 1994). This may be the result of higher levels of fertility, cultural preferences, or a lack of affordable housing for other family members. Table 1 compares households containing at least one person aged 60 or over for different urban districts of Argentina, circa 1990. The first column is taken from a 1990 Gallup survey of 2,000 older people conducted in each provincial capital city. This can be taken as representative of urban conditions in general. The second is taken from a 1986 survey of 223 people living in the poor Buenos Aires slum district of La Boca. The third column refers to the author's 1992-93 survey of 181 elderly residents of three shanty towns, also located in Buenos Aires. The results for La Boca and the shanty towns are very different, even though they both refer to poor elders living in the same city. In La Boca, older people were more likely to be living alone (28 per cent), whereas in the three shanty towns they were less likely to be (11 per cent). Similarly, almost twice as many older people in La Boca (33 per cent) were living just with a partner than was the case in the shanty towns.

These comparisons reveal the dangers of seeking to generalize even from the results of surveys of poor urban neighbourhoods in the same city. It is unlikely that the differences between La Boca and the shanty towns are due to survey methods: while defining household membership is not always a straightforward task, identifying older people living alone should not present many problems. It could be argued that the results are not valid owing to the small number of respondents. However, the sample sizes are large compared to the total number of older people in each site. It is more likely that the different findings reflect the heterogeneity of poor urban neighbourhoods, and hence the varied conditions of older people living in them. La Boca is best described as an "inner-city slum" rather than a shanty town, since it mainly consists of very densely populated tenement blocks. The three shanty towns are more peripherally located, mainly consisting of self-built housing units, and are less densely populated.

TABLE 1. STRUCTURES OF HOUSEHOLDS CONTAINING OLDER PEOPLE IN URBAN DISTRICTS IN ARGENTINA, C. 1990

	Provincial capitals	La Boca	Three shanty towns
		(Percentage)	
Alone	21	28	11
Just with partner	35	33	17
Household of 6 or more	n/a	n/a	24

Sources: Redondo (1990, p. 201); Scipione and others (1992, p. 72); Lloyd-Sherlock (1997).

Table 1 shows that almost a quarter of the respondents from the Buenos Aires shanty towns were living in households of six or more people. This information is not available for the other two surveys, but the figure is significantly higher than that reported for Argentina as a whole in the 1991 census (INDEC, 1993a). Similar results were obtained in a study of shanty towns in São Paulo, where the author interviewed 126 elderly residents in 1995. This second survey found that 31 per cent of respondents were in households of six or more, compared to only 8 per cent in the State of São Paulo as a whole (see Table 2).[1] Taken together, the two shanty town surveys suggest that there is a higher than average probability that older people in such neighbourhoods live in large household units.

TABLE 2. STRUCTURES OF HOUSEHOLDS CONTAINING OLDER PEOPLE IN SÃO PAULO, 1980 AND 1995

	State of São Paulo (1980)	Two shanty towns (1995)
	(Percentage)	
Alone	14	6
2 people	37	19
3 to 5 people	41	44
Household of 6 or more	8	31

Sources: Yazaki, Viera de Melo and Ramos (1991, p. 25); Lloyd-Sherlock (unpublished survey data).

If we accept the above generalization, we can then ask whether larger household sizes influence economic relations between members. Household size may have various implications for the well-being of elders. It is sometimes claimed that larger units may promote intergenerational support and reduce the isolation of old age (Kinsella and Taeuber, 1992; Ramos, 1981). However, in a context of urban poverty, larger households may reflect economic constraints rather than preference, and they may be associated with overcrowding, poor sanitation and abuse.

Household relations are complex and do not lend themselves to objective assessment or systematic analysis. The present paper discusses two sets of criteria. The first is the degree to which older people reported they were economically dependent on other household members. The second set of criteria refers to whether respondents derived a net economic loss or benefit from their household ties. These measurements have important limitations. First, they are based on the subjective judgements of both the interviewees and the author. The measurements refer to the distribution of income and other material goods (such as food and medicines) across households, taking into account the frequency, type and value of exchange. However, they do not include other forms of support that may be of value to elders, such as general care. Nor do they take into account various indirect economic contributions that may be made by elders themselves, such as unpaid domestic labour and care of young children. Nevertheless, these indicators enable a relatively sophisticated level of analysis, as will be seen.

Table 3 shows that only 19 per cent of respondents in Buenos Aires were either completely or substantially dependent on economic support from other household members, and that 60 per cent claimed they experienced no economic dependence at all. Table 4 provides the same information for the São Paulo shanty towns. Here, levels of reported support are somewhat higher, although 69 per cent still claimed no or only slight dependence. It is possible that levels of support were under-reported by these surveys, owing to the lack of willingness of respondents to admit their true levels of dependence. Nevertheless, the converse (overstating support to avoid loss of face associated with "selfish" relatives) is also possible. Taking the findings at face value, it would seem that large households in the shanty towns did not necessarily signify high levels of economic dependence.[2]

TABLE 3. DEGREE OF ECONOMIC DEPENDENCE ON HOUSEHOLD MEMBER
OTHER THAN PARTNER AND DIRECTION OF ECONOMIC TIE,
BUENOS AIRES SHANTY TOWNS, 1992-1993

Degree of economic dependence	(Percentage)	Nature of economic tie	(Percentage)
Complete	4	Benefit	17
Substantial	14	Neutral	30
Slight	22	Contribute	18
None	60	None	35

Source: Lloyd-Sherlock (1997, p. 191).

TABLE 4. DEGREE OF ECONOMIC DEPENDENCE ON HOUSEHOLD MEMBER
OTHER THAN PARTNER AND DIRECTION OF ECONOMIC TIE,
SÃO PAULO SHANTY TOWNS, 1995

Degree of economic dependence	(Percentage)	Nature of economic tie	(Percentage)
Complete	17	Benefit	31
Substantial	14	Neutral	35
Slight	35	Contribute	21
None	34	None	13

Source: Lloyd-Sherlock (unpublished survey data).

A lack of dependence does not discount the possibility that older people
shared economic ties with their households, only that they did not derive any
overall benefit from them. Tables 3 and 4 show that 65 per cent of respondents
in Buenos Aires and 88 per cent in São Paulo reported ties. They also show
that a significant proportion of elders claimed to be making a "net
contribution" to the economic welfare of the household. Indeed, in Buenos
Aires, "net contributors" slightly outnumbered the "net beneficiaries". In the
majority of these cases, older people were the only source of household
income. These typically consisted of elders living with grandchildren and ill or
disabled children. Several respondents mentioned that increases in
unemployment had significantly reduced the capacity of younger household
members to offer them support. A small number complained that other
members held back the bulk of their income for personal expenditure.
However, most referred to some form of pooling mechanism.

These data show that economic ties between respondents and other
household members should not be characterized as unidirectional flows of
support from the latter to the former, and that the notion of older people as a
financial burden on relatives is often inaccurate. Older peoples' contributions
mainly came from two sources: earnings and pensions. The surveys found that
levels of economic activity for older people were substantially higher than

those reported outside the shanty towns. Argentina and Brazil have relatively well-developed old-age pension programmes, which provided benefits to just over half of the respondents (55 per cent in the Buenos Aires survey, 58 per cent in São Paulo). The value of pensions was usually a fraction of basic living requirements, and many forms of economic activity, such as waste recycling, yielded pitiful returns. Nevertheless, in the context of poverty, these could represent a significant contribution to general household income. The survey also found that older people tended to consume fewer household resources than did other members, placing a particularly high priority on the needs of grandchildren and often forgoing necessary medication.

RELATIONS WITH OTHER FAMILY MEMBERS

Tables 5 and 6 give information about family members who did not form part of the respondents' households. Not surprisingly, fewer respondents reported that they were completely dependent on relatives living outside the home. However, a significant proportion did say that they were substantially dependent on them (22 per cent in Buenos Aires, 27 per cent in São Paulo).[3] Also, older people were more likely to be "net beneficiaries" with relatives from outside the home. As such, economic support from relatives beyond the home was often more significant than household ties. One reason for this may have been because economically successful children were more likely to be living away from their parents, since they were able to afford their own accommodation. Two particular cases give extreme examples of this. In both, all the children but one, who was mentally handicapped, had moved away from their elderly parents. Another explanation may be that respondents usually had more children and close relatives living outside the home than in it. This increased the general probability that an outsider relative would be willing and able to help out.

TABLE 5. DEGREE OF ECONOMIC DEPENDENCE ON OTHER FAMILY MEMBERS AND DIRECTION OF ECONOMIC TIES, BUENOS AIRES SHANTY TOWNS, 1992-1993

Degree of economic dependence	(Percentage)	Nature of economic tie	(Percentage)
Complete	2	Benefit	36
Substantial	22	Neutral	16
Slight	28	Contribute	3
None	49	None	45

Source: Lloyd-Sherlock (1997).

TABLE 6. DEGREE OF ECONOMIC DEPENDENCE ON OTHER FAMILY
MEMBERS AND DIRECTION OF ECONOMIC TIES,
SÃO PAULO SHANTY TOWNS, 1995

Degree of economic dependence	(Percentage)	Nature of economic tie	(Percentage)
Complete	4	Benefit	52
Substantial	27	Neutral	5
Slight	26	Contribute	4
None	43	None	42

Source: Lloyd-Sherlock (unpublished survey data).

HOME OWNERSHIP

So far, the present analysis of household economic relations has
excluded indirect economic contributions by older people. The brevity of this
paper allows us to examine just one example of these — the provision of
accommodation. Surveys from both developed and developing countries
report that levels of homeownership are high for elderly people (Chayovan
and Knodel, 1997; Johnson and Falkingham, 1992). As well as comprising a
potential form of economic contribution, homeownership could serve to
reduce the economic vulnerability of elders, and increase their bargaining
powers with other relations.

In the shanty towns studied here the great majority of respondents (77
per cent in Buenos Aires, 74 per cent in São Paulo) owned their own home,
either individually or with their partners. Of these, most were living with other
adults (see table 7). Few respondents attached any importance to their status as
homeowners, and none referred to any form of rental arrangement. It may be
that in the context of an urban slum, where property rights are less well
established and inheritance practices less formalized, homeownership was a
less valuable asset. However, surveys of household expenditure in Buenos
Aires and São Paulo found that accommodation accounted for a high and
increasing share of expenditure in the early 1990s. Also, the absence of legally
constituted property rights did not mean that these houses were without value.
Several respondents referred to informal housing markets and to gradual
improvements they had made to their houses over time, which had often
involved considerable effort and sacrifice. It is possible that if property rights
were more explicit and formalized the status of many older people within their
households would improve considerably.

TABLE 7. HOME OWNERSHIP IN BUENOS AIRES AND SÃO PAULO SHANTY TOWNS

	Buenos Aires	São Paulo
Owner with other adults	69	62
Owner without other adults	8	12
Not owner	18	23
Unclear	5	2

Source: Lloyd-Sherlock (unpublished survey data).

GENDER AND LIVING ARRANGEMENTS

While the elderly populations of many developing countries are not as feminized as those in the developed world, it is clear that old age is a highly "gendered" issue.[4] The economic disadvantage faced by most women during earlier stages of the life course usually continues into old age for a variety of reasons, including large disparities in pension entitlements. Although the elderly populations were clearly feminized in the shanty towns studied here, there was variation (in Buenos Aires, 57 per cent were women and in São Paulo, 70 per cent). Two areas in which gender disparities may be expected are the extent to which older people live alone and their dependence on household support.

Census data for Buenos Aires in 1991 report that older women were more likely to live alone than were men (29 and 11 per cent, respectively) (INDEC, 1993b). There would appear to be a similar imbalance in the shanty towns (27 per cent women and 9 per cent men), although the small numbers involved weaken this finding. It is sometimes argued that living alone increases the economic vulnerability and social isolation of older women (Tan, 1995). However, a recent survey of poor older women in Guadalajara, Mexico, found that relationships between living alone and well-being were more complex and that some respondents preferred to live alone in order to escape abuse or onerous domestic obligations (Varley and Blasco, 1999).

Gender comparisons of household relations produce less predictable results. In São Paulo, 33 per cent of women were either completely or substantially dependent, compared to 26 per cent of men. In Buenos Aires, the respective levels were 37 and 40 per cent. There are several explanations for this lack of variation. First, gender disparities in pension coverage were lower than national levels. This reflected low overall coverage and, in Buenos Aires, the targeting of non-contributory benefits to women. Secondly, more women than men (17 versus 10 per cent) were dependent on economic support from their partners (information not included in tables 3 and 4).

CONCLUSIONS

The present paper does not seek to put forward generalizable findings about the living arrangements of poor older people, since these relationships are often complex, varied and difficult to infer from "raw" demographic data. Within Buenos Aires, comparisons between shanty towns and the poor inner-city slum of La Boca reveal the difficulties in dealing with poor urban elders as a single group. While there was a reasonable level of consistency among the five settlements included in the author's surveys, the condition of older people in other shanty towns may be quite different.

It should not be assumed that larger household sizes translate into greater amounts of direct support for elders. Internal household dynamics depend on more detailed aspects of household composition and the wider environment. Living with young grandchildren or ill relatives is more likely to represent a burden than a benefit. If unemployment is high, healthy young adults may become reliant on a share of pension benefits. Economic support may come from those beyond the household, particularly if other relatives live nearby.

The surveys draw attention to the significant economic contributions made by many respondents to their own households. They challenge the traditional view that older people represent a "burden" to younger family members (as is inherent in the concept of demographic dependency ratios). Respondents often provided significant levels of income, which was pooled at the household level, as well as less obvious contributions, such as the provision of accommodation. This finding is supported by other studies of poor households in both rural and urban contexts (Heslop, 1999; Ofstedal, Knodel and Chayovan, 1999).

The surveys referred to in the present paper are limited both in terms of scale and in terms of the range of issues they deal with. Other concerns that require investigation and analysis include the relationship between health status, income and living arrangements and comparisons of poor elders in rural and urban settings. The author is currently developing projects related to these themes in Thailand and South Africa.

NOTES

[1] Data were not available for São Paulo City. However, the State of São Paulo is itself highly urbanized.

[2] A separate survey of shanty towns in Lapa, São Paulo, produces similar findings, observing that older people "lead their own lives, without depending economically on their children" (Karsch and Baptista, 1992, p. 87).

[3] "Substantial dependence" requires regular provision of substantial material support.

[4] For example, in Brazil, there were 89 men for every 100 women aged 60 or more in 1990, compared to only 67 in the developed regions.

357

Ahlburg, Dennis (1994). Population growth and poverty. In *Population and Development: Old Debates, New Conclusions*, Robert Cassen, ed. Oxford: Transaction Publishers.

Bellardi, Marta, and Aldo De Paula (1986). Villas misera: origen, eradicación y respuestas populares. Buenos Aires: Centro Editor de America Latina.

Chayovan, Napaporn, and John Knodel (1997). A report on the survey of the welfare of the elderly in Thailand. Bangkok: Chulalongkorn University, Institute of Population Studies.

Contreras de Lehr, Esther (1989). Women and old age: status of the elderly woman in Mexico. In *Mid-life and Older Women in Latin America and the Caribbean*. Washington, D.C.: Pan American Health Organization.

Hardoy, Jorge, and David Satterthwaite (1989). *Squatter Citizen: Life in the Urban Third World*. London: Earthscan.

Heslop, Amanda (1999). Poverty and livelihoods in an ageing world. In *The Ageing and Development Report*. London: Earthscan.

INDEC (1993a). Censo nacional de población y vivienda, 1991 (total del país). Buenos Aires: Instituto Nacional de Estadística y Censos.

_____ (1993b). Censo nacional de población y vivienda, 1991 (Capital Federal). Buenos Aires: Instituto Nacional de Estadística y Censos.

Johnson, Paul, and Jane Falkingham (1992). *Ageing and Economic Welfare*. London: Sage.

Karsch, Ursula, and M. Baptista (1992). Social support for the aged in the district of Lapa — São Paulo, Brazil. Pontificia Universidade Católica de São Paulo. Research report.

Kinsella, Kevin, and Cynthia Taeuber (1992). *An Aging World II*. Washington, D.C.: United States Department of Commerce. International population reports, P95/92-3.

Lloyd-Sherlock, Peter (1997). *Old Age and Urban Poverty in the Developing World. The Shanty Towns of Buenos Aires*. London: Macmillan.

_____ (1999). Old age, migration and poverty in the shanty towns of São Paulo, Brazil. *Journal of Developing Areas* (Macomb), vol. 32, No. 4 (summer), pp. 491-514.

Ofstedal, Mary Beth, John Knodel, and Napaporn Chayovan (1999). Intergenerational support and gender: a comparison of four Asian countries. *Elderly in Asia. Research Report*, No. 99-54. Ann Arbor: University of Michigan, Population Studies Research Center.

Ramos, Silvia (1981). *Las Relaciones de Parentesco y de Ayuda Mutua*. Buenos Aires: Centro de Estudios de Estado y Sociedad.

Redondo, Nelida (1990). *Ancianidad y Pobreza. Una Investigación en Sectores Populares Urbanos*. Buenos Aires: Editorial Humanitas.

Scipione, Jorge, and others (1992). Situación de los beneficiarios del sistema nacional de previsión social. Informe de Gallup. Buenos Aires.

Tan, Chang (1995). Social and economic security needs of older women in Asia. *United Nations Bulletin on Ageing*, Nos. 2 and 3.

Varley, Ann, and Maribel Blasco (1999). Reaping what you sow? Older women, housing and family dynamics in urban Mexico. In *Women's Life Cycle and Ageing*. Santo Domingo: International Research and Training Institute for the Advancement of Women.

Yazaki, Lúcia, Aparecida Viera de Melo, and Luiz Ramos (1991). Perspectivas actuais do papel da família frente ao envelhecimento populacional: um estudo de caso. *Informe Demográfico* (São Paulo), vol. 24, pp. 11-96.

LIVING ARRANGEMENTS, POVERTY AND THE HEALTH OF OLDER PERSONS IN AFRICA

*Mapule F. Ramashala**

SUMMARY

The rapid growth in the number of older people worldwide has created an unprecedented global demographic revolution. Improvements in hygiene and water supply and control of infectious diseases during the past century have greatly reduced the risk of premature death. As a consequence, the proportion of the world's population aged 60 and over is increasing more rapidly than in any previous era. In 1950, there were about 200 million people aged 60 and over throughout the world. There are now about 580 million, and by 2025, the number of people over the age of 60 is expected to reach 1.2 billion.

For the first time in history, the majority of those who have survived childhood, in all countries, can expect to live past 50 years of age. Even in the world's poorest countries, those who survive the diseases of infancy and childhood have a very good chance of living to be grandparents. This suggests that the number of older people in developing countries will more than double over the next quarter century, reaching 850 million by 2025, that is, 12 per cent of their total population. By 2050, the proportion of older people is expected to increase to 20 per cent (HelpAge International, 1999).

* University of Durban-Westville, Durban, South Africa.

The growth in life expectancy offers new opportunities but it also creates challenges for the future. In the developing world, populations are now ageing at an unprecedented speed, while most of their poor still live in poverty. Thus, the population ageing occurring in much of the third world is not accompanied by real socio-economic development. Large segments of the population continue to live at the margin. Furthermore, the traditional forms of care available to older generations until recently are under threat (Kalache, 1991). This is in major part because families have suffered from the impact of social changes, including urbanization, geographic spread, the trend towards nuclear families and the participation of women in the workforce. There is a cost for the failure to address the ageing-related problems of any society. Evidence is now emerging that a disproportionate amount of resources is being spent on the elderly population in some countries. Sen (1994) maintains that this is due to a combination of factors:

- The very nature of the problems of the elderly — long-term disabling conditions that often involve high-cost technology;
- Families under strain, faced with chronic and complex problems, put pressure on authorities to institutionalize their elderly who require more extensive care;
- Social and geographic mobility, leading to situations where children are unable to provide the necessary care;
- In the absence of appropriate solutions, decision makers tend to emulate the institutionalized forms of care prevalent in many developed countries;
- Recently, the HIV/AIDS pandemic, which has created a crisis in the family structure in both rural and urban areas. The traditional/cultural practice of depending on children by older people is no longer in place, in large part because the younger generation is "dying off", leaving parents without resources as caregivers of grandchildren. This is having significant impact not only on living arrangements and conditions but also on the quality of life of grandparents.

As the number of older people in Africa continues to increase, particularly those who are aged 75 and over, growing public policy and service delivery attention must, of political and human necessity, be focused on the problems and needs of older people. Clearly, such needs as economic security, access to essential health and human services, adequate housing and personal safety exist, with variations, from region to region in the African continent. The issue of housing and living conditions, considering the rapid urbanization of young families away from parents, is especially illustrative of one of the more acute problems confronting these elders. Little is known about the needs of older people in Africa. Concern about population growth, basic health programmes and provision, mortality and morbidity rates and infectious diseases, especially the HIV/AIDS pandemic, has dominated collective attention in the continent. Therefore, while Africa will still not be an aged continent, it will begin to show signs of ageing, with its consequent benefits and problems. Hence, investing in policies that promote healthy ageing should produce high societal and health returns. One of the major problems confronting planners and policy makers is the absence of systematic reliable data on the needs of older Africans. Some data exist for relatively few countries, but the current lack of reliable national-level data about the older populations presents a major limitation to understanding problems and formulating interventions specifically for older people. Data specific to South Africa (Booysen, 2000) regarding the living conditions and life circumstances of those South Africans aged 65 and over, show that living arrangements and therefore living conditions follow the life patterns of the different racial groups of people in South Africa. Race, gender and place of residence, whether urban or non-urban, remain the most distinguishing features of the society, revealing past discriminatory practices. Data show that Africans constitute the largest group of the aged population (67 per cent).

Because the incidence of chronic illness and disability increases with age, the longer one lives, the more likely one is to experience illness and disability. Chronic illness and disability, in turn, increase the likelihood that many very old people will no longer be able to live independently but will require care. Consequently, crises such as the need to change living arrangements, financial problems and the inability to perform self-care activities are ubiquitous events among the very old.

Policy considerations should take into account a broad-based approach that distinguishes between the well and active elderly, the disabled elderly and the frail elderly. Intervention options should consider inter-sectoral structures and multidisciplinary strategies to ensure that older people are well physically and psychologically and for as long as possible. This means families and local communities must be empowered with resources and technical assistance to care for older persons in the community, and this in turn means access to amenities ranging from water, sanitation, transport, housing, and access to health promotion, disease and disability-prevention strategies. The principal overriding goal should be formulating policies and interventions that result in the elimination of poverty as the first priority. This means we should strive to identify and modify, where possible, the broad range of high-risk situations that have long-term and devastating effects on older people.

National policies must incorporate the issue of ageing and appropriate support mechanisms for older people into the mainstream of their social and economic planning. Policies for employment, health, transport, housing and social care must take into account the variety of needs of older people. These sectoral targets must be integrated into broader social strategies. National Governments should seek the active involvement of older people themselves and of their families, communities and non-governmental organizations in research, planning and policy implementation on all issues that are of concern to older people.

OVERVIEW

Among the most significant demographic trends of the twentieth century has been the continued growth of elderly population age groups both in absolute terms and in relation to other segments of society.

Interest in the study of human ageing has grown steadily throughout the twentieth century, culminating in a spate of academic books and the development of postgraduate courses in social gerontology and geriatrics. Introductions to the study of human ageing have typically emphasized changes in demography, focusing on "the ageing of populations", a trend that has characterized industrialized societies throughout the twentieth century but that in recent years has become a worldwide phenomenon. Even developing countries, with their myriad of challenges, have experienced increases in their older populations. This increase in the number of older people in society and the increase in the proportion of the population who are elderly has resulted in the study of human ageing, focusing on old age in general and the problems and challenges of old age in particular. Throughout the twentieth century, old age has been seen as a "social problem" and this predominant perspective is evident through the language used by policy makers and health and social service planners. While there is no denying either the poor quality of life experienced by many older people or the challenges faced by planners and other professionals in providing health and welfare services for the growing numbers of the frail elderly, it is disconcerting that the joys and triumphs of old age in the latter part of the twentieth century were not promoted with vigour.

Throughout the twentieth century, the proportion of people aged 60 and older has increased in all countries of the world. This trend started earlier in the industrialized countries, but countries in the developing world are experiencing the same changes in population structure. The convening of the World Assembly on Ageing in Vienna in 1982 was an acknowledgement of the fact that ageing could no longer be viewed as a phenomenon of the Western world. The Assembly provided, for the first time, a forum where both developed and developing countries could exchange ideas and information on their experience of the ageing process (Sen, 1994). It was evident from the demographic changes taking place that the ageing process was occurring at an unprecedented rate in most developing countries. By 2000, about two thirds of the estimated 600 million people aged 60 and older will be living in these countries. Kalache (1994) points out that ageing is basically the result of a two-dimensional demographic transformation: on the one hand, overall mortality declines, resulting in longer life expectancy, on the other, declines in fertility result in decreasing the proportion of children and young adults in the population and, consequently, in increasing that of older adults. This dynamic process, usually referred to as the demographic transition, was first observed in post-industrial revolution European societies in the nineteenth century. By and large, it was the result of gradual improvements in living standards among most of the population in countries such as France and the United Kingdom. With limited contributions from medical technology, people benefited from better housing, public sanitation and improved nutritional status: mortality started to fall and, subsequently, fertility decreased. "Ageing was therefore the long-term consequence of socio-economic development" (Sen, 1994). Most importantly, by the time a substantial proportion of the population had reached old age, many of the problems associated with classical under-development had already been solved. Resources were therefore potentially available to be diverted to an increasing elderly population. These were relatively affluent societies, with highly educated populations enjoying the best public services in the world. Yet, population ageing continues to be a significant challenge, requiring adequate societal responses on many fronts. If caring for their elderly remains a challenge for the rich countries, which experienced a process of gradual ageing over many decades, what then about ageing in the developing world (Kalache, 1994)?

The demographic transition in many countries of the third world is now taking place in a much shorter period of time. Unprecedented declines in mortality rates in countries throughout Latin America, Asia and, more recently, Africa are largely the result of the availability of effective treatment and/or prevention of diseases previously responsible for huge numbers of premature deaths. The conditions that lead to these diseases still prevail and the morbidity they cause continues to be high. Population ageing occurring in much of the third world is not accompanied by real socio-economic development. Large segments of the population continue to live at the margin. However, they will live longer than their parents and will have far fewer children. Furthermore, the traditional forms of care available for older generations until recently are not easily available. This is not because families no longer care, but is the result of social changes that include urbanization, geographic spread, the trend towards nuclear families and the participation of women in the workforce (Sen, 1994; Kalache, 1994; Apt and Greico, 1994).

POVERTY, HEALTH AND AGEING

Poverty, with its deleterious effects on health, education, self-esteem, quality of life and lifestyle, is one of the major concerns of older people (Okie, 1991). Okie, in a study specific to the Black elderly in the United States of America, reported that so powerful is the impact of poverty that if differences in income, education and living conditions were eliminated the pattern of vulnerability to cancer would be reversed. The study also found that people of different races show differences in vulnerability to various tumours. But those differences, Okie reports, whether rooted in heredity or culture, are usually outweighed by the much greater influence of poverty, which raises cancer rates by reducing access to health care and education and by determining where and how people live. Health for the elderly may be conceptualized as the ability to live and function effectively in society and to exercise maximum self-reliance and autonomy; it is not necessarily the total absence of disease (Harper, 1988).

According to Rowe (1991), the health of older people has been approached from two different perspectives. The biomedical gerontological and geriatrics model, commonly held by physicians and other medical personnel, defines health in terms of the mechanisms and treatment of age-related diseases and the presence or absence of disease. The functional model, on the other hand, defines health in terms of older people's level of functioning; it is best summarized by a World Health Organization advisory group report:

364

Health in the elderly is best measured in terms of functioning ... Degree of fitness rather than extent of pathology, may be used as a measure of the amount of services the elderly will need from the community (World Health Organization, 1989).

Elderly Africans, like elderly Black Americans, tend to perceive their health according to their ability to perform activities of daily living and not according to laboratory or x-ray findings (Harper, 1988). It may be elderly persons' assessments and perceptions of their health, in both cases, that contribute to their frequent delay in seeking care or reporting discomfort.

The observation that poverty and deprivation are concentrated on a substantial proportion of older people has been a recurring theme of research on ageing in all industrialized societies. In the United Kingdom, for example, older people have been reported to be the largest group in the population living in poverty ever since data were first collected systematically. Subsequent research in other parts of the world has confirmed, repeatedly, the deep-seated nature and extent of poverty in old age. Additional data show that the risk of experiencing poverty is three times greater for older adults than it is for other age groups. Not only does poverty affect a substantial proportion of older people, but when it does, it is likely to be an enduring experience. The high incidence of poverty and low incomes among older people is reflected in other measures as well. Moreover, the problem of poverty in old age is not peculiar to industrialized societies; it is endemic among both Western and Eastern countries as well as third world countries.

Older people are consistently among the poorest in all societies, and material security is therefore one of the greatest preoccupations of old age. Many experience the same lack of physical necessities, assets and income felt by other poor people, but without the resources that younger, fitter and more active adults can use to compensate. The prevalence of poverty among older people is also linked to education levels, including differing levels of literacy (HelpAge International, 1999). Lack of material means is not the only problem of poverty. Another consequence is the inability to participate effectively in economic, social and political life. Older people living in poverty find themselves socially excluded and isolated from decision-making processes. This affects not only their income and wealth but also contributes to poor housing, ill health and personal insecurity.

Efforts to understand poverty have dominated much of the debate on development in recent years, but the poverty experienced by the majority of older people, particularly in developing countries, has been largely ignored. Moreover, during the colonial and post-colonial years in Africa, for example, issues relating to ageing were neglected. Competing interests such as education, health, housing, sanitation and water were considered more pressing. While the rapidly increasing number of older people throughout the world represent a biological success for humanity, the living conditions of the elderly in most countries have by and large lagged behind those enjoyed by the economically active population.

One of the most influential factors on all our lives is the environment in which we live. For older people, this may be particularly so since they spend more time in "the home" than many other groups in society.

Poverty and inadequate incomes are often associated with housing deprivation among older people and often reflect housing provision patterns in earlier life. Moreover, housing deprivation is also the result of paternalistic policies, with few appropriate housing options available to older people.

Although there exists some information about a few countries in the African continent (Apt, 1985, 1991, 1992, 1994, 1995, 1996; Addo, 1972; Brown, 1984; Cox and Mberia, 1977), any discussion of living arrangements in developing countries in general and in Africa in particular must take into consideration a multiplicity of factors. Ageing does not occur in a vacuum. It occurs in a context that includes the needs and resources of individuals, their patterns of activities, their relationships with others and their attachments to their surroundings. Ageing interacts with all these aspects of the physical and social environment. A great deal of what we experience in life is shaped by our circumstances. Considering the limitations of data on living arrangements in Africa in general, the discussion focuses on South Africa, in particular on the cumulative effect of socio-economic factors and their impact on ageing. Even for South Africa, data and therefore policies, with specific reference to living arrangements for older people, are limited. Reasonable-quality data are available mainly for White South Africans owing to selective data-collection policies — the historic legacy of apartheid.

To fully understand ageing in South Africa requires that we appreciate how the South African experience has affected its people, their needs, resources and life experiences.

Inequalities in South African society generated differences in the way Blacks and Whites have adjusted to ageing. These inequalities stem from stratification on the basis of age, sex and the possession of certain resources. Racial characteristics have been used to ascribe inferior status — both social and political — resulting in the unequal treatment of Black South Africans. Until recently, with the achievement of a democratic dispensation in April 1994, discrimination and segregation were used to maintain unequal status throughout the course of the lives of Black South Africans. Living arrangements, therefore, follow these life patterns for the different racial groups of older people in South Africa.

THE IMPACT OF INCOME LEVELS AND POVERTY ON LIVING ARRANGEMENTS OF THE ELDERLY IN AFRICA

An obvious starting point for a discussion on living arrangements for older people, particularly older Africans, given the historical pattern of inequalities in the continent, is the family. In one of the few available studies on the elderly in historical perspective, Cain (1991) examines the situation of the elderly in contemporary South Asia and contrasts it with that of pre-industrial Europe. Cain suggests a strong correlation between the existence of the joint family and the well-being of the elderly in India and Bangladesh; that contrary to what many have suggested, social changes have not eroded the significance of the joint family in the context of South Asia. The majority of old people continue to live in the extended family network.

The historical role played by the family in Africa has been exhaustively presented by Apt (1999), who points out that "historically, African communities had well-articulated caring structures that preserved the quality of life for elder people, but this was linked to the low chance of the survival of large numbers of older persons" (p. 5). She further observes that "migration and urbanization have both separately and jointly been pinpointed as contributing to the destabilization of the value that in the past sustained older persons in a closely knit age-integrated African society" (p. 2). Such a practice had implications for the way older people were perceived within both the family and community structures.

A study initiated by the World Health Organization (WHO) in the mid-1980s and published in the United Kingdom in 1992 examined, from an international perspective, the important issues of providing support to the elderly (Kendig, Hashimoto and Coppard, 1992). This work questions and dispels many of the myths perpetuated by the modernization school, which has been so influential in evaluating the needs of the elderly in both developed and developing countries. The collection, which includes articles from countries as far apart as Sweden and Ghana, shows that the family played a central but very varied role in supporting the elderly. It illustrates that there is a considerable diversity in the experience of ageing owing to different levels of socio-economic and socio-demographic development. But the cases presented in the study also show that, in the absence of other forms of support (pension funds), older people continue to be economically active, particularly in the rural areas. From information based on rural areas, there are strong indications that a much higher proportion of older people are in the labour force in developing countries than in industrialized countries. The authors note that a key issue that requires further exploration is whether extended family households not only provide economies of scale in living costs but also facilitate the role of the aged as providers of child care and socialization.

Apt (1992) places the role of the family in the care of the elderly in the context of the political economy of the country (Ghana), particularly in relation to poverty and uneven development. She further points out that the majority of the population (69 per cent in 1984) continued to live in rural areas. A United Nations report (1979), based on studies of Hong Kong, Jamaica and Lebanon, identifies some of the major problems facing the elderly in terms of their social, economic and psychological needs. The main conclusions are that slums and squatter settlements are an increasingly prominent feature of urban expansion and that a major course of this expansion has resulted from a process of rapid rural-urban migration. Phillips (1988), in his article on accommodation for elderly persons in newly industrialized countries, describes the experience of Hong Kong as an example of the provision of care and accommodation for the elderly in a newly industrialized area. The author shows that Hong Kong has embarked upon a comprehensive and integrated service for its elderly population, with a mixture of public and private enterprise. The developments in Hong Kong are not only related to the historical evolution of its social policy, following trends and developments in the United Kingdom, they are also a pragmatic response to the integration of traditional support for the elderly as a result of rapid social changes over the past decades. Various forms of residential, day and community-based services are provided. Phillips suggests that, while provision for the elderly has advanced quite rapidly in Hong Kong, its replication will only be possible in countries classified as newly industrialized. Among the problems associated with the rapid advance in provision for the elderly are the level of trained and qualified staff.

In a study on the developed world that has relevance for developing countries, Phillipson (1982) argues that the recession in the West of the past three decades affects the elderly as a group owing to the proportionate increase of the 60+ population in the total population. He focuses on social inequalities in the distribution of power in terms of income and property and observes that low income, poor housing and inadequate medical care constitute the main experience of people growing old. Kalache (1991), using Brazil as a case study, shows not only that there has been a rapid ageing of its population but also that the elderly are disproportionately represented among the poorest of the poor. He further points out that in many of the developing countries longevity among females means that poverty and chronic disability conditions affect women disproportionately.

For South Africa, census data (Booysen, 2000) indicate that women are likewise disproportionately represented in the aged population (61.4 per cent females to 38.6 per cent males). Moreover, the condition of functional ageing in the life circumstances of the majority of elderly women means that many could be ageing far earlier than the internationally designated age of either 60 or 65. This has far-reaching implications for the care of the elderly, especially by family members who themselves have few or no resources. In her paper, Apt (1999) has presented an exhaustive discussion on the historical and cultural context of ageing and the African family, with variations from country to country and region to region within the continent. In South Africa, three major factors have affected the living conditions and consequently the living arrangements of older people, particularly older non-Whites:

(a)   Apartheid policies governing the previous urban-rural divide;

(b)   Urbanization of young families;

(c)   Migration labour policies.

These three factors combined have in turn determined the distribution of resources not only by region but by race as well, especially with the following effects:

- Creation of TBV states (Bantu homelands), which were mostly rural and consisted of predominantly older populations;
- The organization of the welfare system, with almost all welfare resources allocated for old-age homes for the White aged;

368

- Migration labour policies, with no pension provision for mining industry workers and other commercial sectors for non-Whites;
- South African labour policies, particularly mining labour policies, which affected not only South Africans but other surrounding African countries as well (Botswana, Lesotho, Malawi, Mozambique, Swaziland, United Republic of Tanzania, Zambia and Zimbabwe);
- The broader policies specific to education, with poor education for Black people resulting in the lack of commercial understanding of retirement and the inability to make claims for retiring. This had a significant impact on older people, who then depended on "dislodged" age-old cultural/traditional patterns of children taking care of parents, with little or no resources; as Apt (1999) explains, this resulted not only in the breakdown of this tradition but also served as a significant stressor on young families;
- The HIV/AIDS pandemic, which has created a crisis in the family structure in both rural and urban areas. The traditional/cultural practice of older people depending on children is no longer intact, in large part because the younger generation is dying, leaving grandparents without resources as caregivers of grandchildren. This has had significant impact not only on the living arrangements of grandparents but on those of grandchildren as well. Unfortunately, data are not available to demonstrate the enormity of the consequences of the HIV/AIDS pandemic on older people in Africa as a whole.

The combination of poverty, natural disasters, violence, social chaos and the disempowered status of women facilitates the transmission of HIV. Conversely, the illness increases the risk of a household or individual becoming even more impoverished, and lowers the general level of health in communities because of its close relationship with other communicable and poverty-related diseases such as tuberculosis. Under apartheid, the poor were shifted to the margins of urban areas and, more importantly, to the margins of the country, thus focusing the core of South Africa's poverty in the rural areas. Moreover, the rural areas of South Africa suffer from a legacy of inappropriate investment decisions. For many rural people in the former homeland areas, economic and social decisions remain conditioned by their unequal and distorted access to markets, services and other opportunities.

THE WAY FORWARD: POLICY IMPLICATIONS

The issue of living arrangements in developing countries in general and in Africa in particular is closely related to the socio-economic empowerment of the people. Wilson and Ramphele (1989, p. 258) observed that poverty is not some morally neutral phenomenon that needs merely to be understood. It is an evil that must be rooted out. No single strategy against poverty is ever likely to be wholly effective. The many dimensions of poverty and its interlocking causes require a multiple strategy attack.

The struggle against poverty in South Africa is intertwined with the struggle against powerlessness. Power lies at the heart of the problem of poverty in southern Africa. Without it, those who are poor remain vulnerable to an ongoing process of impoverishment. A change in the political power structure in South Africa has occurred. What is now necessary is the infusion of a value system that would ensure that the process of transformation and the creation of a new society is of real benefit to all those living in it. There are several examples available in the history of other countries that serve as reminders that a political democracy by itself is not a sufficient condition for ensuring that the poorest, even if they have the right to vote, become full members of a more egalitarian society.

In an address to the National Education Crisis Committee in March 1986, Zwelakhe Sisulu made a distinction between the transfer of power and the shift in the balance of power in South Africa. The trade union movement in the 1970s and 1980s played a significant role in that it made and continues to make a substantial contribution to shifting the balance of forces in favour of the poor. In addition to the trade unions, an entire range of independent organizations not only made a difference in people's lives in the existing circumstances but also helped by transforming power relations to shift the balance of power towards the poor as well as laying foundations that would help determine the shape of South African society in the long run.

Thus, the problems of older people in Africa have to be addressed within a broader context that encompasses reforms at different levels, including legislative and administrative processes that result in benefit structures, health care and educational reforms.

What then are the principal challenges facing us on behalf of the elderly in the new millennium? The present paper has focused more on the relationship between poverty, health and living arrangements, with poverty as the overriding principal factor. Naturally, eliminating poverty is the first priority.

•   We have to acknowledge that there is a serious housing problem for older people in Africa and that the problem will grow in magnitude.

•   Lack of data. Little is known about the needs of older people in Africa. Concerns about population growth, basic health programmes and provision, mortality and morbidity rates and infectious diseases, especially the HIV/AIDS pandemic, have dominated collective attention. An additional concern, although more insidious, is the ageing of the African population. The current lack of reliable national-level data about the older population presents a major limitation to understanding interventions and problems associated with this population. Within the next 20 years, the total number of older people will increase from the current 580 million to over 1 billion. Close to three quarters of these older persons will live in developing countries. The number of Africans 60 years and older will grow from 39 million in 2000 to 80 million in 2025. The number of Africans 65 years of age and older will grow from 25 million in 1999 to 52 million in 2025. While the proportion of Africa's elderly population is growing, it is currently still low. However, it is expected to more than double by 2025 and the population 75 years and older will increase by over 400 per cent in many African regions. Therefore, while

Africa will still not be an aged continent, it will certainly begin to show signs of ageing, with its consequent benefits and problems.

Hence, investing in policies that promote healthy ageing should produce high societal and health returns in developing countries. Healthy older people are a valuable social and economic resource to their families and communities, whereas the alternative is a drain on the already limited human, social and capital resources. Information currently collected by routine sources is fragmented, incomplete or not specific to older populations. Non-routine data sources provide data relevant to the health status of older populations but, again, may not be comprehensive or representative. Demographic, economic and social surveys provide data on proximate causes of impaired functioning such as individual and household earning, health, family and household size and structure, and social and economic roles culturally assigned by age and gender. The data, however, exist for relatively few countries in the African region. The recent strategy by WHO to encourage the collection of minimum data sets for the continent, with a specific focus on countries of sub-Saharan Africa, is encouraging. But we have to ensure that data include information that would provide the basis for more creative policies, including strategies for poverty reduction, housing older people in a dignified way and providing a wide range of options that facilitate both healthy ageing and "ageing in place".

- The options have to distinguish between the well and active elderly, the disabled elderly and the frail elderly.

- The options have to be based on intersectoral structures to ensure that older people are well physically and psychologically and for as long as possible. What this means is that local communities must be empowered with resources and technical expertise to care for older persons in the community, and this in turn means access to amenities ranging from water, sanitation, transport, housing, and access to health promotion, disease and disability-prevention strategies.

- Options for disabled older people who are living at home under the care of family members. Studies have demonstrated that care for disabled older people, frequently around the clock, is a burden and a major stressor to younger people and in some cases results in neglect and abuse. Every effort should be made by the health and welfare sectors to provide community-based supportive care to older people as well as to caregivers. The limited data available from South Africa indicate that the institutionalization of older people is not a recommended strategy.

- The frail elderly who require intensive around-the-clock care need several levels of care, ranging from the provision of community-based respite care to short-term hospitalization, specifically focusing on physical and psychological problems.

- Most of the diseases that afflict older persons are the so-called lifestyle diseases, conditions like lung cancer, diabetes and heart disease, which are strongly linked to risk factors such as cigarette smoking, poor nutrition, lack of regular exercise and chronic stress. Simple preventative measures can significantly reduce the negative impact of lifestyle diseases on older people.

- The highest rates of accidental death and injury occur among older people. Relatively simple and inexpensive accident-prevention measures can significantly reduce the risk of accidental injury and death among older people.
- Strategies need to be devised for the reduction of crime and victimization and abuse of older people.
- Older people are in need of political empowerment and advocacy.
- Opportunities for the employment of older people should be enhanced.
- Gender-sensitive policies for older people need to be developed, recognizing particular vulnerabilities to long-term poverty in old age that result from women's lifelong disadvantages in health and nutrition, limited labour force participation and discrimination in the area of property ownership.
- Family support. In practice, family care remains the most widely used survival strategy for the majority of the world's older people, whether in the context of extended families or co-residence of parents with adult children.
- The rights of older people need to be respected.

CONCLUSION

As the number of older people in Africa continues to increase, particularly those who are 75 years of age and older, growing public policy and service delivery attention must, of political and human necessity, be focused on the problems and needs of older adults. Clearly, such needs as economic security, access to essential health and human services, adequate housing and personal safety exist without regard to region. For the rapidly growing number of Black elderly in South Africa, for example, many of these needs and the related problems are more acute. The area of housing, or living arrangements, considering the rapid urbanization of young families away from parents, is especially illustrative of one of the more acute problems confronting these elders.

One of the gaps in our knowledge and in our array of services for older people is alternative living arrangements, especially for the frail, the slightly impaired and those who need a range of sheltered housing but do not need nursing care. Almost everyone in the ageing field is aware of the concept that there is a continuum of living arrangements, ranging from living independently in one's own home to complete institutionalization.

Old age, has for many years, been seen as a social problem (MacIntyre, 1977) and this perspective has helped perpetuate ageism. As a result, in any discussion of living arrangements for older people there has usually been more emphasis on the needs of the frail elderly than on elderly people in general. Most older people live in "normal housing". Yet, generally, in everyday life, we associate old age with special housing. The variety of housing accommodation in the United States of America, for example, available to elderly people is matched by the variety of institutional care used by very frail elderly people (Bond, 1990). Data that show the high concentration of older people in particular areas are often seen as supporting the predominant view that old age is a problem. Thus, we are regularly confronted with the "problems" associated with concentrations of people from different groups. To planners, such variations make the task of planning more difficult and challenging. Meeting the needs of a population with a high proportion of older people is not a short-term challenge. Meeting the needs of a population with a high proportion of older people who are poor and have health problems is even more complex, especially in a country or society with competing urgent needs for health care, education, sanitation, nutrition, housing and so forth, as is the case in South Africa.

Inadequate housing conditions are particularly problematic for older people who are impaired, handicapped or disabled. The unnecessary admission of older dependent people in homes for senior citizens has been attributed to the lack of adequate housing. One policy response to the severe reduction in public expenditures on housing has been the concept of "ageing in place". This policy aims at helping older people remain in their own homes more satisfactorily, through the work of voluntary non-governmental organizations, societies, and local authorities, rather than central or national Governments.

Policy on the provision of housing for older people has to take into consideration a range of issues, such as degree of dependence, health status, proximity to family and so forth, thus suggesting a continuum of living arrangements across the board. Awareness that there must be a variety of living arrangements to meet the needs of the older population is related to the heterogeneity of older people (Streib, 1982), who differ in income, family arrangements, level of health, mobility, and attitudes and personality. Providing supportive services to permit people to remain in their homes is considered the best option by many persons in the field of gerontology. For countries in Africa, it is perhaps the only option. Expensive institutional care is not an option for developing countries.

There have been a number of attempts to devise new family arrangements for older people as a means of solving many of their problems of economic security, dependency and isolation.

Policy makers and planners responsible for the quality of life, in the broader sense, of older people must envision a society that has large numbers of older persons of varying cultural and social backgrounds and having similar expectations from the public sector. Increasingly, the elderly will rely more on public service and welfare programmes than on family to meet some of their most serious needs. These needs relate to health care, housing, nutrition, safety and security and so on. The family will continue to meet some of the social and emotional needs of the elderly in any given society. Services can complement and, in many ways, enhance later-life individual and family relationships.

The field of alternate "continuum" living arrangements is just beginning. Policy makers, planners, managers and those who work in the field of gerontology, as well as families and communities, need all the ingenuity and initiative they can muster, and the flexibility to provide a range of services for older people to achieve healthy ageing and ageing in place.

REFERENCES

Primary sources

Booysen, D. (2000). Profiling those South Africans aged 65 years and older. Paper presented at the WHO workshop to create a minimum data set for research, policy and action on ageing and older adults in Africa, Harare, 22-24 January.

HelpAge International (1999). *The Ageing and Development Report: A Summary. Poverty, Independence and the World's Older People. Leading Global Action on Ageing.* London: Saffron Hill.

Secondary sources

Addo, N. O. (1972). Urban population and employment in Ghana. In *Population Growth and Economic Development in Africa*, S. Ominde and C. N. Ejiogu, eds. London: Heineman.

Apt, N. A. (1985). The role of grandparents in the care of children. In *Problems and Aspirations of Ghanaian Children: Implications for Policy Planning in Action*, P. A. Twumasi, and others, eds. Project report for Ghana National Commission on Children.

_____ (1991). Ghanaian Youth on Ageing. *Bold* (Malta), vol. 1, pp. 3-11.

_____ (1992). Family support to elderly people in Ghana. In *Family Support for the Elderly: The International Experience*, H. L. Kendig, A. Hashimoto and L. Coppard, eds. New York: Oxford University Press.

_____ (1994). The situation of elderly women in Ghana. Report to the United Nations. New York.

_____ (1995). Ageing in Africa: toward a redefinition of caring. In *An Ageing Population, an Ageing Planet and a Sustainable Future*, Stanley Engman, and others, eds., vol. 1, chap. 9. Texas Institute for Research and Education on Aging.

_____ (1996). *Coping with Old Age in a Changing Africa.* Aldershot, United Kingdom: Avebury.

_____ (1999). Rapid urbanization and living arrangements of older persons in Africa. Paper presented at the United Nations Technical Meeting on Population Ageing and Living Arrangements of Older Persons: Critical Issues and Policy Responses, New York, 8-10 February 2000.

_____, and M. Greico (1994). Urbanization, caring for the elderly and the changing African family: the challenge to social welfare and social policy. *International Social Security Review.* Geneva, pp. 111-122.

Bond, J. (1990). Living arrangements of elderly people. In *Ageing in Society: An Introduction to Social Gerontology*, J. Bond, and P. Coleman, eds. London: Sage Publications.

Brown, C. K. (1984). Improving the social protection of the ageing population in Ghana. Legon: University of Ghana, Institute of Statistical, Social and Economic Research.

Cain, M. (1991). Welfare, institutions in comparative perspective, the fate of the elderly in contemporary South Asia and pre-industrial Western Europe. In *Life, Death and the Elderly: Historical Perspective*, M. H. Pelling and R. M. Smith, eds. London: Routledge.

Cox, F. M. and N. U. Mberia (1977). *Ageing in a Changing Society: A Kenyan Experience*. New York: International Federation on Ageing.

Dowd, E., and P. Kowal (2000). Creation of "minimum data sets" for research on ageing in countries of the African region (with emphasis on countries of sub-Saharan Africa). Paper presented at the WHO workshop to create a minimum data set for research, policy and action on ageing and older adults in Africa, Harare, 22-24 January.

Harper, M. S. (1988). Behavioural, social and mental health aspects of home care for older Americans. *Home Health Care Services Quarterly*, vol. 9, No. 4, pp. 61-124.

Kalache, A. (1991). Ageing in developing countries. In *Principles and Practice of Geriatric Medicine*, 2nd edition, M. S. J. Pathy, ed. Chichester, United Kingdom: J. Wiley.

_____ (1994). Forward. In *Ageing: Debates on Demographic Transition and Social Policy*, by Kasturi Sen. London: Zed Books Ltd.

Kendig, H. L., A. Hashimoto, and L. Coppard, eds. (1992). *Family Support for the Elderly: The International Experience*. New York: Oxford University Press.

MacIntyre, S. (1977). Old age as a social problem. In R. Dingwall, and others, eds. *Health Care and Health Knowledge*, London: Croom Helm, pp. 46-63.

Okie, S. (1991). Study links cancer and poverty: Blacks' higher rates are tied to income. *Washington Post* (April 17), pp. A1 and A6.

Phillips, D. R. (1988). Accommodation for elderly persons in newly industrialized countries. *International Journal of Health Services*, vol. 18, No. 2.

Phillipson, C. (1982). *Capitalism and the Construction of Old Age*. London: Macmillan.

Rowe, J. W. (1991). Reducing the risk of usual ageing. *Generations*, vol. 15, No. 1, pp. 25-28.

Sen, K. (1994). *Ageing: Debates on Demographic Transition and Social Policy*. London: Zed Books Ltd.

Streib, G. F. (1982). The continuum of living arrangements. In *Ageing and The Human Condition*, vol. II. Frontiers in Ageing Series. Springfield, Illinois: Sangamon State University. New York: Human Sciences Press Inc.

United Nations (1979). The ageing in slums and squatter settlements. New York.

Wilson, F., and M. Ramphele (1989). *Uprooting Poverty: The South African Challenge*, a Report for the Second Carnegie Inquiry into Poverty and Development in South Africa. Cape Town/Johannesburg: David Phillip.

World Health Organization (1984). Health of the Elderly. WHO technical report series. Geneva.

_____ (1989). The uses of epidemiology in the study of the elderly. Report of a WHO scientific group on the epidemiology of ageing. Geneva.

LIVING ARRANGEMENTS AND WELL-BEING OF THE OLDER POPULATION: FUTURE RESEARCH DIRECTIONS

*Victoria A. Velkoff**

Living arrangements are influenced by a variety of factors, including marital status, financial well-being, health status, and family size and structure, as well as cultural traditions such as kinship patterns, the value placed on living independently or with family members, the availability of social services and social support, and the physical features of housing stock and local communities. In turn, living arrangements affect life satisfaction, health, and most importantly for those living in the community, the chances of institutionalization. One's living arrangements are dynamic, they change over the life course, adapting to changing life circumstances.

Some significant observations emerge from a cross-national comparison of living arrangements of the older population. First, women in developed countries are much more likely than men to live alone as they age (see figure I); older men are likely to live in family settings, typically with a spouse. Secondly, there has been an increase in the proportion of the older population that is living alone in developed countries (see figure II). Thirdly, both older men and women in developing countries usually live with adult children (see figure III). Fourthly, the use of non-family institutions for care of the frail elderly varies widely around the world but is relatively low everywhere (see figure IV).

Given the above information on the living arrangements of the older population, what can be said about the well-being of older people? Are the older women who are living alone in developed countries worse or better off than their counterparts who are living with a spouse or other relative? Does the fact that older men and women in many developing countries still live with their adult children mean that they are cared for by their co-resident children? Do we know anything about the quality or type of relationship between the co-resident parent and adult child? Although information on living arrangements is useful, such data do not necessarily reveal much about the nature of social and/or intergenerational relationships that pertain to older people, and whether those relationships enhance older people's well-being. Descriptive statistics on living arrangements also do not inform us about the motivations and preferences for different living arrangements among older people.

---

* United States Bureau of the Census.

Figure I. Percentage of United States population in older ages living alone, by sex: March 1998

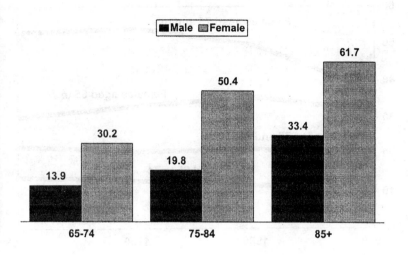

Figure II. Percentage of United States population aged 65 and over living alone, by age and sex: 1970-1998

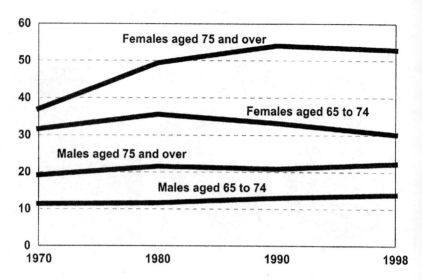

Source: United States Bureau of the Census, CPS reports, *Marital Status and Living Arrangements*, March 1994 (pp. 20-484) and March 1998 (Update) (pp. 20-514).

Figure III. Percentage of population aged 60 and over living with
children, in four Asian countries: circa 1996

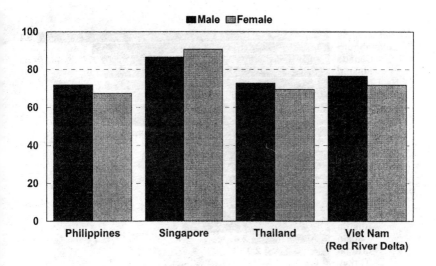

Source: Anh and others (1997), Chan (1997), Knodel and Chayovan (1997) and Natividad and Cruz (1997).

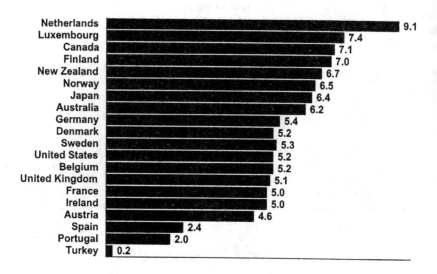

Figure IV. Percentage of the older population in residential care: circa 1991

Netherlands	9.1
Luxembourg	7.4
Canada	7.1
Finland	7.0
New Zealand	6.7
Norway	6.5
Japan	6.4
Australia	6.2
Germany	5.4
Denmark	5.2
Sweden	5.3
United States	5.2
Belgium	5.2
United Kingdom	5.1
France	5.0
Ireland	5.0
Austria	4.6
Spain	2.4
Portugal	2.0
Turkey	0.2

Source: OECD (1996).

There is a need to go beyond the descriptive statistics on living arrangements to investigate the factors that influence one's living arrangements and explore the impact those different living arrangements have on older people's lives. Hermalin (1997) suggests the need to "distinguish between the *form* and *function* of familial arrangements, and not infer the content from the structure". In other words, objective measures of living arrangements should not be used to hypothesize about subjective measures of well-being or quality of relationships between co-resident family members.

As population ageing increases in both developed and developing countries, issues surrounding support and care of older persons are receiving more attention. The living arrangements of the older population can have an influence on the demand for formal and informal support systems. Given the competing demands for scarce resources, examination of the factors influencing the living arrangements and social support systems of the older population can aid policy makers trying to address the needs of the older population. While there are several areas that warrant future research when discussing the living arrangements of the older population and their well-being, the present paper will focus on three areas: (a) changing family structure; (b) familial resource transfers; and (c) older people's preference in terms of living arrangements and care.

Changing family structures will have an impact on the well-being of the older population now and into the future. Changing family structures also influence the need for formal support systems. There are several alternative forms of family and generational structure that are shaped by changes in marital status, fertility, mortality and migration. Much of the research has focused on the *traditional* paths through the life course (e.g., marriage, bearing children and widowhood) and has not considered the alternative pathways and their consequences on living arrangements and well-being in later life.

Declines in fertility, often quite rapid, now characterize most developing countries. Research on and microsimulation of kin availability suggests that tomorrow's elderly will have fewer children upon whom to rely, though this may be offset by increased joint survival of spouses (Kinsella, 1996). In the Republic of Korea, for example, Lee and Palloni (1992) have shown that, although declining fertility results in an increase in the proportion of Korean women with no surviving son, increased male longevity means that the proportion of elderly widows also will decline (i.e., their husbands will live longer). Thus, from the older women's viewpoint, family status may not deteriorate significantly in the coming years. From society's perspective, however, the demands for support of older people will increase, because the momentum of rapid population ageing means that the fraction of the overall population that is older (especially sonless and childless widows) will increase among successive cohorts. Given the strong trend towards the nuclearization of family structure in the Republic of Korea and the traditional absence of state involvement in socio-economic support, the future standard of living for a growing number of elderly widows could be tenuous.

In contrast to the fertility decline in many developing countries, the post-war baby booms in developed countries have led to older people currently having more kin (children) available than did their counterparts in the past (Crimmins and Ingegneri, 1990; Wolf, 1995). Although there is a link between the number of kin and co-residence and care of older people, the decision process about who provides the care goes beyond sheer numbers. Decisions about co-residence and care are made within a family network and the socio-demographic characteristics of the parties involved are important in the decision-making process (Wolf, Freedman and Soldo, 1997; Wolf and Soldo, 1988).

The increase in divorce over the past few decades is also changing the shape and structure of the family and there is currently a lack of research that focuses on the impact that divorce has, not only on the living arrangements and well-being of the older population, but also on the relationships between adult children and their divorced parents. The increase in divorce and the subsequent blended families that are formed could have a positive benefit of leading to more kin who are potentially available to care for older people. Microsimulations have shown that the increase in stepchildren in the future may offset the decline in fertility in terms of children who are available to care for older people (Wachter, 1998). Whether the increase in number of available kin (through acquiring stepchildren) will translate into an increase in support for the older population has yet to be investigated thoroughly. There is some evidence that the non-custodial parent in a divorce, who in many countries has typically been the father, may not have the support of his children as he ages (Bulcroft and Bulcroft, 1991; Cooney and Uhlenberg, 1990).

In addition to the declines in fertility and the increases in divorce, there are other aspects of family structure that warrant further research. For instance, there are increases in migration (largely rural-to-urban) that may reduce the potential for direct support of older persons. Relatively little is known about remittance flows from younger migrants to older parents, about multistage migration of family members (e.g., parents following children to urban areas) and about cyclical or return migration. Insufficient attention has been given to the prevalence and characteristics of never-married and/or childless older people and the types of social support they rely on (Koropeckyj-Cox, 1998; Wu and Pollard, 1998). In parts of Africa, the HIV/AIDS epidemic has decimated adult populations, leaving many older persons with few if any living children. Grandparents have been thrust back into direct child-rearing roles. One study of AIDS orphans in Kinshasa found that the principal guardian for 35 per cent of the orphans was a grandparent (Ryder and others, 1994). Further research is needed on the impact that AIDS is having on the older population in terms of the support they may not be receiving because their children are dead as well as the support they may be called upon to provide for their grandchildren.

FAMILIAL RESOURCE TRANSFERS

Since most physical, emotional and economic care to older individuals is provided by family members, the demography of population ageing has increasingly been concerned with understanding and modelling kin availability. However, modelling of kin availability is complicated by the fact that while demographic forces impose constraints on family, household and kin structures, these structures also are determined by social and cultural factors that are difficult to measure (Myers, 1992). Little is known about the complex decision-making process behind transfers of physical, emotional and economic care between family members, and microlevel data can assist in understanding how these decisions are made and the types of support/care that are provided by the family (Wolf, Freedman and Soldo, 1997).

One reason for examining data on the living arrangements of the older population is because co-residence is viewed as one type of intergenerational transfer. However, as mentioned above, data on co-residence alone does not provide information about the motivation for living together, the effects of living together, who is benefiting from co-residence, or conversely, who is being harmed by co-residence. Often, there is an assumption that co-residence is based on the needs of the older person, but research has shown that co-residence is typically mutually beneficial to both generations (Casterline and others, 1991; Chan, 1997). Families also provide critical support that is not captured in data on living arrangements.

Many older people receive financial help from adult children. However, in most societies, support does not flow in only one direction. In countries with well-established pension and social security programmes, many older adults give support (including financial help, shelter, childcare and the wisdom of experience) to their adult children and grandchildren. Older people in developing countries appear less likely than in developed countries to provide financial help; data from the Malaysian Family Life Survey indicate that the main direction of monetary transfers between non-co-resident parents and children is from the latter to the former (Lillard and Willis, 1997). Beyond the financial realm, it seems clear that older persons in developing countries make substantial contributions to family well-being, in ways ranging from socialization to housekeeping and childcare. Such activities free younger adult women for employment as unpaid family help in agricultural production as well as for paid employment (Hashimoto, 1991; Apt, 1992).

Intergenerational transfers are not well documented. Little is known about the motivation for the transfers, the effects of the transfers and the volume and direction of the transfers. Ongoing research in Asia is beginning to reveal the complexity of familial exchange, not just between parents and children, but among wider family and social networks as well (Agree, Biddlecom and Valente, 1999). Knowing more about the familial exchange network may be useful in helping anticipate the need for formal care in a society.

PREFERENCES ABOUT LIVING ARRANGEMENTS

There is a need for more research on the preferences and attitudes of older people in terms of their living arrangements (Kinsella, 1990; Myers, 1996). The increase in older people living alone that has been observed in many developed countries has often been attributed to the improved economic resources of the older population, which has enabled them to act on their preference for independent living. Assumptions are often made about older people's preferences for living arrangements that are based on past norms. This is particularly true in developing countries, where it is often assumed that the preferred living arrangement for older people is co-residence with their children. However, recent research in the Philippines found that many older people, although co-residing with children, would prefer to live alone or with a spouse only (Natividad and Cruz, 1997). They live with children either because of their needs or the needs of their children or a combination of both. Having more information on the actual, rather than the assumed, preferences of older people would assist in designing policies that would better serve the needs and wants of the older population.

CONCLUSION

Changes over time in living arrangements and caregiving patterns appear as responses to changes in other spheres of life. Demographic trends in fertility, mortality and migration have an impact on family size and household structure, especially as these trends interact with changing gender roles, increased education and expanding employment opportunities. In "older" industrialized countries, current elderly cohorts have lived through a complexity of twentieth-century changes, and this is reflected in the pattern and diversity of living arrangements that have emerged. The major question today in industrialized societies is whether the observed trends in living and care arrangements will (and, in a qualitative sense, "should") continue. In less industrialized countries, many of the social changes associated with modern economic development are fairly recent phenomena: the overarching question in these countries is whether the basic family structures will come to resemble those of the so-called Western model. These questions have policy implications as government and other agencies grapple with how best to plan for the inevitable growth in the older population.

REFERENCES

Agree, E. M., A. E. Biddlecom and T. W. Valente (1999). Multi-generational exchanges in Taiwan and the Philippines: a social network approach. Paper presented at the 1999 annual meeting of the Population Association of America.

Anh, T. S., and others (1997). Living arrangements, patrilineality and sources of support among elderly Vietnamese. *Asia-Pacific Population Journal* (Bangkok), vol. 12, No. 4 (December), pp. 69-88.

Apt, N. A. (1992). Family support to elderly people in Ghana. In *Family Support for the Elderly*, Hal L. Kendig, Akiko Hashimoto and Larry C. Coppard, eds. Oxford: Oxford University Press, pp. 203-212.

Bulcroft, K. A., and R. A. Bulcroft (1991). The timing of divorce: effects on parent-child relationships in later life. *Research on Aging*, vol. 13, pp. 226-243.

Casterline, J. B., and others (1991). Differences in the living arrangements of the elderly in four Asian countries: the interplay of constraints and preferences. *Comparative Study of the Elderly in Asia*. Research report. Ann Arbor: University of Michigan, Population Studies Center.

Chan, A. (1997). An overview of the living arrangements and social support exchanges of older Singaporeans. *Asia-Pacific Population Journal* (Bangkok), vol. 12, No. 4 (December), pp. 35-50.

Cooney, T. M., and P. Uhlenberg (1990). The role of divorce in men's relations with their adult children after mid-life. *Journal of Marriage and the Family*, vol. 52, pp. 677-688.

Crimmins, E. M., and D. G. Ingegneri (1990). Interaction and living arrangements of older parents and their children: Past trends, present determinants, future implications. *Research on Aging*, vol. 12, No. 1 (March), pp. 3-35.

Hashimoto, A. (1991). Living arrangements of the aged in seven developing countries: a preliminary analysis. *Journal of Cross-Cultural Gerontology*, vol. 6, No. 4, pp. 359-382.

Hermalin, A. I. (1997). Drawing policy lessons for Asia from research on ageing. *Asia-Pacific Population Journal* (Bangkok), vol. 12, No. 4 (December), pp. 89-102.

Kinsella, K. G. (1990). *Living Arrangements of the Elderly and Social Policy: A Cross-national Perspective*. Center for International Research, staff paper No. 52. Washington, D.C.: United States Bureau of the Census.

_____ (1996). Aging and the family: present and future demographic issues. In *Aging and the Family: Theory and Research*, Rosemary Blieszner and Victoria Hilkevitch Bedford, eds. Westport, Connecticut: Praeger, pp. 32-56.

Knodel, J., and N. Chayovan (1997). Family support and living arrangements of Thai elderly. *Asia-Pacific Population Journal* (Bangkok), vol. 12, No. 4 (December), pp. 51-68.

Koropeckyj-Cox, T. (1998). Loneliness and depression in middle and old age: Are the childless more vulnerable. *Journal of Gerontology: Social Sciences*, vol. 53B, No. 6, pp. S303-S312.

Lee, R., and A. Palloni (1992). Changes in the family status of elderly women in Korea. *Demography*, vol. 29, No. 1, pp. 69-92.

Lillard, L. E., and R. J. Willis (1997). Motives for intergenerational transfers: evidence from Malaysia. *Demography*, vol. 34, No. 1 (February), pp. 115-134.

Myers, G. C. (1992). Demographic aging and family support for older persons. In *Family Support for the Elderly*, Hal L. Kendig, Akiko Hashimoto and Larry C. Coppard, eds. Oxford: Oxford University Press, pp. 31-68.

_____ (1996). Aging and the social sciences: research directions and unresolved issues. In *Handbook of Aging and the Social Sciences*, Robert H. Binstock and Linda K. George, eds. San Diego, CA: Academic Press, pp.1-11.

Natividad, J. N., and G. T. Cruz (1997). Patterns in living arrangements and familial support for the elderly in the Philippines. *Asia-Pacific Population Journal* (Bangkok), vol. 12, No. 4 (December), pp. 17-34.

OECD (1996). *Caring for Frail Elderly People*, Social Policy Studies No. 19. Paris: Organisation for Economic Cooperation and Development.

Ryder, R. W., and others (1994). AIDS orphans in Kinshasa, Zaire: incidence and socio-economic consequences. *Current Science*, vol. 8, No. 5 (May), pp. 673-680.

Wachter, K. W. (1998). Kinship resources for the elderly: an update. Berkeley: University of California, Department of Demography.

Wolf, D. A. (1995). Changes in the living arrangements of older women: an international study. *The Gerontologist*, vol. 35, No. 6, pp. 724-731.

_____, V. Freedman and B. Soldo (1997). The division of family labor: care for elderly parents. *Journal of Gerontology*, series B, vol. 52B, pp. 102-109.

Wolf, D. A., and B. J. Soldo (1988). Household composition choices of older unmarried women. *Demography*, vol. 25, No. 3 (August), pp. 387-403.

Wu, Z., and M. S. Pollard (1998). Social support among unmarried childless elderly persons. *Journal of Gerontology: Social Sciences*, vol. 53B, No. 6, pp. S324-S335.

NOTE ON STATISTICAL ANALYSIS AND MICROSIMULATION FOR STUDYING LIVING ARRANGEMENTS AND INTERGENERATIONAL TRANSFERS

*Douglas A. Wolf**

ON MODELS FOR THE ANALYSIS OF LIVING ARRANGEMENTS AND INTRA-FAMILY TRANSFERS

In the area of multivariate modelling of living arrangements and family transfers, we are inevitably led towards a desire, or need, for complexity in model specification and hence difficulty in estimation. This complexity arises because we generally wish to represent the situations of multiple actors (decision makers), for example, an older person or couple and their several children, and, possibly, the children's parents-in-law as well. Furthermore, each actor may engage in one or more of a set of multiple activities of interest, including co-residence, financial transfers, or the provision of personal-care services. The spatial proximity of members of a kin group may be a further outcome of interest. Thus, we are faced with jointly modelling what may be an array of discrete and continuous (or truncated) outcomes of varying numbers over varying numbers of individual decision makers (when we look across observations in, say, a cross-sectional data file).

Yet, the econometrics literature provides a number of tools with which to formulate estimable models, and provides estimation algorithms, for most or all of the situations that might arise in the preceding substantive context. Software with which to estimate all the potential variants of these models may not be readily available, which can be a major problem. Nonetheless, the binding constraint at the margins of applied work in this area is more likely to come from data limitations than from a lack of suitable econometric machinery. Data sets may not include information on all the actors of interest, or may do so but provide too little information on each to permit interesting analysis. Furthermore, not all resource flows may be represented.

Paradoxically, while available data typically have numerous shortcomings with respect to their ability to support the estimation of complex resource flows in multiple domains in multi-actor family networks, available data have generally not been much exploited with respect to the analyses they

---

* Syracuse University, United States of America.

could potentially support. As an example, Aykan and Wolf (2000), use Turkish Demographic and Health Surveys (DHS) data to model the competition between a married woman's parents and parents-in-law for co-residence with the woman and her husband; the DHS standard design was intended to inform research on fertility, family planning, child development and maternal and child health, yet the Turkish survey adopted optional questions on the survivorship of respondents' parents and parents-in-law, permitting our analysis with its "ageing" focus. There are no doubt numerous other instances of available data that could support unexpected analyses in domains far from their originally intended range of topics.

A difficult issue that arises in the specification of models that depict outcomes in multiple domains is that of endogeneity, or simultaneity. But, these issues can easily be misunderstood. If two outcomes are both viewed as choice variables under the control of a single actor, then it does not make sense to think of them as reciprocally causally related (i.e., that a change in A causes a change in B, while B similarly produces its own distinctive causal response in A). Instead, they should be treated as "jointly determined". This will give the statistical specification of the model the appearance of a reduced form. Variables A and B are still jointly endogenous, and presumably depend, in part, on common unmeasured variables (i.e., exhibit correlated disturbances) but do not appear as each other's regressors. For example, an area of considerable research activity at present is the question whether women's hours of paid employment and their hours of familial caregiving activity are negatively related. If a woman is viewed as the sole decision maker, and her decision is made conditional on exogenously given prices (e.g., market wages, household productivity, and costs of market substitutes for her own caregiving time), a fixed "care production technology", and fixed preferences, then the two time-use outcomes are jointly determined.

However, there are many cases of outcome variables that are simultaneously determined, for example a woman's parent-care hours and her sister's parent-care hours, or, an older person's health and co-residence status, or, an older person's co-residence status and co-resident child's labour supply. In these cases, outcomes reflect the decisions of multiple actors, and one can imagine an exogenous change that would lead one actor to adjust, for example, her care hours, while that change would lead to a reaction on the part of some other actor's care hours.

Estimation of these reciprocal causal relationships demands identifying restrictions, that is, suitable instruments with which to identify the effects of endogenous variables. A great challenge — two challenges, in fact — is to decide which variables can be used as instruments in this type of model, and to ensure the presence in data sets of such variables. The theories on which choice models are based often offer little help in pointing out such instrumental variables; theories are more likely to suggest what factors do belong in a relationship than to suggest that some other factor definitely does not belong in that relationship. Ethnographic, or other qualitative and intensive, field efforts might help to produce the sort of empirical evidence that would support decisions about how to identify simultaneous-equations models.

Two final points about endogeneity deserve mention. First, longitudinal data, which might provide a temporal sequence of values for both independent and dependent variables, does not automatically provide a way out of the problem of establishing causality. Yet, many analysts seem to assume that the observed temporal sequence is the same as the causal sequence. However, actors make plans, they have expectations about the future, and they take steps today that reflect their plans about the future. Thus, there is a sense in which events in the future "cause" events in the present. Secondly, "contextual" variables are not necessarily exogenous. Multilevel modelling is, at present, a popular and rapidly developing analytic tool, but as context is virtually always location-specific, one must recognize that the inclusion of contextual variables introduces possible endogeneity bias, as actors are to some extent free to choose their location. They may choose their location so as to achieve a favourable context, for example, older persons may migrate to a service-rich area (or to their child's neighbourhood) in anticipation of future care needs. If so, the contextual variables are not exogenous. This criticism is often made; solutions to the problem are far more rare.

ON MICROSIMULATION, IN THE CONTEXT OF FAMILY/KIN NETWORKS AND INTRA-FAMILY TRANSFERS

It makes sense to turn from a discussion of model specification to microsimulation, since microsimulation must be preceded by model specification and estimation.

What is microsimulation? The essential ingredients are the use of computer-based sampling, and an analysis that is conducted at the maximally disaggregated level, that is, that of the individual (which might be a person, a couple, a firm or organization — whatever is the fundamental analytic unit at hand). The "sampling" is, in fact, a process of making stochastic assignments of values to variables. These remarks pertain to a situation in which the "model" is a set of relationships among observed and unobserved factors (in the demographic domain, primarily); the unobserved factors are assumed to come from particular distributions; the model produces a distribution of possible values for the outcome of interest, and the computer program — the sampling algorithm — selects a particular value from that distribution. The sampling process may be repeated many times for a particular individual, and there may be many individuals (e.g., a sample, and even, perhaps, everyone in some population) to which the sampling algorithm is applied.

An interesting question is the following: is microsimulation a complement to, or an alternative to, "macro" simulation? Before addressing this question, it should be noted that the distinguishing features of "macro" versus "micro" simulation is not deterministic versus stochastic (stochastic aggregate population forecasting techniques, for example, are currently gaining increased attention), nor "expected value" versus "frequency distribution" (although advocates of microsimulation often give as a rationale for doing microsimulation the fact that it can produce an estimate of the population frequency distribution of some outcome, while macro models generally produce just the expectation), but, instead, aggregated versus disaggregated. To make progress towards answering the question posed above, there are areas where microsimulation has been shown to be useful, and others where macrosimulation has little or nothing to say. The best-known area in which microsimulation has proved useful is in depicting the details of kinship networks, and the best-known work in this area is by Kenneth Wachter and his colleagues (Hammel, Wachter and McDaniel, 1981; Wachter, 1997).

Microsimulation could, in addition, be used to conduct a conventional population projection, but it is hard to imagine that anyone would seriously want to. Situations in which microsimulation does reveal its value include those characterized by (a) complex models — for example, multiple-equation models in which multiple actors make decisions about multiple interrelated domains of behaviour, such as the intra-familial transfer situations described above; (b) situations involving interactions between individual members of a population, for example the workings of mating markets; (c) models that explicitly represent "unmeasured heterogeneity", such as the "frailty" models of human mortality developed by Vaupel and colleagues (Vaupel and Yashin, 1985; Vaupel, Manton and Stallard, 1979) or the random-mixture models of Hutterite fertility developed by Heckman and Walker (1987); (d) the analyst's wishes to quantify the various sources of uncertainty, or forecast variance, in a model. Microsimulation can also be a way to extend the range of lessons that can be learned from some types of models. For example, in a conventional linear single-equation regression setting, most of what one might want to learn from the estimated model can be learned from the coefficients themselves, or simple transformations of them. Forecasts are also easy to carry out. In contrast, a Markov renewal model of, say, labour market transitions may incorporate a set of age- and duration-dependent hazard functions for transitions among states "never worked", "working", "unemployed", and "retired". Further complexity can be introduced by distinguishing between different jobs held over the worklife. Having estimated all the parameters of such a model (even a simple one, with only a few time-invariant covariates), the analyst can draw only a limited set of conclusions about the overall life-course process from the parameters of the hazard functions themselves. But with microsimulation, the analyst is free to compute numbers that answer questions as detailed as "what are the chances that someone who entered the labour market at age 24 is in his seventh job at age 47?" and so on.

Since microsimulation is fundamentally an exercise in sampling, it is crucial that the simulator pay attention to the issue of sampling error. A run of a microsimulation computer program produces, typically, a microdata file full of randomly assigned variable values. The values might purport to represent the situation at some future date, starting from an observed starting point for some well-defined population. If a sample of equivalent size could be drawn from the actual future population, it would be possible to proceed to compute estimated standard errors for any summary statistics based on that sample data. The same should be done if the data are simulated.

It is also important to remember, as noted above, that for each individual whose future is being simulated, the "model" (embedded in the computer program) generates a probability distribution over possible values of each variable in the future, while one run of the simulation program produces one draw from this distribution for each person. These draws do not represent, on their own, the expected value of that person's variable, but rather a randomly-selected particular value of that variable. The value assigned may be far from the expected value but can still be "correct" (in a probabilistic sense). The expected value (for the person) may, in fact, not be an admissible value in the random-assignment algorithm. For example, the expected value of survivorship in some future year is a survival probability, whereas a run of a microsimulation program will assign to each person either a "zero" or a "one", corresponding to survivorship and non-survivorship respectively. Nonetheless, when everyone's simulated values are averaged, it is possible, in principle, to treat the resulting summary statistic as an estimate of the expected value of the variable in the population (just as it would be in a sample from a real population).

There are many sources of variability, or uncertainty, in the projections that come from a microsimulation exercise. Many people appear to think that the "Monte Carlo" variation is the primary such source of uncertainty, but it is probably not, and may even be so small as to be disregarded. The Monte Carlo variation refers to the fact that different runs of the computer program will assign different values to a given outcome for a given individual, because different random numbers (corresponding to different points on the support of the distribution of possible values of that variable) were used in different runs. Each of the different values is equally valid (conditional on the appropriateness of the model structure overall). If the exercise were repeated often enough, the set of values assigned for an individual would gradually converge to the theoretical probability distribution of the variable for that individual. The average of all those values is probably a good estimate of the expected value of that person's value. And, the sample average of those expected values is probably a good estimate of the population mean. But, it may not be necessary to run the computer program many times, or, possibly, more than once, since the "sampling error" present in one person's stochastic assignment is balanced by an offsetting error in some other person's assignment, and so on. This is the same reasoning that is used to develop an intuitive understanding of the central limit theorem. A more likely limiting factor than the Monte Carlo variation in determining the sampling error in summary statistics based on simulated data is classical sampling error in the data file that represents the starting point for the microsimulation. Other important sources of variation in simulated microdata are item and unit imputation error in the starting population, and sampling errors associated with the parameters of equations that make up the projection model. Efforts to quantify this uncertainty is an area of current research.

Despite the relatively undeveloped nature of our knowledge about dealing with microsimulation uncertainty, the preceding considerations lead me to two views that are sharply at odds with some current practice. First, the practice of "calibrating" microsimulation programs is dubious. This practice tends to consist of imposing ad hoc ex post adjustments (such as adding or subtracting constants from the intercepts of regression equations) in order to ensure that summary statistics from microsimulations match some "target", which is typically a number from someone else's projection. There is no reason to expect even a "perfect" model to generate a sample whose sample mean is exactly equal to its expected value in the population. Simple random sampling produces summary statistics to which are attached standard errors. Attempts should be made to compute the standard error of any sample statistic that is based on simulated microdata, as well as a confidence interval (chosen to represent a pre-specified confidence level), in order to determine whether the simulated summary statistic's confidence interval covers the target value. Its failure to do so signals an inadequacy in the model, and may suggest the need for respecification or re-estimation of the model.

Secondly, "variance reduction" techniques are inappropriate in the context of stochastic simulation models. Some practitioners of demographic microsimulation (e.g., van Imhoff and Post, 1998) advocate the use of variance-reduction techniques. The author questions this view, for two reasons. First of all, it appears to imply that for each person we want to ensure that the value randomly assigned to him or her is close to its expected value. But as noted above, one run of the simulation program produces not an estimate of a person's expected value but a draw from the full relative frequency distribution for that variable. Limiting the range of values potentially assigned to an individual might not bring the assigned value closer to its expectation. More importantly, if it is agreed that the computation of standard errors is important, then bias should not be introduced into the estimate of the population variance of the variable in question. If an asterisk (*) is used to denote a simulated value, then by analogy to usual sampling theory, the standard error of a simulated sample mean is

$$SE\,(\overline{Y}^*) = \frac{\sigma_Y^*}{\sqrt{N}} \, ,$$

in which the unknown population standard deviation for the variable has been replaced by its (simulated) sample counterpart, and N is the number of individuals simulated (not the number of repetitions of the simulation algorithm). Variance reduction techniques, applied to individual values of Y, will inappropriately shrink the estimate of the population variance, and lead to downward-biased estimates of standard errors.

Aykan, Hakan, and Douglas A. Wolf (2000). Traditionality, modernity, and household composition: parent-child co-residence in contemporary Turkey. *Research on Aging*, vol. 22, No. 4 (July), pp. 395-421.

Hammel, E. A., K. W. Wachter and C. K. McDaniel (1981). The kin of the aged in AD 2000. In *Aging: Social Change*, S. Kiesler, J. Morgan and V. Oppenheimer, eds. New York: Academic Press, pp. 11-40.

Heckman, James J., and James R. Walker (1987). Using goodness of fit and other criteria to choose among competing duration models: a case study of Hutterite data. In *Sociological Methodology 1987*, Clifford C. Clogg, ed. Washington, D.C.: American Sociological Association.

Van Imhoff, Evert, and Wendy Post (1998). Microsimulation methods for population projection. *Population: An English Selection*, vol. 10, No. 1, pp. 97-138.

Vaupel, J. W., K. Manton and E. Stallard (1979). The impact of heterogeneity in individual frailty on the dynamics of mortality. *Demography*, vol. 16 (August), pp. 439-454.

Vaupel, James W., and Anatoli I. Yashin (1985). The deviant dynamics of death in heterogeneous populations. In *Sociological Methodology 1985*, Nancy Brandon Tuma, ed. San Francisco: Jossey Bass Publishers, pp. 179-211.

Wachter, Kenneth W. (1997). Kinship resources for elderly. *Philosophical Transactions of the Royal Society of London* (series B), vol. 352, pp. 1811-1817.

كيفية الحصول على منشورات الأمم المتحدة

يمكن الحصول على منشورات الأمم المتحدة من المكتبات ودور التوزيع في جميع أنحاء العالم . استعلم عنها من المكتبة
التي تتعامل معها أو اكتب إلى : الأمم المتحدة ، قسم البيع في نيويورك أو في جنيف .

如何购取联合国出版物

联合国出版物在全世界各地的书店和经售处均有发售。请向书店询问或写信到纽约或日内瓦的
联合国销售组。

HOW TO OBTAIN UNITED NATIONS PUBLICATIONS

United Nations publications may be obtained from bookstores and distributors throughout the
world. Consult your bookstore or write to: United Nations, Sales Section, New York or Geneva.

COMMENT SE PROCURER LES PUBLICATIONS DES NATIONS UNIES

Les publications des Nations Unies sont en vente dans les librairies et les agences dépositaires
du monde entier. Informez-vous auprès de votre libraire ou adressez-vous à : Nations Unies,
Section des ventes, New York ou Genève.

КАК ПОЛУЧИТЬ ИЗДАНИЯ ОРГАНИЗАЦИИ ОБЪЕДИНЕННЫХ НАЦИЙ

Издания Организации Объединенных Наций можно купить в книжных магазинах
и агентствах во всех районах мира. Наводите справки об изданиях в вашем книжном
магазине или пишите по адресу: Организация Объединенных Наций, Секция по
продаже изданий, Нью-Йорк или Женева.

COMO CONSEGUIR PUBLICACIONES DE LAS NACIONES UNIDAS

Las publicaciones de las Naciones Unidas están en venta en librerías y casas distribuidoras en
todas partes del mundo. Consulte a su librero o diríjase a: Naciones Unidas, Sección de Ventas,
Nueva York o Ginebra.

Litho in United Nations, New York
00-82069—December 2001—6,450
ISBN 92-1-151358-8

United Nations publication
Sales No. E.01.XIII.16
ST/ESA/SER.N/42-43